READINGS IN THE MODERN ESSAY

EDITED BY
EDWARD S. NOYES

Essay Index Reprint Series

BOOKS FOR LIBRARIES PRESS
FREEPORT, NEW YORK

INTERNATIONAL STANDARD BOOK NUMBER:
0-8369-2008-2

LIBRARY OF CONGRESS CATALOG CARD NUMBER:
70-121494

PRINTED IN THE UNITED STATES OF AMERICA

CONTENTS

GROUP ONE

ON THINKING AND WRITING

AUTHOR	TITLE	PAGE
JAMES HARVEY ROBINSON	On Various Kinds of Thinking	3
THOMAS HENRY HUXLEY	The Method of Scientific Investigation	23
ELLWOOD HENDRICK	Adventures in Philosophy	33
HERBERT SPENCER	The Relativity of All Knowledge	53
SIR A. T. QUILLER-COUCH	On Jargon	59
FRANK MOORE COLBY	Our Refinement	79
SUGGESTIONS FOR READING		91

GROUP TWO

ON POLITICAL, SOCIAL, AND SCIENTIFIC TOPICS

AUTHOR	TITLE	PAGE
ALDOUS HUXLEY	The Idea of Equality	95
HAROLD J. LASKI	A Plea for Equality	119
BERTRAND EARL RUSSELL	Political Ideals	141
WALTER LIPPMANN	Bryan and the Dogma of Majority Rule	157
JAMES TRUSLOW ADAMS	Our Changing Characteristics	171
WILLIAM ALLEN WHITE	Cheer Up, America!	189
NORMAN THOMAS	The Essential Condition of Economic Planning	205
STUART CHASE	The Nemesis of American Business	219
SIR ARTHUR STANLEY EDDINGTON	Introduction to The Nature of the Physical World	241
SIR JAMES HOPWOOD JEANS	The Study of Astronomy	251
WILLIAM BEEBE	A Chain of Jungle Life	267
ROBERT LOUIS STEVENSON	Pulvis et Umbra	285

AUTHOR	TITLE	PAGE
{ WILL DURANT..................	*Is Progress a Delusion?*	295
{ J. B. S. HALDANE......................	*Man's Destiny*	315
SUGGESTIONS FOR READING.........................		320

GROUP THREE
FAMILIAR ESSAYS

H. M. TOMLINSON...	*Some Hints for Those About to Travel*	325
G. LOWES DICKINSON...............	*A Sacred Mountain*	337
WILLIAM BOLITHO..........................	*Believe It*	345
J. B. PRIESTLEY.....................	*The Disillusioned*	351
GEORGE MACAULAY TREVELYAN...............	*Walking*	357
MAX BEERBOHM.................	*Going Out for a Walk*	379
	The Golden Drugget	383
SAMUEL McCHORD CROTHERS		
	Every Man's Natural Desire to be Somebody Else	391
C. E. MONTAGUE.............	*Autumn Tints in Chivalry*	405
ROBERT BENCHLEY................	*Cleaning out the Desk*	417
STEPHEN BUTLER LEACOCK...........	*Oxford As I See It*	423
SUGGESTIONS FOR READING.........................		444

GROUP FOUR
ON LITERARY TYPES

CARL VAN DOREN.................	*A Note on the Essay*	449
ELIZABETH A. DREW.................	*The Plain Reader*	453
G. K. CHESTERTON..................	*On Detective Novels*	471
LUDWIG LEWISOHN...................	*A Note on Tragedy*	477
	A Note on Comedy	481
JOHN GALSWORTHY....	*Some Platitudes Concerning Drama*	487
ANDRÉ MAUROIS................	*The Modern Biographer*	499
IOLO A. WILLIAMS......................	*Poetry Today*	521
CHAUNCEY BREWSTER TINKER.......	*Figures in a Dream*	537
SUGGESTIONS FOR READING.........................		560

INTRODUCTION

SINCE there are already in print so many collections of modern essays, the editor of a new anthology should be able to give some good reason for adding to the number. Clearly, his fundamental reason is that he believes his own collection better, for his purposes at least, than any other. It is equally clear that this reason may not, to other teachers, with somewhat different purposes, appear sufficient. The fact, nevertheless, that a collection was planned for a specific course — as I have planned this collection — does not necessarily make it valueless for other courses, whereas it does, after all, insure a plan.

That plan can best be explained by a brief description of the course for which this book was designed. Offered to Sophomores or Juniors in the Sheffield Scientific School of Yale University, this course is intended to encourage in its students wider and more intelligent reading, through a study of modern literary types, beginning with the essay. The present collection, therefore, presents essays, by modern authors, ranging from the more formal discussion of contemporary political and social problems to the more personal and informal interpretation of a mood, light or serious. Literary criticism, philosophical speculation, scientific statement, and humor are all included. A glance at the Table of Contents will show the scope and variety of topics.

Modern fiction, drama, and poetry are also studied in this course. I have therefore included a final group of essays, on different types of literature, which may be used either as introductory or as concluding discussions for this study — as points of departure or as opportunities for a final summing up. Without reference to their strategic purpose, however, I believe that these essays merit inclusion, merely as essays.

In the course of which I have been speaking much attention is also devoted to composition. Students are required to present, regularly, themes based on their reading outside of class. Hence the first group of essays in this book is intended to assist them in their thinking and writing. I neither expect nor desire that these essays should be regarded as in any way equivalent to the formal study of psychology, logic, and literary expression. In experience, however, I have found them valuable in helping students to clarify their own thinking and to avoid some of the confused ideas, woolly abstract terms, and genteelisms which disfigure much undergraduate writing.

In the years during which the course has gradually taken its present shape, my colleagues and I have used several collections somewhat similar to the present one. In each we found valuable material, together with some essays which seemed to us relatively inferior for our work. This volume is, in part, an attempt to gather into one collection the essays which have proved, in the classroom, their unusual value. Sixteen of the thirty-nine have appeared in other anthologies; some have been rather frequently reprinted; that they have on that account lost their freshness, I do not believe. The rest, though written by authors often represented in collections, have not, to my knowledge (I do not pretend to have examined all anthologies), been so reprinted. At least, the teacher who is looking for new material should not be disappointed in this book.

To some extent, the essays fall naturally into pairs, especially in the second group, where, for example, Mr. Aldous Huxley and Professor Laski present the idea of equality from decidedly different points of view. To carry throughout the collection such a scheme of contrasting essays would have resulted in too strict a limitation of its scope. Yet an attempt has been made to utilize as far as possible that conflict of opinion which stimulates not only discussion in the classroom but outside reading as well. To encourage such further investigation, I have added some suggestions for reading. These are intended, not to be exhaustive, but to point out books and articles which undergraduates have found interesting and worth while.

By bracketing titles in the Table of Contents, I have sought to indicate comparisons and contrasts in this second group. It begins with essays on some important problems of modern politics, proceeds to social and economic criticism, expounds, for the layman, some aspects of modern science, and terminates in a discussion of the always fascinating question of the future of mankind. Whenever feasible, I have chosen essays likely to provoke debate and dissent, rather than to produce a lethargic agreement with whatever appears in print. The familiar essays in the third group are less adaptable to a set arrangement. It will not be difficult, however, to discover some connecting threads. Mr. Lowes Dickinson, for instance, has evidently, however unconsciously, put into practice some of Mr. Tomlinson's *Hints*; Mr. Bolitho and Mr. Priestley, and Mr. Trevelyan and Mr. Beerbohm seem to be on opposite sides of their respective fences.

The foregoing account of my plan will, I hope, make manifest that the collection has possibilities for usefulness not limited to any one course. Its material should be sufficiently varied for a study of the modern essay. Its contents should provide suggestions both in style and, with the reading lists, in subject-matter for courses in composition. It may conceivably have value as a means of unifying a course in the study of literary types.

Although I have had much advice in planning the book, for its defects, whatever they may be, I must assume entire responsibility. Aside from the formal acknowledgments of permission to reprint which are made with the separate essays, I should like to state here my gratitude for the courtesy of the authors and publishers through whom the essays have been made available. Professors Randall Stewart and William Clyde DeVane have been helpful with suggestions. For his unfailing kindness, I wish especially to thank Professor Jack R. Crawford, to whose counsel and aid the collection owes its being.

EDWARD S. NOYES

YALE UNIVERSITY

GROUP ONE
ON THINKING AND WRITING

JAMES HARVEY ROBINSON

Born in Illinois, Dr. Robinson graduated from Harvard in 1887, and received the degree of Ph.D. from the University of Freiburg, Germany, in 1890. For some twenty-five years he was professor of history at Columbia University; he was one of the founders of the New School for Social Research in New York, and he has become widely known as author and lecturer. His Development of Modern Europe (1907) *and* Medieval and Modern Times (1915) *are standard texts.* To the general reading public, however, he is probably best known as the author of The Humanizing of Knowledge (1923) *and* The Mind in the Making (1921), *from the latter of which the following essay is taken.* Clear organization and apt illustration, conspicuous in this essay, are found equally throughout the book, and partly explain its remarkable and enduring popularity. Many have found it unsurpassed as a means toward a better understanding, not merely of the development of liberal thought, but also of the way in which their own minds work.

The following essay is reprinted from The Mind in the Making, *by James Harvey Robinson, Harper and Brothers, publishers. By permission of the publishers.*

JAMES HARVEY ROBINSON

ON VARIOUS KINDS OF THINKING

WE DO not think enough about thinking, and much of our confusion is the result of current illusions in regard to it. Let us forget for the moment any impressions we may have derived from the philosophers, and see what seems to happen in ourselves. The first thing that we notice is that our thought moves with such incredible rapidity that it is almost impossible to arrest any specimen of it long enough to have a look at it. When we are offered a penny for our thoughts we always find that we have recently had so many things in mind that we can easily make a selection which will not compromise us too nakedly. On inspection we shall find that even if we are not downright ashamed of a great part of our spontaneous thinking it is far too intimate, personal, ignoble or trivial to permit us to reveal more than a small part of it. I believe this must be true of everyone. We do not, of course, know what goes on in other people's heads. They tell us very little and we tell them very little. The spigot of speech, rarely fully opened, could never emit more than driblets of the ever renewed hogshead of thought — *noch grösser wie's Heidelberger Fass.*[1] We find it hard to believe that other people's thoughts are as silly as our own, but they probably are.

We all appear to ourselves to be thinking all the time during our waking hours, and most of us are aware that we go on thinking while we are asleep, even more foolishly than when awake. When uninterrupted by some practical issue we are engaged in what is now known as a *reverie.*

[1] Even larger than the Heidelberg tun (famous for its size). *Ed.*

This is our spontaneous and favorite kind of thinking. We allow our ideas to take their own course and this course is determined by our hopes and fears, our spontaneous desires, their fulfillment or frustration; by our likes and dislikes, our loves and hates and resentments. There is nothing else anything like so interesting to ourselves as ourselves. All thought that is not more or less laboriously controlled and directed will inevitably circle about the beloved Ego. It is amusing and pathetic to observe this tendency in ourselves and in others. We learn politely and generously to overlook this truth, but if we dare to think of it, it blazes forth like the noontide sun.

The reverie or "free association of ideas" has of late become the subject of scientific research. While investigators are not yet agreed on the results, or at least on the proper interpretation to be given to them, there can be no doubt that our reveries form the chief index to our fundamental character. They are a reflection of our nature as modified by often hidden and forgotten experiences. We need not go into the matter further here, for it is only necessary to observe that the reverie is at all times a potent and in many cases an omnipotent rival to every other kind of thinking. It doubtless influences all our speculations in its persistent tendency to self-magnification and self-justification, which are its chief preoccupations, but it is the last thing to make directly or indirectly for honest increase of knowledge.[1] Philosophers usually talk as if such thinking did

[1] The poet-clergyman, John Donne, who lived in the time of James I, has given a beautifully honest picture of the doings of a saint's mind: "I throw myself down in my chamber and call in and invite God and His angels thither, and when they are there I neglect God and His angels for the noise of a fly, for the rattling of a coach, for the whining of a door. I talk on in the same posture of praying, eyes lifted up, knees bowed down, as though I prayed to God, and if God or His angels should ask me when I thought last of God in that prayer I cannot tell. Sometimes I find that I had forgot what I was about, but when I began to forget it I cannot tell. A memory of yesterday's pleasures, a fear of tomorrow's dangers, a straw

not exist or were in some way negligible. This is what makes their speculations so unreal and often worthless.

The reverie, as any of us can see for himself, is frequently broken and interrupted by the necessity of a second kind of thinking. We have to make practical decisions. Shall we write a letter or no? Shall we take the subway or a bus? Shall we have dinner at seven or half past? Shall we buy U.S. Rubber or a Liberty Bond? Decisions are easily distinguishable from the free flow of the reverie. Sometimes they demand a good deal of careful pondering and the recollection of pertinent facts; often, however, they are made impulsively. They are a more difficult and laborious thing than the reverie, and we resent having to "make up our mind" when we are tired, or absorbed in a congenial reverie. Weighing a decision, it should be noted, does not necessarily add anything to our knowledge, although we may, of course, seek further information before making it.

RATIONALIZING

A third kind of thinking is stimulated when anyone questions our belief and opinions. We sometimes find ourselves changing our minds without any resistance or heavy emotion, but if we are told that we are wrong we resent the imputation and harden our hearts. We are incredibly heedless in the formation of our beliefs, but find ourselves filled with an illicit passion for them when anyone proposes to rob us of their companionship. It is obviously not the ideas themselves that are dear to us, but our self-esteem, which is threatened. We are by nature stubbornly pledged to defend our own from attack, whether it be our person, our family, our property, or our opinion. A

under my knee, a noise in mine ear, a light in mine eye, an anything, a nothing, a fancy, a chimera in my brain troubles me in my prayer." — Quoted by ROBERT LYND, *The Art of Letters*, pp. 46–47.

United States Senator once remarked to a friend of mine that God Almighty could not make him change his mind on our Latin-America policy. We may surrender, but rarely confess ourselves vanquished. In the intellectual world at least peace is without victory.

Few of us take the pains to study the origin of our cherished convictions; indeed, we have a natural repugnance to so doing. We like to continue to believe what we have been accustomed to accept as true, and the resentment aroused when doubt is cast upon any of our assumptions leads us to seek every manner of excuse for clinging to them. *The result is that most of our so-called reasoning consists in finding arguments for going on believing as we already do.*

I remember years ago attending a public dinner to which the Governor of the state was bidden. The chairman explained that His Excellency could not be present for certain "good" reasons; what the "real" reasons were the presiding officer said he would leave us to conjecture. This distinction between "good" and "real" reasons is one of the most clarifying and essential in the whole realm of thought. We can readily give what seem to us "good" reasons for being a Catholic or a Mason, a Republican or a Democrat, an adherent or opponent of the League of Nations. But the "real" reasons are usually on quite a different plane. Of course the importance of this distinction is popularly, if somewhat obscurely, recognized. The Baptist missionary is ready enough to see that the Buddhist is not such because his doctrines would bear careful inspection, but because he happened to be born in a Buddhist family in Tokio. But it would be treason to his faith to acknowledge that his own partiality for certain doctrines is due to the fact that his mother was a member of the First Baptist church of Oak Ridge. A savage can give all sorts of reasons for his belief that it is dangerous to step on a man's shadow, and a newspaper editor can advance plenty of arguments against the Bolsheviki. But neither of them may realize why he happens to be defending his particular opinion. The "real" reasons for our beliefs are concealed from ourselves as well as from others. As we grow up we simply adopt the ideas presented to us in regard to such matters as religion, family relations, property, business, our country, and the state. We unconsciously absorb them from our environment. They are persistently whispered in our ear by the group in which we happen to live. Moreover, as Mr. Trotter has pointed out, these judgments, being the product of suggestion and not of reasoning, have the quality of perfect obviousness, so that to question them

> ... is to the believer to carry skepticism to an insane degree, and will be met by contempt, disapproval, or condemnation, according to the nature of the belief in question. When, therefore, we find ourselves entertaining an opinion about the basis of which there is a quality of feeling which tells us that to inquire into it would be absurd, obviously unnecessary, unprofitable, undesirable, bad form, or wicked, we may know that that opinion is a nonrational one, and probably, therefore, founded upon inadequate evidence.[1]

Opinions, on the other hand, which are the result of experience or of honest reasoning do not have this quality of "primary certitude." I remember when as a youth I heard a group of business men discussing the question of the immortality of the soul, I was outraged by the sentiment of doubt expressed by one of the party. As I look back now I see that I had at the time no interest in the matter, and certainly no least argument to urge in favor of the belief in which I had been reared. But neither my personal indifference to the issue, nor the fact that I had

[1] *Instincts of the Herd*, p. 44.

previously given it no attention, served to prevent an angry resentment when I heard *my* ideas questioned.

This spontaneous and loyal support of our preconceptions — this process of finding "good" reasons to justify our routine beliefs — is known to modern psychologists as "rationalizing" — clearly only a new name for a very ancient thing. Our "good" reasons ordinarily have no value in promoting honest enlightenment, because, no matter how solemnly they may be marshaled, they are at bottom the result of personal preference or prejudice, and not of an honest desire to seek or accept new knowledge.

In our reveries we are frequently engaged in self-justification, for we cannot bear to think ourselves wrong, and yet have constant illustrations of our weaknesses and mistakes. So we spend much time finding fault with circumstances and the conduct of others, and shifting on to them with great ingenuity the onus of our own failures and disappointments. *Rationalizing is the self-exculpation which occurs when we feel ourselves, or our group, accused of misapprehension or error.*

The little word *my* is the most important one in all human affairs, and properly to reckon with it is the beginning of wisdom. It has the same force whether it is *my* dinner, *my* dog, and *my* house, or *my* faith, *my* country, and *my* God. We not only resent the imputation that our watch is wrong, or our car shabby, but that our conception of the canals of Mars, of the pronunciation of "Epictetus," of the medicinal value of salicine, or the date of Sargon I, are subject to revision.

Philosophers, scholars, and men of science exhibit a common sensitiveness in all decisions in which their *amour propre* is involved. Thousands of argumentative works have been written to vent a grudge. However stately their reasoning, it may be nothing but rationalizing, stimulated by the most commonplace of all motives. A history of philosophy and theology could be written in terms of grouches, wounded pride, and aversions, and it would be far more instructive than the usual treatments of these themes. Sometimes, under Providence, the lowly impulse of resentment leads to great achievements. Milton wrote his treatise on divorce as a result of his troubles with his seventeen-year-old wife, and when he was accused of being the leading spirit in a new sect, the Divorcers, he wrote his noble *Areopagitica* to prove his right to say what he thought fit, and incidentally to establish the advantage of a free press in the promotion of Truth.

All mankind, high and low, thinks in all the ways which have been described. The reverie goes on all the time not only in the mind of the mill hand and the Broadway flapper, but equally in weighty judges and godly bishops. It has gone on in all the philosophers, scientists, poets, and theologians that have ever lived. Aristotle's most abstruse speculations were doubtless tempered by highly irrelevant reflections. He is reported to have had very thin legs and small eyes, for which he doubtless had to find excuses, and he was wont to indulge in very conspicuous dress and rings and was accustomed to arrange his hair carefully.[1] Diogenes the Cynic exhibited the impudence of a touchy soul. His tub was his distinction. Tennyson in beginning his "Maud" could not forget his chagrin over losing his patrimony years before as the result of an unhappy investment in the Patent Decorative Carving Company. These facts are not recalled here as a gratuitous disparagement of the truly great, but to insure a full realization of the tremendous competition which all really exacting thought has to face, even in the minds of the most highly endowed mortals.

[1] Diogenes Lærtius, book v.

And now the astonishing and perturbing suspicion emerges that perhaps almost all that had passed for social science, political economy, politics, and ethics in the past may be brushed aside by future generations as mainly rationalizing. John Dewey has already reached this conclusion in regard to philosophy.[1] Veblen[2] and other writers have revealed the various unperceived presuppositions of the traditional political economy, and now comes an Italian sociologist, Vilfredo Pareto, who, in his huge treatise on general sociology, devotes hundreds of pages to substantiating a similar thesis affecting all the social sciences.[3] This conclusion may be ranked by students of a hundred years hence as one of the several great discoveries of our age. It is by no means fully worked out, and it is so opposed to nature that it will be very slowly accepted by the great mass of those who consider themselves thoughtful. As a historical student I am personally fully reconciled to this newer view. Indeed, it seems to me inevitable that just as the various sciences of nature were, before the opening of the seventeenth century, largely masses of rationalizations to suit the religious sentiments of the period, so the social sciences have continued even to our own day to be rationalizations of uncritically accepted beliefs and customs.

It will become apparent as we proceed that the fact that an idea is ancient and that it has been widely received is no argument in its favor, but should immediately suggest the necessity of carefully testing it as a probable instance of rationalization.

[1] *Reconstruction in Philosophy.*

[2] *The Place of Science in Modern Civilization.*

[3] *Traité de Sociologie Générale, passim.* The author's term "*derivations*" seems to be his precise way of expressing what we have called the "good" reasons, and his "*residus*" correspond to the "real" reasons. He well says, "*L'homme éprouve le besoin de raisonner, et en outre d'étendre un voile sur ses instincts et sur ses sentiments*" — hence, rationalization. (P. 788.) His aim is to reduce sociology to the "real" reasons. (P. 791.)

HOW CREATIVE THOUGHT TRANSFORMS THE WORLD

This brings us to another kind of thought which can fairly easily be distinguished from the three kinds described above. It has not the usual qualities of the reverie, for it does not hover about our personal complacencies and humiliations. It is not made up of the homely decisions forced upon us by everyday needs, when we review our little stock of existing information, consult our conventional preferences and obligations, and make a choice of action. It is not the defense of our own cherished beliefs and prejudices just because they are our own — mere plausible excuses for remaining of the same mind. On the contrary, it is that peculiar species of thought which leads us to *change* our mind.

It is this kind of thought that has raised man from his pristine, subsavage ignorance and squalor to the degree of knowledge and comfort which he now possesses. On his capacity to continue and greatly extend this kind of thinking depends his chance of groping his way out of the plight in which the most highly civilized peoples of the world now find themselves. In the past this type of thinking has been called Reason. But so many misapprehensions have grown up around the word that some of us have become very suspicious of it. I suggest, therefore, that we substitute a recent name and speak of "creative thought" rather than of Reason. *For this kind of meditation begets knowledge, and knowledge is really creative inasmuch as it makes things look different from what they seemed before and may indeed work for their reconstruction.*

In certain moods some of us realize that we are observing things or making reflections with a seeming disregard of our personal preoccupations. We are not preening or defending ourselves; we are not faced by the necessity of any practical decision, nor are we apologizing for believing this or that. We are just wondering and looking and mayhap seeing what we never perceived before.

Curiosity is as clear and definite as any of our urges. We wonder what is in a sealed telegram or in a letter in which some one else is absorbed, or what is being said in the telephone booth or in low conversation. This inquisitiveness is vastly stimulated by jealousy, suspicion, or any hint that we ourselves are directly or indirectly involved. But there appears to be a fair amount of personal interest in other people's affairs even when they do not concern us except as a mystery to be unraveled or a tale to be told. The reports of a divorce suit will have "news value" for many weeks. They constitute a story, like a novel or play or moving picture. This is not an example of pure curiosity, however, since we readily identify ourselves with others, and their joys and despair then become our own.

We also take note of, or "observe," as Sherlock Holmes says, things which have nothing to do with our personal interests and make no personal appeal either direct or by way of sympathy. This is what Veblen so well calls "idle curiosity." And it is usually idle enough. Some of us when we face the line of people opposite us in a subway train impulsively consider them in detail and engage in rapid inferences and form theories in regard to them. On entering a room there are those who will perceive at a glance the degree of preciousness of the rugs, the character of the pictures, and the personality revealed by the books. But there are many, it would seem, who are so absorbed in their personal reverie or in some definite purpose that they have no bright-eyed energy for idle curiosity. The tendency to miscellaneous observation we come by honestly enough, for we note it in many of our animal relatives.

Veblen, however, uses the term "idle curiosity" somewhat ironically, as is his wont. It is idle only to those who fail to realize that it may be a very rare and indispensable thing from which almost all distinguished human achievement proceeds, since it may lead to systematic examination and seeking for things hitherto undiscovered.   For research is but diligent search which enjoys the high flavor of primitive hunting.   Occasionally and fitfully idle curiosity thus leads to creative thought, which alters and broadens our own views and aspirations and may in turn, under highly favorable circumstances, affect the views and lives of others, even for generations to follow.   An example or two will make this unique human process clear.

Galileo was a thoughtful youth and doubtless carried on a rich and varied reverie.   He had artistic ability and might have turned out to be a musician or painter. When he had dwelt among the monks at Vallombrosa he had been tempted to lead the life of a religious.   As a boy he busied himself with toy machines and he inherited a fondness for mathematics.   All these facts are of record. We may safely assume also that, along with many other subjects of contemplation, the Pisan maidens found a vivid place in his thoughts.

One day when seventeen years old he wandered into the cathedral of his native town.   In the midst of his reverie he looked up at the lamps hanging by long chains from the high ceiling of the church.   Then something very difficult to explain occurred.   He found himself no longer thinking of the building, worshipers, or the services; of his artistic or religious interests; of his reluctance to become a physician as his father wished.   He forgot the question of a career and even the *graziosissime donne*.   As he watched the swinging lamps he was suddenly wondering if mayhap their oscillations, whether long or short, did not occupy the same time.   Then he tested this hypothesis by counting his pulse, for that was the only timepiece he had with him.

This observation, however remarkable in itself, was not enough to produce a really creative thought.   Others may have noticed the same thing and yet nothing came of it. Most of our observations have no assignable results. Galileo may have seen that the warts on a peasant's face formed a perfect isosceles triangle, or he may have noticed with boyish glee that just as the officiating priest was uttering the solemn words, *ecce agnus Dei*, a fly lit on the end of his nose. To be really creative, ideas have to be worked up and then "put over," so that they become a part of man's social heritage. The highly accurate pendulum clock was one of the later results of Galileo's discovery. He himself was led to reconsider and successfully to refute the old notions of falling bodies. It remained for Newton to prove that the moon was falling, and presumably all the heavenly bodies. This quite upset all the consecrated views of the heavens as managed by angelic engineers. The universality of the laws of gravitation stimulated the attempt to seek other and equally important natural laws and cast grave doubts on the miracles in which mankind had hitherto believed. In short, those who dared to include in their thought the discoveries of Galileo and his successors found themselves in a new earth surrounded by new heavens.

On the 28th of October, 1831, three hundred and fifty years after Galileo had noticed the isochronous vibrations of the lamps, creative thought and its currency had so far increased that Faraday was wondering what would happen if he mounted a disk of copper between the poles of a horseshoe magnet. As the disk revolved an electric current was produced. This would doubtless have seemed the idlest kind of an experiment to the stanch business men of the time, who, it happened, were just then denouncing the child-labor bills in their anxiety to avail themselves to the full of the results of earlier idle curiosity. But should the dynamos and motors which have come into being as the outcome of Faraday's experiment be stopped this evening, the business man of today, agitated over labor troubles, might, as he trudged home past lines of "dead" cars, through dark streets to an unlighted house, engage in a little creative thought of his own and perceive that he and his laborers would have no modern factories and mines to quarrel about had it not been for the strange practical effects of the idle curiosity of scientists, inventors, and engineers.

The examples of creative intelligence given above belong to the realm of modern scientific achievement, which furnishes the most striking instances of the effects of scrupulous, objective thinking. But there are, of course, other great realms in which the recording and embodiment of acute observation and insight have wrought themselves into the higher life of man. The great poets and dramatists and our modern story-tellers have found themselves engaged in productive reveries, noting and artistically presenting their discoveries for the delight and instruction of those who have the ability to appreciate them.

The process by which a fresh and original poem or drama comes into being is doubtless analogous to that which originates and elaborates so-called scientific discoveries; but there is clearly a temperamental difference. The genesis and advance of painting, sculpture, and music offer still other problems. We really as yet know shockingly little about these matters, and indeed very few people have the least curiosity about them.[1] Nevertheless, creative intelligence in its various forms and activities is what makes man. Were it not for its slow, painful, and constantly discouraged operations through the ages man

---

[1] Recently a re-examination of creative thought has begun as a result of new knowledge which discredits many of the notions formerly held about "reason." See, for example, *Creative Intelligence*, by a group of American philosophic thinkers; John Dewey, *Essays in Experimental Logic* (both pretty hard books); and Veblen, *The Place of Science in Modern Civilization*. Easier than these and very stimulating are Dewey, *Reconstruction in Philosophy*, and Woodworth, *Dynamic Psychology*.

would be no more than a species of primate living on seeds, fruit, roots, and uncooked flesh, and wandering naked through the woods and over·the plains like a chimpanzee.

The origin and progress and future promotion of civilization are ill understood and misconceived. These should be made the chief theme of education, but much hard work is necessary before we can reconstruct our ideas of man and his capacities and free ourselves from innumerable persistent misapprehensions. There have been obstructionists in all times, not merely the lethargic masses, but the moralists, the rationalizing theologians, and most of the philosophers, all busily if unconsciously engaged in ratifying existing ignorance and mistakes and discouraging creative thought. Naturally, those who reassure us seem worthy of honor and respect. Equally naturally those who puzzle us with disturbing criticisms and invite us to change our ways are objects of suspicion and readily discredited. Our personal discontent does not ordinarily extend to any critical questioning of the general situation in which we find ourselves. In every age the prevailing conditions of civilization have appeared quite natural and inevitable to those who grew up in them. The cow asks no questions as to how it happens to have a dry stall and a supply of hay. The kitten laps its warm milk from a china saucer, without knowing anything about porcelain; the dog nestles in the corner of a divan with no sense of obligation to the inventors of upholstery and the manufacturers of down pillows. So we humans accept our breakfasts, our trains and telephones and orchestras and movies, our national Constitution, or moral code and standards of manners, with the simplicity and innocence of a pet rabbit. We have absolutely inexhaustible capacities for appropriating what others do for us with no thought of a "thank you." We do not feel called upon to make any least contribution to the merry game ourselves.

Indeed, we are usually quite unaware that a game is being played at all.

We have now examined the various classes of thinking which we can readily observe in ourselves and which we have plenty of reasons to believe go on, and always have been going on, in our fellow-men. We can sometimes get quite pure and sparkling examples of all four kinds, but commonly they are so confused and intermingled in our reverie as not to be readily distinguishable. The reverie is a reflection of our longings, exultations, and complacencies, our fears, suspicions, and disappointments. We are chiefly engaged in struggling to maintain our self-respect and in asserting that supremacy which we all crave and which seems to us our natural prerogative. It is not strange, but rather quite inevitable, that our beliefs about what is true and false, good and bad, right and wrong, should be mixed up with the reverie and be influenced by the same considerations which determine its character and course. We resent criticisms of our views exactly as we do of anything else connected with ourselves. Our notions of life and its ideals seem to us to be *our own* and as such necessarily true and right, to be defended at all costs.

We very rarely consider, however, the process by which we gained our convictions. If we did so, we could hardly fail to see that there was usually little ground for our confidence in them. Here and there, in this department of knowledge or that, some one of us might make a fair claim to have taken some trouble to get correct ideas of, let us say, the situation in Russia, the sources of our food supply, the origin of the Constitution, the revision of the tariff, the policy of the Holy Roman Apostolic Church, modern business organization, trade unions, birth control, socialism, the League of Nations, the excess-profits tax, preparedness, advertising in its social bearings; but only a very exceptional person would be entitled to opinions on all of even these few matters. And yet most of us have opinions on all these, and on many other questions of equal importance, of which we may know even less. We feel compelled, as self-respecting persons, to take sides when they come up for discussion. We even surprise ourselves by our omniscience. Without taking thought we see in a flash that it is most righteous and expedient to discourage birth control by legislative enactment, or that one who decries intervention in Mexico is clearly wrong, or that big advertising is essential to big business and that big business is the pride of the land. As godlike beings why should we not rejoice in our omniscience?

It is clear, in any case, that our convictions on important matters are not the result of knowledge or critical thought, nor, it may be added, are they often dictated by supposed self-interest. Most of them are *pure prejudices* in the proper sense of that word. We do not form them ourselves. They are the whisperings of "the voice of the herd." We have in the last analysis no responsibility for them and need assume none. They are not really our own ideas, but those of others no more well informed or inspired than ourselves, who have got them in the same careless and humiliating manner as we. It should be our pride to revise our ideas and not to adhere to what passes for respectable opinion, for such opinion can frequently be shown to be not respectable at all. We should, in view of the considerations that have been mentioned, resent our supine credulity. As an English writer has remarked:

"If we feared the entertaining of an unverifiable opinion with the warmth with which we fear using the wrong implement at the dinner table, if the thought of holding a prejudice disgusted us as does a foul disease, then the dangers of man's suggestibility would be turned into advantages."[1]

The purpose of this essay is to set forth briefly the way in which the notions of the herd have been accumulated. This seems to me the best, easiest, and least invidious educational device for cultivating a proper distrust for the older notions on which we still continue to rely.

The "real" reasons, which explain how it is we happen to hold a particular belief, are chiefly historical. Our most important opinions — those, for example, having to do with traditional, religious, and moral convictions, property rights, patriotism, national honor, the state, and indeed all the assumed foundations of society — are, as I have already suggested, rarely the result of reasoned consideration, but of unthinking absorption from the social environment in which we live. Consequently, they have about them a quality of "elemental certitude," and we especially resent doubt or criticism cast upon them. So long, however, as we revere the whisperings of the herd, we are obviously unable to examine them dispassionately and to consider to what extent they are suited to the novel conditions and social exigencies in which we find ourselves today.

The "real" reasons for our beliefs, by making clear their origins and history, can do much to dissipate this emotional blockade and rid us of our prejudices and preconceptions. Once this is done and we come critically to examine our traditional beliefs, we may well find some of them sustained by experience and honest reasoning, while others must be revised to meet new conditions and our more extended knowledge. But only after we have undertaken such a critical examination in the light of experience and modern knowledge, freed from any feeling of "primary certitude," can we claim that the "good" are also the "real" reasons for our opinions.

[1] Trotter, *op. cit.*, p. 45. The first part of this little volume is excellent.

I do not flatter myself that this general show-up of man's thought through the ages will cure myself or others of carelessness in adopting ideas, or of unseemly heat in defending them just because we have adopted them. But if the considerations which I propose to recall are really incorporated into our thinking and are permitted to establish our general outlook on human affairs, they will do much to relieve the imaginary obligation we feel in regard to traditional sentiments and ideals. Few of us are capable of engaging in creative thought, but some of us can at least come to distinguish it from other and inferior kinds of thought and accord to it the esteem that it merits as the greatest treasure of the past and the only hope of the future.

THOMAS HENRY HUXLEY

Thomas Henry Huxley (1825–1895) was born in a suburb of London, received the degree of M.B. from London University in 1845, and then served for several years as assistant surgeon in the Royal Navy. His later life is a record of extraordinary activity and success as teacher, lecturer, and scientific investigator. He was for thirty-two years professor of natural history in the Royal School of Mines; his own discoveries in natural science were numerous and fruitful; more learned societies than can easily be enumerated invited him into their membership. Yet his chief service to science lay not so much in his own research as in his unequaled ability to make clear to the public at large the results and the significance of the work of other scientists, and the importance and dignity of the scientific attitude of mind. It is characteristic that of the thirteen volumes of his collected works, four are filled with his scientific monographs, whereas nine are made up of essays and addresses. The following essay, taken from The Method of Discovery, *is typical of Huxley's ability to give to the ordinary reader a clear, concrete explanation of abstract terms and ideas.*

THOMAS HENRY HUXLEY
THE METHOD OF SCIENTIFIC
INVESTIGATION

THE method of scientific investigation is nothing but the expression of the necessary mode of working of the human mind. It is simply the mode at which all phenomena are reasoned about, rendered precise and exact. There is no more difference, but there is just the same kind of difference, between the mental operations of a man of science and those of an ordinary person, as there is between the operations and methods of a baker or of a butcher weighing out his goods in common scales, and the operations of a chemist in performing a difficult and complex analysis by means of his balance and finely graduated weights. It is not that the action of the scales in the one case, and the balance in the other, differ in the principles of their construction or manner of working; but the beam of one is set on an infinitely finer axis than the other, and of course turns by the addition of a much smaller weight.

You will understand this better, perhaps, if I give you some familiar example. You have all heard it repeated, I dare say, that men of science work by means of Induction and Deduction, and that by the help of these operations, they, in a sort of sense, wring from Nature certain other things, which are called Natural Laws, and Causes, and that out of these, by some cunning skill of their own, they build up Hypotheses and Theories. And it is imagined by many, that the operations of the common mind can be by no means compared with these processes, and that they have to be acquired by a sort of special apprenticeship to

the craft.   To hear all these large words, you would think
that the mind of a man of science must be constituted
differently from that of his fellow-men; but if you will not
be frightened by terms, you will discover that you are quite
wrong, and that all these terrible apparatus are being used
by yourselves every day and every hour of your lives.

There is a well-known incident in one of Molière's plays,
where the author makes the hero express unbounded delight on being told that he had been talking prose during
the whole of his life.   In the same way, I trust that you
will take comfort, and be delighted with yourselves, on the
discovery that you have been acting on the principles of
inductive and deductive philosophy during the same
period.   Probably there is not one here who has not in the
course of the day had occasion to set in motion a complex
train of reasoning, of the very same kind, though differing
of course in degree, as that which a scientific man goes
through in tracing the causes of natural phenomena.

A very trivial circumstance will serve to exemplify this.
Suppose you go into a fruiterer's shop, wanting an apple —
you take up one, and, on biting it, you find it sour; you
look at it, and see that it is hard and green.   You take up
another one, and that too is hard, green, and sour.   The
shopman offers you a third; but, before biting it you examine it, and find that it is hard and green, and you immediately say that you will not have it, as it must be sour,
like those that you have already tried.

Nothing can be more simple than that, you think; but
if you will take the trouble to analyze and trace out into its
logical elements what has been done by the mind, you will
be greatly surprised.   In the first place, you have performed the operation of Induction.   You found that, in
two experiences, hardness and greenness in apples went
together with sourness.   It was so in the first case, and it
was confirmed by the second.   True, it is a very small

basis, but still it is enough to make an induction from; you generalize the facts, and you expect to find sourness in apples where you get hardness and greenness. You found upon that a general law, that all hard and green apples are sour; and that, so far as it goes, is a perfect induction. Well, having got your natural law in this way, when you are offered another apple which you find is hard and green, you say, "All hard and green apples are sour; this apple is hard and green, therefore this apple is sour." That train of reasoning is what logicians call a syllogism, and has all its various parts and terms — its major premise, its minor premise, and its conclusion. And, by the help of further reasoning, which, if drawn out, would have to be exhibited in two or three other syllogisms, you arrive at your final determination, "I will not have that apple." So that, you see, you have in the first place, established a law by Induction, and upon that you have founded a Deduction, and reasoned out the special conclusion of the particular case. Well now, suppose, having got your law, that at some time afterward, you are discussing the qualities of apples with a friend: you will say to him, "It is a very curious thing — but I find that all hard and green apples are sour!" Your friend says to you, "But how do you know that?" You at once reply, "Oh, because I have tried them over and over again, and have always found them to be so." Well, if we were talking science instead of common sense, we should call that an Experimental Verification. And, if still opposed, you go further, and say, "I have heard from the people in Somersetshire and Devonshire, where a large number of apples are grown, that they have observed the same thing. It is also found to be the case in Normandy, and in North America. In short, I find it to be the universal experience of mankind wherever attention has been directed to the subject." Whereupon, your friend, unless he is a very unreasonable man, agrees with you, and is convinced that you are quite right in the conclusion you have drawn. He believes, although perhaps he does not know he believes it, that the more extensive verifications are — that the more frequently experiments have been made, and results of the same kind arrived at — that the more varied the conditions under which the same results are attained, the more certain is the ultimate conclusion, and he disputes the question no further. He sees that the experiment has been tried under all sorts of conditions, as to time, place, and people, with the same result; and he says with you, therefore, that the law you have laid down must be a good one, and he must believe it.

In science we do the same thing — the philosopher exercises precisely the same faculties, though in a much more delicate manner. In scientific inquiry it becomes a matter of duty to expose a supposed law to every possible kind of verification, and to take care, moreover, that this is done intentionally, and not left to a mere accident, as in the case of the apples. And in science, as in common life, our confidence in a law is in exact proportion to the absence of variation in the result of our experimental verifications. For instance, if you let go your grasp of an article you may have in your hand, it will immediately fall to the ground. That is a very common verification of one of the best established laws of Nature — that of gravitation. The method by which men of science establish the existence of that law is exactly the same as that by which we have established the trivial proposition about the sourness of hard and green apples. But we believe it in such an extensive, thorough, and unhesitating manner because the universal experience of mankind verifies it, and we can verify it ourselves at any time; and that is the strongest possible foundation on which any natural law can rest.

So much, then, by way of proof that the method of establishing laws in science is exactly the same as that pursued in common life. Let us now turn to another matter (though really it is but another phase of the same question), and that is, the method by which, from the relations of certain phenomena, we prove that some stand in the position of causes toward the others.

I want to put the case clearly before you, and I will therefore show you what I mean by another familiar example. I will suppose that one of you, on coming down in the morning to the parlor of your house, finds that a teapot and some spoons which had been left in the room on the previous evening are gone — the window is open, and you observe the mark of a dirty hand on the window-frame, and perhaps, in addition to that, you notice the impress of a hob-nailed shoe on the gravel outside. All these phenomena have struck your attention instantly, and before two seconds have passed you say, "Oh, somebody has broken open the window, entered the room, and run off with the spoons and the tea-pot!" That speech is out of your mouth in a moment. And you will probably add, "I know there has; I am quite sure of it!" You mean to say exactly what you know; but in reality you are giving expression to what is, in all essential particulars, an Hypothesis. You do not *know* it at all; it is nothing but an hypothesis rapidly framed in your own mind! And, it is an hypothesis founded on a long train of inductions and deductions.

What are those inductions and deductions, and how have you got at this hypothesis? You have observed, in the first place, that the window is open; but by a train of reasoning involving many Inductions and Deductions, you have probably arrived long before at the General Law — and a very good one it is — that windows do not open of themselves; and you therefore conclude that something has opened the window. A second general law that you have

arrived at in the same way is, that tea-pots and spoons do
not go out of a window spontaneously, and you are satisfied
that, as they are not now where you left them, they have
been removed.   In the third place, you look at the marks
on the window-sill, and the shoe-marks outside, and you
say that in all previous experience the former kind of mark
has never been produced by anything else but the hand
of a human being; and the same experience shows that no
other animal but man at present wears shoes with hob-
nails in them such as would produce the marks in the
gravel.   I do not know, even if we could discover any of
those "missing links" that are talked about, that they
would help us to any other conclusion!   At any rate the
law which states our present experience is strong enough
for my present purpose.   You next reach the conclusion,
that as these kinds of marks have not been left by any other
animals than men, or are liable to be formed in any other
way than by a man's hand and shoe, the marks in question
have been formed by a man in that way.   You have, further, a general law, founded on observation and experience
— and that, too, is, I am sorry to say, a very universal and
unimpeachable one — that some men are thieves; and you
assume at once from all these premises — and that is what
constitutes your hypothesis — that the man who made the
marks outside and on the window-sill, opened the window,
got in the room, and stole your tea-pot and spoons.   You
have now arrived at a *Vera Causa;* you have assumed a
Cause which it is plain is competent to produce all the
phenomena you have observed.   You can explain all these
phenomena only by the hypothesis of a thief.   But that is
a hypothetical conclusion, of the justice of which you have
no absolute proof at all; it is only rendered highly probable
by a series of inductive and deductive reasonings.

I suppose your first action, assuming that you are a man
of ordinary common sense, and that you have established

this hypothesis to your own satisfaction, will very likely be to go off for the police, and set them on the track of the burglar, with the view to the recovery of your property. But just as you are starting with this object, some person comes in, and on learning what you are about, says, "My good friend, you are going on a great deal too fast. How do you know that the man who really made the marks took the spoons? It might have been a monkey that took them, and the man may have merely looked in afterward." You would probably reply, "Well, that is all very well, but you see it is contrary to all experience of the way tea-pots and spoons are abstracted; so that, at any rate, your hypothesis is less probable than mine." While you are talking the thing over in this way, another friend arrives, one of that good kind of people that I was talking of a little while ago. And he might say, "Oh, my dear sir, you are certainly going on a great deal too fast. You are most presumptuous. You admit that all these occurrences took place when you were fast asleep, at a time when you could not possibly have known anything about what was taking place. How do you know that the laws of Nature were not suspended during the night? It may be that there has been some kind of supernatural interference in this case." In point of fact, he declares that your hypothesis is one of which you cannot at all demonstrate the truth, and that you are by no means sure that the laws of Nature are the same when you are asleep as when you are awake.

Well, now, you cannot at the moment answer that kind of reasoning. You feel that your worthy friend has you somewhat at a disadvantage. You will feel perfectly convinced in your own mind, however, that you are quite right, and you say to him, "My good friend, I can only be guided by the natural probabilities of the case, and if you will be kind enough to stand aside and permit me to pass, I will go and fetch the police." Well, we will suppose that your journey is successful, and that by good luck you meet with a policeman; that eventually the burglar is found with your property on his person, and the marks correspond to his hand and of the shoes. Probably any jury would consider those facts a very good experimental verification of your hypothesis, touching the cause of the abnormal phenomena observed in your parlor, and would act accordingly.

Now, in this supposititious case, I have taken phenomena of a very common kind, in order that you might see what are the different steps in an ordinary process of reasoning, if you will only take the trouble to analyze it carefully. All the operations I have described, you will see, are involved in the mind of any man of sense in leading him to a conclusion as to the course he should take in order to make good a robbery and punish the offender. I say that you are led, in that case, to your conclusion by exactly the same train of reasoning as that which a man of science pursues when he is endeavoring to discover the origin and laws of the most occult phenomena. The process is, and always must be, the same; and precisely the same mode of reasoning was employed by Newton and Laplace in their endeavors to discover and define the causes of the movements of the heavenly bodies, as you, with your own common sense, would employ to detect a burglar. The only difference is, that the nature of the inquiry being more abstruse, every step has to be most carefully watched, so that there may not be a single crack or flaw in your hypothesis. A flaw or crack in many of the hypotheses of daily life may be of little or no moment as affecting the general correctness of the conclusions at which we may arrive; but in a scientific inquiry a fallacy, great or small, is always of importance, and is sure to be in the long run constantly productive of mischievous, if not fatal results.

Do not allow yourselves to be misled by the common notion that an hypothesis is untrustworthy simply because it is an hypothesis. It is often urged, in respect to some scientific conclusion, that, after all, it is only an hypothesis. But what more have we to guide us in nine-tenths of the most important affairs of daily life than hypotheses, and often very ill-based ones? So that in science, where the evidence of an hypothesis is subjected to the most rigid examination, we may rightly pursue the same course. You may have hypotheses and hypotheses. A man may say, if he likes, that the moon is made of green cheese: that is an hypothesis. But another man, who has devoted a great deal of time and attention to the subject, and availed himself of the most powerful telescopes and the results of the observations of others, declares that in his opinion it is probably composed of materials very similar to those of which our own earth is made up: and that is also only an hypothesis. But I need not tell you that there is an enormous difference in the value of the two hypotheses. That one which is based on sound scientific knowledge is sure to have a corresponding value; and that which is a mere hasty, random guess, is likely to have but little value. Every great step in our progress in discovering causes has been made in exactly the same way as that which I have detailed to you. A person observing the occurrence of certain facts and phenomena asks, naturally enough, what process, what kind of operation known to occur in nature applied to the particular case, will unravel and explain the mystery? Hence you have the scientific hypothesis; and its value will be proportionate to the care and completeness with which its basis had been tested and verified. It is in these matters as in the commonest affairs of practical life: the guess of the fool will be folly, while the guess of the wise man will contain wisdom. In all cases, you see that the value of the result depends on the patience and faithfulness with which the investigator applies to his hypothesis every possible kind of verification.

ELLWOOD HENDRICK

Ellwood Hendrick (1861–1930) was born in Albany, New York. After preliminary schooling there, he went to Switzerland to special-ize in the study of chemistry, graduating from the University of Zürich in 1881. *For four years after his return to America, he was manager of a chemical works in Albany; for sixteen years more, in the insurance business; and from* 1900 *to* 1915, *a member of the New York Stock Exchange firm of Pomeroy Brothers. Later, he became a consulting editor of* Chemical and Metallurgical Engi-neering, *while from* 1924 *to his death he was Curator of the Chandler Chemical Museum of Columbia University. Two of his books,* Everyman's Chemistry (1917) *and* Opportunities in Chemistry (1919), *won unusual popularity because of their "successful at-tempts to make chemistry popular to the layman." That, with him, specialization did not mean narrowness is proved not only by his varied career, but by the scope of ideas in his many articles on non-scientific subjects. The essay which follows is taken from* Percola-tor Papers, *a collection of his magazine essays, copyright,* 1919, *by Harper and Brothers. Reprinted by permission of the publishers.*

ELLWOOD HENDRICK

ADVENTURES IN PHILOSOPHY

I. A LITTLE HOMILY ON THE TRUTH

WE SORELY need a clearer conception of the truth. We need it in the business of living; especially as a means of avoiding misunderstandings. If we have an abstract idea of what the truth is we are less likely to err in the belief that we are right before we know the truth. In adventuring upon a theory which for the past few years has seemed to me to hold we shall hardly be charged with applying new meanings to old words if we say that facts and the truth are not the same. Facts are parts of the truth, just as wheels, rods, levers, and the like are parts of a machine. If we say "the whole truth" every time we refer to the truth, it might make the idea more clear, but let us agree to consider it so, without the need of saying two words where one will do.

If you strike me, that becomes a fact as soon as you have done it. Whether you have struck me or not is a question of fact and not a question of truth. The truth may be that you struck me to call my attention to impending danger, or you may have struck me in anger, or the blow may be an unimportant episode in a long fight between us.

The truth, as I conceive it, is all the facts in their right or correct relation, the relation which they must bear to one another when the truth is attained. Thus the truth becomes an abstract thing, because we know *what* it is, although we may not know *it*. Rarely, indeed, are we able to gather all the facts in relation to a subject, on the one hand, or to correlate them, on the other; nevertheless, we must do this if we would know the truth.

If this definition is unfamiliar, if we are not accustomed to consider the truth in this sense, I think it will do us no harm to bear it in mind. In courts of law, according to current practice, it might not hold, but we are, fortunately, under no obligation to order our thinking according to processes of law.

If we exalt the truth and reverence it, the glib and hysterical brothers and sisters who, grasping a single fact, proceed to preach that and that only as the truth, will cause less annoyance. We may acknowledge their facts as facts, which is all they ask of us. If we still remain unconvinced of the truth of their preachments we shall be contradicting no one. The truth is very great, very large, and when Lessing prayed that to him be given the privilege to seek the truth rather than to know it, because to know it he was not worthy, he spoke as one of the wisest of men. To seek it, to get nearer to it, sometimes perhaps to get a glimpse of it, is all that we may hope for; it is the best that we can do.

Suppose you and I look at a tree on a hillside. We see only the leaves, and we observe that the tree is green. The tree *is* green; that is a fact. Let us make a note of it. Then suppose we go a distance away and look at it again. The tree is blue. It is idle for us to say, "It seems blue, but it really is green," because our very organs which gave the reaction of green a while ago now give the reaction of blue. By the same token that the tree was green when we saw it near by it is blue when we see it from afar. So let us make a second note: the tree is blue. Here we have two contradictory statements of fact, neither false, and yet neither the whole truth. The truth about the color of the tree involves a great range of subjects, including the physics of light, the anatomy and physiology of the human eye, photo-chemistry — in short, a vast store of learning and understanding.

Many facts which seem irreconcilable become har-

monious parts of the truth when all the facts are arranged
in their right order. So the truth should make us humble
and patient with one another. None of us has faculties of
universal coördination, and our blind spots, instead of
being little delinquencies of perception, are in reality vast
areas. The most we can claim is that we have a few
sighted spots. To see all the facts in their right relation is
what we might call the Olympian Vision.

II. THE GREEN TREE

The first time I visited Charlotte, North Carolina, I had
some business to transact with a charming, soft-spoken old
gentleman who wore a broad-brimmed felt hat. When our
business was completed for the day we walked leisurely
about the town. "Charlotte," said the gentleman of the
sombrero, "is all to' up over a dispute which is ragin' among
our people."

"What is the cause of it?" I asked.

"Free grace and fo'ordination," he answered.

I was delighted, and wrote a long letter home about it
that night. Charlotte seemed so very archaic! This was
many years ago, and since then Charlotte has grown to
be a great manufacturing town with a grand hotel and
clubs and all the things that modern industry and wealth
bring about. In those days there were the Presbyterians
and Baptists on the one side and the Methodists and Lu-
therans on the other, and the adherents of the little
Episcopal Church, who were divided on the question.
These included substantially the whole white population.
Now, unless I am sorely mistaken, Charlotte has ceased
to worry over "free grace and fo'ordination"; she is modern and up-to-date. But if my surmise be correct, she has
gone backward intellectually; she only thinks herself modern; she has become commercial and has ceased to participate in the intellectual life of the day. For the old

question whereby Charlotte was "all to' up" abides in philosophy. Turn whichever way we will, we meet that same old nagging problem, teasing us, on the one hand, with what seems to be proof that we have no free will at all, and insisting, on the other, that a very good reason why we have free will is because we know we have it.

Many of us have ceased to be Presbyterians or Baptists or Methodists or Episcopalians, but as soon as we venture into biology we find ourselves urged to join either the Mechanist or the Vitalist denomination, and there we find the same old dispute raging again among our biological people.

This is, indeed, the comedy domain of philosophy. The Greeks used to dispute over it. Saint Paul appeared to have the problem solved, and so did Saint Augustine. Pelagius differed from them, and so did his followers — with some warmth. The harmony between Luther and John Calvin over the matter was not striking; Servetus had an opinion which went up in smoke; the savants of Charlotte, North Carolina, talked themselves out over it — and now behold the biologists in battle array! If it were given to us to live to a prodigious number of years and to observe the earth from afar, we should see the philosophers in dispute over this problem throughout the ages, never agreeing and never persuading one another. It is a very enduring subject.

But is not this dispute over the question whether we have free will or not very like a dispute that we might engage in over the color of a tree — whether it be green or blue? It hardly seems worth while to boast or to grow angry in protesting that we have absolute free will, when a little surgical operation of one sort or another, or a shock, or a blow upon the head, may change our nature entirely. Why not proceed along the mechanistic way seeking the mechanical, physical, and chemical causes of every act, and thus gather as many facts as we can? If every act seems to be a response to a stimulus, why deny it? We shall not have achieved the truth when we have learned the exact process of every act, but we shall be much wiser than we are now. We shall advance toward the truth when we learn the relation to one another of those processes of which we are now so ignorant. And if from the study of the facts at hand we reach the conclusion that we have no free will at all, but are mere automata, with no power of choice or selection throughout our lives, is it not time to pause and admit that we may not have all the facts yet? Also that such as we have may not be in their right order before our vision?

There are some verses by John Godfrey Saxe, called "The Blind Men and the Elephant," which are very instructive. According to Saxe, six wise men of Indostan, all of them very wise, but all of them blind, went to see the elephant. One examined its side and declared the elephant was very like a wall; another, feeling its trunk, was sure the elephant was very like a snake; another concluded from its leg that it was very like a tree; another, examining one of its tusks, knew that the elephant was very like a spear; the expert who examined its ear found it to resemble a fan, and the authority who grasped its tail was equally certain that the elephant was very like a rope. According to the legend, they are still disputing over it.

Now the truth is bigger than an elephant, and our vision of it is narrower than the observations of each of the blind men. And we should bear in mind that they were right, every one of them. Each had a fact; none knew the truth. None had a theory of the truth; each knew what he knew, and that was enough for him. We can well imagine one of them saying, "If a thing is so, it's so, and you can't get around it; my senses bear me witness; the elephant is very like a snake."

If we have a good working method of dealing with facts it is a good thing to hold to it just as we do well to hold fast to the fact that the tree is green when we look at it near by. It seems to be a part of the truth. And the mechanistic theory, which will have nothing to do with spooks or ghosts or with vital sparks with qualities that are not material, is helpful, wholesome, and illuminating. It makes for clean thinking. It will not countenance the Pickwickian point of view, which is very popular and current in our day. It provides that facts be gathered by observation and the study of cause and effect. It also seems to lead to the conclusion that every act is the only one possible under conditions as they exist. Now if this reasoning appears sound, let us, instead of frothing at the mouth and denouncing the sincere men who have reached these conclusions, admit it — as a part of the truth.

If through another chain of reasoning, or through consciousness, or by any other means, we come to a conclusion opposed to this, there is no occasion to boast that the first conclusion is disproved. If we reach both conclusions, we may know that we have not yet achieved the truth, but, for aught we know, both may be right. That we have free will and that we have not free will may be, both of them, parts of the truth, just as the opposed statements that the tree is green and that it is blue are parts of the truth.

We may say that the whole organization of human conduct is based upon the free will of the individual; but the organization of human conduct, like many another good thing, is based in large part upon fancy. When we consider acts from anear we might as well admit that free will seems to play very little, if any, part in them. Here is the human machine with its equipment, the consciousness including a part of that group of records and nerve centers which are "connected up," the connecting up occurring automatically along the line of least resistance; and then, given the stimulus, the one and only reaction which can occur does occur. There would need to be a difference in the equipment or the stimulus to bring about a different reaction. The conclusion, you observe, is precisely the same as that reached by the late and occasionally lamented John Calvin, except that he maintained that every current through the colloidal content of every nerve was a special, volitional act of the Deity, "for His own glory."

This view, that every act is automatic if considered by itself, has great merit. If we consider it to be a part of the truth, we are likely to have far more abundant charity for one another. By it we enlarge our sympathy. For instance, we may say that everybody always does his best at the time he acts. If he does evil, there is a reason for it, a structural reason. His sympathetic equipment may be atrophied. Or he may be angry. In either case we are dealing with facts close at hand and our business is with his condition. The cause of it may be due to his grandfather, or to a false leading in his early childhood. We should diagnose his case and determine what part of his equipment is atrophied or what part so congested that his way was the path of crime. And if he is angry we should regard him as a nervous invalid until his attack is over and the anger bodies are eliminated from his system or until his injured brain cells are restored.

There is an illuminating book by Doctor Crile, of Cleveland, on *The Origin and Nature of the Emotions*, that is very enlightening about anger. He postulates that by evolution we have developed what he calls "nociceptors," which give the warning of pain in the presence of danger, and that these warnings are given according to the experience of the race. The equipment provides against such external injuries as the goring and tearing by an animal's teeth in far greater measure than against the more modern devices of swift-moving bullets and very sharp instruments, because the experience of the race against teeth is so much greater than with bullets and swords. It is imaginable that if a sword were sharp enough and thin enough and swung with sufficient speed, the old Chinese legend of the master headsman might almost escape fiction. In this, it may be recalled, the executioner graciously gave a pinch of snuff to each of his victims, who remained comfortably unaware that his head had been severed from his body. By the sneezes which followed the perfect swordsmanship was revealed; the heads rolled off, and the surprised offenders proceeded to die with all haste and propriety.

Another interesting warning is found in the fact that we are ticklish in our ears and nostrils and on the soles of our feet, where buzzing insects are likely to sting.

Now in danger these warnings elicit the response either of flight or of turning and facing it, and so we become either afraid or angry. Doctor Crile notes two features in connection with these emotions which are interesting in regard to what we are discussing: he finds that during the processes of anger and fear we suffer inhibitions of all other faculties than those which are of value in fighting or running away. We are useless, inefficient, incompetent, in every other respect. When we are angry we have not our normal equipment because the greater part is blocked off, and we are no more our complete selves than when, if ever, we are very drunk. The second observation is that under anger or fear there occurs a destruction of brain cells that are but slowly repaired, and, under stress of severe and prolonged emotion, the brain is permanently injured. These notes have been vastly illuminating to me in regard to the dreadful war which now rages, and I think we may well pause to consider how difficult the recovery will be after it is over, when so many minds that are crippled by passion must attempt the work that calls for entire men.

The Man of Wrath with a great lust to kill ceases to inspire us. We know that he is of value in hand-to-hand combats, but he is a nuisance, and even worse, in a fight where cool heads and steady hands are needed for machine-guns. He is potential in instigating war, but he is incompetent to end it. He is a drum-major of anarchy.

We also learn that the emotional hurrah of the man in high authority is evidence that he is unfit for his job, because under emotion his qualities of judgment are paralyzed and his sense of co-ordination is atrophied.

While confining ourselves to the mechanistic point of view we may describe judgment as the operation of selecting the best thing available to do at the time — just as the tree reaches out toward the light — and we may regard it as mechanical. As in a Jacquard loom the woof is run through those openings that are before it, so the judgment, the determining bobbin, as we might call it, passes through those channels of the mind that are open to it, and determines the act which we mechanically perform.

We may regard impulse as something different from reason if we want to, but to me the difference seems to be in name rather than in fact. If judgment is automatic it may operate so rapidly that it skips consciousness, but that is no ground for calling it a thing apart. Under impulse we act rapidly, so that consciousness is often skipped in the process, and usually there is an emotional drive to it. An impulse seems to me to be a quick, emotional leading or drive to an act, and as much of an automatic response to stimulus as to eat when we are hungry or to drink when we are thirsty. In doing many things we skip consciousness after we are used to doing them, although at first, when we are learning how, they involve great effort.

There are also automatic vanities which we have dis-

cussed elsewhere, of which a notable example is our disposition to justify ourselves, any time and all the time.
We are apt to think that we thought, when we were acting
so rapidly that the act skipped consciousness. And in explaining afterward, our sense of veracity is under the
greatest strain. We fool ourselves into the belief that we
deliberated over every possibility, when in fact we were
following blindly the drive within us to do that which was
the only possible thing that we could do under existing conditions.

III. THE BLUE TREE

Free will is a long way from our acts, yet we have a constructive faculty. Although often within a very narrow
range, we have the ordering of our lives in our hands.
This constructive faculty is in use when we are conjuring
up our ideals. We can of our own volition say, "I will
plan my life to do this thing." We can of our own will select a picture in our minds and hold it in our consciousness
as a stimulus. More likely than not we get the idea from
some one else; but such ideas, as they are given to us, become our property, to do with as we will, to adopt as ideas
or to reject. Many things influence us in this; we are not as
free as we think we are; we generate our own energy, and
some of us are equipped with very low-power dynamos;
but the process of selecting those purposes and ways of
life which we project into our consciousness by our own
will is the occasion of our greatest freedom.

As we grow older we become either more firm of purpose
or more obedient to any stimulus; what we have made of
our lives becomes more fixed; but at no time are we complete. We may change our whole nature at fifty as well
as at thirty or fifteen — but we are less likely to. This
business of combining impressions and setting them up as
ideals is the substance of our free will. We may fall short

of our ideals, we may be entirely different from what we meant to be, and yet be following them as nearly as we can. The question of responsibility is: With what earnestness do we select our ideals, and with what effort do we project them into our consciousness?

The difference between achieving an ideal and performing an act is rather hazy, I'll admit; but I imagine the one to be the little push we give of our own desire and choice when a picture comes into consciousness that we want to have represent us. "That is mine!" we say, and we proceed to conform to the picture, to drive it into consciousness, to recall it, to urge it upon ourselves until in the end we act that way, and this because we want to. The picture is the stimulus, but the process of selection seems supermechanical. Although I cannot imagine how we can think without our thinking-machines, it seems that somewhere in the process freedom has entered in and we thus become, let us say, the navigating officers of our lives. On the other hand, the direct performance of an act seems an automatic response to the strongest stimulus in the mind at the time.

This may seem like arguing in a circle, because the mechanism that we employ when we are selecting our ideals is substantially the same as that which we use when we perform an act. But the stimulus comes from within. Responsibility is a quality that we recognize, and to consider it a fiction seems premature — as though we had not yet a clear vision of the truth of the matter.

In the late Christian Herter's remarkable and, in many respects, illuminating book called *Biologic Aspects of Human Problems* he develops consciousness as an "awareness of self" that arises in a certain complexity of organism under certain conditions. This awareness of self becomes more abundant as what we might call the harmonious complexity of the organism increases. Now, responsibility, or the capacity to choose of our own accord, like consciousness, is a quality that seems to be present in us. It would be futile to deny consciousness because we do not understand just how and where it begins. And it seems equally idle to deny responsibility. It seems to me to be a late accompaniment of this awareness of self which we know we have, and to my way of thinking it functions when we order our lives.

So we conceive these two statements as being parts of the truth — that whatever anyone does, it seems the best that he can do at the time, and also that whatever anyone does is qualified by the manner in which he has ordered his life. This idealizing ego, then, is as much a part of ourselves as are our fingers and toes. It is also selective. Now, if it appears that we have no free will when we commit an act, but have free will when we order our lives, we surely have not the whole truth in hand, but the theory may lead us nearer to it.

IV. THE GOD IN THE MACHINE

Here I respectfully ask your pardon. Despite my protestations I have already burdened you with a definition of the truth that is not in the dictionaries, and now I am about to ask you to consider religion from a point of view that does not seem to be current. I admit frankly that it is not only distressing to the reader, but also that it makes for confusion, to frame new definitions for old words as one proceeds; but, "*Gott hilf mir; ich kann nicht anders!*"

It seems to me that, so far as our civilization is concerned, the concept of religion *per se* is modern. There is no Germanic word for it; in English, German, Dutch, and Scandinavian, the Latin word has been imported and substituted for faith, belief, and even for dogma and theology. In the sense in which I want to use the word there is no plural. Christianity, Buddhism, Brahminism, Judaism, Mohammedanism are not so many religions (although I

ADVENTURES IN PHILOSOPHY   45

must admit that the Latins, who gave us the word, would have used it in this sense); they are, let us say, faiths or beliefs or confessions. At all events, if we agree to call them such, it will leave us free to use the word religion without thinking of the minister, the Sunday-school, or the choir in which we used to sing. Of course, the minister and the Sunday-school and the church choir may have functioned as parts of religion, but to think of them as the substance of it might get them out of their right relation to the idea which I am trying to express.

In the chapter called "The Blue Tree" we considered how we may, of our own free will, select impressions or ideas, and by making ideals of them drive them into consciousness so that they shall serve both as stimuli and inhibitions to our actions. We called this the ordering of life. In the process we are open to impressions, although we determine within ourselves, subject, of course, to our limitations, which of these impressions we shall select. Now, the function of providing ideals and offering them and teaching them, so that we may order our lives aright and thus approach the truth, seems to me to be the great province of religion. We may practice religion either with or without dogma. The man of faith may have great religious value, and again he may have no religious value at all. There are, for example, religious Christians, and, on the other hand, Christians of great piety who are not religious. The anchorite who whips and distresses himself to save his own soul is not practising religion; he is exercising his faith. The Samaritan who picks up the fallen wanderer by the wayside and by his act also enlarges the vision of the man he helps, so that the stimulus of sympathy enters into him, is doing a religious act. Faith may be a stimulus to religious acts, and we know that it often is; but since often it is not, we may as well address ourselves to that aspect of religion which we can understand, regarding it as having to do with the ordering of our lives, and not as related to dogma or faith save as dogma or faith may induce it. Then we find that everybody has the religious equipment, just as he has a sympathetic equipment although both may be greatly atrophied. With his mind, although we cannot fail to recognize a conflict between science and the Bible and science and dogma, there is no conflict between science and religion.

This view of religion takes the subject out of the domain of metaphysics and mysteries and recognizes it as a specific department of human life. By it we reach the conclusion that it is a necessary function, in which we are all interested. The truly religious man is he who helps you and me to be of positive value to the world in which we live and, in one way or another, to approach the truth. Whether he be a Christian or a Jew or anything else is his affair — his faith, his profession. His religion is in his ideals and his use of them.

We must have ideals. We can do nothing without them. And this essay is written in the sincere belief that as we approach the truth with understanding, one human problem after another will be solved. Only, we must order our lives aright or else we cannot approach the truth. We cannot, otherwise, get the facts into focus. So all the world needs religion — today, it would seem, more than ever before. Dogmas that we cannot believe will not answer the purpose. Apologetics often offend more than they aid. Religion is bigger than any church or any creed or any faith, and its business is the development of a wiser and a better humanity.

V. INTO THE UNKNOWN

We have discussed the problem of free will and found it not very free, and yet I have tried to develop the idea that we have the ordering of our lives in our own hands. Now let us adventure farther, and this time into the unknown, with analogy as our guide.

We have seen how facts are parts of the truth and that we reap confusion if we consider them as substitutes for it. We might postulate a law of arrangement, a law of order, that holds good in regard to the truth and applies also to animate and inanimate things. We see this ordering of the composite parts into their right relation in the formation of a crystal. We need not question now why the molecules join according to a mathematical scale to form a symmetrical body; suffice it for the present to observe that they do. The molecules are individual, but they group themselves into something that is not a molecule — into a crystal. We may compare a crystal to the truth, and the molecules to the facts which constitute it. Until the molecules are in their right order there is no crystal. Until the facts are in their right order there is no truth.

We, as men and women, are composed of innumerable particles of many different kinds. Their good condition and orderly arrangement are necessary to our being. Let us consider, for example, our white blood corpuscles or leucocytes. They work with what almost appears to be intelligence in overcoming disease. They are not simple little things by any means; they are marvelously complex. They respond to a stimulus and go to work, just as we do. Sometimes they are weak, inefficient, and sick; and then we languish or die because they do not do their work. They are mechanical entities, and are subject to physical and chemical laws.

Now we are mechanical entities and we constitute something greater than ourselves. We group ourselves artificially into nations which a congress has power to change by moving a boundary line from one side of us to the other. We divide humanity into other groups, as into families, because of immediate consanguinity, and into races, based on what appears to be a remoter consanguinity. We divide ourselves again into long-headed and broad-headed classes. The facts upon which these groupings are based do not accord with one another, nor do they tell us much about what humanity means. They are desirable facts and, in a way, it is worth knowing that some of us are of one nation and some of another; some long-headed and some broad; some one thing and others something else; but a new and greater meaning might be applied to us by a master mind, the greater anthropologist who could explain the human family as it has not been explained before.

The news of battles does not tell us what is really happening to us all; and there are problems ahead even graver and more important than who shall win. Is not victory itself a curse to the winner who lacks the character to meet his obligations? Some day, let us hope, a wiser generation will follow that will refuse to accept the wrath and hate that we cherish, and will work diligently to repair the havoc of this war. Then perhaps the greater anthropologist will come.

Collective humanity is, indeed, a strange phenomenon. Constantly destroying itself, it is at war with half of nature and cultivates as richly as it can the other half. It has a marvelous faculty for helping itself, and then, when a part of it has achieved a high order of living and gathered in those things of the earth which it desires, there is usually a great fall, and as the years roll on, the dull, stupid toiler guides his plow over the land that once was Carthage and Nineveh. What is it that makes collective humanity sick? What was the disease of Babylon and of the forgotten city that underlies it? After all the analyses, what was the sickness of Rome? Why did Europe go to sleep for a thousand years, and what was it that killed the intellect of the Saracens? Why did Persia die?

Collective humanity is a thing, a being that grows well

and is strong and becomes godlike, and then again sickens and becomes foolish, and the spirit of it fades away until slavery under a benign master would be an advantage. Collective humanity as we see it is a great jumble of parts, related, unrelated, and in dire confusion.   What is it doing? Not one of us can tell.

Now let us imagine leucocytes to have consciousness and vision, and let us consider a single one of them.   Its abode is in the blood of somebody — of you, let us say; and its life is very exciting for it because it never knows what its path will be.   Sometimes it is driven into one of your fingers, again into one of your toes; it may be busy on a little scratch well covered up, or it may suddenly have to do battle with a tetanus bacillus.   Ask a leucocyte what it knows of life, and it might well answer that it is a continuous problem; it would tell you all sorts of interesting things about your interior — which is its whole world — but it could not tell anything about you.   Even so simple a detail as that, for instance, you do not like parsnips, could not occur to this leucocyte, because you do not eat them, and so it has no experience with parsnips.   Really, the leucocytes with consciousness, which I am imagining, are very like us; they are in their world and we in ours. And we may be very like them — parts of a Great Intelligence as much beyond us as we are beyond the leucocytes which form parts of us.

Humanity has always been speculating about this Greater Intelligence, and yet speculation has always been discouraged on the ground that the matter is all settled. This conservatism is what gives us such amazing dicta as the Westminster Shorter Catechism and the Thirty-nine Articles.   The usual human concept of the Greater Intelligence is as of one apart from us and appearing in all manifestations of power.   It has been proposed that we may come into sight and communication with it after death; and the fear of it, described as the beginning of wisdom, has also been used to make us do strange things in accordance with traditions and myths older than history.

Even analogy will only help us occasionally here, and otherwise we have nothing to guide us in these vaster regions but the imagination. And yet, if we can imagine some relation between human beings and a possible Greater Intelligence, a relation which does not seem false or impossible, we may be taking steps in advance. If we imagine this and imagine that and then something else, it may be that some day somebody will imagine a working hypothesis which does not seem to offend against the truth.

Now suppose the working hypothesis should involve the conception of human beings as minute particles of the Greater Intelligence, citing the analogy of the leucocytes or any other swarm of microscopic units. We need not then restrict ourselves to their reactions in the human body. We are different, are differently constructed, and this remarkable quality of consciousness is, at all events, far greater in the human being than it is, for instance, in a leucocyte. Without doubt it reaches farther. Nor need we restrict the Greater Intelligence to our own limitations. We are not conscious of our blood corpuscles, but that is no reason why the Greater Intelligence may not be conscious of us. We know, as we have said, that if our white blood corpuscles are weak, inefficient, or sick, we languish, and that our welfare requires that they be in health. So, if we consider collective humanity and observe that it advances in knowledge, in understanding, in order, and in righteousness, we may then feel that it is well with the Greater Intelligence of which we are a part. But if we live in idleness and waste and hatred and cruelty and malice, and cause misery and degradation, it would seem that we are offending and injuring the Greater Intelligence, the God of all of us. This makes the Greater Intelligence in a way dependent upon us, so that it loses health and welfare and power when we undermine the health and welfare of one another.

Sometimes when we know more than we do now, there may be available a working hypothesis along these lines and in accord with familiar facts.   It is interesting to speculate upon what the results may be.   Hebrew poetry has given us a tradition and a conception of a deity apart from ourselves and pregnant with the greatest conceivable measure of power.   The Christian, Jewish, and Mohammedan peoples worship an Almighty Divinity that rules the stars and the uttermost heavens, the nebulæ as well as the sun and its planets, including the earth.   The thought of any other is condemned.   Beginning with a tribal master of its fate inspired by selfishness, lust, and wrath, humanity has magnified its conception of its god until it has exalted him beyond the earth and projected him through the ether into a million other worlds.   It may be that we shall be guided back again to a God of all men and women, exercising vast powers of the spirit when in health and when His component particles are doing their work as they should, but losing power to lead or guide if mankind is wayward and corrupt.

HERBERT SPENCER

Herbert Spencer (1820–1903) *was born in Derby, England, and educated at Hinton Charterhouse, near Bath. An assistant schoolmaster at seventeen, he turned within a year to the more congenial occupation of civil engineering, for which he showed great aptitude. He began as author by contributing, to various periodicals, essays on political, scientific, and economic subjects. It would be absurd to try, in the space available here, to follow the development of his thought, or even to list his publications. Conscious of the rapid increase in many branches of learning, he made a magnificent effort to comprehend all the knowledge of his day in a single philosophical system based on the principles of evolutionary science. Whatever the permanent value of that system, there can be no doubt of his influence as an original thinker in many fields, and as a fellow worker with Huxley, Darwin, and Tyndall in spreading the doctrine of evolution, social as well as organic. The following selection is taken from Part I of* First Principles, *the opening volume of* A System of Philosophy (1862).

HERBERT SPENCER

THE RELATIVITY OF ALL KNOWLEDGE

IF, WHEN walking through the fields some day in September, you hear a rustle a few yards in advance, and on observing the ditch side where it occurs, see the herbage agitated, you will probably turn toward the spot to learn by what this sound and motion are produced. As you approach there flutters into the ditch, a partridge; on seeing which your curiosity is satisfied — you have what you call an *explanation* of the appearances. The explanation, mark, amounts to this: that whereas throughout life you have had countless experiences of disturbance among small stationary bodies, accompanying the movement of other bodies among them, and have generalized the relation between such disturbances and such movements, you consider this particular disturbance explained, on finding it to present an instance of the like relation. Suppose you catch the partridge; and, wishing to ascertain why it did not escape, examine it, and find at one spot a slight trace of blood upon its feathers. You now *understand*, as you say, what has disabled the partridge. It has been wounded by a sportsman — adds another case to the many cases already seen by you, of birds being killed or injured by the shot discharged at them from fowling-pieces. And in assimilating this case to other such cases consists your understanding of it. But now, on consideration, a difficulty suggests itself. Only a single shot has struck the partridge, and that not in a vital place: the wings are uninjured, as are also those muscles which move them; and the creature proves by its struggles that it has abundant strength. Why then, you inquire of yourself, does it not fly? Occasion favoring, you put the question to an anatomist, who furnishes you with a *solution*. He points out that this solitary shot has passed close to the place at which the nerve supplying the wing-muscles of one side diverges from the spine; and that a slight injury to this nerve, extending even to the rupture of a few fibres, may, by preventing a perfect co-ordination in the actions of the two wings, destroy the power of flight. You are no longer puzzled. But what has happened? — what has changed your state from one of perplexity to one of *comprehension?* Simply the disclosure of a class of previously known cases, along with which you can include this case. The connection between lesions of the nervous system and paralysis of the limbs has been already many times brought under your notice; and you here find a relation of cause and effect that is essentially similar.

Let us suppose you are led on to make further inquiries concerning organic actions, which, conspicuous and remarkable as they are, you had not before cared to understand. How is respiration effected? you ask — why does air periodically rush into the lungs? The answer is that in the higher vertebrata, as in ourselves, influx of air is caused by an enlargement of the thoracic cavity, due partly to depression of the diaphragm, partly to elevation of the ribs. But how does elevation of the ribs enlarge the cavity? In reply the anatomist shows you that the plane of each pair of ribs makes an acute angle with the spine; that this angle widens when the movable ends of the ribs are raised; and he makes you realize the consequent dilatation of the cavity by pointing out how the area of a parallelogram increases as its angles approach to right angles — you understand this special fact when you see it to be an instance of a general geometrical fact. There still arises, however, the question — why does the air rush into this enlarged cavity? To which comes the answer that, when the thoracic cavity is enlarged, the contained air, partially relieved from pressure, expands, and so loses some of its resisting power; that hence it opposes to the pressure of the external air a less pressure; and that as air, like every other fluid, presses equally in all directions, motion must result along any line in which the resistance is less than elsewhere; whence follows an inward current. And this *interpretation* you recognize as one, when a few facts of like kind, exhibited more plainly in a visible fluid such as water, are cited in illustration. Again, when it was pointed out that the limbs are compound levers acting in essentially the same way as levers of iron or wood, you might consider yourself as having obtained a partial *rationale* of animal movements. The contraction of a muscle, seeming before utterly unaccountable, would seem less unaccountable were you shown how, by a galvanic current, a series of soft iron magnets could be made to shorten itself, through the attraction of each magnet for its neighbors: — an alleged analogy which especially answers the purpose of our argument, since, whether real or fancied, it equally illustrates the mental illumination that results on finding a class of cases within which a particular case may possibly be included. And it may be further noted how, in the instance here named, an additional feeling of comprehension arises on remembering that the influence conveyed through the nerves to the muscles is, though not positively electric, yet a form of force nearly allied to the electric. Similarly when you learn that animal heat arises from chemical combinations — when you learn that the absorption of nutrient fluids through the coats of the intestines is an instance of osmotic action — when you learn that the changes undergone by food during digestion are like changes artificially producible in the laboratory, you regard yourself as *knowing* something about the natures of these phenomena.

Observe now what we have been doing. Turning to the

general question, let us note where these successive interpretations have carried us.   We began with quite special
and concrete facts.   In explaining each, and afterwards
explaining the more general facts of which they are instances, we have got down to certain highly general facts:
to a geometrical principle or property of space, to a simple
law of mechanical action, to a law of fluid equilibrium —
to truths in physics, in chemistry, in thermology, in electricity.   The particular phenomena with which we set out
have been merged in larger and larger groups of phenomena; and as they have been so merged, we have arrived
at solutions that we consider profound in proportion as this
process has been carried far.   Still deeper explanations are
simply further steps in the same direction.   When, for instance, it is asked why the law of action of the lever is what
it is, or why fluid equilibrium and fluid motion exhibit the
relations which they do, the answer furnished by mathematicians consists in the disclosure of the principle of
virtual velocities — a principle holding true alike in fluids
and solids — a principle under which the others are comprehended.   And similarly, the insight obtained into the
phenomena of chemical combination, heat, electricity, etc.,
implies that a rationale of them, when found, will be the
exposition of some highly general fact respecting the constitution of matter, of which chemical, electrical, and ther-
mal facts are merely different manifestations.

Is this process limited or unlimited?   Can we go on forever explaining classes of facts by including them in larger
classes; or must we eventually come to a largest class?
The supposition that the process is unlimited, were any one
absurd enough to espouse it, would still imply that an ultimate explanation could not be reached, since infinite time
would be required to reach it.   While the unavoidable conclusion that it is limited (proved not only by the finite
sphere of observation open to us, but also by the diminution

in the number of generalizations that necessarily accompanies increase of their breadth) equally implies that the ultimate fact cannot be understood. For if the successively deeper interpretations of nature which constitute advancing knowledge are merely successive inclusions of special truths in general truths, and of general truths in truths still more general, it obviously follows that the most general truth, not admitting of inclusion in any other, does not admit of interpretation. Manifestly, as the *most* general cognition at which we arrive cannot be reduced to a *more* general one, it cannot be understood. Of necessity, therefore, explanation must eventually bring us down to the inexplicable. The deepest truth which we can get at must be unaccountable. Comprehension must become something other than comprehension before the ultimate fact can be comprehended.

Sir A. T. QUILLER-COUCH

Sir Arthur Thomas Quiller-Couch, educated at Trinity College, Oxford, holds, among many other testimonies of his ability as scholar, author, and teacher, the degree of M.A. from Oxford and from Cambridge, that of Litt.D. from Bristol, and that of LL.D. from Aberdeen and Edinburgh. Since 1912 he has been King Edward VII Professor of English Literature in Cambridge University, where he is also a Fellow of Jesus College. The list of his published works, including essays, fiction, and poetry, runs to some fifty titles; he has edited such well-known anthologies as The Oxford Book of Ballads *and* The Oxford Book of Victorian Verse, *besides providing such admirable introductions as that to the* World's Classics *edition of the poems of Matthew Arnold. That he is eminently qualified to lecture on the art of writing is proved, however, not so much by the necessarily abridged account just given of his academic honors and literary accomplishments as by the lectures themselves. Republished as essays, they have not lost their charm, but show the good taste, good judgment, and good humor characteristic of their author.*

The following essay is reprinted from On the Art of Writing, *by A. T. Quiller-Couch, published by G. P. Putnam's Sons. By permission of the publishers.*

ON JARGON

WE PARTED, Gentlemen, upon a promise to discuss the capital difficulty of Prose, as we have discussed the capital difficulty of Verse. But, although we shall come to it, on second thoughts I ask leave to break the order of my argument and to interpose some words upon a kind of writing which, from a superficial likeness, commonly passes for prose in these days, and by lazy folk is commonly written for prose, yet actually is not prose at all; my excuse being the simple practical one that, by first clearing this sham prose out of the way, we shall the better deal with honest prose when we come to it. The proper difficulties of prose will remain; but we shall be agreed in understanding what it is, or at any rate what it is not, that we talk about. I remember to have heard somewhere of a religious body in the United States of America which had reason to suspect one of its churches of accepting spiritual consolation from a coloured preacher — an offence against the laws of the Synod — and despatched a Disciplinary Committee with power to act; and of the Committee's returning to report itself unable to take any action under its terms of reference, for that while a person undoubtedly coloured had undoubtedly occupied the pulpit and had audibly spoken from it in the Committee's presence, the performance could be brought within no definition of preaching known or discoverable. So it is with that infirmity of speech — that flux, that determination of words to the mouth, or to the pen — which, though it be familiar to you in parliamentary debates, in newspapers, and as the staple language of Blue Books,

Committees, Official Reports, I take leave to introduce to you as prose which is not prose and under its real name of Jargon.

You must not confuse this Jargon with what is called Journalese. The two overlap, indeed, and have a knack of assimilating each other's vices. But Jargon finds, maybe, the most of its votaries among good douce people who have never written to or for a newspaper in their life, who would never talk of "adverse climatic conditions" when they mean "bad weather"; who have never trifled with verbs such as "obsess," "recrudesce," "envisage," "adumbrate," or with phrases such as "the psychological moment," "the true inwardness," "it gives furiously to think." It dallies with Latinity — "sub silentio," "de die in diem," "cui bono?" (always in the sense, unsuspected by Cicero, of "What is the profit?") — but not for the sake of style. Your journalist at the worst is an artist in his way; he daubs paint of this kind upon the lily with a professional zeal; the more flagrant (or, to use his own word, arresting) the pigment, the happier is his soul. Like the Babu he is trying all the while to embellish our poor language, to make it more floriferous, more poetical — like the Babu for example who, reporting his mother's death, wrote, "Regret to inform you, the hand that rocked the cradle has kicked the bucket."

There is metaphor; *there* is ornament; *there* is a sense of poetry, though as yet groping in a world unrealised. No such gusto marks — no such zeal, artistic or professional, animates — the practitioners of Jargon, who are, most of them (I repeat), douce respectable persons. Caution is its father; the instinct to save everything and especially trouble; its mother, Indolence. It looks precise, but is not. It is, in these times, *safe*: a thousand men have said it before and not one to your knowledge had been prosecuted for it. And so, like respectability in Chicago, Jargon stalks unchecked in our midst. It is becoming the language of Parliament; it has become the medium through which Boards of Government, County Councils, Syndicates, Committees, Commercial Firms, express the processes as well as the conclusions of their thought and so voice the reason of their being.

Has a Minister to say "No" in the House of Commons? Some men are constitutionally incapable of saying no; but the Minister conveys it thus: "The answer to the question is in the negative." That means "no." Can you discover it to mean anything less, or anything more except that the speaker is a pompous person? — which was no part of the information demanded.

That is Jargon, and it happens to be accurate. But as a rule Jargon is by no means accurate, its method being to walk circumspectly around its target; and its faith, that having done so it has either hit the bull's-eye or at least achieved something equivalent, and safer.

Thus the clerk of a Board of Guardians will minute that —

In the case of John Jenkins deceased the coffin provided was of the usual character.

Now this is not accurate. "In the case of John Jenkins deceased," for whom a coffin was supplied, it is wholly superfluous to tell us that he is deceased. But actually John Jenkins never had more than one case, and that was the coffin. The clerk says he had two — a coffin in a case; but I suspect the clerk to be mistaken, and I am sure he errs in telling us that the coffin was of the usual character; for coffins have no character, usual or unusual.

For another example (I shall not tell you whence derived) —

In the case of every candidate who is placed in the first class [So you see the lucky fellow gets a case as well as a first-class.

> He might be a stuffed animal: perhaps he is] — In the case of every candidate who is placed in the first class the class-list will show by some convenient mark (1) the Section or Sections for proficiency in which he is placed in the first class and (2) the Section or Sections (if any) in which he has passed with special distinction.

"The Section or Sections (if any)" — But how, if they are not any, could they be indicated by a mark however convenient?

> The Examiners will have regard to the style and method of the candidate's answers, and will give credit for excellence in *these respects.*

Have you begun to detect the two main vices of Jargon? The first is that it uses circumlocution rather than short straight speech. It says: "In the case of John Jenkins deceased, the coffin" when it means "John Jenkins's coffin"; and its yea is not yea, neither is its nay nay; but its answer is in the affirmative or in the negative, as the foolish and superfluous "case" may be. The second vice is that it habitually chooses vague woolly abstract nouns rather than concrete ones. I shall have something to say by-and-by about the concrete noun, and how you should ever be struggling for it whether in prose or in verse. For the moment I content myself with advising you, if you would write masculine English, never to forget the old tag of your Latin Grammar —

> Masculine will only be
> Things that you can touch and see.

But since these lectures are meant to be a course in First Aid to writing, I will content myself with one or two extremely rough rules; yet I shall be disappointed if you do not find them serviceable.

The first is: Whenever in your reading you come across one of these words, *case, instance, character, nature, condi-*

tion, persuasion, degree — whenever in writing your pen betrays you to one or another of them — pull yourself up and take thought. If it be "case" (I choose it as Jargon's dearest child — "in Heaven yclept Metonomy") turn to the dictionary, if you will, and seek out what meaning can be derived from *casus*, its Latin ancestor; then try how, with a little trouble, you can extricate yourself from that case. The odds are, you will feel like a butterfly who has discarded his chrysalis.

Here are some specimens to try your hand on:

(1) All those tears which inundated Lord Hugh Cecil's head were dry in the case of Mr. Harold Cox.

Poor Mr. Cox! left gasping in his aquarium!

(2) [From a cigar-merchant.] In any case, let us send you a case on approval.

(3) It is contended that Consols have fallen in consequence: but such is by no means the case.

"*Such*," by the way, is another spoilt child of Jargon, especially in Committee's Rules — "Co-opted members may be eligible as such; such members to continue to serve for such time as" — and so on.

(4) Even in the purely Celtic areas only in two or three cases do the Bishops bear Celtic names.

For "cases" read "dioceses."

Instance. In most instances the players were below their form.

But what were they playing at? Instances?

Character — Nature. There can be no doubt that the accident was caused through the dangerous nature of the spot, the hidden character of the by-road, and the utter absence of any warning or danger signal.

Mark the foggy wording of it all! And yet the man hit something and broke his neck! Contrast that explanation with the verdict of a coroner's jury in the west of England on a drowned postman: "We find that deceased met his death by an act of God, caused by sudden overflowing of the river Walkham and helped out by the scandalous neglect of the way-wardens."

The Aintree course is notoriously of a trying nature.

On account of its light character, purity, and age, Usher's whiskey is a whiskey that will agree with you.

Order. The mésalliance was of a pronounced order.

Condition. He was conveyed to his place of residence in an intoxicated condition.

"He was carried home drunk."

Quality and *Section.* Mr. ——, exhibiting no less than five works, all of a superior quality, figures prominently in the oil section.

— This was written of an exhibition of pictures.

Degree. A singular degree of rarity prevails in the earlier editions of this romance.

That is Jargon. In prose it runs simply "The earlier editions of this romance are rare" — or "are very rare" — or even (if you believe what I take leave to doubt), "are singularly rare"; which should mean that they are rarer than the editions of any other work in the world.

Now what I ask you to consider about these quotations is that in each the writer was using Jargon to shirk prose, palming off periphrases upon us when with a little trouble he could have gone straight to the point. "A singular degree of rarity prevails," "the accident was caused through the dangerous nature of the spot," "but such is by no means the case." We may not be capable of much; but we can all write better than that, if we take a little trouble. In place of, "the Aintree course is of a trying nature" we can surely say "Aintree is a trying course" or "the Aintree course is a trying one" — just that and nothing more.

Next, having trained yourself to keep a lookout for these worst offenders (and you will be surprised to find how quickly you get into the way of it), proceed to push your suspicions out among the whole cloudy host of abstract terms. "How excellent a thing is sleep," sighed Sancho Panza; "it wraps a man round like a cloak" — an excellent example, by the way, of how to say a thing concretely; a Jargoneer would have said that "among the beneficent qualities of sleep its capacity for withdrawing the human consciousness from the contemplation of immediate circumstances may perhaps be accounted not the least remarkable." How vile a thing — shall we say? — is the abstract noun! It wraps a man's thoughts round like cotton wool.

Here is a pretty little nest of specimens, found in *The Times* newspaper by Messrs. H. W. and F. G. Fowler, authors of that capital little book *The King's English*:

> One of the most important reforms mentioned in the rescript is the unification of the organization of judicial institutions and the guarantee for all the tribunals of the independence necessary for securing to all classes of the community equality before the law.

I do not dwell on the cacophony; but, to convey a straightforward piece of news, might not the editor of *The Times* as well employ a man to write:

> One of the most important reforms is that of the Courts, which need a uniform system and to be made independent. In this way only can men be assured that all are equal before the law.

I think he might.

A day or two ago the musical critic of the *Standard* wrote this:

MR. LAMOND IN BEETHOVEN
Mr. Frederick Lamond, the Scottish pianist, as an interpreter of Beethoven has few rivals. At this second recital of

the composer's works at Bechstein Hall on Saturday afternoon
he again displayed a complete sympathy and understanding of
his material that extracted the very essence of æsthetic and
musical value from each selection he undertook.   The delightful intimacy of his playing and his unusual force of individual
expression are invaluable assets, which, allied to his technical
brilliancy, enable him to achieve an artistic triumph.   The two
lengthy Variations in E flat major (Op. 35) and in D major, the
latter on the Turkish March from *The Ruins of Athens*, when
included in the same programme, require a master hand to
provide continuity of interest.   *To say that Mr. Lamond successfully avoided moments that might at times, in these works,
have inclined to comparative disinterestedness, would be but a
moderate way of expressing the remarkable fascination with which
his versatile playing endowed them*, but *at the same time* two of
the sonatas given included a similar form of composition, and
no matter how intellectually brilliant may be the interpretation, the extravagant use of a certain mode is bound in time to
become somewhat ineffective.   In the Three Sonatas, the E
major (Op. 109), the A major (Op. 2), No. 2, and the C minor
(Op. 111), Mr. Lamond signalized his perfect insight into the
composer's varying moods.

Will you not agree with me that here is no writing, here is
no prose, here is not even English, but merely a flux of
words to the pen?

Here again is a string, a concatenation — say, rather,
a tiara of gems of purest ray serene from the dark un-
fathomed caves of a Scottish newspaper:

> The Chinese viewpoint, as indicated in this letter, may not
> be without interest to your readers, because it evidently is
> suggestive of more than an academic attempt to explain an
> unpleasant aspect of things which, if allowed to materialize,
> might suddenly culminate in disaster resembling the Chang-
> Sha riots.   It also ventures to illustrate incidents having their
> inception in recent premature endeavours to accelerate the
> development of Protestant missions in China; but we would
> hope for the sake of the interests involved that what my cor-
> respondent describes as "the irresponsible ruffian element"
> may be known by their various religious designations only
> within very restricted areas.

Well, the Chinese have given it up, poor fellows! and are asking the Christians — as today's newspapers inform us — to pray for them. Do you wonder? But that is, or was, the Chinese "viewpoint" — and what a willow-pattern viewpoint! Observe its delicacy. It does not venture to interest or be interesting; merely "to be not without interest." But it does "venture to illustrate incidents" — which, for a viewpoint, is brave enough; and this illustration "is suggestive of something more than an academic attempt to explain an unpleasant aspect of things which, if allowed to materialise, might suddenly culminate." *What* materialises? The unpleasant aspect? or the things? Grammar says the "things," "things which if allowed to materialise." But things are materialised already, and as a condition of their being things. It must be the aspect, then, that materialises. But, if so, it is also the aspect that culminates, and an aspect, however unpleasant, can hardly do that, or at worst cannot culminate in anything resembling the Chang-Sha riots.... I give it up.

Let us turn to another trick of jargon; the trick of Elegant Variation, so rampant in the sporting press that there, without needing to attend these lectures, the undergraduate detects it for laughter:

> Hayward and C. B. Fry now faced the bowling, which apparently had no terrors for the Surrey crack. The old Oxonian, however, took some time in settling to work....

Yes, you all recognise it and laugh at it. But why do you practise it in your essays? An undergraduate brings me an essay on Byron. In an essay on Byron, Byron is (or ought to be) mentioned many times. I expect, nay exact, that Byron shall be mentioned again and again. But my undergraduate has a blushing sense that to call Byron Byron twice on one page is indelicate. So Byron, after starting bravely as Byron, in the second sentence turns into "that great but unequal poet" and thenceforward I have as much trouble with Byron as ever Telemachus with Proteus to hold and pin him back to his proper self. Half-way down the page he becomes "the gloomy master of Newstead"; overleaf he is reincarnated into "the meteoric darling of society"; and so proceeds through successive avatars — "this arch-rebel," "the author of *Childe Harold*," "the apostle of scorn," "the ex-Harrovian, proud, but abnormally sensitive of his club-foot," "the martyr of Missolonghi," "the pageant-monger of a bleeding heart." Now this again is jargon. It does not, as most jargon does, come of laziness; but it comes of timidity, which is worse. In literature as in life he makes himself felt who not only calls a spade a spade but has.the pluck to double spades and redouble.

For another rule — just as rough and ready, but just as useful: Train your suspicions to bristle up whenever you come upon "as regards," "with regard to," "in respect of," "in connection with," "according as to whether," and the like. They are all dodges of jargon, circumlocutions for evading this or that simple statement; and I say that it is not enough to avoid them nine times out of ten, or nine-and-ninety times out of a hundred. You should never use them. That is positive enough, I hope? Though I cannot admire his style, I admire the man who wrote to me, "Re Tennyson — your remarks anent his *In Memoriam* make me sick"; for though *re* is not a preposition of the first water, and "anent" has enjoyed its day, the finish crowned the work. But here are a few specimens far, very far, worse:

> The special difficulty in Professor Minocelsi's case [our old friend "case" again] arose *in connexion with* the view he holds *relative to* the historical value of the opening pages of Genesis.

That is jargon. In prose, even taking the miserable sentence as it stands constructed, we should write "the difficulty arose over the views he holds about the historical value," etc.

From a popular novelist:

> I was entirely indifferent *as to* the results of the game, caring nothing at all *as to* whether *I had losses or gains* —

Cut out the first "as" in "as to," and the second "as to" altogether, and the sentence begins to be prose — "I was indifferent to the results of the game, caring nothing whether I had losses or gains."

But why, like Dogberry, have "had losses"? Why not simply "lose." Let us try again. "I was entirely indifferent to the results of the game, caring nothing at all whether I won or lost."

Still the sentence remains absurd; for the second clause but repeats the first without adding one jot. For if you care not at all whether you win or lose, you must be entirely indifferent to the results of the game. So why not say, "I was careless if I won or lost," and have done with it?

> A man of simple and charming character, he was fitly *associated with* the distinction of the Order of Merit.

I take this gem with some others from a collection made three years ago, by the *Oxford Magazine*; and I hope you admire it as one beyond price. "He was associated with the distinction of the Order of Merit" means "he was given the Order of Merit." If the members of that Order make a society then he was associated with them; but you cannot associate a man with a distinction. The inventor of such fine writing would doubtless have answered Canning's Needy Knife-grinder with:

> I associate thee with sixpence! I will see thee in another association first!

But let us close our *florilegium* and attempt to illustrate jargon by the converse method of taking a famous piece of

English (say Hamlet's soliloquy) and remoulding a few lines of it in this fashion:

> To be, or the contrary? Whether the former or the latter be preferable would seem to admit of some difference of opinion; the answer in the present case being of an affirmative or of a negative character according as to whether one elects on the one hand to mentally suffer the disfavour of fortune, albeit in an extreme degree, or on the other to boldly envisage adverse conditions in the prospect of eventually bringing them to a conclusion. The condition of sleep is similar to, if not indistinguishable from that of death; and with the addition of finality the former might be considered identical with the latter: so that in this connection it might be argued with regard to sleep that, could the addition be effected, a termination would be put to the endurance of a multiplicity of inconveniences, not to mention a number of downright evils incidental to our fallen humanity, and thus a consummation achieved of a most gratifying nature.

That is jargon: and to write jargon is to be perpetually shuffling around in the fog and cotton-wool of abstract terms; to be for ever hearkening, like Ibsen's Peer Gynt, to the voice of the Boyg exhorting you to circumvent the difficulty, to beat the air because it is easier than to flesh your sword in the thing. The first virtue, the touchstone of masculine style, is its use of the active verb and the concrete noun. When you write in the active voice, "They gave him a silver teapot," you write as a man. When you write "He was made the recipient of a silver teapot," you write jargon. But at the beginning set even higher store on the concrete noun. Somebody — I think it was Fitz-Gerald — once posited the question, "What would have become of Christianity if Jeremy Bentham had had the writing of the Parables?" Without pursuing that dreadful enquiry I ask you to note how carefully the Parables — those exquisite short stories — speak only of "things which you can touch and see" — "A sower went forth to sow," "The Kingdom of Heaven is like unto leaven, which a woman took" — and not the Parables only, but the Sermon on the Mount and almost every verse of the Gospel. The Gospel does not, like my young essayist, fear to repeat a word, if the word be good. The Gospel says "Render unto Cæsar the things that are Cæsar's" — not "Render unto Cæsar the things that appertain to that potentate." The Gospel does not say "Consider the growth of the lilies," or even "Consider how the lilies grow." It says, "Consider the lilies, how they grow."

Or take Shakespeare. I wager you that no writer of English so constantly chooses the concrete word, in phrase after phrase forcing you to touch and see. No writer so insistently teaches the general through the particular. He does it even in *Venus and Adonis* (as Professor Wendell, of Harvard, pointed out in a brilliant little monograph on Shakespeare, published some ten years ago). Read any page of *Venus and Adonis* side by side with any page of Marlowe's *Hero and Leander* and you cannot but mark the contrast: in Shakespeare the definite, particular, visualised image, in Marlowe the beautiful generalisation, the abstract term, the thing seen at a literary remove. Take the two openings, both of which start out with the sunrise. Marlowe begins:

> Now had the Morn espied her lover's steeds:
> Whereat she starts, puts on her purple weeds,
> And, red for anger that he stay'd so long,
> All headlong throws herself the clouds among.

Shakespeare wastes no words on Aurora and her feelings, but gets to his hero and to business without ado:

> Even as the sun with purple-colour'd face —

(You have the sun visualised at once)

> Even as the sun with purple-colour'd face
> Had ta'en his last leave of the weeping morn,
> Rose-cheek'd Adonis hied him to the chase;
> Hunting he loved, but love he laugh'd to scorn.

When Shakespeare has to describe a horse, mark how
definite he is:

> Round-hoof'd, short-jointed, fetlocks shag and long,
> Broad breast, full eye, small head and nostril wide,
> High crest, short ears, straight legs and passing strong,
> Thin mane, thick tail, broad buttock, tender hide.

Or again, in a casual simile, how definite:

> Upon this promise did he raise his chin,
> Like a dive-dipper peering through a wave,
> Which, being look'd on, ducks as quickly in.

Or take, if you will, Marlowe's description of Hero's first
meeting Leander:

> It lies not in our power to love or hate,
> For will in us is over-ruled by fate...

and set against it Shakespeare's description of Venus' last
meeting with Adonis, as she came on him lying in his blood:

> Or as a snail whose tender horns being hit
> Shrinks backward in his shelly cave with pain,
> And there, all smother'd up, in shade doth sit,
> Long after fearing to creep forth again;
> So, at his bloody view —

I do not deny Marlowe's lines (if you will study the whole
passage) to be lovely.   You may even judge Shakespeare's
to be crude by comparison.   But you cannot help noting
that whereas Marlowe steadily deals in abstract, nebulous
terms, Shakespeare constantly uses concrete ones, which
later on he learned to pack into verse, such as:

> Sleep that knits up the ravell'd sleeve of care.

Is it unfair to instance Marlowe, who died young?
Then let us take Webster for the comparison; Webster, a
man of genius or of something very like it, and commonly
praised by the critics for his mastery over definite, detailed, and what I may call *solidified sensation*.   Let us take
this admired passage from his *Duchess of Malfy*:

Ferdinand. How doth our sister Duchess bear herself
In her imprisonment?
    Basola.   Nobly: I'll describe her.
She's sad as one long wed to 't, and she seems
Rather to welcome the end of misery
Than shun it: a behaviour so noble
As gives a majesty to adversity.[1]
You may discern the shape of loveliness
More perfect in her tears than in her smiles;
She will muse for hours together;[2] and her silence
Methinks expresseth more than if she spake.

Now set against this the well-known passage from *Twelfth
Night* where the Duke asks and Viola answers a question
about someone unknown to him and invented by her — a
mere phantasm, in short: yet note how much more definite is the language:

Viola. My father had a daughter lov'd a man;
As it might be, perhaps, were I a woman,
I should your lordship.
    Duke.   And what's her history?
Viola. A blank, my lord.   She never told her love,
But let concealment, like a worm i' the bud,
Feed on her damask cheek; she pined in thought,
And with a green and yellow melancholy
She sat like Patience on a monument
Smiling at grief.   Was not this love indeed?

Observe (apart from the dramatic skill of it) how, when
Shakespeare *has* to use the abstract noun "concealment,"
on an instant it turns into a visible worm "feeding" on the
visible rose; how, having to use a second abstract word
"patience," at once he solidifies it in tangible stone.
    Turning to prose, you may easily assure yourselves that
men who have written learnedly on the art agree in treat-
ing our maxim — to prefer the concrete term to the abstract,
the particular to the general, the definite to the vague —

[1] Note the abstract term.
[2] Here we first come on the concrete: and beautiful it is.

as a canon of rhetoric. Whately has much to say on it.
The late Mr. E. J. Payne, in one of his admirable prefaces to Burke (prefaces too little known and valued, as
too often happens to scholarship hidden away in a school-
book), illustrated the maxim by setting a passage from
Burke's speech *On Conciliation with America* alongside a
passage of like purport from Lord Brougham's *Inquiry
into the Policy of the European Powers.* Here is the deadly
parallel:

BURKE	BROUGHAM
In large bodies the circulation of power must be less vigorous at the extremities. Nature has said it. The Turk cannot govern Ægypt and Arabia and Curdistan as he governs Thrace; nor has he the same dominion in Crimea and Algiers which he has in Brusa and Smyrna. Despotism itself is obliged to truck and huckster. The Sultan gets such obedience as he can. He governs with a loose rein, that he may govern at all; and the whole of the force and vigour of his authority in his centre is derived from a prudent relaxation in all his borders.	In all the despotisms of the East, it has been observed that the further any part of the empire is removed from the capital, the more do its inhabitants enjoy some sort of rights and privileges: the more inefficacious is the power of the monarch; and the more feeble and easily decayed is the organisation of the government.

You perceive that Brougham has transferred Burke's
thought to his own page; but will you not also perceive how
pitiably, by dissolving Burke's vivid particulars into smooth
generalities, he has enervated its hold on the mind?

"This particularising style," comments Mr. Payne,
"is the essence of poetry; and in prose it is impossible not
to be struck with the energy it produces. Brougham's
passage is excellent in its way: but it pales before the

flashing lights of Burke's sentences." The best instances of this energy of style, he adds, are to be found in the classical writers of the seventeenth century. "When South says, 'An Aristotle was but the rubbish of an Adam, and Athens but the rudiments of Paradise,' he communicates more effectually the notion of the difference between the intellect of fallen and of unfallen humanity than in all the philosophy of his sermons put together."

You may agree with me, or you may not, that South in this passage is expounding trash; but you will agree with Mr. Payne and me that he uttered it vividly.

Let me quote to you, as a final example of this vivid style of writing, a passage from Dr. John Donne far beyond and above anything that ever lay within South's compass:

> The ashes of an Oak in the Chimney are no epitaph of that Oak, to tell me how high or how large that was; it tells me not what flocks it sheltered while it stood, nor what men it hurt when it fell. The dust of great persons' graves is speechless, too; it says nothing, it distinguishes nothing. As soon the dust of a wretch whom thou wouldest not, as of a prince whom thou couldest not look upon will trouble thine eyes if the wind blow it thither; and when a whirlewind hath blown the dust of the Churchyard into the Church, and the man sweep out the dust of the Church into the Churchyard, who will undertake to sift those dusts again and to pronounce, This is the Patrician, this is the noble flowre [flour], this the yeomanly, this the Plebeian bran? So is the death of *Iesabel* (*Iesabel* was a Queen) expressed. They shall not say *This is Iesabel;* not only not wonder that it is, nor pity that it should be; but they shall not say, they shall not know, *This is Iesabel.*

Carlyle noted of Goethe, "his emblematic intellect, his never-failing tendency to transform into *shape*, into *life*, the feeling that may dwell in him. Everything has form, has visual excellence: the poet's imagination bodies forth the forms of things unseen, and his pen turns them into shape."

Perpend this, Gentlemen, and maybe you will not here-

after set it down to my reproach that I wasted an hour of a
May morning in a denunciation of jargon, and in exhorting
you upon a technical matter at first sight so trivial as the
choice between abstract and definite words.

A lesson about writing your language may go deeper
than language; for language (as in a former lecture I tried to
preach to you) is your reason, your λόγος. So long as you
prefer abstract words, which express other men's sum-
marised concepts of things, to concrete ones which lie as
near as can be reached to things themselves and are the
first-hand material for your thoughts, you will remain, at
the best, writers at second-hand. If your language be
jargon, your intellect, if not your whole character, will almost certainly correspond. Where your mind should go
straight, it will dodge: the difficulties it should approach
with a fair front and grip with a firm hand it will be seeking
to evade or circumvent. For the style is the man, and
where a man's treasure is there his heart, and his brain, and
his writing, will be also.

FRANK MOORE COLBY

Frank Moore Colby (1865–1925) *graduated from Columbia University in* 1888. *After a year of post-graduate study leading to the degree of M.A., he taught history and economics, first at Amherst, next at Columbia, and finally at New York University, resigning his professorship in* 1900 *to devote himself to editorial work. Already in* 1898 *he had begun to act as editor of* The International Year Book, *a position which he held until his death; from* 1900 *to* 1903 *he was one of three editors responsible for the* New International Encyclopædia, *and from* 1913 *to* 1915 *he alone supervised the second edition of that work. Of these labors he said that they were making him into "a chute down which tons of general information plunged annually in a long, deafening roar, leaving only a trail of dust behind." Despite the dust, however, he found energy to contribute frequently to such periodicals as* The Bookman, The New Republic, *and* The North American Review, *and to publish three volumes of collected essays. An outspoken critic of American life and letters, he attacked frequently the timid propriety, the lack of originality in thought and word, in contemporary literary magazines. For these evils he held his former colleagues, the college professors, largely responsible. Whether or not he was justified in this opinion, his pungent criticism of a certain type of "literary" essay is worth reading.*

The following essay is reprinted from The Margin of Hesitation *by Frank Moore Colby, copyright,* 1921, *by Dodd, Mead and Company, Inc. Used by permission of Dodd, Mead and Company, Inc.*

FRANK MOORE COLBY

OUR REFINEMENT

I DO NOT object to that excellent lady who is to be found at intervals in the literary columns of a serious magazine wondering sweetly what the May-fly thinks in June. On the contrary, a May-fly is a good enough excuse for wonder, and wonder is a good enough excuse for the most exciting kind of imaginative exercise. There is no reason why the intimations of immortality conveyed by May-flies should not be a permanent part of every serious magazine on earth.

I do not object, that is to say, to the situation itself. I object only to one appalling circumstance. It is always the same lady and she is always saying exactly the same sweet things, and the language she says them in is not a living human language. The objectionable thing is the awful iterativeness of its subhuman literary propriety.

And it is the same way with all those other things expressive of literary refinement, expressive of nothing else, but recurring with a deadly certainty, weekly, monthly, perennially, and perhaps eternally. Those pious papers on the comic spirit, by American professors of English; those happy thoughts on the pleasures of reading good books rather than bad; on the imperishable charm of that which is imperishably charming; on the superiority of the "things of the spirit" over other things not mentioned but presumably gross, such as things on the dinner table; humorous apologues of Dame Experience conceived as a school-mistress; tender souvenirs of quaint great-uncles; peeps at a sparrow, nesting — it would be a sin to blame them from any other point of view than that of the future

of the English language, for the subjects are irreproachable
and the motives that actuate the writers on them are as
pure as the driven snow.   But they are the mimetic gentilities of what may be called our upper middle literary class
and they are not expressed in any living language.   Indeed they tend to rob a language of any hope to live.

Not, of course, that English style is a mere matter of
vocabulary or that the most rollicking use of the American
vernacular in utter Shakespearean defiance of propriety
would bring Shakespearean results.   But distinguishable
writing does after all derive from an immense catholicity
and a freedom of choice, not only from among words that
are read, but among words that are lived with.   Nor can it
possibly dispense with what the French call the "green"
language — least of all in this country where the "green"
language has already acquired a vigor and variety that is
not to be found in books.

Take for example a passage from almost any serious article in an American magazine, say in regard to the reconstruction of American education after the war, for nobody
had the slightest notion what he was writing about when
he was writing on that subject, and there is never any idea
in the article that might distract attention from the words.

> It can scarcely be denied that the vital needs of the hour
> call for something more than the disparate and unco-ordinated
> efforts which were unhappily often the mark of educational
> endeavor in the past.   That looms large in the lesson of the
> war.   If it has taught us nothing else, the war has at least
> taught us the necessity for a synthetic direction of educational
> agencies towards a definite and realized goal, humanistic in the
> broad and permanent sense of that term, humanistic, that is to
> say, with due reference to the changing conditions of Society.
> The policy of drift must be abandoned once and for all and for
> it must be substituted a policy of steadfast, watchful — etc.

Not that I have seen this particular passage in an article on
the reconstruction of education, but it might be found in

any of them. It is exactly in the vein of all that I have happened to read; and in the best American magazines you will sometimes find four pages of eight hundred words apiece all made up of just such sentences.

Compare it for imaginative energy, ingenuity, humor, any literary quality you like, with the following selection from a recent volume on Americanisms and slang:

> See the elephant, crack up, make a kick, buck the tiger, jump on with both feet, go the whole hog, know the ropes, get solid, make the fur fly, put a bug in the ear, haloo, halloa, hello, and sometimes holler, get the dead-wood on, die with your boots on, hornswoggle, ker-flap, ker-splash, beat it, butt in, give a show-down, cut-up, kick-in, start-off, run-in, and jump off, put it over, put it across, don't be a high-brow, road-louse, sob-sister, lounge-lizard, rube, boob, kike, or has-been.

The style of this paragraph is by no means so good as would have resulted from a more careful selection, for the words are taken at random and most of them are stale. Moreover, the words are not nearly so imaginative or vigorous as seventeenth-century terms, since forgotten by the mincing generations. The text, for example, is not for a moment to be compared with that of Sir Thomas Urquhart's *Rabelais*. But even as it is, it is immeasurably better than my educational extract and it is just as pertinent to the subject of education — probably more so. The substitution of these lists for the usual university president's magazine contribution on educational reconstruction problems would have helped just as much, if not more, to the solution of those problems, besides being pleasanter to read. Such lists might, I think, replace with advantage much of what is called "inspirational literature." "New Thought," for example, might have spared itself thousands upon thousands of pages by the simple repetition of these lists.

There were many barkeepers — in better days, of course

— who, if they could have learned the literary language without losing grip of their own, might have made good writers. There are no professors of English literature who could learn to write the language even if you gave them all the advantages of barkeepers. They lack the barkeeper's fine, reckless imagination in the use of words. They cannot appropriate a word, or stretch it, or make it do something it had not done before, or still less create it out of nothing. They could not even interest themselves in the "green" language; their interest arises only when it is dry. Never, like a washwoman, or a poet, could they add to the capacities of human speech. Their lives are spent in reducing them. Language would never grow if ruled by the American upper middle literary class. It would stiffen and die. Our college chairs of English and our magazines for "cultured" persons probably do more to prevent the adequate use of our common speech than any other influences.

Distinguishable English sometimes may be found in an American newspaper; it is never found in an American literary magazine. In some corner of a newspaper you may find a man writing with freedom and a sort of natural tact, choosing the words he really needs without regard to what is vulgar or what is polite. People are apt to read it aloud to you without knowing why; they like the sound of it. That never happens in a literary magazine. Nobody in a literary magazine fits words to thought; he fits his thoughts to a borrowed diction. Nobody in a literary magazine cares a hang about the right word for the expression of his thought, but he is worried to death about diction. All the best contemporary literary essays are written in diction and there is no more telling the writers apart, so far as their style is concerned, than if they were all buried in the same good taste by the same undertaker.

Diction is the great funereal American substitute for style. Indeed that is what they mean when they praise an author's style. They do not mean that he has his own style of writing; they mean that he is *in the style* of writing.

Measured by the vitality of masterpieces, newspaper English is sometimes fairly good; literary magazine English is never good. Bad English is English about to die, such as you see in the magazines; the worst English is the English that has never lived — it is the English of American belles-lettres.

That is one of the reasons why I hate the self-improved, traveled American whom I meet in books and periodicals. I hate him also for what seems to me the servility of his spirit in the presence of other people's past. I dare say it may be because I envy him his advantages. That is what the cultivated person always implies, and he wonders how anyone, in view of the national crudity, can have the heart to find fault with these missionaries of taste from a riper culture who have learned the value of artistic *milieux* and literary backgrounds. After all, he says, what Henry James would call the "European scene" may still be commended to Americans, and surely it is just as well that they should be reminded now and then of what Professor Barrett Wendell used so admirably to term their "centuries of social inexperience." Nevertheless as he goes on I not only feel that I am coarse, but I like the feeling of it; and for the sake of other people of my own coarse type I will present here the excuses of vulgarity.

I have never been in Paterson, New Jersey, and I have never been in Venice, and so far as direct esthetic personal consequences to myself of golden hours of dalliance in the two places are concerned, I am therefore unable to offer a comparison. But during my life I have met many returned travelers from Venice and from Paterson, and I have read or listened to their narratives with as much attention as they could reasonably demand. Theoretically, I accept the opinion of enlightened persons that Venice is superior, in respect to what educators call its "cultural value," to Paterson. Practically, and judging merely from the effects upon the respective visitors, I am all for Paterson. I have never met a man who returned from Paterson talking like the stray pages of a catalogue, of which he had a complete copy before he started. Paterson never took away part of a man's mind and replaced it with a portion of an encyclopedia. Nobody ever came back from Paterson damaged as a man and yet inferior as a magazine article. For the careless person, I should recommend Venice; for the culture-seeker, Paterson. Overstrain, that misery of the conscientious self-improving man, with its disagreeable effects upon other people, could be avoided in Paterson. Out of ten essays on Venice that I have read, nine were written by fish out of water who might have swum easily and perhaps with grace in the artistic currents of Paterson.

A self-improved American delivered an apologetic discourse the other day on the American deficiency in backgrounds. Culture cannot take root, he said; families float; everybody dies in a town he was not born in; art bombinates in a vacuum; literature gathers no moss; manners, when they exist at all, are accidental; history is clean gone out of our heads, while every Englishman is familiar with Bannockburn; poetry cannot be written, and it is foolish to try, on account of the dearth of venerable circumstances; no traditions, no memories, no inheritance — in fact, no past at all; not even a present of any consequence, but only a future; and into this future every man, woman, and child in the whole foolish country is moving — though it is not through any fault of theirs, for the unfortunate inhabitants really have no other place to go to.

I bear no grudge against the author of this discourse as an individual, but only as a type. Indeed, I am not sure that he is an individual or that I have reported him cor-

rectly, for no sooner does anyone begin in this manner than
his words run into the words of others, forming a river of
sound, and I think not of one man, but of strings of them —
all worrying about the lack of backgrounds, like the man
who cast no shadow in the sun. I deny that it is anyone's
voluntary attitude; it is a lockstep that began before I was
born, and I have no doubt it will continue indefinitely.
Seven centuries after Columbus's injudicious discovery
they will still be complaining, with a Baedeker in their
hands, of the fatal youth of North America. For they live
long, these people, because, as in certain lower orders of
animal life, apparently, there is hardly any life worth
losing, and the family likeness they bear to one another is
astonishing. The very ones that George William Curtis
used to satirize as shining in society are still to be found
among us at this moment, but they are engaged for the
most part in contributing to the magazines. In one respect they seem more the slaves of other people's backgrounds even than Mrs. Potiphar was. Mrs. Potiphar
only believed that the right sort of liveries were not produced in this country — or at least not till our backgrounds are ever so many centuries thicker than they are
now. I am unable, looking back, to see any value whatever in these decades of sheer sterile complaint of sterility,
because no ruins can be seen against the sky, because no
naiads are dreamed of in the Hudson or mermaids in Cape
Cod Bay, and because most people who are born in In-
dianapolis seem glad to get away from it when they can.

For one sign that we have changed too fast I can produce two signs that we have not changed half fast enough.
If there is no moss here on the walls of ancient battle-
ments there is plenty of moss in our heads, and, so far as
tenacity of tradition is concerned, I can produce a dozen
United States Senators who are fully as picturesque, if
only you regard them internally, as the quaintest peas-

ant in the quaintest part of France.   Backgrounds are
not lost here just because we move about; backgrounds
are simply worn inside, often with the ivy clustering on
them.   Who has not talked with some expatriated Boston
man and found him as reposeful, as redolent of sad, forgotten, far-off things, as any distant prospect of Stoke-
Pogis?   In fact, it seems as if these pale expositors of backgrounds had merely visited the monuments they praise —
inside some Boston man — and that, I confess, is the most
irritating thing to me about them.   They have never
really looked at anything themselves, but only learned
from others what they ought to seem to see.   And it is absurd to tax us with a lack of memory, when in some of our
most exclusive literary circles there is notoriously nothing
but a memory to be seen.   There is too much Stoke-Pogis
in a Boston man, if anything, in proportion to other things.
Even the casual foreign visitor has noticed it.

I have great respect for the religion of the Quakers,
whose name, I understand, comes from the phrase of a
founder about quaking and shaking in the fear of the Lord.
And if that is the real reason why they quake, I believe
they are justified not only in their quaking, but in trying
to make other people quake.   But these Delsartean
literary quakers correctly tremulous in the presence of antiquity, these "cultured" minds, not only palsied by their
own advantages, but intent on palsying others, bring back
no good report to anybody in regard to the good things in
the world.

I do not know whether a poet, like a sugar beet, requires a soil with peculiar properties; and, in regard to the
poet, I do not know what the peculiar properties ought to
be.   Zoning of verse, comparative literary crop statistics,
mean annual density of ideas, ratio of true poetry to
square miles and population within a given period, are all
outside my limitations.   The theory that bone-dust fer-

tilizers are the things for poets does not always seem to work, even when the bone-dust is that of the Crusaders, and I have read lyrics from cathedral towns, which, though infinitely more decorous than the brass band of my native village, were equally remote from literature. Still there may be something in it. But I do know, even better than I wish I did, two generations of writers on the theme, who have been saying, with hardly any deviation in their phrases, that this is the land where poets cannot grow; and I know them for the sort of persons who, if by chance a poet should grow in defiance of their theory, could not tell him from a sugar beet. They are unaware of any growing thing which stands before them unaccompanied by a bibliography. Unless there were antecedent books about an object, they would not know that the object was a poet.

As the words "culture" and "refinement" have been applied and as they have been exemplified in American letters, they have come to carry a curse for all save little bands of unpleasant and self-conscious persons who are themselves fidgeting about it. "Culture" is not absorbed, but packed in, always with a view to being taken out again without a wrinkle in it, and it does nothing to the man who gets it, but he means to do a lot with it to you. It is absurd to suppose that the human container of it takes any personal interest in his contents.

Of course I am not speaking of the essence of the thing, but only of the implications of the word as they have been seared into our social experience. I do not mean that humane learning blasts an American, but I do mean that among those who are known as cultured Americans learning is not humane. And I am not condemning the present moment. It has nothing to do with the rudeness of young people, jazz bands, the corruption of the English language, war psychology, the Bolshevism of college professors, fox-trotting, the neglect of the classics, movies, commercialism, syndicalism, indecencies on the stage, popular novels, feminism, or any other of the unheard-of horrors that the middle-aged mind associates with the break-down of civilization.   There is no sign that American civilization is breaking down in this respect, for the simple reason that there is no sign that American civilization in this respect ever existed.   There is no sign that among any considerable body of cultured Americans learning was ever humane, and it is lucky for us that vivacious men at every period of our national life have revolted from it.   Ten years of Greek study would not have hurt Mark Twain, but ten years' contact with the sort of persons who studied Greek would have destroyed him.   Historical studies would not have suffocated Walt Whitman; even after reading Bishop Stubbs he might have remained our poet of democracy. But association with modern historians would have done for him.   Had Walt Whitman taken the same course I did at a school of political science, he would have gone mad or become a college president.

What was it that so pinched the mind of Henry Adams, readers of the *Education of Henry Adams* are always asking, though one would think the answer could not be missed. It was Boston and Cambridge in the eighteen-fifties and an acute personal consciousness of membership in the Adams family.   It was a lucky thing for both Jews and Christians that Moses was not a cultured Boston man, for the Ten Commandments would not only have been multiplied by fifty, but a supplemental volume of thousands of really indispensable gentilities would have come out every year.   No man knew better than the late W. D. Howells the Sinaitic rigor of the social scruple when the descendent of the Puritans once turned his conscience away from God and bent it upon culture.   The genial tale of *The Lady of the Aroostook* might well have been a tragedy.   Indeed, the passion of a man bred in the right Boston set and im-

mensely conscious of it — a man who read the right books
in the right way, knew the right people, visited the right
places abroad — the passion of such a man for a girl who not
only said "I want to know," but who had never heard of a
chaperon — there is a situation not only tragic in itself,
but close to the edge of violence, terminable, one would
say, only by accidental death, murder, or suicide.
Desdemona was smothered for less. That Mr. Howells
should see it to a comparatively cheerful end without calling
down the lightning proves merely the magic of his hand.
But Mr. Howells did not conceal one painful consequence.
Hero and heroine both were outcasts from culture for-
evermore. Never again did they enter the doors of the
right people of Cambridge. "He's done the wisest thing
he could by taking her out to California. She never would
have gone down here." This was the doom that culture
pronounced in the final chapter. For, although at nine-
teen years of age Lydia ceased to say she wanted to know,
the early stain remained. She bore it to the grave. And
this ending was entirely just and Mr. Howells did not ex-
aggerate in the slightest degree the rigors of the law, for,
though Lydia as he made her was the most natural and
adorable creature imaginable, he was right in saying that
in the cultured circles of the time and place she would
not have gone down.

The taboo of culture is of course no new thing, but dates
from a comparatively recent grudge in our brief literary
history. People are ashamed of their culture nowadays, a
friend of mine was saying, and he went on to cite instances
of the exclusion from human intercourse of all those
matters of general interest which make intercourse human. And why are you so afraid of general ideas? one
visiting Frenchman after another has asked me, and I
have never yet been able to think of a suitable reply.
And they go back to France on no better terms with the

English language than when they came. It is impossible to arouse any enthusiasm for our spoken language in a Frenchman, for he does not believe that conversation in his sense of the word is ever carried on in it. And he is certainly right. The range of a quite ordinary Frenchman's everyday talk is not generally permitted in this country. Religion may be discussed with a French chauffeur on a footing of naturalness absolutely out of place at an American authors' club. You may confess a literary taste to a French washwoman, but not to a New York banker. The philosophic speculations of French barber shops would be shockingly pedantic at our dinner tables,

Of course the main reason why the conversation of a novelist does not differ from that of a shoe manufacturer is simply because as a rule there is no real difference between them. But there is sometimes another side to it. The man of letters who excludes letters from his talk is not necessarily ashamed of them. But he knows the traditional association in this country of culture with ennui, and he knows that it is amply justified. Acquaintance with the personalities of cultured groups naturally disposes a sensitive mind to the cultivation of an appearance of illiteracy. Thought is not a social nuisance in this country, but thinkers generally are. Hence, when seized by an irresistible impulse to express any sort of an idea, a well-bred man will always leave the room, just as he would do if seized by an uncontrollable fit of coughing.

SUGGESTIONS FOR READING

Editor's Note: These suggestions should not be regarded as in any way exhaustive, nor as equivalents of the systematic study of psychology or philosophy. They are presented because students without opportunities for such study have found these books valuable in opening "a door to new worlds in the brain."

I. *On Thinking*
   Arnold Bennett: *Controlling the Mind* (Chapter VIII in *How to Live on Twenty-Four Hours a Day*).
   John Dewey: *Human Nature and Conduct*.
   Ernest Dimnet: *The Art of Thinking*.
   Irwin Edman: *Human Traits*.
   William James: *Reasoning* (in *Principles of Psychology*).
   Everett Dean Martin: *The Behavior of Crowds*.
   James Harvey Robinson: *The Mind in the Making*.
   Bertrand Russell: *Mysticism and Logic*.

II. *An Approach to Philosophy*
   Will Durant: *The Story of Philosophy*.
   William James: *Some Problems of Philosophy*.
   H. A. Larrabee: *What Philosophy Is*.
   Bertrand Russell: *Problems of Philosophy*.

III. *On Writing*
   Whoever is interested in writing will equip himself with the necessary reference books. These should include, at least, a good dictionary and a thesaurus. Fowler's *Modern English Usage* is not only useful but entertaining; there are numerous textbooks of composition, among which Woolley's *Handbook* and *Writing and Thinking*, by Foerster and Steadman, are especially well arranged. The reading of essays on style can never take the place of actual practice, as a means toward acquiring grace and precision in writing. Yet hints furnished by authors may prove useful supplements to that practice.
   W. T. Brewster: *Writing English Prose* (Home University Library).
   Sir Arthur T. Quiller-Couch: *The Art of Writing*.
   Brander Matthews: *Essays on English*.
   Robert Littell: *Some Advice to Writers* (originally an essay in *The New Republic*, reprinted in *Models and Values*, edited by Phillips, Crane, and Byers).

Warner Taylor: *Types and Times in the Essay*, Section V.
   This entire section is composed of letters and essays, by
   modern authors, on the art of writing.
Virginia Woolf: *The Patron and the Crocus* (from *The Common
   Reader*).

o

GROUP TWO
ESSAYS ON POLITICAL, SOCIAL, AND SCIENTIFIC TOPICS

ALDOUS HUXLEY

Born in 1894, Aldous Huxley was educated at Eton and at Balliol College, Oxford. A grandson of the famous scientist (see Essay 2 and introductory note), he has been on the editorial staff of The Athenæum *and has acted also as dramatic critic of* The Westminster Gazette. *The list of his publications in book form already runs to some twenty-one titles, including novels, short stories, and critical essays, to most of which the adjectives "brilliant" and "penetrating" have been applied by discerning critics.* Brave New World *(1932), his most recent novel, is a fantasy of the future, satirizing the trend toward standardization (even children are produced, in laboratories, according to the type desired). The title of the collection of essays from which the following essay is taken is* Proper Studies, *presumably from Pope's famous line, "The proper study of mankind is man." In the Introduction to that volume, Mr. Huxley states his purpose:*

"These essays represent an attempt on my part to methodize the confused notions, which I have derived from observation and reading, about a few of the more important aspects of social and individual life."

"The Idea of Equality" is reprinted from Proper Studies *by Aldous Huxley, published by Chatto & Windus, 1927. By permission of the author.*

ALDOUS HUXLEY

THE IDEA OF EQUALITY

SUNDAY FAITH AND WEEKDAY FAITH

THAT all men are created equal is a proposition to which, at ordinary times, no sane human being has ever given his assent. A man who has to undergo a dangerous operation does not act on the assumption that one doctor is just as good as another. Editors do not print every contribution that reaches them. And when they require Civil Servants, even the most democratic governments make a careful selection among their theoretically equal subjects. At ordinary times, then, we are perfectly certain that men are not equal. But when, in a democratic country, we think or act politically, we are no less certain that men are equal. Or at any rate — which comes to the same thing in practice — we behave as though we were certain of men's equality. Similarly, the pious mediæval nobleman who, in church, believed in forgiving enemies and turning the other cheek, was ready, as soon as he had emerged again into the light of day, to draw his sword at the slightest provocation. The human mind has an almost infinite capacity for being inconsistent.

The amount of time during which men are engaged in thinking or acting politically is very small when compared with the whole period of their lives; but the brief activities of man the politician exercise a disproportionate influence on the daily life of man the worker, man at play, man the father and husband, man the owner of property. Hence the importance of knowing what he thinks in his political capacity and why he thinks it.

THE EQUALITARIAN AXIOM

Politicians and political philosophers have often talked about the equality of man as though it were a necessary and unavoidable idea, an idea which human beings must believe in, just as they must, from the very nature of their physical and mental constitution, believe in such notions as weight, heat, and light. Man is "by nature free, equal, and independent," says Locke, with the calm assurance of one who knows he is saying something that cannot be contradicted. It would be possible to quote literally thousands of similar pronouncements. One must be mad, says Babeuf, to deny so manifest a truth.

EQUALITY AND CHRISTIANITY

In point of historical fact, however, the notion of human equality is of recent growth, and, so far from being a directly apprehended and necessary truth, is a conclusion logically drawn from pre-existing metaphysical assumptions. In modern times the Christian doctrines of the brotherhood of men and of their equality before God have been invoked in support of political democracy. Quite illogically, however. For the brotherhood of men does not imply their equality. Families have their fools and their men of genius, their black sheep and their saints, their worldly successes and their worldly failures. A man should treat his brothers lovingly and with justice, according to the deserts of each. But the deserts of every brother are not the same. Neither does men's equality before God imply their equality as among themselves. Compared with an infinite quantity, all finite quantities may be regarded as equal. There is no difference, where infinity is concerned, between one and a thousand. But leave infinity out of the question, and a thousand is very different from one. Our world is a series of finite quantities, and where worldly matters are concerned, the fact that all men are equal in relation to the infinite quantity which is God is entirely irrelevant. The Church has at all times conducted its worldly policy on the assumption that it was irrelevant. It is only recently that the theorists of democracy have appealed to Christian doctrine for a confirmation of their equalitarian principles. Christian doctrine, as I have shown, gives no such support.

EQUALITY AND THE PHILOSOPHER

The writers who in the course of the eighteenth century supplied our modern political democracy with its philosophical basis did not turn to Christianity to find the doctrine of human equality. They were, to begin with, almost without exception anti-clerical writers, to whom the idea of accepting any assistance from the Church would have been extremely repugnant. Moreover, the Church, as organized for its worldly activities, offered them no assistance, but a frank hostility. It represented, even more clearly than the monarchical and feudal state, that mediæval principle of hierarchical, aristocratic government against which, precisely, the equalitarians were protesting.

The origin of our modern idea of human equality is to be found in the philosophy of Aristotle. The tutor of Alexander the Great was not, it is true, a democrat. Living as he did in a slave-holding society, he regarded slavery as a necessary state of affairs. Whatever is, is right; the familiar is the reasonable; and Aristotle was an owner of slaves, not a slave himself; he had no cause to complain. In his political philosophy he rationalized his satisfaction with the existing state of things, and affirmed that some men are born to be masters (himself, it went without saying, among them) and others to be slaves. But in saying this he was committing an inconsistency. For it was a fundamental tenet of his metaphysical system that specific qualities are the same in every member of a species. Individuals of one species are the same in essence or substance. Two human beings differ from one another in matter, but are the same in essence, as being both rational animals. The essential human quality which distinguishes the species Man from all other species is identical in both.

INCONSISTENCIES

How are we to reconcile this doctrine with Aristotle's statement that some men are born to be masters and others slaves? Clearly, no reconciliation is possible; the doctrines are contradictory. Aristotle said one thing when he was discussing the abstract problems of metaphysics and another when, as a slave-owner, he was discussing politics. Such inconsistencies are extremely common, and are generally made in perfectly good faith. In cases where material interests are at stake, where social and religious traditions, inculcated in childhood, and consequently incorporated into the very structure of the mind, can exercise their influence, men will naturally think in one way; in other cases, where their interests and their early-acquired beliefs are not concerned, they will naturally and inevitably think in quite a different way. A man who thinks and behaves as an open-minded, unprejudiced scientist so long as he is repairing his automobile, will be outraged if asked to think about the creation of the world or the future life except in terms of the mythology current among the barbarous Semites three thousand years ago; and though quite ready to admit that the present system of wireless telegraphy might be improved, he will regard anyone who desires to alter the existing economic and political system as either a madman or a criminal. The greatest men of genius have not been exempt from these curious inconsistencies. Newton created the science of celestial me-

chanics; but he was also the author of *Observations on the Prophecies of Daniel and the Apocalypse of Saint John*, of a *Lexicon Propheticum* and a *History of the Creation*. With one part of his mind he believed in the miracles and prophecies about which he had been taught in childhood; with another part he believed that the universe is a scene of order and uniformity. The two parts were impenetrably
° divided one from the other. The mathematical physicist never interfered with the commentator on the Apocalypse; the believer in miracles had no share in formulating the laws of gravitation. Similarly, Aristotle the slave-owner believed that some men are born to command and others to serve; Aristotle the metaphysician, thinking in the abstract, and unaffected by the social prejudices which influenced the slave-owner, expounded a doctrine of specific essences, which entailed belief in the real and substantial equality of all human beings. The opinion of the slave-owner was probably nearer the truth than that of the metaphysician. But it is by the metaphysician's doctrine that our lives are influenced today.

APPLIED METAPHYSICS

That all members of a species are identical in essence was still, in the Middle Ages, a purely metaphysical doctrine. No attempt was made to apply it practically in politics. So long as the feudal and ecclesiastical hierarchies served their purpose of government, they seemed, to all but a very few, necessary and unquestionable. Whatever is, is right; feudalism and Catholicism *were*. It was only after what we call the Reformation and the Renaissance, when, under the stress of new economic and intellectual forces, the old system had largely broken down, that men began to think of applying the metaphysical doctrine of Aristotle and his mediæval disciples to politics. Feudalism and ecclesiastical authority lingered on, but as the merest ghosts of themselves.   They had, to all intents and purposes, ceased to be, and not being, they were wrong.

It was not necessary, however, for the political thinkers of the eighteenth century to go back directly to Aristotle and the Schoolmen.   They had what was for them a better authority nearer home.   Descartes, the most influential philosopher of his age, had reaffirmed the Aristotelian and Scholastic doctrine in the most positive terms.   At the beginning of his *Discourse on Method* we read that "what is called good sense or reason is equal in all men," and a little later he says, "I am disposed to believe that [reason] is to be found complete in each individual; and on this point to adopt the opinion of philosophers who say that the difference of greater or less holds only among the accidents, and not among the forms or natures of individuals of the same species."   Descartes took not the slightest interest in politics, and was concerned only with physical science and the theory of knowledge.   It remained for others to draw the obvious political conclusions from what was for him, as it had been for Aristotle and the Schoolmen, a purely abstract metaphysical principle.   These conclusions might have been drawn at any time during the preceding two thousand years.   But it was only in the two centuries immediately following Descartes' death that political circumstances in Europe, especially in France, were favourable to such conclusions being drawn.   The forms of government current during classical antiquity and the Middle Ages had been efficient and well adapted to the circumstances of the times.   They seemed, accordingly, right and reasonable.   In the eighteenth century, on the other hand, particularly on the continent of Europe, the existing form of government was not adapted to the social circumstances of the age.   At a period when the middle classes were already rich and well educated, absolute monarchy and the ineffectual remains of feudalism were unsuitable as

forms of government.   Being unsuitable, they therefore
seemed utterly unreasonable and wrong.   Middle-class
Frenchmen wanted a share in the government.   But men
are not content merely to desire; they like to have a logical
or a pseudo-logical justification for their desires; they like
to believe that when they want something, it is not merely
for their own personal advantage, but that their desires
are dictated by pure reason, by nature, by God Himself.
The greater part of the world's philosophy and theology is
merely an intellectual justification for the wishes and the
day-dreams of philosophers and theologians.   And practically all political theories are elaborated, after the fact, to
justify the interests and desires of certain individuals,
classes, or nations.   In the eighteenth century, middle-
class Frenchmen justified their very natural wish to participate in the government of the country by elaborating a
new political philosophy from the metaphysical doctrine of
Aristotle, the Schoolmen, and Descartes.   These philosophers had taught that the specific essence is the same in all
individuals of a species.   In the case of *Homo Sapiens* this
specific essence is reason.   All men are equally reasonable.
It follows that all men have an equal capacity, and therefore an equal right, to govern; there are no born slaves nor
masters.   Hence, monarchy and hereditary aristocracy
are inadmissible.   Nature herself demands that government shall be organized on democratic principles.   Thus
middle-class Frenchmen had the satisfaction of discovering
that their desires were endorsed as right and reasonable,
not only by Aristotle, Saint Thomas, and Descartes, but
also by the Creator of the Universe in person.

MAKING THE FACTS FIT

Even metaphysicians cannot entirely ignore the obvious
facts of the world in which they live.   Having committed
themselves to a belief in this fundamental equality of all

men, the eighteenth-century political philosophers had to invent an explanation for the manifest inequalities which they could not fail to observe on every side. If Jones, they argued, is an imbecile and Smith a man of genius, that is due, not to any inherent and congenital differences between the two men, but to purely external and accidental differences in their upbringing, their education, and the ways in which circumstances have compelled them to use their minds. Give Jones the right sort of training, and you can turn him into a Newton, a Saint Francis, or a Cæsar according to taste. "The diversity of opinions," says Descartes, "does not arise from some being endowed with a larger share of reason than others, but solely from this, that we conduct our thoughts along different ways, and do not fix our attention on the same objects." "Intelligence, genius, and virtue," says Helvétius, whose work, *De l'Esprit*, was published in 1758, and exercised an enormous contemporary influence, "are the products of education." And again (*De l'Esprit*, Discours III. ch. 26): "*La grande inégalité d'esprit qu'on aperçoit entre les hommes dépend donc uniquement et de la différente éducation qu'ils reçoivent, et de l'enchaînement inconnu et divers dans lesquels ils se trouvent placés,*" [1] and so on.

The political and philosophical literature of the eighteenth century teems with such notions. It was only to be expected; for such notions, it is obvious, are the necessary corollaries of the Cartesian axiom that reason is the same and entire in all men. They followed no less necessarily from the *tabula rasa* theory of mind elaborated by Locke. Both philosophers regarded men as originally and in essence equal, the one in possessing the same specific faculties and innate ideas, the other in possessing no innate ideas.

[1] "The great inequality of intelligence which one perceives among men results, then, only from the different education which they receive and from the unknown and varied environment in which they are placed."

It followed from either assumption that men are made or marred exclusively by environment and education. Followers whether of Locke or of Descartes, the eighteenth-century philosophers were all agreed in attributing the observed inequalities of intelligence and virtue to inequalities of instruction. Men were naturally reasonable and therefore good; but they lived in the midst of vice and abject superstition. Why? Because evil-minded legislators — kings and priests — had created a social environment calculated to warp the native reason and corrupt the morals of the human race. Why priests and kings, who, as human beings, were themselves naturally reasonable and therefore virtuous, should have conspired against their fellows, or why their reasonable fellows should have allowed themselves to be put upon by these crafty corrupters, was never adequately explained. The democratic religion, like all other religions, is founded on faith as much as on reason. The king-priest theory in its wildest and most extravagant form is the inspiration and subject of much of Shelley's finest poetry. Poor Shelley, together with large numbers of his less talented predecessors and contemporaries, seems seriously to have believed that by getting rid of priests and kings you could inaugurate the golden age.[1]

THE TESTS OF EXPERIMENT

The historical and psychological researches of the past century have rendered the theory which lies behind the practice of modern democracy entirely untenable. Reason is not the same in all men; human beings belong to a variety of psychological types separated one from another by irreducible differences. Men are not the exclusive products of their environments. A century of growing

[1] For a magnificent expression of this idea, read the final speech of the Spirit of the Hour, in Act III of Shelley's *Prometheus Unbound*.

democracy has shown that the reform of institutions and the spread of education are by no means necessarily followed by improvements in individual virtue and intelligence. At the same time biologists have accumulated an enormous mass of evidence tending to show that physical peculiarities are inherited in a perfectly regular and necessary fashion. Body being indissolubly connected with mind, this evidence would almost be enough in itself to prove that mental peculiarities are similarly heritable. Direct observation on the history of families reinforces this evidence, and makes it certain that mental idiosyncrasies are inherited in exactly the same way as physical idiosyncrasies. Indeed, mind being in some sort a function of brain, a mental idiosyncrasy is also a physical one, just as much as red hair or blue eyes. Faculties are heritable: we are born more or less intelligent, more or less musical, mathematical, and so on. From this it follows that men are not essentially equal, and that human beings are at least as much the product of their heredity as of their education.

THE BEHAVIOURIST REACTION

Recently, it is true, Helvétius's doctrine of the all-effectiveness of nurture and the unimportance of nature and heredity has been revived by psychologists of the Behaviourist School. Unlike the philosophers of the eighteenth century, the Behaviourists have no political axe to grind and are not metaphysicians. If they agree with Helvétius, it is not because they want the vote (they have it), nor, presumably, because they accept the authority of Aristotle, the Schoolmen, and Descartes on the one hand, or of Locke on the other. They agree with Helvétius on what they affirm to be scientific grounds. Helvétius's theory, according to the Behaviourists, is in accordance with the observed facts. Before going further, let us briefly examine their claims.

"The Behaviourist," writes Mr. J. B. Watson, the leader of the school, "no longer finds support for hereditary patterns of behaviour nor for special abilities (musical, art, etc.), which are supposed to run in families. He believes that, given the relatively simple list of embryological responses which are fairly uniform in infants, he can build (granting that both internal and external environment can be controlled) any infant along any specified line — into rich man, poor man, beggar man, thief." Taken literally, this last statement is merely silly. No one was ever such a fool as to suggest that riches and poverty were heritable in the sense that a Roman nose or a talent for music may be said to be heritable. Opulent fathers have long anticipated this great discovery of the Behaviourists, and have "built their children into rich men" by placing large cheques to their account at the bank. We must presume, in charity to Mr. Watson, that he does not mean what he says, and that when he says "rich man, poor man, beggar man, thief," he really means something like intelligent man, imbecile, mathematician and non-mathematician, musical person and unmusical person, etc. Presuming that this is what he does mean, let us examine the Behaviourists' hypothesis, which is identical with that of the philosophers who, in the eighteenth century, elaborated the theory of modern democracy. The first thing that strikes one about the Behaviourists' hypothesis is, that the observations on which it is based are almost exclusively observations on small children, not on fully grown men and women. It is on the ground that all infants are very much alike that the Behaviourists deny the hereditary transmission of special aptitudes, attributing the enormous differences of mental capacity observable among grown human beings exclusively to differences in environment, internal and external. Now it is an obvious and familiar fact, that the younger a child, the less individually differentiated it is. Physically, all

new-born children are very much alike: there are few fathers who, after seeing their new-born infant once, could
recognize it again among a group of other infants.   Mr.
Watson will not, I suppose, venture to deny that physical peculiarities may be inherited.   Yet the son who at
twenty will have his father's aquiline nose and his mother's
dark, straight hair may be as snubnosed and golden at two
as another child whose father is pugfaced and his mother
blonde, and who will grow up to be like them.   If the Behaviourists had made their observations on children a few
months before they were born, they would have been able
to affirm not only the psychological identity of all men and
women, but also their physical identity.   Three days after
their respective conceptions, Pocahontas, Shakespeare, and
a Negro congenital idiot would probably be indistinguishable from one another, even under the most powerful microscope.   According to Behaviourist notions, this should
be regarded as a conclusive proof of the omnipotence of
nurture.   Since they are indistinguishable at conception,
it must be environment that turns the fertilized ova into
respectively a Red-Indian woman, an English man of
genius, and a Negro idiot.

    Mind and body are closely interdependent: they come
to maturity more or less simultaneously.   A mind is not
fully grown until the body with which it is connected
through the brain has passed the age of puberty.   The
mind of a young child is as much undifferentiated and un-
individualized as its body.   It does not become completely
itself until the body is more or less fully grown.   A child
of two has neither his father's nose nor his maternal grandfather's talent for mathematics.   But that is no argument
against his developing both when he is a few years older.
A young child looks and thinks like other children of the
same age and not like his parents.   Later on he will certainly look like his parents.   What reason is there to sup-

pose that his mind will not also be like theirs? If he has his father's nose, why not his father's brain, and with it his father's mentality? The Behaviourists give us no answers to these questions. They merely state, what we already knew, that small children are very much alike. But this is entirely beside the point. Two fertilized ova may be indistinguishable; but if one belongs to a Negress and the other to a Japanese, no amount of nurture will make the Japanese egg develop into a Negro, or *vice versa*. There is no more valid reason for supposing the two very similar infants who were to become Shakespeare and Stratford's village idiot could have been educated into exchanging their adult parts. To study human psychology exclusively in babies is like studying the anatomy of frogs exclusively in tadpoles. That environment may profoundly influence the course of mental development is obvious. But it is no less obvious that there is a hereditarily conditioned development to be modified. Environment no more creates a mental aptitude in a grown boy than it creates the shape of his nose.

EQUALITY OF VIRTUE

We have dealt so far with the primary assumption from which the whole theory and practice of democracy flows — that all men are substantially equal; and with one of its corollaries — that the observed differences between human beings are due to environment; and that education, in the widest sense of the term, is all-powerful. It is now necessary to touch briefly on one or two other corollaries. Men being in essence equally reasonable, it follows that they are also in essence equally moral. For morality (according to the philosophers who formulated the theory of democracy) is absolute and exists in itself, apart from any actual society of right- or wrong-doing individuals. The truths of morality can be apprehended by reason.

All men are equally reasonable: therefore all are equally
capable of grasping the absolute truths of moral science.
They are therefore, in essence, equally virtuous, and if,
in practice, they behave badly, that is merely an accident,
due to corrupting surroundings. Man must be delivered
from his corrupting surroundings (and for the most ardent
and ruthlessly logical spirits all government, all law, and
organized religion are corrupting influences). Finding
himself once more in that idyllic "state of nature" from
which he should never have tried to rise, man will become,
automatically, perfectly virtuous. There are few people
now, I suppose, who take the theories of Rousseau very
seriously. But though our intellect may reject them, our
emotions are still largely influenced by them. Many
people still cherish a vague sentimental belief that the
poor and uncultivated, who are nearer to the "state of
nature" than the cultured and the rich, are for that reason
more virtuous.

DEMOCRATIC POT AND CATHOLIC KETTLE

Pots have a diverting way of calling kettles black, and
the prophets of the democratic-humanitarian religion have
at all times, from the eighteenth century down to the
present day, denounced the upholders of Christian orthodoxy as anti-scientific. In certain important respects, however, the dogmas and the practice of orthodox Catholic
Christianity were and are more nearly in accordance with
the facts than the dogmas and practice of democratic-
humanitarianism. The doctrine of Original Sin is,
scientifically, much truer than the doctrine of natural
reasonableness and virtue. Original Sin, in the shape of
anti-social tendencies inherited from our animal ancestors,
is a familiar and observable fact. Primitively, and in a
state of nature, human beings were not, as the eighteenth-
century philosophers supposed, wise and virtuous: they
were apes.

Practically, the wisdom of the Church displays itself in a recognition among human beings of different psychological types. It is not every Tom, Dick, or Harry who is allowed to study the intricacies of theology. What may strengthen the faith of one may bewilder or perhaps even disgust another. Moreover, not all are called upon to rule; there must be discipline, a hierarchy, the subjection of many and the dominion of few. In these matters the theory and practice of the Church is based on observation and long experience. The humanitarian democrats who affirm that men are equal, and who on the strength of their belief distribute votes to everybody, can claim no experimental justification for their beliefs and actions. They are men who have a faith, and who act on it, without attempting to discover whether the faith corresponds with objective reality.

THE RELATION OF THEORY TO ACTION

It is in the theory of human equality that modern democracy finds its philosophic justification and some part, at any rate, of its motive force. It would not be true to say that the democratic movement took its rise in the theories propounded by Helvétius and his fellows. The origin of any widespread social disturbance is never merely a theory. It is only in pursuit of their interests, or under the influence of powerful emotions, that large masses of men are moved to action. When we analyse any of the historical movements in favour of democracy and self-determination, we find that they derive their original impetus from considerations of self-interest on the part of the whole or a part of the population. Autocracy and the rule of foreigners are often (though by no means invariably) inefficient, cruel, and corrupt. Large masses of the subjects of despots or strangers find their interests adversely affected by the activities of their rulers. They desire to

change the form of government, so that it shall be more
favourable to their particular national or class interests.
But the discontented are never satisfied with mere discontent and desire for change. They like, as I have already pointed out, to justify their discontent, to find
exalted and philosophical excuses for their desires, to feel
that the state of affairs most agreeable to them is also
the state of affairs most agreeable to Pure Reason, Nature, and the Deity. Violent oppression begets violent
and desperate reaction. But if their grievances are only
moderate, men will not fight whole-heartedly for their re-
dress, unless they can persuade themselves of the absolute
rightness, the essential reasonableness of what they desire. Nor will they be able, without some kind of intellectual rationalization of these desires, to persuade other
men, with less immediate cause for discontent, to join them.
Emotion cannot be communicated by a direct contagion.
It must be passed from man to man by means of a verbal
medium. Now words, unless they are mere onomatopœic
exclamations, appeal to the emotions through the understanding. Feelings are communicated by means of ideas,
which are their intellectual equivalent; at the sound of the
words conveying the ideas the appropriate emotion is
evoked. Thus, theory is seen to be doubly important,
first, as providing a higher, philosophical justification for
feelings and wishes, and second, as making possible the
communication of feeling from one man to another. "The
equality of all men" and "natural rights" are examples of
simple intellectual generalizations which have justified
emotions of discontent and hatred, and at the same time
have rendered them easily communicable. The rise and
progress of any democratic movement may be schemat-
ically represented in some such way as this: Power is in the
hands of a government that injures the material interests,
or in some way outrages the feelings, of all, or at least

an influential fraction of its subjects. The subjects are discontented and desire to change the existing government for one which shall be, for their purposes, better. But discontent and desire for change are not in themselves enough to drive men to action. They require a cause which they can believe to be absolutely, and not merely relatively and personally, good. By postulating (quite gratuitously) the congenital equality of all men, by assuming the existence of certain "natural rights" (the term is entirely meaningless), existing absolutely, in themselves and apart from any society in which such rights might be exercised, the discontented are able to justify their discontent, and at the same time to communicate it by means of easily remembered intellectual formulas to their less discontented fellows.

THEORY GETS OUT OF HAND

The invention of transcendental reasons to justify actions dictated by self-interest, instinct, or prejudice would be harmless enough if the justificatory philosophy ceased to exist with the accomplishment of the particular action it was designed to justify. But once it has been called into existence, a metaphysic is difficult to kill. Men will not let it go, but persist in elaborating the system, in drawing with a perfect logic ever fresh conclusions from the original assumptions. These assumptions, which are accepted as axiomatic, may be demonstrably false. But the arguments by which conclusions are reached may be logically flawless. In that case, the conclusions will be what the logicians call "hypothetically necessary." That is to say that, granted the truth of the assumptions, the conclusions are necessarily true. If the assumptions are false, the conclusions are necessarily false. It may be remarked, in passing, that the hypothetical necessity of the conclusions of a logically correct argument has often and quite unjustifiably been regarded as implying the absolute necessity of the assumptions from which the argument starts.

In the case of the theory of democracy the original assumptions are these: that reason is the same and entire in all men, and that all men are naturally equal. To these assumptions are attached several corollaries: that men are naturally good as well as naturally reasonable; that they are the product of their environment; that they are indefinitely educable. The main conclusions derivable from these assumptions are the following: that the state ought to be organized on democratic lines; that the governors should be chosen by universal suffrage; that the opinion of the majority on all subjects is the best opinion; that education should be universal, and the same for all citizens. The primary assumptions, as we have seen, are almost certainly false; but the logic by which the metaphysicians of democracy deduced the conclusions was sound enough. Given the assumptions, the conclusions were necessary.

In the early stages of that great movement which has made the whole of the West democratic, there was only discontent and a desire for such relatively small changes in the mode of government as would increase its efficiency and make it serve the interests of the discontented. A philosophy was invented to justify the malcontents in their demand for change; the philosophy was elaborated; conclusions were relentlessly drawn; and it was found that, granted the assumptions on which the philosophy was based, Logic demanded that the changes in the existing institutions should be, not small, but vast, sweeping, and comprehensive. Those who rationalize their desires for the purpose of persuading themselves and others that these desires are in accord with nature and reason find themselves persuading the world of the rightness and reasonableness of many ideas and plans of action of which they had, originally, never dreamed. Whatever is, is right. Becoming familiar, a dogma automatically becomes right. Notions which for one generation are dubious novelties become for the next absolute truths, which it is criminal to deny and a duty to uphold. The malcontents of the first generation invent a justifying philosophy. The philosophy is elaborated, conclusions are logically drawn. Their children are brought up with the whole philosophy (remote conclusion as well as primary assumption), which becomes, by familiarity, not a reasonable hypothesis, but actually a part of the mind, conditioning and, so to speak, canalizing all rational thought. For most people, nothing which is contrary to any system of ideas with which they have been brought up since childhood can possibly be reasonable. New ideas are reasonable if they can be fitted into an already familiar scheme, unreasonable if they cannot be made to fit. Our intellectual prejudices determine the channels along which our reason shall flow.

Of such systems of intellectual prejudices some seem merely reasonable, and some are sacred as well as reasonable. It depends on the kind of entity to which the prejudices refer. In general it may be said that intellectual prejudices about non-human entities appear to the holder of them as merely reasonable, while prejudices about human entities strike him as being sacred as well as reasonable. Thus, we all believe that the earth moves round the sun, and that the sun is at a distance of some ninety million miles from our planet. We believe, even though we may be quite incapable of demonstrating the truth of either of these propositions — and the vast majority of those who believe in the findings of modern astronomy do so as an act of blind faith, and would be completely at a loss if asked to show reasons for their belief. We have a prejudice in favour of modern astronomy. Having been brought up with it, we find it reasonable, and any new idea which contradicts the findings of contemporary astronomy strikes us as absurd. But it does not strike us as morally reprehensible. Our complex of what may be called astronomy-prejudices is only reasonable, not sacred.

THE NEARER, THE MORE SACRED

There was a time, however, when men's astronomy-prejudices were bound up with a great human activity — religion. For their contemporaries the ideas of Copernicus and Galileo were not merely absurd, as contradicting the established intellectual prejudices, they were also immoral. The established prejudices were supported by high religious authority. For its devotees, the local and contemporary brand of religion is "good," "sacred," "right," as well as reasonable and true. Anything which contradicts any part of the cult is therefore not only false and unreasonable, but also bad, unholy, and wrong. As the Copernican ideas became more familiar, they seemed less frightful. Brought up in a heliocentric system, the religious folk of ensuing generations accepted without demur the propositions which to their fathers had seemed absurd and wicked. History repeated itself when, in the middle of the nineteenth century, Darwin published his *Origin of Species*. The uproar was enormous. The theory of natural selection seemed much more criminal than the Copernican theory of planetary motion. Wickedness in these matters is proportionate to the distance from ourselves. Copernicus and Galileo had propounded unorthodox views about the stars. It was a crime, but not a very grave one; the stars are very remote. Darwin and the Darwinians propounded unorthodox views about man himself. Their crime was therefore enormous. The dislike of the Darwinian hypothesis is by no means confined to those who believe in the literal truth of the Book of Genesis. One does not have to be an orthodox Christian to object to what seems an assault on human dignity, uniqueness, and superiority.

DEMOCRACY AS A RELIGION

The prejudices in favour of democracy belong to the second class; they seem, to those who cherish them, sacred as well as reasonable, morally right as well as true. Democracy is natural, good, just, progressive, and so forth. The opponents of it are reactionary, bad, unjust, antinatural, etc. For vast numbers of people the idea of democracy has become a religious idea, which it is a duty to try to carry into practice in all circumstances, regardless of the practical requirements of each particular case. The metaphysic of democracy which was in origin the rationalization of certain French and English men's desires for the improvement of their governments, has become a universally and absolutely true theology which it is all humanity's highest duty to put into practice. Thus, India must have democracy, not because democratic government would be better than the existing undemocratic government — it would almost certainly be incomparably worse — but because democracy is everywhere and in all circumstances right. The transformation of the theory of democracy into theology has had another curious result: it has created a desire for progress in the direction of more democracy among numbers of people whose material interests are in no way harmed, and are even actively advanced, by the existing form of government which they desire to change. This spread of socialism among the middle classes, the spontaneous granting of humanitarian reforms by power-holders to whose material advantages it would have been to wield their power ruthlessly and give none of it away — these are phenomena which have become so familiar that we have almost ceased to comment on them.   They show how great the influence of a theory can be when by familiarity it has become a part of the mind of those who believe in it.   In the beginning is desire; desire is rationalized; logic works on the rationalization and draws conclusions; the rationalization, with all these conclusions, undreamed of in many cases by those who first desired and rationalized, becomes one of the prejudices of men in the succeeding generations; the prejudice determines their judgment of what is right and wrong, true and false; it gives direction to their thoughts and desires; it drives them into action.   The result is, that a man whose interests are bound up with the existing order of things will desire to makes changes in that order much more sweeping than those desired by his grandfather, though the latter's material interests were genuinely injured by it.   Man shall not live by bread alone.   The divine injunction was unnecessary.   Man never has lived by bread alone, but by every word that proceeded out of the mouth of every conceivable God.   There are occasions when it would be greatly to man's advantage if he did confine himself for a little exclusively to bread.

H. J. LASKI

Born in 1893, H. J. Laski is a graduate of Oxford University (New College). Rapidly gaining distinction by his writings in the field of history and political economy, he was appointed Lecturer in History at Harvard, from 1916 to 1920, in which latter year he simultaneously filled a similar position at Yale. From 1922 to 1925 he was Lecturer in Political Science at Magdalen College, Oxford; since 1926 he has been Professor of Political Science at the University of London, with leave of absence in 1931, when he acted as Visiting Professor at Yale. During this busy and extraordinarily successful career as teacher and lecturer, he has found time to write numerous books which have been widely read by laymen as well as by students of economics and history. Among the most popular of these are A Grammar of Politics *(1925) and* Introduction to Politics *(1931).*

The following essay is reprinted from The Dangers of Obedience, *by Harold J. Laski, with the permission of Harper & Brothers, publishers (1930).*

H. J. LASKI

A PLEA FOR EQUALITY

AT NO period since the French Revolution has there
been a skepticism of democracy so profound as at
the present time. Its unquestioned supremacy as
an ideal is gone, and there are few now so poor as to do it
reverence. Some speak with contempt of the bourgeois
notions it embodies; others insist upon its futile in-
efficiency; to others, again, democracy has broken upon the
impregnable rock of scientific analysis. It is based, we
are told, upon the exploded myth of equality. It is the
unnatural offspring of Romanticism, the fruit of a dubious
marriage between Envy and Rousseau. Its principles, it
is insisted, do not survive examination. Liberty is meaningless save in terms of law; and law demands authority
and subordination as conditions of its life. Equality,
could it be realized, would merely level the claims of the
best to the plane of mediocrity; and it would compel the
able and the energetic to fit a Procrustes' bed of identity
for which Nature did not create them. Fraternity, moreover, is simple folly in a world where ruthless struggle is
the law of life; we cannot love our fellow-men until we
have won security, and in the uneasy pyramid of society
there is no security save as we trample upon our neighbors.
All over the world the institutional system which, to the
nineteenth century was the pattern laid up in heaven for
emulation, has been challenged; and there is no way to
gain a reputation so easily as by insisting that the age of
enthusiasm for democratic institutions is now drawing to its
close.

Yet a shrewd observer would be a little skeptical of this

temper. The democratic movement is not an historic accident. It arose from intelligible causes, and it is still referable to intelligible principle. It arose as a protest
against the possession of privilege by men whose supremacy
was not found to be intimately connected with the well-
being of society. Men discovered at long last that exclusion from privilege is exclusion from benefit. They learned
that if, over any considerable period, they are governed by
a section of themselves, it is in the interest of that section
that they will be governed. Grim experience taught them
that power is poisonous to its possessors; that no dynasty
and no class can exclusively control the engines of power
without ultimately confusing their private interest with the
public well-being. They learned that interest elevates
prejudice to the level of principle, and that reason is then
used, not to satisfy objective need, but to justify postponement of desirable change. They found, in a word,
that if popular well-being is to be the purpose of government, popular control is the essential condition of its fulfillment.

Almost a century and a half has passed since 1789, and
we can begin to assess the results of that gigantic up-
heaval. Broadly, it may be said to have brought the
middle-class business man to power; and its chief consequence has been the abolition of that political privilege
which was the chief obstacle to his ascent. In the
Western world, at least, men can now enjoy the major
political freedoms. There is universal suffrage; there is a
relatively wide liberty of speech and association; there is
opportunity for the humble to elevate themselves to a part
in the governance of the state. The old view of government as the natural field of an hereditary aristocracy has
been definitely relegated to the museum of historic anti-
quities; and it is certainly difficult not to feel that the
scale of life today is for the average man ampler than at

any previous time. Given political-mindedness, he can hope to play his little part upon the national stage. Given the sense of organization, and any will widely representative of popular desire can expect to find its place, after due effort, in the statute book. The political state is a democratic state in the important sense that it is no longer built upon a system of deliberate exclusions.

But if the political state is democratic, it cannot be said that we are members of a democratic society. The outstanding fact in the political sphere is equality. Bismarck's insistence that the best form of government is a benevolent and rational absolutism no longer commands general assent because historic experience has shown that no absolutism is ever capable of continuing either benevolent or rational. Any form of government other than the democratic suffers from the fatal defect of preventing the natural expansion of the human spirit. It thwarts the progress of civilization because it belittles men. It elevates the few at the expense of the many in terms which reason cannot justify. When the monarchy governed France, when the aristocracy governed England, those who obtained the fruits of the adventure were rarely those who toiled for its enlargement. The democratic principle had at least this major advantage that it offered a plane where the claims of men to a share in the common good could be admitted as equal. Personality as such was dignified by its recognition as citizenship. To open to ordinary men new avenues of creative effort was not merely to raise their moral stature; it enlarged also the quality of the political state by enabling it to base its experiments on a far wider induction than at any previous time. Political democracy, as Tocqueville regretfully admitted, more securely civilized the masses than has ever been the case under alternative systems.

II

But political democracy implies only political equality; and though it is not necessary to minimize the significance of political equality, neither is it necessary to magnify it. In most states of the modern world it has not been followed by equality either in the social or in the economic spheres. And since politics, after all, is relatively a small part of life, the ambit of territory within which the continuous expansion of personality is permitted, in which, that is to say, the spirit of the individual has genuine elbow-room, remains notably small. The distribution of wealth is notoriously unequal; the distribution of educational opportunities hardly less so. The degree to which occupations in the modern world are, America apart, stereotyped from father to son is astonishing to the observer. The democratic political state has, so far, been curiously unable to alter the inequalities of the social fabric. The result everywhere is grave dissatisfaction, a sense that political institutions are less capable of themselves effecting basic social change than merely of recording in legislation changes that have been effected by revolutionary means. The nineteenth century preached the doctrine that the ballot-box was the highroad to the realization of social good. The twentieth century seems not unlikely to urge that violence is the true midwife of radical betterment. That difference in outlook — with all the dangers it implies — is born of nothing so much as our failure to apply the idea of equality outside the merely political sphere. For without equality there cannot be liberty, and without liberty there cannot be the humanization of mankind.

Without equality, I say, there cannot be liberty. All history goes to show that interdependence. For if liberty means the continuous power of expansion in the human spirit, it is rarely present save in a society of equals. Where there are rich and poor, educated and uneducated, we find always masters and servants.   To be rich is to be powerful, to be educated is to have authority.   To live in subordination by reason of poverty or ignorance is to be like a tree in the shade which perishes because it cannot reach the light.   Poverty and ignorance benumb the faculties and depress the energies of men.   It is, of course, true that there are those who by the very strength of the conditions which suppress them are goaded to conquest of their environment.   But with ordinary men this is not the case.   On the contrary, the sense of inferiority which an unequal society inflicts upon them deprives them of that hope which is the spur of effort.   They remain contented with a condition in which they cannot make the best of themselves.   The distance which separates them from the wealthy and the cultured is so vast that they are never stimulated to make the effort to overpass it.   They remain uncivilized because power and consideration are objects too refined for their understanding.   They are satisfied with the crude in arts and letters, the brutal in sensual pleasures, the material and the vulgar in objects of desire. And because of their inferiority, they are judged incapable of advancement.   Aristocracies, whether of wealth or birth, have never understood the secret of this degradation. In part, they have accepted it as proof of their own superiority; and in part they have welcomed it as a safeguard of their security.   They take the deference they are accorded as the proof of their inherent worth; and they do not examine into the causes of its reception.

Aristocracies, historically, have always suffered from an incapacity for ideas.   They cannot share the wants or the instincts of the rest of the society of which they are a part.   And they always fail, accordingly, to realize that the desire of equality is one of the most permanent passions of mankind.   At the very birth of political science, Aristotle had already seen that a failure to satisfy it is one of the major causes of revolutions: it is not less so today. For where there are wide differences in the habits of men, there are wide differences in their thoughts. To think differently is to lose hold of a basis of social unity. A house divided against itself, the Bible says, cannot stand; a nation divided into rich and poor is a house divided against itself. It is only where men have an equal interest in the result of the common effort that there is a bond of genuine fellowship between them. A realization of unequal interest means, inevitably, the growth of a sense of injustice. That sense fastens itself upon the perception of an unequal return to effort; and an abyss is precipitated between classes of which, in the end, revolution is always the outcome.

It appears, therefore, that the less obvious the differences between men in the gain of living, the greater the bond of fellowship between them. And in a society like our own the differences between men are intensified by the fact that they are rarely referable to rational principle. We have wealthy men and women who have never contributed a day's effort to the sum of productivity; and we have poor men and women who have never known relaxation from unremitting toil. Wealth, with us, is so often the result of accident, of corruption, of a power to satisfy demand not inherently social in character, that there is little relation between its possession and a criterion of social benefit. The economic inequalities of society, that is to say, do not so explain themselves that men can regard them as just. Those who support them as necessary are always on the defensive; and they are always occupied in searching for possible concessions to the poor whereby they can be the better preserved. Philanthropy and social legislation are the taxes the rich must pay to keep the poor in order; and instead of a stimulus to cease from poverty they act as an incentive to remain in a routine where the service performed prevents by its character the emergence of a civilized quality in the performer. Our inegalitarian system corrodes the conscience of the rich by extracting ransom from them; and it destroys the creativeness of the poor by emphasizing their inferiority in the very conference of benefit. The rich hate the process of giving, and the poor hate them because they are compelled to receive.

The system, moreover, weakens from decade to decade. It weakens because in the first place it is no longer supported by the authority of religion, and, in the second, because the growth of education is increasingly destructive of the habit of deference. Where poverty was accompanied by deep religious feeling it rarely awoke envy, either because the poor man felt in duty bound to accept the will of God, or because he had an intimate assurance of a due reward in the after life. But he has no longer the sense of being selected for salvation; and despite the development of an increasingly Corybantic Christianity, he insists more and more that his heaven must be realized in the present life. It is necessary, moreover, continually to raise the standard of education, in part because an intelligent worker is a condition of our scale of productive effort, and in part because an educated democracy is a primary condition of social peace. Yet the first result of education among the masses is the perception that whatever inequalities may be justified by social needs, the present inequalities are incapable of justification. The more we educate, in short, the more we reveal to the multitude the inadequacy of the moral principle upon which our civilization is based. Since we have given political power to that multitude, either it will use the institutions of democracy to rectify the inadequacy or it will search for some other institutional principle whereby the rectification can be made.

III

"Our inequality," said Matthew Arnold, "materializes our upper class, vulgarizes our middle class, brutalizes our lower." It does this, moreover, in proportion to the degree of inequality that exists among us. Anyone who considers the habits of our plutocracy will see how the crass stupidity of their standards is reflected in every nook and cranny of society. The fact that they govern because they are rich means that wealth is the mark of consideration. What is held out to other classes for admiration is not elevation of mind, dignity of character, or beauty of life, but position, show, luxury, or any other mark by which riches may be displayed. There is absent, that is to say, from an admiration for this plutocracy any quality that is likely to ennoble the mind. Those who feel it merely develop in themselves the zest for ostentation, crude as it is, that they admire. By maintaining inequality, in fact, we maintain the conditions which inhibit the process of civilizing men. For where those who are held up to us for emulation are those whose only qualities are either a genius for acquisition or a capacity to preserve what someone else had acquired, there cannot be growth of spiritual stature. The religion of inequality, indeed, has not even the advantage of mysticism; it is too solid, crude, brutal for that. And, like all religions void of graciousness, it fashions its acolytes in its own image.

There is, moreover, another aspect from which our religion of inequality must be regarded. One of the first considerations in any society is the need for the equal protection of the laws. What is certain in our society is that an unequal distribution of wealth means unequal protection in the courts. The rich man can almost always secure bail; not so the poor. A fine means nothing to the rich; but it may well destroy the poor man's home, or, in default, send him to prison. The rich man has at his disposal all the resources of legal technic; the poor man, for the most part, must either take what lawyer he can get, or rely on the power of the judge to penetrate through his own stumbling inarticulateness. Nor does the difference end here. What we call embezzlement in a junior clerk becomes high finance in a millionaire. What is disorderly conduct in the East End of London becomes high spirits west of Temple Bar. What is theft in Poplar is kleptomania in Kensington. We have no conscience about the fate of Sacco and Vanzetti; but Mr. Thaw's millions enable him to escape their fate. There is, in fact, equality before the law only when there is equal wealth in the parties; and the measure of justice they will obtain is very largely a function of their balance at the bank.

Or consider, from the same angle, the consequence of inequality in the sphere of education. Even where we have conquered illiteracy, education, for the overwhelming majority, ends at fourteen years of age; which means, for most, that the necessary tools of intellectual analysis are incapable of being used. Knowledge and the power to make experience articulate become the monopoly of the few. An inability in the uneducated to state their wants leads, at its lower levels, to a wantlessness which utterly degrades the human spirit. Most men and women go through life completely ignorant of the intellectual heritage of civilization. Yet, personal relations apart, no one who has been vouchsafed companionship in the investigation of that heritage but knows it as the source of the main joy life can offer. To deprive men of access to it does not destroy the impulse of curiosity; it merely deflects it into channels from which no social good can emerge. Education is the great civilizer. and it is, above all, absence of education which provokes the brute in man. The price we pay for that absence anyone can see in Manchester or the underworld of Chicago. Above all, an inequality in this sphere is paid for by the inability of the ignorant to realize the fragility of civilization. They have a sense of angry despair or sodden disillusion; they do not know how to formulate the source either of their anger or their hopelessness. We leave them to destroy because we have not taught them how to fulfill.

There is, moreover, a psychological result of inequality upon which too much stress can hardly be laid. Inequality divides our society into men who give and men who receive orders. The second class, being deprived of initiative, is robbed of the possibility of freedom. Its members spend their lives as prisoners of an inescapable routine they have had no part in making. When their life is compared with that of their governors, whose power of self-controlled initiative is continuous and unbroken, it is obvious enough that distinctiveness of personality has there little chance of survival. And the orders received are irresponsible since, in general, they are born, not of function, but of the possession of wealth. The farm laborer, the domestic servant, the factory worker realize in a high degree that definition of an animate tool which Aristotle insisted was the quintessence of slavery. In the psychological sphere their experience means a continuous inhibition of natural impulse, a want of room to experiment with themselves, which is disastrous to the expansion of personality. Economic equality, for them, would mean the end of government by a narrow oligarchy of wealth whose sole purpose in life is personal pleasure or personal gain. We can understand the need for obedience to a doctor, a tax-collector, a policeman. There, as we can realize, the rules they enforce are born of principles of which they, not less than we, are servants; and their relation to the result is a disinterested one. But the orders of the narrow group who own economic power are rarely disinterested and never born of principle unless they choose so to make them. The result is the loss of freedom in those whom they command because they dictate the rules of authority to ends in which their servants cannot share.

It is partly a result of this dictation that it should be incompatible also with freedom in the sphere of the mind. To preserve inequality in social life, the pattern of mental experience must be controlled for the majority. The press, broadly speaking, is a servile instrument of wealthy men. Owned by them, in a degree ever more concentrated, dependent for its profits on wealthy advertisers whom it dare not offend, it pours forth a stream of tendencious news the main purpose of which is to maintain an atmosphere favorable to the maintenance of inequality. Our governors may well adapt to themselves the aphorism of Fletcher of Saltoun and say that they care not who has the making of the nation's laws so long as they have the making of its news. It is difficult for any observer, however much he strive for impartiality, to see the facts through the clouds of bias, suggestion, and suppression with which he is confronted; and it is the deliberate purpose of those clouds to screen from view the actual workings of a system of which inequality is the basic principle to be defended.

In a less degree, yet still very notably, the same is true of the educational system. It is dangerous in school and university alike to obtain a reputation for political or economic radicalism. The authorities who control appointments are the nominees of the conquerors; and, from dismissal to loss of the chance of promotion, they have at their disposal weapons which effectively prevent any ultimate freedom of thought in their servants. Anyone who scrutinizes the long list of investigations by the American Association of University Professors, or who analyzes the history of those teachers who have affiliated themselves to trade unions, will realize amply enough that liberty of thought in the teaching world is, at the point where the thought touches the existing disposition of social forces, broadly impossible for most. There have not, perhaps, been in England some of the more egregious outrages which have characterized American experience; but that is because there the selection has been more carefully made and dismissal, *a priori*, has been less necessary. For in the theological realm the English record is not an honorable one; and even today, in Oxford and Cambridge, theological teaching is a jealously guarded monopoly of the Church of England. In the result, both in school and university, the picture of the system presented is bound in the overwhelming majority of the cases to be that intellectually necessary for the preservation of the existing order. Exactly as in Soviet Russia where truth means "communist" truth, with a *ne varietur* written over the halls of instruction, so, if more subtly, the actual institutions of an unequal society are presented as though they were the inescapable inevitabilities of the social order. Our educational system is used, not to train the mind as an instrument of critical enquiry, but to bend it to the services of certain presuppositions profitable to the oligarchy which lives by their results.

IV

The price we pay for this inequality is a heavy one. The masses are dehumanized. The middle class is, in general, so wrapped up in its pursuit and worship of property that it has hardly the time, and rarely the inclination, for continuous experience of spiritual values. The wealthy pass their lives in feverish search for aimless pleasures which satiate at the moment of their attainment. Social prestige and conventional respectability are not ideals likely to produce a great civilization when they are regarded as ends in themselves. Yet they are the inevitable outcome of a society which regards inequality as its first and most natural law.   For what it must do to maintain them as ideals is to frown upon those who do not follow the beaten track.   Our personalities must be cast into molds which satisfy the norms of this pitiful principle.   Even our charities are thought of, not in terms of their objects, but of those who support them.   An English social worker who desires to raise funds for his organization knows perfectly well that he can double his subscriptions if he can persuade the Prince of Wales to permit the use of his name.   A theatrical performance for charity in New York in one of the great houses, with members of the Junior League as its pathetic exponents, would raise far more money than one given by the Theatre Guild.   Incredible organizations like the Primrose League in England and the Daughters of the American Revolution in America live by their ministration to the instinct for snobbery in an unequal society. What are so curiously termed the great hostesses entertain Mr. Shaw and Mr. Wells, Professor Einstein, and Mr. Ramsay MacDonald, not out of interest in, or sympathy for, their ideas, but for the advertising value of their presence at a social function.

The unequal society demands a standardized and uniform outlook as the condition of its preservation.   It is fatal to individuality, because individuality implies the novel and the unexpected; and these are dangerous to conventional habits.   It has to impose upon its members beliefs, ideas, habits, rules which prevent that affirmation of self from which the increase of civilization flows.   To offer us the type of life our acquisitive society practices is to offer us a religion which leaves unsatisfied the claims alike of knowledge, of beauty, and of manners.   The claims of knowledge: for we cannot afford the truth about social or economic organization.   We cannot give more than the smatterings of education to the multitude if it is to remain properly subservient to its masters.   On most of the vital aspects of sex we maintain a deliberate conspiracy of silence; and the very implications of the phrase "a good marriage" are tragi-comic evidence of the way in which the ideal of sexual comradeship is perverted. The claims, also, of beauty: for these always make room — as our slums, our factories, and our egregious villadom proclaim — to the demands of property. Successful art is either art which meets a vulgar demand or that which receives temporary canonization because it pleases the powerful; and when England wants a trustee of the National Gallery, it selects, not Roger Fry, but Lord Curzon, not Laurence Binyon, but Sir Philip Sassoon. The claims, finally, of manners: at the base, it is clear enough that manners will not emerge where overcrowding makes impossible the observance of the elementary decencies of life. The middle and the apex of the pyramid have been amply described for us by Mr. Galsworthy and Proust. Manners do not mean, as our system makes them mean, the uneasy and apprehensive search to maintain one's social position which gives to New York and London, to Paris and Rome, their pathetically elaborate code of trivialities, their ludicrous formalism, their contemptible craving for the publicity of the social column. The Duc de Guermantes, who calls for his ticket at the theatre and is able to show a greater courtesy to the attendant than a nobleman of lesser rank because he has a more assured social prestige, is a real symbol of our society.

We live in terror of doing the wrong thing instead of in hope of finding the right. We lack a healthy individualism which might give us the courage to experiment with ourselves. Instead of developing a self-respect born of a satisfied and harmonious personality, we sacrifice ourselves on the Procrustes' bed of traditional conventions, each one of which thwarts impulses that are basic to our character. We are trying to have our cake and eat it — a matter of impossibility in affairs of social logic. We have given the people power in the realm of politics, and we are trying to pretend to ourselves that the equalization of authority therein implied may rightly cease at its boundaries. The pretense is folly. The whole principle of democracy is nothing less than the affirmation by the people of its own essence; and this is incompatible with irrational privilege in any sphere. The law of democracy is the attachment of prestige, not to the accident of birth or wealth, but to the performance of social function. A democracy can understand why the President of the United States is important; but sensibly enough, it resents the attachment of importance and power to a leisured aristocracy with no duties save the pursuit of pleasure. It will give its respect to great artists, poets, scientists, philosophers, but it sees no reason to revere Commodore Vanderbilt or that Duke of Norfolk upon whose marriage the London *Times* of half a century ago bestowed the incredible epithalamium of a leading article.

The democratic demand for social and economic equality is, in fact, built upon the simple insistence that without it first things cannot come first. And that simple insistence is impossible in any community where, because the rights of property are unequally distributed, all other rights are modeled in their image. That is not, it is perhaps worth while to remark, the affirmation of dangerous radicalism. Conservative philosophers like Aristotle, publicists of genius like Harrington in England and Madison in America, critics of society like Matthew Arnold, all alike have insisted that as the rights of property are, so the complexion of society will be. Make the first unequal, and all else in life for which men strive will adjust itself to those terms. If, doubtless, the distribution of property were built upon a principle of unquestionable justice so that each man received in proportion to his contribution to the common stock, it would not greatly matter that there were differences of position in society. Inequality would be a function of merit, intelligible and defensible. But this is so demonstrably not the case, that inequality everywhere is the nurse of envy and hate and corruption; and of these, everywhere as well, the outcome is revolution. So that states which seek the postponement of equality have always within themselves a festering sore which is bound to break out sooner or later. They lack the essential condition of stable government, which is a widespread sense of allegiance to the constitution as the protector of the equal rights of men.

"The surest way to prevent seditions," said Bacon, "is to take away the matter of them." Where we have a state in which no man is so rich that he can buy his neighbor and none so poor that he must sell himself, we have present the fundamental condition of security. For men who can purchase others are free only at the cost of these; and men who are driven to sell themselves turn naturally to revolution as the alternative to slavery. In an equal state we confer upon all citizens the effective hope of bettering their conditions. We elevate the quality of their effort by giving them the right to aspire. We prevent that persistent frustration of impulse which is the major consequence of inequality. The divisions of society build themselves on the actual service they perform. Upon any other basis this is not the case. Intrust, as we intrust, the governance of the state to an aristocracy, whether of wealth or birth, and it is bound, in the end, to govern badly. For it cannot escape temptation and flattery. It is unacquainted with the realities of life as these are experienced by those over whom it rules. It is driven to elevate its own sense of superiority to the position of a social axiom; and it entirely fails to observe that the axiom is in fact the narrowest of inductions from the most partial of evidence, the substance of its own desires. The proof of this is simple enough. Confront any aristocracy with novelty, and it is patently incapable of its rational examination. The nobility of the *ancien régime* in France, the Romanoff dynasty in Russia, the English landowner in Ireland, the Austrian conqueror in Italy — these had before their eyes the evidence of a new and inescapable temper with which terms had to be made; and they could only equate it with original sin. Yet great agitations are not marks of popular crime; popular crime is only a mark of great agitation born of some suffering too grievous to be endured. And the root of great passions is the unchanging passion for equality.

The skeptic, of course, is horrified at a panegyric of this sort. All that we know, he argues, teaches us that men are different in taste and different in talent; to treat them as equals is to fly in the face of elementary principles of nature. But this is to mistake equality with identity. Equality does not mean that the differences of men are to be neglected; it means only that those differences are to be selected for emphasis which are deliberately relevant to the common good. It refuses to recognize the legitimacy of barriers which are born, not of the nature of things, but of accident illegitimate in its social consequence. It does not mean that the Heaven-sent painter shall be compelled to the study of advanced mathematics; but merely that the Heaven-sent painter shall not be driven to waste his talent through the absence of organized opportunity. It means a shift in the emphasis of social action from the few to the many. It implies the utilization, of set purpose, of the national resources to the elevation of quality in the ordinary man. It is built upon a belief that when the ordinary man is trained to co-operate in the government of society, his powers are quickened, his self-respect increased. He is something more than a passive spectator of the social process. His individuality becomes articulate; he contributes his little stock of experience and wisdom to the common store. The tradition he inherits is widened and quickened by his knowledge and opinion. The power of social adaptation is strengthened by the wider induction that can be made.

We need not doubt, with the skeptic, that a single individual of outstanding ability will often perform better the functions of government than the members of a democratic state. Cæsar, Cromwell, Napoleon, Lenin had, doubtless, more energy, more perseverance, more capacity to plan in a wholesale way, and more art to perfect the details of their planning. But the answer to this is at least twofold. The energy, the perseverance, the capacity of the great dictators are almost always from the outset, and, in the end, invariably, purchased at the expense of the growth of those qualities in those over whom they rule. Democracy is not the most efficient form of government, neither is it the most capable of conceiving the greatest ideas. But a democratic government provokes in its citizens that which no other political system is able to secure. There flows from its equality in citizenship a restless energy, a pervasive vitality, more favorable to individuality than any other qualities. The knowledge there that the road lies open to power is a spur and an incentive which neither the favors of a dictatorship nor the prestige of an aristocracy can evoke. And the equalization of citizenship in the political field is itself a safeguard of the public interest. The political leader in a democratic state may be, often enough, less able or less honorable than the leader of an aristocracy. But his tenure of power is subject always to the condition that he must, in the end, submit himself to the will of the majority. His interest is in the democratic system more securely merged with the interest of the whole than is the case in any alternative scheme. The government of an aristocracy is, at its best, always in some sort a conspiracy against the nation. The very fact that it is protecting the privileged interest of a minority tends to make it shape institutions to its own ends and to protect them against invasion for the benefit of the whole. That has been, of course unconsciously, the history of the interpretation of the American Constitution by the Supreme Court; and, still more notably and again unconsciously, the history of the interpretation of trade-union law by English judges. Minority government always narrows public policy to mean the perpetuation of its own power.

Nor, finally, must we forget the significance of the historical aspect of the problem. Englishmen, to whom equality is still a strange ideal, Americans, who rarely observe the growth of a privileged aristocracy among themselves, too often forget that the history of society is supremely the history of the abolition of differences which reason cannot explain and justice cannot excuse. That has been the case in the sphere of religion; it has been, in Western civilization, predominantly the case in politics. Everyone has read the half-dozen remarkable pages in which Tocqueville explained how the movement of French history has been the evolution of an irresistible tendency to equalization of conditions. "Those who have knowingly labored in its cause," he wrote, "and those who have served it unwittingly; those who have fought for it and those who have announced themselves its opponents; all have been driven along the same track;... the gradual development of equal conditions... possesses all the characteristics of a divine decree; it is universal; it is desirable; it constantly eludes all human interference; and all events as well as all men contribute to its progress."

Certainly it does not appear likely that a democracy which has established equality in religion and politics; which has overthrown the power of churches and kings and aristocracies; will leave untouched the economic and the social field. Yet nothing is more dangerous in social philosophy than the postulation of inevitable victories. The power of inequality is still immense, the interests it protects gigantic. To be optimistic about the prospect of its abdication is folly; to believe that it is certain of defeat is overconfidence. It is the tragedy of modern society that science has made social conflict the parent of social disaster; for the forces of democracy in this new realm to try their strength with the forces of privilege may well make the second state worse than what they seek to overthrow. We must rather have faith in the power of reason to direct the human spirit to the prospects of concession and sacrifice. We must rather seek to persuade our masters that our equality is their freedom.

BERTRAND RUSSELL

Bertrand Russell, grandson of the eminent political reformer and statesman, Lord John Russell, was born in Monmouthshire, in 1872. He graduated first class in Mathematics and in Moral Sciences from Trinity College, Cambridge, where he later served as Fellow and as Lecturer in Mathematical Logic. In 1914 he was Exchange Professor at Harvard; since that time he has twice visited the United States as lecturer. It needs only the partial list of his writings here given to show that few living men equal him in the range of intellectual interests. Primarily a mathematician and a scientist (The ABC of Relativity, 1925, The Outlook for Science, 1931), he has written also on philosophy (Mysticism and Logic, 1918), on socialism (German Social Democracy, 1907, Proposed Roads to Freedom, 1918), on international affairs (The Problem of China, 1922), on education (Education and the Good Life, 1926), and on religion (What I Believe, 1925). Despite their diversity of subjects, these books unite in revealing a fearless, logical mind, a warmly altruistic and liberal spirit, and a remarkable clarity of expression. The title, Earl Russell, which he recently inherited, is justly famous; the name, Bertrand Russell, he had already made famous.

The essay which follows is reprinted from Political Ideals, by Bertrand Russell. Copyright, 1917, by The Century Company.

BERTRAND RUSSELL

POLITICAL IDEALS

IN DARK days, men need a clear faith and a well-grounded hope; and as the outcome of these, the calm courage which takes no account of hardships by the way. The times through which we are passing have afforded to many of us a confirmation of our faith. We see that the things we had thought evil are really evil, and we know more definitely than we ever did before the directions in which men must move if a better world is to arise on the ruins of the one which is now hurling itself into destruction. We see that men's political dealings with one another are based on wholly wrong ideals, and can only be saved by quite different ideals from continuing to be a source of suffering, devastation, and sin.

Political ideals must be based upon ideals for the individual life. The aim of politics should be to make the lives of individuals as good as possible. There is nothing for the politician to consider outside or above the various men, women, and children who compose the world. The problem of politics is to adjust the relations of human beings in such a way that each severally may have as much of good in his existence as possible. And this problem requires that we should first consider what it is that we think good in the individual life.

To begin with, we do not want all men to be alike. We do not want to lay down a pattern or type to which men of all sorts are to be made by some means or another to approximate. This is the ideal of the impatient administrator. A bad teacher will aim at imposing his opinion, and turning out a set of pupils all of whom will give the

same definite answer on a doubtful point.   Mr. Bernard
Shaw is said to hold that *Troilus and Cressida* is the best
of Shakespeare's plays.   Although I disagree with his
opinion, I should welcome it in a pupil as a sign of individuality; but most teachers would not tolerate such a hetero-
dox view.   Not only teachers, but all commonplace persons
in authority, desire in their subordinates that kind of uniformity which makes their actions easily predictable and
never inconvenient.   The result is that they crush initiative
and individuality when they can, and when they cannot,
they quarrel with it.

It is not one ideal for all men, but a separate ideal for
each separate man, that has to be realized if possible.
Every man has it in his being to develop into something
good or bad; there is a best possible for him, and a worst
possible.   His circumstances will determine whether his
capacities for good are developed or crushed, and whether
his bad impulses are strengthened or gradually diverted
into better channels.

But although we cannot set up in any detail an ideal of
character which is to be universally applicable — although
we cannot say, for instance, that all men ought to be
industrious, or self-sacrificing, or fond of music — there
are some broad principles which can be used to guide our
estimates as to what is possible or desirable.

We may distinguish two sorts of goods, and two corresponding sorts of impulses.   There are goods in regard to
which individual possession is possible, and there are goods
in which all can share alike.   The food and clothing of one
man is not the food and clothing of another; if the supply
is insufficient, what one man has is obtained at the expense
of some other man.   This applies to material goods generally, and therefore to the greater part of the present
economic life of the world.   On the other hand, mental
and spiritual goods do not belong to one man to the

exclusion of another. If one man knows a science, that does not prevent others from knowing it; on the contrary, it helps them to acquire the knowledge. If one man is a great artist or poet, that does not prevent others from painting pictures or writing poems, but helps to create the atmosphere in which such things are possible. If one man is full of good-will toward others, that does not mean that there is less good-will to be shared among the rest; the more good-will one man has, the more he is likely to create among others. In such matters there is no *possession*, because there is not a definite amount to be shared; any increase anywhere tends to produce an increase everywhere.

There are two kinds of impulses, corresponding to the two kinds of goods. There are *possessive* impulses, which aim at acquiring or retaining private goods that cannot be shared; these center in the impulse of property. And there are *creative* or constructive impulses, which aim at bringing into the world or making available for use the kind of goods in which there is no privacy and no possession.

The best life is the one in which the creative impulses play the largest part and the possessive impulses the smallest. This is no new discovery. The Gospel says: "Take no thought, saying, What shall we eat? or What shall we drink? or, Wherewithal shall we be clothed?" The thought we give to these things is taken away from matters of more importance. And what is worse, the habit of mind engendered by thinking of these things is a bad one; it leads to competition, envy, domination, cruelty, and almost all the moral evils that infest the world. In particular, it leads to the predatory use of force. Material possessions can be taken by force and enjoyed by the robber. Spiritual possessions cannot be taken in this way. You may kill an artist or a thinker, but you cannot acquire his art or his thought. You may put a man to death because he loves his fellowmen, but you will not by so doing acquire the love which made his happiness. Force is impotent in such matters; it is only as regards material goods that it is effective. For this reason the men who believe in force are the men whose thoughts and desires are preoccupied with material goods.

The possessive impulses, when they are strong, infect activities which ought to be purely creative. A man who has made some valuable discovery may be filled with jealousy of a rival discoverer. If one man has found a cure for cancer and another has found a cure for consumption, one of them may be delighted if the other man's discovery turns out a mistake, instead of regretting the suffering of patients which would otherwise have been avoided. In such cases, instead of desiring knowledge for its own sake, or for the sake of its usefulness, a man is desiring it as a means to reputation. Every creative impulse is shadowed by a possessive impulse; even the aspirant to saintliness may be jealous of the more successful saint. More affection is accompanied by some tinge of jealousy, which is a possessive impulse intruding into the creative region. Worst of all, in this direction, is the sheer envy of those who have missed everything worth having in life, and who are instinctively bent on preventing others from enjoying what they have not had. There is often much of this in the attitude of the old toward the young.

There is in human beings, as in plants and animals, a certain natural impulse of growth, and this is just as true of mental as of physical development. Physical development is helped by air and nourishment and exercise, and may be hindered by the sort of treatment which made Chinese women's feet small. In just the same way mental development may be helped or hindered by outside influences. The outside influences that help are those that merely provide encouragement or mental food or opportunities for exercising mental faculties. The influences that hinder are those that interfere with growth by applying any kind of force, whether discipline or authority or fear or the tyranny of public opinion or the necessity of engaging in some totally incongenial occupation. Worst of all influences are those that thwart or twist a man's fundamental impulse, which is what shows itself as conscience in the moral sphere; such influences are likely to do a man an inward danger from which he will never recover.

Those who realize the harm that can be done to others by any use of force against them, and the worthlessness of the goods that can be acquired by force, will be very full of respect for the liberty of others; they will not try to bind them or fetter them; they will be slow to judge and swift to sympathize; they will treat every human being with a kind of tenderness, because the principle of good in him is at once fragile and infinitely precious. They will not condemn those who are unlike themselves; they will know and feel that individuality brings differences and uniformity means death. They will wish each human being to be as much a living thing and as little a mechanical product as it is possible to be; they will cherish in each one just those things which the harsh usage of a ruthless world would destroy. In one word, all their dealings with others will be inspired by a deep impulse of *reverence*.

What we shall desire for individuals is now clear: strong creative impulses, overpowering and absorbing the instinct of possession; reverence for others; respect for the fundamental creative impulse in ourselves. A certain kind of self-respect or native pride is necessary to a good life; a man must not have a sense of utter inward defeat if he is to remain whole, but must feel the courage and the hope and the will to live by the best that is in him, whatever outward or inward obstacles it may encounter. So far as it lies in a man's own power, his life will realize its best possibilities if it has three things: creative rather than possessive impulses, reverence for others, and respect for the fundamental impulse in himself.

Political and social institutions are to be judged by the good or harm that they do to individuals. Do they encourage creativeness rather than possessiveness? Do they embody or promote a spirit of reverence between human beings? Do they preserve self-respect?

In all these ways the institutions under which we live are very far indeed from what they ought to be.

Institutions, and especially economic systems, have a profound influence in molding the characters of men and women. They may encourage adventure and hope, or timidity and the pursuit of safety. They may open men's minds to great possibilities, or close them against everything but the risk of obscure misfortune. They may make a man's happiness depend upon what he adds to the general possessions of the world, or upon what he can secure for himself of the private goods in which others cannot share. Modern capitalism forces the wrong decision of these alternatives upon all who are not heroic or exceptionally fortunate.

Men's impulses are molded, partly by their native disposition, partly by opportunity and environment, especially early environment. Direct preaching can do very little to change impulses, though it can lead people to restrain the direct expression of them, often with the result that the impulses go underground and come to the surface again in some contorted form. When we have discovered what kinds of impulse we desire, we must not rest content with preaching, or with trying to produce the outward manifestation without the inner spring; we must try rather to alter institutions in the way that will, of itself, modify the life of impulse in the desired direction.

At present our institutions rest upon two things: property and power. Both of these are very unjustly distributed; both, in the actual world, are of great importance to the happiness of the individual. Both are possessive goods; yet without them many of the goods in which all might share are hard to acquire as things are now.

Without property, as things are, a man has no freedom, and no security for the necessities of a tolerable life; without power, he has no opportunity for initiative. If men are to have free play for their creative impulses, they must be liberated from sordid cares by a certain measure of security, and they must have a sufficient share of power to be able to exercise initiative as regards the course and conditions of their lives.

Few men can succeed in being creative rather than possessive in a world which is wholly built on competition, where the great majority would fall into utter destitution if they became careless as to the acquisition of material goods, where honor and power and respect are given to wealth rather than to wisdom, where the law embodies and consecrates the injustice of those who have toward those who have not. In such an environment even those whom nature has endowed with great creative gifts become infected with the poison of competition. Men combine in groups to attain more strength in the scramble for material goods, and loyalty to the group spreads a halo of quasi-idealism round the central impulse of greed. Trade-unions and the Labor party are no more exempt from this vice than other parties and other sections of society; though they are largely inspired by the hope of a radically better world. They are too often led astray by the immediate object of securing for themselves a large share of material goods. That this desire is in accordance with justice, it is impossible to deny; but something larger and more constructive is needed as a political ideal, if the victors of tomorrow are not to become the oppressors of the day after. The inspiration and outcome of a reforming movement ought to be freedom and a generous spirit, not niggling restrictions and regulations.

The present economic system concentrates initiative in the hands of a small number of very rich men. Those who are not capitalists have, almost always, very little choice as to their activities when once they have selected a trade or profession; they are not part of the power that moves the mechanism, but only a passive portion of the machinery. Despite political democracy, there is still an extraordinary degree of difference in the power of self-direction belonging to a capitalist and to a man who has to earn his living. Economic affairs touch men's lives, at most times, much more intimately than political questions. At present the man who has no capital usually has to sell himself to some large organization, such as a railway company, for example. He has no voice in its management, and no liberty in politics except what his trade-union can secure for him. If he happens to desire a form of liberty which is not thought important by his trade-union, he is powerless; he must submit or starve.

Exactly the same thing happens to professional men. Probably a majority of journalists are engaged in writing for newspapers whose politics they disagree with; only a man of wealth can own a large newspaper, and only an accident can enable the point of view or the interests of those who are not wealthy to find expression in a newpaper. A large part of the best brains of the country are in the civil service, where the condition of their employment is silence about the evils which cannot be concealed from them. A Nonconformist minister loses his livelihood if his views displease his congregation; a member of Parliament loses his seat if he is not sufficiently supple or sufficiently stupid to follow or share all the turns and twists of public opinion. In every walk of life, independence of mind is punished by failure, more and more as economic organizations grow larger and more rigid. Is it surprising that men become increasingly docile, increasingly ready to submit to dictation and to forego the right of thinking for themselves? Yet along such lines civilization can only sink into a Byzantine immobility.

Fear of destitution is not a motive out of which a free creative life can grow, yet it is the chief motive which inspires the daily work of most wage-earners. The hope of possessing more wealth and power than any man ought to have, which is the corresponding motive of the rich, is quite as bad in its effects; it compels men to close their minds against justice, and to prevent themselves from thinking honestly on social questions, while in the depths of their hearts they uneasily feel that their pleasures are bought by the miseries of others. The injustices of destitution and wealth alike ought to be rendered impossible. Then a great fear would be removed from the lives of the many, and hope would have to take on a better form in the lives of the few.

But security and liberty are only the negative conditions for good political institutions. When they have been won, we need also the positive condition: encouragement of creative energy. Security alone might produce a smug and stationary society; it demands creativeness as its counterpart, in order to keep alive the adventure and interest of life, and the movement toward perpetually new and better things. There can be no final goal for human institutions; the best are those that most encourage progress toward others still better. Without effort and change, human life cannot remain good. It is not a finished Utopia that we ought to desire, but a world where imagination and hope are alive and active.

It is a sad evidence of the weariness mankind has suffered from excessive toil that his heavens have usually been places where nothing ever happened or changed. Fatigue produces the illusion that only rest is needed for happiness; but when men have rested for a time, boredom drives them to renewed activity. For this reason, a happy life must be one in which there is activity. If it is also to be a useful life, the activity ought to be as far as possible creative, not merely predatory or defensive. But activity requires imagination and originality, which are apt to be subversive of the *status quo*. At present, those who have power dread a disturbance of the *status quo*, lest their unjust privileges should be taken away. In combination with the instinct for conventionality, which man shares with the other gregarious animals, those who profit by the existing order have established a system which punishes originality and starves imagination from the moment of first going to school down to the time of death and burial. The whole spirit in which education is conducted needs to be changed, in order that children may be encouraged to think and feel for themselves, not to acquiesce passively in the thoughts and feelings of others. It is not rewards after the event that will produce initiative, but a certain mental atmosphere. There have been times when such an atmosphere existed; the great days of Greece, and Elizabethan England, may serve as examples. But in our own day the tyranny of vast machine-like organizations, governed from above by men who know and care little for the lives of those whom they control, is killing individuality and freedom of mind, and forcing men more and more to conform to a uniform pattern.

Vast organizations are an inevitable element in modern life, and it is useless to aim at their abolition, as has been done by some reformers, for instance, William Morris. It is true that they make the preservation of individuality more difficult, but what is needed is a way of combining them with the greatest possible scope for individual initiative.

One very important step toward this end would be to render democratic the government of every organization. At present, our legislative institutions are more or less democratic, except for the important fact that women are excluded. But our administration is still purely bureaucratic, and our economic organizations are monarchial or oligarchic. Every limited liability company is run by a small number of self-appointed or co-opted directors. There can be no real freedom or democracy until the men who do the work in a business also control its management.

Another measure which would do much to increase liberty would be an increase of self-government for subordinate groups, whether geographical or economic or defined by some common belief, like religious sects. A modern state is so vast and its machinery is so little understood that even when a man has a vote he does not feel himself any effective part of the force which determines its policy. Except in matters where he can act in conjunction with an exceptionally powerful group, he feels himself almost impotent, and the government remains a remote impersonal circumstance, which must be simply endured, like the weather. By a share in the control of smaller bodies, a man might regain some of that sense of personal opportunity and responsibility which belonged to the citizen of a city-state in ancient Greece or medieval Italy.

When any group of men has a strong corporate consciousness — such as belongs, for example, to a nation or a trade or a religious body — liberty demands that it should be free to decide for itself all matters which are of great importance to the outside world. This is the basis of the universal claim for national independence. But nations are by no means the only groups which ought to have self-government for their internal concerns. And nations, like other groups, ought not to have complete liberty of action in matters which are of equal concern to foreign nations. Liberty demands self-government, but not the right to interfere with others. The greatest degree of liberty is not secured by anarchy. The reconciliation of liberty with government is a difficult problem, but it is one which any political theory must face.

The essence of government is the use of force in accordance with law to secure certain ends which the holders of power consider desirable. The coercion of an individual or a group by force is always in itself more or less harmful. But if there were no government, the result would not be an absence of force in men's relations to each other; it would merely be the exercise of force by those who had strong predatory instincts, necessitating either slavery or a perpetual readiness to repel force with force on the part of those whose instincts were less violent. This is the state of affairs at present in international relations, owing to the fact that no international government exists. The results of anarchy between states should suffice to persuade us that anarchism has no solution to offer for the evils of the world.

There is probably one purpose, and only one, for which the use of force by a government is beneficent, and that is to diminish the total amount of force used in the world. It is clear, for example, that the legal prohibition of murder diminishes the total amount of violence in the world. And no one would maintain that parents should have unlimited freedom to ill-treat their children. So long as some men wish to do violence to others, there cannot be complete liberty, for either the wish to do violence must be restrained, or the victims must be left to suffer. For this reason, although individuals and societies should have the utmost freedom as regards their own affairs, they ought not to have complete freedom as regards their dealings with others. To give freedom to the strong to oppress the weak is not the way to secure the greatest possible amount of freedom in the world. This is the basis of the socialist revolt against the kind of freedom which used to be advocated by *laissez-faire* economists.

Democracy is a device — the best so far invented — for diminishing as much as possible the interference of governments with liberty. If a nation is divided into two sections which cannot both have their way, democracy theoretically insures that the majority shall have their way. But democracy is not at all an adequate device unless it is accompanied by a very great amount of devolution. Love of uniformity, or the mere pleasure of interfering, or dislike of differing tastes and temperaments, may often lead a majority to control a minority in matters which do not really concern the majority. We should none of us like to have the internal affairs of Great Britain settled by a parliament of the world, if ever such a body came into existence. Nevertheless, there are matters which such a body could settle much better than any existing instrument of government.

The theory of the legitimate use of force in human affairs, where a government exists, seems clear. Force should only be used against those who attempt to use force against others, or against those who will not respect the law in cases where a common decision is necessary and a minority are opposed to the action of the majority. These seem legitimate occasions for the use of force; and they should be legitimate occasions in international affairs, if an international government existed. The problem of the legitimate occasions for the use of force in the absence of a government is a different one, with which we are not at present concerned.

Although a government must have the power to use force, and may on occasion use it legitimately, the aim of the reformers to have such institutions as will diminish the need for actual coercion will be found to have this effect. Most of us abstain, for instance, from theft, not because it is illegal, but because we feel no desire to steal. The more men learn to live creatively rather than possessively, the less their wishes will lead them to thwart others or to attempt violent interference with their liberty. Most of the conflicts of interests, which lead individuals or organizations into disputes, are purely imaginary, and would be seen to be so if men aimed more at the good in which all can share, and less at those private possessions that are the source of strife. In proportion as men live creatively, they cease to wish to interfere with others by force. Very many matters in which, at present, common action is thought indispensable, might well be left to individual decision. It used to be thought absolutely necessary that all the inhabitants of a country should have the same religion, but we now know that there is no such necessity. In like manner it will be found, as men grow more tolerant in their instincts, that many uniformities now insisted upon are useless and even harmful.

Good political institutions would weaken the impulse toward force and domination in two ways: first, by increasing the opportunities for the creative impulses, and by shaping education so as to strengthen these impulses; secondly, by diminishing the outlets for the possessive instincts. The diffusion of power, both in the political and the economic sphere, instead of its concentration in the hands of officials and captains of industry, would greatly diminish the opportunities for acquiring the habit of command, out of which the desire for exercising tyranny is apt to spring. Autonomy, both for districts and for organizations, would leave fewer occasions when governments were called upon to make decisions as to other people's concerns. And the abolition of capitalism and the wage system would remove the chief incentive to fear and greed, those correlative passions by which all free life is choked and gagged.

Few men seem to realize how many of the evils from which we suffer are wholly unnecessary, and that they could be abolished by a united effort within a few years. If a majority in every civilized country so desired, we could, within twenty years, abolish all abject poverty, quite half the illness in the world, the whole economic slavery which binds down nine tenths of our population; we could fill the world with beauty and joy, and secure the reign of universal peace. It is only because men are apathetic that this is not achieved, only because imagination is sluggish, and what always has been is regarded as what always must be. With good-will, generosity, intelligence, these things could be brought about.

WALTER LIPPMANN

Walter Lippmann entered Harvard with the class of 1910, *but finished his four years' course in three, incidentally winning membership in Phi Beta Kappa. In four years more he had already become well known as a writer on political affairs.* A Preface to Politics *appeared in* 1913. *In* 1917 *Mr. Lippmann was appointed assistant to the Secretary of War; during the World War he served as Captain in the Military Intelligence Division, attached to General Headquarters, A.E.F.; following the Armistice, he became secretary of the organization headed by Colonel E. M. House to assemble data for the Peace Conference at Versailles. Such experiences have enabled him to speak authoritatively on national and international policies. As chief editorial writer for* The New York World *until that paper went out of existence in February,* 1931, *he added still further to his reputation as a keen and candid critic. Now, as special writer for* The New York Herald Tribune, *he continues to influence the political thought of a large group of readers. Recent among his published books are* The Phantom Public (1925), American Inquisitors (1928), *and* A Preface to Morals (1929).

The following essay is reprinted from Men of Destiny (1927), *by Walter Lippmann, by permission of The Macmillan Company, publishers.*

BRYAN AND THE DOGMA OF MAJORITY RULE

URING the Dayton trial there was much discussion about what had happened to Mr. Bryan. How had a progressive democrat become so illiberal? How did it happen that the leader of the hosts of progress in 1896 was the leader of the hosts of darkness in 1925?

It was said that he had grown old. It was said that he was running for President. It was said that he had the ambition to lead an uprising of fundamentalists and prohibitionists. It was said that he was a beaten orator who had found his last applauding audience in the backwoods. And it was said that he had undergone a passionate religious conversion.

No matter whether the comment was charitable or malicious, it was always an explanation. There was always the assumption that Mr. Bryan had changed, and that, in changing, he had departed from the cardinal tenets of his political faith. Mr. Bryan vehemently denied this and, on reflection, I am now inclined to think he was right. We were too hasty. Mr. Bryan's career was more logical and of a piece than it looked. There was no contradiction, as most of us assumed, in the spectacle of the Great Commoner fighting for the legal suppression of scientific teaching.

He argued that a majority of the voters in Tennessee had the right to decide what should be taught in their schools. He had always argued that a majority had the right to decide. He had insisted on their right to decide on war and peace, on their right to regulate morals, on their right to make and unmake laws and lawmakers and executives and judges. He had fought to extend the suffrage so that the largest possible majority might help to decide; he had fought for the direct election of senators, for the initiative and referendum and direct primary, and for every other device which would permit the people to rule. He had always insisted that the people should rule. And he had never qualified this faith by saying what they should rule and how. It was no great transformation of thought, and certainly it was not for him an abandonment of principle to say that, if a majority in Tennessee was fundamentalist, then the public schools in Tennessee should be conducted on fundamentalist principles.

To question this right of the majority would have seemed to him as heretical as to question the fundamentalist creed. Mr. Bryan was as true to his political as he was to his religious faith. He had always believed in the sanctity of the text of the Bible. He had always believed that a majority of the people should rule. Here in Tennessee was a majority which believed in the sanctity of the text. To lead this majority was the logical climax of his career, and he died fighting for a cause in which the two great dogmas of his life were both at stake.

Given his two premises, I do not see how it is possible to escape his conclusions. If every word of the first chapter of Genesis is directly inspired by an omniscient and omnipotent God, then there is no honest way of accepting what scientists teach about the origin of man. And if the doctrine of majority rule is based on the eternal and inherent rights of man, then it is the only true basis of government, and there can be no fair objections to the moral basis of a law made by a fundamentalist majority in Tennessee. It is no answer to Mr. Bryan to say that the law is absurd, obscurantist, and reactionary. It follows from his premises, and it can be attacked radically only by attacking his premises.

This first premise — that the text of the Bible was written, as John Donne put it, by the Secretaries of the Holy Ghost — I shall not attempt to discuss here. There exists a vast literature of criticism. I am interested in his second premise: that the majority is of right sovereign in all things. And here the position is quite different. There is a literature of dissent and of satire and of denunciation. But there exists no carefully worked-out higher criticism of a dogma which, in theory at least, constitutes the fundamental principle of nearly every government in the Western world. On the contrary, the main effort of political thinkers during the last few generations has been devoted to vindicating the rights of masses of men against the vested rights of clerics and kings and nobles and men of property. There has been a running counter-attack from those who distrusted the people, or had some interest in opposing their enfranchisement, but I do not know of any serious attempt to reach a clear understanding of where and when the majority principle applies.

Mr. Bryan applied it absolutely at Dayton, and thereby did a service to democratic thinking. For he reduced to absurdity a dogma which had been held carelessly but almost universally, and thus demonstrated that it was time to reconsider the premises of the democratic faith. Those who believed in democracy have always assumed that the majority should rule. They have assumed that, even if the majority is not wise, it is on the road to wisdom, and that with sufficient education the people would learn how to rule. But in Tennessee the people used their power to prevent their own children from learning, not merely the doctrine of evolution, but the spirit and method by which learning is possible. They had used their right to rule in order to weaken the agency which they had set up in order that they might learn how to rule. They had founded popular government on the faith in popular education.

And they had used the prerogatives of democracy to destroy the hopes of democracy.

After this demonstration in Tennessee it was no longer possible to doubt that the dogma of majority rule contains within it some sort of deep and destructive confusion.

II

In exploring this dogma it will be best to begin at the very beginning with the primitive intuition from which the whole democratic view of life is derived. It is a feeling of ultimate equality and fellowship with all other creatures.

There is no worldly sense in this feeling, for it is reasoned from the heart; "There you are, sir, and there is your neighbor. You are better born than he, you are richer, you are stronger, you are handsomer, nay, you are better, wiser, kinder, more likable; you have given more to your fellow men and taken less than he. By any and every test of intelligence, of virtue, of usefulness, you are demonstrably a better man than he, and yet — absurd as it sounds — these differences do not matter, for the last part of him is untouchable and incomparable and unique and universal." Either you feel this or you do not; when you do not feel it, the superiorities that the world acknowledges seem like mountainous waves at sea; when you do feel it they are slight and impermanent ripples upon a vast ocean. Men were possessed by this feeling long before they had imagined the possibility of democratic government. They spoke of it in many ways, but the essential quality of feeling is the same from Buddha to Saint Francis to Whitman.

There is no way of proving the doctrine that all souls are precious in the eyes of God, or, as Dean Inge recently put it, that "the personality of every man and woman is sacred and inviolable." The doctrine proceeds from a mystical intuition. There is felt to be a spiritual reality

behind and independent of the visible character and behavior of a man.   We have no scientific evidence that this
reality exists, and in the nature of things we can have none.
But we know, each of us, in a way too certain for doubting,
that, after all the weighing and comparing and judging of
us is done, there is something left over which is the heart
of the matter.   Hence our conviction when we ourselves are judged that mercy is more just than justice.
When we know the facts as we can know only the facts
about ourselves, there is something too coarse in all the concepts of the intelligence and something too rough in all the
standards of morality.   The judgments of men fall upon
behavior.   They may be necessary judgments, but we do
not believe they are final.   There is something else, which
is inadmissible, perhaps, as evidence in this world, which
would weigh mightily before divine justice.

Each of us knows that of himself, and some attribute the
same reserved value to others.   Some natures with a
genius for sympathy extend it to everyone they know and
can imagine; others can barely project it to their wives and
children.   But even though few really have this sympathy
with all men, there is enough of it abroad, re-enforced perhaps with each man's dread of his fate in the unknown, to
establish the doctrine rather generally.   So we execute the
murderer, but out of respect for an inviolable part of him
we allow him the consolation of a priest and we bury him
respectfully when he is dead.   For we believe that, however terrible was his conduct, there is in him, nevertheless,
though no human mind can detect it, a final quality which
makes him part of our own destiny in the universe.

I can think of no inherent reason why men should entertain this mystical respect for other men.   But it is easy
to show how much that we find best in the world would be
lost if the sense of equality and fellowship were lost.   If
we judged and were judged by our visible behavior alone, the

inner defenses of civility and friendship and enduring love would be breached. Outward conduct is not good enough to endure a cold and steady analysis. Only an animal affection become habitual and reflected in mystical respect can blind people sufficiently to our faults. They would not like us enough to pardon us if all they had to go on was a strict behaviorist account of our conduct. They must reach deeper, blindly and confidently, to something which they know is likable although they do not know why. Otherwise the inequalities of man would be intolerable. The strong, the clever, the beautiful, the competent, and the good would make life miserable for their neighbors. They would be unbearable with their superiorities, and they would find unbearable the sense of inferiority they implanted in others. There would be no term upon the arrogance of the successful and the envy of the defeated. For without the mystic sense of equality the obvious inequalities would seem unalterable.

These temporal differences are seen in perspective by the doctrine that in the light of eternity there are no differences at all.

III

It is not possible for most of us, however, to consider anything very clearly or steadily in the light of eternity. The doctrine of ultimate human equality cannot be tested in human experience; it rests on a faith which transcends experience. That is why those who understood the doctrine have always been ascetic; they ignored or renounced worldly goods and worldly standards. These things belonged to Cæsar. The mystical democrat did not say that they should not belong to Cæsar; he said that they would be of no use to Cæsar ultimately, and that, therefore, they were not to be taken seriously now.

But in the reception of this subtle argument the essential

reservation was soon obscured. The mystics were preaching equality only to those men who had renounced their carnal appetites; they were welcomed as preachers of equality in this world. Thus the doctrine that I am as good as you in eternity, because all the standards of goodness are finite and temporary, was converted into the doctrine that I am as good as you are in this world by this world's standards. The mystics had attained a sense of equality by transcending and renouncing all the standards with which we measure inequality. The populace retained its appetites and its standards and then sought to deny the inequalities which they produced and revealed.

The mystical democrat had said, "gold and precious stones are of no account"; the literal democrat understood him to say that everybody ought to have gold and precious stones. The mystical democrat had said, "beauty is only skin deep"; and the literal democrat preened himself and said, "I always suspected I was as handsome as you." Reason, intelligence, learning, wisdom, dealt for the mystic only with passing events in a temporal world, and could help men little to fathom the ultimate meaning of creation; to the literal democrat this incapacity of reason was evidence that one man's notion was intrinsically as good as another's.

Thus the primitive intuition of democracy became the animus of a philosophy which denied that there could be an order of values among men. Any opinion, any taste, any action was intrinsically as good as any other. Each stands on its own bottom and guarantees itself. If I feel strongly about it, it is right; there is no other test. It is right not only as against your opinion, but against my own opinions, about which I no longer feel so strongly. There is no arbitrament by which the relative value of opinions is determined. They are all free, they are all equal, all have the same rights and powers.

Since no value can be placed upon an opinion, there is no way in this philosophy of deciding between opinions except to count them. Thus the mystical sense of equality was translated to mean in practice that two minds are better than one mind and two souls better than one soul. Your true mystic would be horrified at the notion that you can add up souls and that the greater number is superior to the lesser. To him souls are imponderable and incommensurable; that is the only sense in which they are truly equal. And yet in the name of that sense of equality which he attains by denying that the worth of a soul can be measured, the worldly democrats have made the mere counting of souls the final arbiter of all worth. It is a curious misunderstanding; Mr. Bryan brought it into high relief during the Tennessee case. The spiritual doctrine that all men will stand at last equal before the throne of God meant to him that all men are equally good biologists before the ballot-box of Tennessee. That kind of democracy is quite evidently a gross materialization of an idea that in essence cannot be materialized. It is a confusing interchange of two worlds that are not interchangeable

IV

Although the principle of majority rule derives a certain sanctity from the mystical sense of equality, it is really quite unrelated to it. There is nothing in the teachings of Jesus or Saint Francis which justifies us in thinking that the opinions of fifty-one per cent of a group are better than the opinions of forty-nine per cent. The mystical doctrine of equality ignores the standards of the world and recognizes each soul as unique; the principle of majority rule is a device for establishing standards of action in this world by the crude and obvious device of adding up voters. Yet owing to a confusion between the two, the mystical doctrine has been brutalized and made absurd, and the principle of majority rule has acquired an unction that protects it from criticism. A mere political expedient, worth using only when it is necessary or demonstrably useful to the conduct of affairs, has been hallowed by an altogether adventitious sanctity due to an association of ideas with a religious hope of salvation.

Once we succeed in disentangling this confusion of ideas, it becomes apparent that the principle of majority rule is wholly alien to what the humane mystic feels. The rule of the majority is the rule of force. For while nobody can seriously maintain that the greatest number must have the greatest wisdom or the greatest virtue, there is no denying that under modern social conditions they are likely to have the most power. I say likely to have, for we are reminded by the recent history of Russia and of Italy that organized and armed minorities can under certain circumstances disfranchise the majority. Nevertheless, it is a good working premise that in the long run the greater force resides in the greater number, and what we call a democratic society might be defined for certain purposes as one in which the majority is always prepared to put down a revolutionary minority.

The apologists of democracy have done their best to dissemble the true nature of majority rule. They have argued that by some mysterious process, the opinion to which a majority subscribes is true and righteous. They have even attempted to endow the sovereign majority with the inspiration of an infallible church and of kings by the grace of God. It was a natural mistake. Although they saw clearly that the utterances of the church were the decisions of the ruling clergy, and that the divine guidance of the king was exercised by his courtiers, they were not prepared to admit that the new sovereign was a purely temporal ruler. They felt certain they must ascribe to the majority of the voters the same supernatural excellence which had

always adhered to the traditional rulers. Throughout
the nineteenth century, therefore, the people were flattered
and mystified by hearing that deep within a fixed percentage of them there lay the same divine inspiration and the
same gifts of revelation which men had attributed previously to the established authorities.

And then just as in the past men had invented a mythical ancestry for their king, tracing his line back to David
or Æneas or Zeus himself, so the minnesingers of democracy
have invented their own account of the rise of popular
government. The classic legend is to be found in the
theory of the Social Contract, and few naïve democrats are
without traces of belief in this legend. They imagine that
somehow "the people" got together and established nations and governments and institutions. Yet the historic
record plainly shows that the progress of democracy has
consisted in an increasing participation of an increasing
number of people in the management of institutions they
neither created nor willed. And the record shows, too,
that new numbers were allowed to participate when they
were powerful enough to force their way in; they were enfranchised not because "society" sought the benefits of
their wisdom, and not because "society" wished them to
have power; they were enfranchised because they had
power, and giving them the vote was the least disturbing
way of letting them exercise their power. For the principle of majority rule is the mildest form in which the force
of numbers can be exercised. It is a pacific substitute for
civil war in which the opposing armies are counted and the
victory awarded to the larger before any blood is shed.

Except in the sacred tests of democracy and in the incantations of the orators, we hardly take the trouble to pretend that the rule of the majority is not at the bottom a
rule of force. What other virtue can there be in fifty-one
per cent except the brute fact that fifty-one is more than

forty-nine? The rule of fifty-one per cent is a convenience; it is for certain matters a satisfactory political device, it is for others the lesser of two evils, and for still others it is acceptable because we do not know any less troublesome method of obtaining a political decision. But it may easily become an absurd tyranny if we regard it worshipfully, as though it were more than a political device. We have lost all sense of its true meaning when we imagine that the opinion of fifty-one per cent is in some high fashion the true opinion of the whole hundred per cent, or indulge in the sophistry that the rule of a majority is based upon the ultimate equality of man.

v

At Dayton Mr. Bryan contended that in schools supported by the state the majority of the voters had the right to determine what should be taught. If my analysis is correct, there is no fact from which that right can be derived except the fact that the majority is stronger than the minority. It cannot be argued that the majority in Tennessee represented the whole people of Tennessee; nor that fifty-one Tennesseans are better than forty-nine Tennesseans; nor that they were better biologists, or better Christians, or better parents, or better Americans. It cannot be said that they are necessarily more in tune with the ultimate judgments of God. All that can be said for them is that there are more of them, and that in a world ruled by force it may be necessary to defer to the force they exercise.

When the majority exercises that force to destroy the public schools, the minority may have to yield for a time to this force, but there is no reason why they should accept the result. For the votes of a majority have no intrinsic bearing on the conduct of a school. They are external facts to be taken into consideration like the weather or the hazard of fire. Guidance for a school can come ultimately only from educators, and the question of what shall be taught as biology can be determined only by biologists. The votes of a majority do not settle anything here and they are entitled to no respect whatever. They may be right or they may be wrong; there is nothing in the majority principle which will make them either right or wrong. In the conduct of schools, and especially as to the details of the curriculum, the majority principle is an obvious irrelevance. It is not even a convenient device as it is in the determination say of who shall pay the taxes.

VI

But what good is it to deny the competence of the majority when you have admitted that it has the power to enforce its decisions? I enter this denial myself because I prefer clarity to confusion, and the ascription of wisdom to fifty-one per cent seems to me a pernicious confusion. But I do it also because I have some hope that the exorcising of the superstition which has become attached to the majority principle will weaken its hold upon the popular imagination, and tend therefore to keep it within convenient limits. Mr. Bryan would not have won the logical victory he won at Dayton if educated people had not been caught in a tangle of ideas which made it seem as if the acknowledgment of the absolutism of the majority was necessary to faith in the final value of the human soul. It seems to me that a rigorous untangling of this confusion might help to arm the minority for a more effective resistance in the future.

JAMES TRUSLOW ADAMS

James Truslow Adams, after graduating from the Polytechnic Institute in Brooklyn, in 1898, *took post-graduate courses at Yale, receiving the degree of Master of Arts in* 1900. *Until* 1912 *he was a member of a New York Stock Exchange firm; during the World War, he served as Captain in the Military Intelligence Division, on the General Staff. Like Mr. Lippmann, he was detailed to special duty with Colonel House's Commission before and during the Peace Conference at Versailles. He has since the war become well known both as a historian and as a commentator on modern America and its ways.* The Founding of New England *won the Pulitzer Prize in History for* 1921; Revolutionary New England 1691–1776 (1923) *and* The Epic of America (1931) *are later historical studies, the latter of which has been especially widely read. In* Our Business Civilization (1929) *and* The Tempo of Modern Life (1931), *as well as in many magazine articles, Mr. Adams has sought to describe and to criticize our own day, from a point of view which has been reached through his own experiences and his thorough historical research.*

The essay which follows is reprinted from The Tempo of Modern Life, *by James Truslow Adams, with permission of Albert and Charles Boni, Inc., publishers.*

JAMES TRUSLOW ADAMS

OUR CHANGING CHARACTERISTICS

THERE are few things more difficult to generalize about without danger of valid objections than national character. The exceptions to any generalization at once begin to appear destructively numerous. A concept of a Frenchman must include not only such diverse types as the Gascon, the Parisian, and the Breton, but also the innumerable differences between individuals of these and other types in what is a rather small country which for long has been culturally and politically unified. When we attempt the task in America it would seem to be hopeless. Who *is* an American? Is he the descendant of a Boston Brahman, of a Georgian cotton planter, or a newly arrived Armenian, Hungarian, or Italian? Is the typical American a clerk on the fifty-fourth story of a Wall Street office building or a farm hand of the Machine Age guiding in isolation a power plow along a furrow which stretches endlessly over the horizon? Is he a scientist working for pitiful pay and the love of science in some government bureau in Washington, or a one hundred per cent go-getter in a Chamber of Commerce whose ideas of progress are limited to increase of wealth and population? Is he Hamilton or Jefferson, Lincoln or Harding, Roosevelt or Coolidge, Emerson or Barnum?

The task of defining national character in such a conflicting welter of opposites is dismaying enough, and yet a fairly clear notion is of prime importance for any number of very practical purposes. The modern business man doing business on a national scale, making mass appeal to our whole hundred and twenty millions at once; the statesman, domestic or foreign, trying to forecast the success or failure of an idea or a policy; the genuine patriot interested in the highest development of his civilization — these and others must all take account of that real if vague concept which we call the national character. It is from the third point of view that we are concerned with the topic in the present article.

There are many signs that our world is approaching a new and critical stage. Deeply embedded in the structure of the universe there is a power or force that is continually at work molding chaos into cosmos, formlessness into forms. These forms, or patterns, belong to the spiritual as well as to the physical plane of reality. A scale of values, an ethical system, a philosophy of life appear to be as "natural" and inevitable a part of the web and woof of that strange and inexplicable phantasmagoria that we call the universe as are crystals, corals, or living embodiments of the form-producing force in the plant or animal body.

For generations now we have been witnessing the gradual breakdown of old forms until we have reached the very nadir of formlessness in our whole spiritual life. But there are, as I have said, many indications that we are about to witness a new stage, the embryo stage of new forms.

For the most part this play of cosmic forces is independent of consciousness or will in individuals. The atoms know not and care not why or how they combine to make quartz crystals or a living cell of protoplasm. To a greater extent than we care to admit, perhaps, the higher forms — our scales of values, our philosophies — are also independent of conscious molding by ourselves. They are not wholly so, however, and if, as has recently been said, more and more of us here in America as elsewhere "are looking for a new set of controlling ideas capable of restoring value to human existence," it is evidence of the interplay between the blind form-making force of physical nature and the consciousness of man. What these ideas will be will depend largely upon the soil in which they will be rooted, the soil of our national character.

It is also clear that the form in which life, either physical or spiritual, is embodied is of transcendent importance for the individual. If living cells are arranged in the form of a bird, both the powers and limitations of the individual are wholly different from those of the individual when they are arranged in the form of a fish. Similarly in the spiritual world, powers and limitations depend largely upon the forms within which the spirit has its being. Because they are so largely intangible, we are likely to lose sight of the fact that these forms — scales of values, systems of thought, philosophies of life — all afford the spirit peculiar powers and impose peculiar limits.

What of the new forms? Arising from and in large part molded by the national character, are they likely to afford wider scope for man's highest aspirations, to enlarge the powers of the spirit, or to place limits and bind them closer to the earth? What of the national character itself?

Let us for the present discussion avoid the more difficult problem of a complete analysis and seek to establish a trend, often a simpler task, in the spiritual as in the physical world. Are our characteristics changing, and, if so, in what direction? Can we, in the first place, establish any definite points of reference which will be tangible and certain? I think we can.

Man expresses himself in his arts, and among these none is more illuminating than the earliest and most practical, that of architecture. It is one, moreover, in which we as Americans excel.

We need not greatly concern ourselves with the inchoate beginnings of our nationality in the first few generations of early settlement in the wilderness of the Atlantic seaboard. The physical tasks were almost overwhelmingly hard and there was little opportunity for a distinctly American expression of either old or new spiritual life. By the time there was, we find that the spirit of the colonies had expressed itself in an architectural form, characteristic with minor variations throughout all of them.

When we speak of "colonial architecture," what at once comes to our mind is the home, the dwelling house of Georgian type, modeled on the English but with a delicacy and refinement surpassing most of the models overseas. From New England to the Far South these homes had outwardly a perfection of form and inwardly a proportion, a refinement of detail, a simplicity that all clearly sprang from the spirit of the time.

We may note quickly in passing several points in regard to them. The high point of the architecture was domestic. They were homes. They had an air of spaciousness, of dignity. They were aristocratic in the best sense. They were restrained and disciplined. Display or vulgarity were unthinkable in connection with them. They evidenced an ordered and stratified society. They held peace and rest. They were simple, unostentatious, and profoundly satisfying. They were shelters for a quiet life, alien from haste.

Let us, using the same architectural measure, pass from this first flowering of the American spirit to the very instant of today. The great contribution of twentieth century America to the art of building is the skyscraper, of which we may take the office building as both the earliest and most typical example. What are some of its usual characteristics?

The buildings are commercial, not domestic. Their very *raison d'être* is financial, the desire to get the most money possible from a given plot of ground. Their bulk is huge but they are not spacious, save perhaps for their entrance halls in some instances. They are democratic in the physical sense of herding within their walls thousands of persons of every possible sort. In their primary insistence upon mere size and height regardless of every other element, they are undisciplined and unrestrained. Peace or rest are unthinkable within their walls with the incessant movement of thousands of hurrying individuals, and elevators moving at incredible speed.

They are lavish in their ostentation of expense on the ground floor, bare and unsatisfying above. A "front" of vulgar cost is built to hide the emptiness of the countless floors beyond the reach of the first casual glance from the street. Yet every small and growing community cries for them and we hold them to the world as our characteristic achievement in art, as our most significant contribution in that most telltale of all arts, the housing of man's chief interest.

II

Here, then, we have two points of reference tangible enough to be noted by all men, because they are physical in structure, yet full of spiritual implications for our task. When we turn to other means of establishing our trend, such as literature, newspapers, our methods of living, the wants we create and strive to satisfy, our social ways of contact, our national ideals as expressed in political campaigns and policies, and other means less obvious than the buildings in which we live or work or express our spiritual aspirations, what do we find? I think we find the same trends indicated above, amplified and emphasized.

It is, if I may repeat myself to prevent misunderstanding, only with these trends and not with the whole complex national character that I am here concerned. As a historian, and with no wish to make a case but only to report what I find, certain trends in the past century appear to me to be clearly indicated. Let me note them just as from time to time I have jotted them down, without at first trying either to order or explain them.

These trends are the substitution of self-expression for self-discipline; of the concept of prosperity for that of liberty; of restlessness for rest; of spending for saving; of show for solidity; of desire for the new or novel in place of affection for the old and tried; of dependence for self-reliance; of gregariousness for solitude; of luxury for simplicity; of ostentation for restraint; of success for integrity; of national for local; of easy generosity for wise giving; of preferring impressions to thought, facts to ideas; of democracy for aristocracy; of the mediocre for the excellent.

For the most part I do not think any observer would quarrel with the validity of most of the above list. Discipline, self or other, has almost completely vanished from our life. In earlier days it was amply provided by school, family, and social life, by ideals and religious beliefs. Today it is not only absent in all these quarters but is preached against by psychologists and sociologists, decried by the new pedagogy, and even legislated against in school and prison.

Nothing is imposed any longer, from learning one's ABC's to honoring one's parents. Everything is elective, from college courses to marital fidelity. The man or woman who casts all discipline to the winds for the sake of transient gratification of selfish desires, who denies obligations and duties, is no longer considered a libertine or a cad but merely a modernist pursuing the legitimate end of self-expression.

For a considerable time evidence has been accumulating that the national rallying cry has become an economic balance sheet. Perhaps one of the chief values of the whole prohibition muddle has been to serve as a mirror for the American soul. In the arguments advanced for and against, in the spiritual tone of the discussion, we can see all too well reflected the moving ideals of the American people, and the argument that carries most weight would clearly appear to be that of prosperity. Balanced against this, the questions of personal liberty, class legislation, or constitutional propriety are but as straw weighed against iron.

Prohibition is only one of the many mirrors that reflect the same truth. In innumerable cases of business practice and of legislation it has become evident that when personal freedom and initiative have to be balanced against the prosperity of the moment according to the business methods of the moment, prosperity wins. The one liberty that is still valued is the liberty to exploit and to acquire. That liberty will be defended to the death, but other liberties, such as freedom of thought and speech, have become pale and unreal ghosts, academic questions of no interest to the practical man.

Who cares in the slightest about the innumerable cases of encroachment on personal liberties on the part of both state and federal governments in the past ten years so long as business is good? Who cares about the methods employed by our police? Who is willing to give thought to the treatment frequently meted out to foreigners by our immigration officials — treatment that could hardly be surpassed by the old Russian régime at its worst, treatment that we could not stand a moment if accorded to *our* citizens by any foreign government? No, personal liberty as a rallying cry today receives no answer. But we will elect any man President who will promise us prosperity.

There is as little question of our growing restlessness. By rail, boat, automobile, or plane we are as restless as a swarm of gnats in a summer sunbeam. "We don't know where we're going but we're on our way" is the cry of all. Even the babies get their rest by traveling at forty miles an hour swung in cradles in Ford cars. That much of the movement is mere restlessness and does not spring from a desire to see and learn may easily be observed by watching the speed of our new tourists when they travel and listening to their comments when they have to stop to look at anything. As for the "nature" they claim to go to see, they are ruining our whole countryside with appalling indifference.

The home itself has yielded and has ceased to afford any sense of permanence and security. In the old days a home was expected to serve for generations. In the South, frequently property was entailed and the family was assured of a continuing center where it could cluster. A year ago, on October first, a hundred thousand families in New York City moved from one apartment to another, in many instances for no better reason than that they were bored with the one they had occupied a twelvemonth. Our multimillionaires build palaces, and in a few years abandon them to country clubs or office buildings.

As for thrift and saving, with the entire complex of spiritual satisfactions that go with an assured future, they have not only notoriously been thrown overboard but are vigorously denounced by advertising experts like Bruce Barton and great industrial leaders like Henry Ford. "We should use, not save," the latter teaches the American people while they mortgage their homes, if they own them, to buy his cars. On every side we are being taught not to save but to borrow. The self-respect and satisfaction of the man of a generation ago who did not owe a penny in the world is being replaced by the social-respect and deep dissatisfaction of the man who has borrowed to the limit to live on the most expensive scale that hard cash and bank credit will allow.

With this has naturally come a preference for show to solidity. A witty and observing foreigner has said that

Americans put all their goods in the shop window. In every vein the insidious poison is at work. A man who toiled and saved to own his home would see to it that it was well built and substantial. The man who expects to move every year cares for nothing more than that the roof will not fall until he gets out, provided the appearance is attractive. In an advertisement of houses for sale in a New York suburb recently one of the great advantages pointed out was that the roofs were guaranteed for three years.

The first thing that every business firm thinks of is show. Its office or shop must look as if there were unlimited resources behind it. Even a savings bank, whose real solidity should be seen in its list of investments and whose object is to encourage thrift, will squander hugely on marbles and bronze in its banking room to impress the depositor.

The same motive is at work in our intellectual life. One has only to glance at the advertisements of the classics, of language courses, of "five foot shelves" and note the motives that are appealed to for desiring culture. Nor are our schools and colleges exempt from the same poison. The insistence on degrees after a teacher's name, the regulating of wage scales in accordance with them, the insistence on a professor's publishing something which can be listed are as much part of the same trend as is the clerk's wanting to be cultured so as to pass from a grilled window to an assistant-assistant executive's desk.

III

We could expand the above examples almost indefinitely and continue through the remainder of the list. But it is all obvious enough to anyone who will observe with fresh eyes, and ponder. Both for those who may agree or disagree with me, let us pass to some of the other questions that arise in connection with the trends I have noted. Do they in any way hang together? Do they make a unified whole or are they self-contradictory and hence probably mistaken? Do they derive from any conditions in our history that would make them natural and probable, or are they opposed to those conditions? If they are real, do they represent a transient phase or a permanent alteration in our character?

As we study them carefully, it seems to me that they do hang together remarkably and ominously well. A person, for example, who is restless, rather than one who cares for rest and permanence, would naturally prefer the new to the old, the novel for the tried, impressions instead of difficult and sustained thought. Both these characteristics, again, naturally cohere with the desire for show rather than solidity, and for self-expression rather than self-discipline.

With these same qualities would go the love of gregariousness rather than solitude, of luxury rather than simplicity, and, easily belonging to the same type of character, we would find the desire to spend ousting the desire to save, and the substitution of prosperity for liberty and of success for integrity. With such a succession of substitutions, that of dependence for self-reliance is not only natural but inevitable, and so with the other items in the trend. They all fit into a psychological whole. There is no self-contradiction to be found among them.

But is there any connection to be found between them and our history? Are they qualities that might be found to have developed with more or less logical and psychological necessity from the conditions of American life which have separated the period of the colonial home from that of the seventy-story office building? I think here again we find confirmation rather than contradiction.

I have no intention to rival Mr. Coolidge by writing the history of America in five hundred words. All I can do in my limited space is to point to certain facts and influences.

Until well into the eighteenth century, there had been no very great change in the character of the American to mark him off from his English cousin. The wilderness and remoteness had, indeed, had some effect, but this was small compared with the later effects of what we have come to call "the West." Leaving out a few minor strains — such as the Dutch, Swedes, and the earlier Germans — the settlers were almost wholly British, who sought, in a somewhat freer atmosphere and with somewhat wider economic opportunity, to reproduce the life they had left.

The continent open to them was of limited extent. Beyond a comparatively narrow strip lay the long barrier of the Appalachians and the claims of the French. The strip itself contained no great natural resources to arouse cupidity or feverish activity. The character of the colonists had become a little more democratic, a little more pliant, a little more rebellious and self-reliant than that of their cousins of similar social ranks at home. That was all. They might differ with the majority of both Englishmen and Parliament over questions of politics and economics, but those were differences of interest and policy, not of character.

There lay ahead, however, the operation of two factors that were to prove of enormous influence — the exploitation of the American continent, and the immigration from Europe. We cannot here trace this influence step by step chronologically, but we must summarize it. "The West" — there were successively many of them — unlike the colonial America, was of almost limitless extent and wealth. There were whole empires of farm land and forest, mines that made fortunes for the lucky almost overnight, reservoirs of gas and oil that spawned cities and millionaires.

All did not happen in a day, but it did happen within what might almost be the span of one long life. In ages past an Oriental conqueror might sack the riches of a rival's state, a king of Spain might draw gold from a Peruvian hoard, but never before had such boundless opportunities for sudden wealth been opened to the fortunate among a whole population which could join in the race unhampered.

In the rush for opportunity, old ties and loyalties were broken. A restlessness entered the American blood that has remained in it ever since. In American legend, the frontier has become the Land of Romance and we are bid to think of the pioneers as empire-builders. A very few may have dreamed of the future glory of America rather than of private gain, but it is well not to gild too much the plain truth, which is that in the vast majority of instances, the rush was for riches to be made as quickly as might be. In the killing of a million buffaloes a year, in the total destruction of forests without replanting, in the whole of the story in all its aspects there were few thoughts for a national destiny not linked with immediate personal gain at any expense to the nation. In this orgy of exploitation it is not difficult to discover the soil in which some of the elements of the changed trend in American character had its roots.

Another factor was also at work which combined with the above in its effects. The racial homogeneity of our earlier colonial days was broken by the millions of immigrants who came to us of racial stocks other than our own. Our first character had been that of seventeenth and eighteenth-century Englishmen, not greatly altered until the Revolution. It was unified and stable, but the West and Europe both operated to undermine its stability.

On the one hand, the influence of the West, with the loosening of old bonds, its peculiar population, and its opportunities of limitless expansion and wealth greatly altered old ideals and standards of value. On the other, the steady infusion in large numbers of Germans, Irish,

Swedes, Norwegians, Jews, Russians, Italians, Greeks, and other races also bore a conspicuous part in making the national character less uniform and stable. I am not concerned with their several contributions of value, but merely with the fact that the introduction of such foreign swarms tended to destroy a unified national character.

By the latter part of the nineteenth century, two things had thus happened. In the first place, the real America had become the West, and its traits were becoming dominant. One of these was restlessness, not only a willingness but a desire to try any new place or thing and make a complete break with the old. Moreover, although the frontier may breed some fine qualities, it is a good deal like the farm in the respect that although it may be a fine place to come from, it is a soul-killing place in which to remain. It bred emotion rather than thought, and to a considerable extent substituted new material values for the spiritual ones of the older America.

In the rush for wealth — whether won from forests or mines; farms tilled, raped, and abandoned for fresher soil; real estate values from fast-growing cities; lands fraudulently obtained from a complaisant government — restraint, self-discipline, thought for the future ceased to be virtues. With all this came a vast optimism, a belief that everything would become bigger and better, and, because the standards of success were economic, better because bigger. Wealth was the goal, and the faster things got bigger — towns, cities, the piles of slain buffaloes, the area of forests destroyed — the quicker one's personal wealth accumulated. Statistics took on a new significance and spelled the letters of one's private fate.

At the same time, by the latter half of the nineteenth century another thing had happened, as we have said. Partly from the effects of the West and partly from immigration, the old, stable American-English character had become unstable, soft, pliant, something which could be easily molded by new influences. It could readily take the impress of an emotion, a leader, a new invention. It was full of possibility, both of good and evil.

Suddenly this new, unformed, malleable national character, already warped to a large degree toward material values, was called upon to feel the full force of the influences flowing from the fruition of the Industrial Revolution. Invention followed invention with startling rapidity. Life itself became infinitely more mobile. Scientists, engineers, manufacturers threw at the public contrivance after contrivance of the most far-reaching influence upon man's personal and social life without a thought of what that influence might be beyond the profit of the moment to the individual manufacturer.

Choice became bewildering in its complexity. The national character had become unstable. It was in a real sense unformed and immature, far more so than it had been a century earlier. It had also lost belief in the necessity of restraint and discipline. It had accepted material standards and ideals. It was in far more danger of being overwhelmed by the ideals of a new, raw, and crude Machine Age than was perhaps any other nation of the civilized group.

With an ingenuity that would have been fiendish had it not been so unthinking and ignorant, the leaders of the new era used every resource of modern psychology to warp the unformed character of the people, to provide the greatest possible profit to the individuals and corporations that made and purveyed the new "goods." Our best and worst qualities, our love of wife and children, our national pride, our self-respect, our snobbery, our fear of social opinion, our neglect of the future, our lack of self-restraint and discipline, our love of mere physical comfort have all been played upon to make mush of our characters in order that big business might thrive. Even our national government, whether wittingly or not, undertook to inflame our American love of gambling and our desire to "get rich quick" regardless of effect on character.

IV

Taking all the molding influences of the past century and more into account, it is little wonder, perhaps, that our national characteristics exhibit the trend noted. The situation, serious as it is, might be less so had it occurred at a time when the spiritual forms in the world at large — its scales of values, its ethical systems, its philosophies of life — were intact. But as we have noted, they have been largely destroyed; and at the very time when new forms are in process of arising, largely to be molded by the national characters of the peoples among whom they arise, our own is in the state pictured above. The question whether our new characteristics are temporary or permanent thus becomes of acute significance.

Race is a word of such vague and undefined content as to be of slight help to us, but if we take the whole history of the Western nations from which we derive, I think we may say that the characteristics noted above may be classed as acquired and not inherited. Biologists consider such not to be permanent and heritable, though the analogy with biology again is so vague as to afford little comfort.

More hopeful, I think, is the fact that these new characteristics appear to have derived directly from circumstances, and that these circumstances themselves have been in large part such as have passed and will not recur again. Immigration and "the West" have ceased to be continuing factors in our development. Their effects remain and must be dealt with, but neither factor will continue to intensify them. The tides of immigration have been shut off. There is significance in the fact that "the Wests" which won under Jefferson, Jackson, and Lincoln were defeated in 1896 under Bryan.

"The West" of today is a new West in which conditions, and to a large extent ideals, are different. Yet its greatest contribution to our national life and character remains that broadening and deepening of the dream of a better and a richer life for all of every class which was the cause of its earlier victories and which goes far to redeem its less noble influences. The nation as a whole is entering upon a new era in which all the conditions will be different from any experienced heretofore. Territory, resources, opportunities are none of them any longer unexploited and boundless. What the future may hold, we cannot tell, but in fundamental influences it will be different from the past. The menacing factor that remains is that of mass production and the machine.

Also, we have spoken thus far only of the trend in characteristics, not of our character as a whole. In that there are certain noble traits which remain unaltered, or have matured and strengthened. It is possible, now the warping influences of the past century have to some extent disappeared, that the national character may develop around them as a core, that we shall forget in manhood the wild oats sown in our youth.

But age acquires no value save through thought and discipline. If we cannot reinstate those, we are in danger of hampering rather than aiding in that reconstruction of the spiritual life of man that is the inevitable and most vital task now before the nations. We must either forward or retard it. We are too great to live aloof. We could not if we would, and upon the trend of our character depends to a great extent the future of the world.

Nor let us forget that although fortune has poured her favors in our lap, there is a Nemesis that dogs the steps of all, and we cannot lightly scorn the growing enmity of half the world. Are we to treat the Machine Age and mass production only as a new and different "West," or are we at last, in growing up, to learn wisdom and restraint? Are we going to change the trend in our character or is it to become fixed in its present form, a danger to ourselves and a menace to mankind? Few questions could be more difficult to answer or more pregnant with consequence.

WILLIAM ALLEN WHITE

Born in the then pioneer town of Emporia, Kansas, in 1868, William Allen White began to work as a printer before he went to college. On completing his course at Kansas State University, he became a reporter; at twenty-four he was already an editorial writer for the Kansas City Star. *In 1895 he bought the* Emporia Gazette, *as he says, "on credit, without a cent of money, and chiefly with the audacity and impudence of youth." In his long career as editor and proprietor he has made that paper known throughout the country. Its steady growth in influence has been due mainly to Mr. White's vigorous and fearless editorial comment, and his breadth of vision. As a citizen of Emporia, Kansas, he has concerned himself with local politics without ever forgetting that he is also a citizen of the United States and of the world. Thus, in 1917 he served as official observer in France for the American Red Cross, and he has acted in the public service in ways too numerous to mention here. Besides his editorials and frequent contributions to periodicals, he has published five volumes of short stories [including* The Court of Boyville (1896) *and* In Our Town (1906)], *political essays,* The Old Order Changeth (1910), *two novels, of which* A Certain Rich Man (1909) *is the better known, and a* Life of Woodrow Wilson (1924).*

The following essay is reprinted from Harper's Magazine, *March, 1927, through the courtesy of the author.*

WILLIAM ALLEN WHITE

CHEER UP, AMERICA!

I

FOR four months, half a hundred workmen at the corners of Thirty-Second and Thirty-Third Streets and Park Avenue in New York City have been tearing down an old temple — a temple of hospitality, the old Park Avenue Hotel. The old temple was filled with sentiment and surrounded by traditions, in so far as two or three American generations can hallow a temple. In January of 1927, after four months' work, the temple had been reduced to a sort of ground plan of its ruins. It looked like Pompeii. In the midst of the ruins two great machines, somehow reminding one of sentient beings, sank their great tusks into the earth, biting out huge steel basketloads of brick and dust, boards and stone, scrap iron and mortar. The steel beasts, swishing their plumy steam tails into the cool winter air, hummed their eternal work song. The workmen, scurrying about the débris, were busy with a dozen kinds of tasks. Each small group was doing its work with three or four foremen over the lot, directing the force. On a cold day the workmen were overcoated, gloved, warmly clad. A dozen, and sometimes a score of idlers, leaned against the railings that strung about the vacant lot, watching the workers. The idlers were clad about as the workers were, and the workers were clad about as the men hurrying along to the Avenue on business errands. A shabbier, dustier, more worn brown appeared in the workers' clothes, and a few more wrinkles than appeared on the clothes of the wayfarers; but that dusty brown made the chief difference between those who were working with their hands and those who idled or hurried into the offices that rose ten, fifteen, twenty stories in the buildings nearby. The foremen were not distinguished from the workers in either clothing or in the manner of their occupation. They all worked; no man idled. Few gave orders. The orders were reasonably polite.

Four years ago I saw wreckers working around a temple in Egypt near Luxor. They were digging it out. Thirty or forty boys between the ages of eight and twenty, naked save for a loincloth, grubbing up the débris and talus of another age, uncovering some ancient temple with a tradition hallowed in Egypt about as the Park Avenue Hotel was hallowed in Manhattan. The foreman, turbanned and draped in long dark skirts, stood over the youths, yelling at them, cursing them, urging them to their tasks. They, watching the tail of his eye with snakelike cunning, did as little clawing in the earth as possible, filled as few leaky baskets as possible, under which their comrades groaned as they carried them out of the excavation. Occasionally, and when a white man came along, to emphasize the abysmal difference yawning between the foreman and the workers, the turbanned man cracked his whip and let the lash fall upon the naked back of some boy who jumped and winced and began to claw eagerly in the earth. Another foreman, or superintendent, much more gorgeously turbanned, much more splendidly robed, sat aloof, as far from the slave driver as the slave driver was from his prey. And occasionally, strolling into the work, came another man, an Egyptian apparently, of the scholarly cast, whose eyes scorned the superintendent and could not even see the foreman and had no social consciousness whatever of the naked creatures groveling in the dust — ages in time behind him and unspeakably beneath. By way of diversion some American tourists threw a handful of copper coins at the grubbing boys. They started to pounce upon the coins like hungry pups, when the foreman's lash cracked, driving them away, and he stooped down and gathered up the loot. Somewhere in the contrast between those pictures lies all that is worth while in America. Before going into the obvious contrasts between the pictures, let us find the common points in each. Probably, at least typically, there was profit for the employer in both jobs. Upon his profit both bosses lorded it over those who walked and worked in the economic rank just beneath the bosses. Probably there were fewer unsatisfied wants among the barebacked boys of Thebes in their breechcloths than would be found among the men at Thirty-Third Street and Park Avenue. The workmen on each job most likely slept well, ate well according to the tradition and environment of the times and place, fought easily, lived and loved according to the distinction of each man's temperament, whether he came from an east side tenement or from a mud hovel along the Nile. The boys in Thebes did not seem to mind the lash. The men on Park Avenue did not seem to be oppressed by the compulsion which made them work and allowed the idlers to gaze at them. Very likely and typically, there may have been in each job, the one in Thebes, the one in Park Avenue, considerable favoritism, a little graft, some downright dishonesty, if each transaction were all unraveled and put under the magnifying glass of a cantankerous sociologist. And yet, despite these similarities which might be spun out still further, the two pictures revealed two civilizations, each civilization founded upon a deeply different social philosophy. In Egypt are the beginnings of human progress; from America, looking back, we can measure man's advance. He has not come to the end of the trail, of course. But he seems to have been moving, and in the various civilizations still functioning on the globe, we may trace the windings of man's trail of progress.

II

Now it is fair to ask what is the chief gain which man has made on his long journey. It is reasonable to presume that the journey has been an upward journey. What has man found in these later, and probably higher, levels which he did not have when he left the woods and settled in the open valley with his herd, his plow, and his boat upon the stream and inland sea? What, in this Mediterranean civilization, of which America is the direct descendant, has man found that is new and worth while? Why, indeed, is it better for man, taking him as merely a two-legged, burden-bearing animal, to live in America than to live on the banks of the Nile?

Man has marked his progress not so much by the material aspects of his civilization as he has marked it by his philosophy of life, considering the material things about him as the outward and visible sign of his inner and spiritual attitude toward life. Now man's spiritual attitude which marks his progress is chiefly toward his fellows, but somewhat toward the things outside himself which he fancies make for his security and happiness. The attitude which marks and makes the difference between the boys under the lash of Thebes and the men under orders at Thirty-Third Street and Park Avenue, New York City, United States of America, is the attitude of good will manifest in mutual consideration. This mutual consideration which dominates our Western civilization — the civilization of Europe and America, with all its imperfections too obvious to enumerate — has enlarged one quality in man which makes the Western man different from his fellows on the planet. The Western man has self-respect. That is "the pearl of great price." That is the thing for which man in the West ideally would lose his life that he might save it. Because of the fact that in America men may easily be self-respecting, the millions have come flocking to the United

States from all over the globe. Self-respect is bought with many things, but the common coin with which men today seek to buy it is gold, wealth, the thing epitomized in the word capital. To be free from the lash for one day, for one year, for one life is the chief end of man. Not because of the ease it brings, but because of the freedom it brings. Freedom is another name for self-respect. Democracy is institutionalized self-respect — nothing more, and, ideally, little less. It is odd to watch man in the ages between Thebes and New York City, nosing about for five thousand years against the hard wall of time and circumstance, burrowing for a quick passage through to self-respect. He tried here, a military empire under Rome; there, a feudal system; yonder, a hierarchy; beyond, a limited monarchy; each attempt coming a little nearer to the ideal in his heart. It is not hard to find fault with the tunnel man has made, to show that he has doubled back many times, to see where he has futilely followed blind leads. It is absurdly easy to look into man's heart today in the quest for democracy and find there evidences of envy, of greed, of blindness, of malice, of all the lusts of the flesh. The mean spirit that ever chains man to his clay prison is always flaunting itself. So, of course, democracy, and particularly American democracy, is crass, is crammed with injustices, strident with disharmony, marred with ugliness, cursed with selfishness. Bernard Shaw in *Pygmalion* makes his hero ask a lady, "if she fancied it would be agreeable if the hero came out frankly with all the things in his mind." The lady twitters that it might be cynical, and the hero shrieks, "It would not be decent." Every wise man knows this and yet he understands that beneath the indecencies in the mind of humanity are humanity's deep aspirations, its struggling nobility, its unrealized ideals.

So it is with democracy. Who can doubt that our American democracy has built into stone and steel, brick and wood, even into the institutions of commerce and of government, of religion and social usage, a million aspects of our animal indecencies? Always man has made his obscene gods, but he has always fashioned his glorious vision; always he has tempered his ideal justice with palpable inequity. To point out in American civilization its banality; to stress our commercial greed, our ravening imperialism on the sea whereon the flag follows the bargain; to fall down in despair before boodlers and grafters in politics; to grow gloomy in the face of social climbers; to surrender all hope for America because of the tabloid newspapers, jazz in the radio, and the demagogue in public life — in short, to stress the indecencies obvious in the scum of our consciousness, is to see life as a child sees it and to miss its meaning. The same child, looking at "the glory that was Greece and the grandeur that was Rome" would forget also the vast cruelties of those civilizations which outbalanced for the common man the superficial beauties that survive those civilizations. Progress in a civilization must be measured by its effect upon man in the average if we are to accept what seems to be man's aim in his struggle with his environment since the dawn of history. In some other age another man may aspire to something better than self-respect. He may seek some attitude finer than his own soul's freedom. But since man first began making his record in the world, it seems fairly clear that he has been striving for just one thing — the right to be his own and not another's.

It is pathetic to observe the various objects which man has brought in his hand with which to pay the gods of life in his quest for self-respect. He walked through countless unrecorded ages bringing two things — the soldier's sword and the priest's mitre. Through war and religion he sought to establish himself over his fellows and so maintain his soul's dignity. Then he came with the ballot in its various forms which produce self-government. Now he comes bringing capital. Each price — war, religion, democracy, capitalism — has represented a change in man's philosophic expression of the same ideal, his yearning for the thing called equality of opportunity. Of course, envy of his fellows has motivated much of man's activity in seeking that equality of opportunity which makes for self-respect. But envy does not debase all of his conduct. If envy debased everything in the struggle for self-respect there would be no heroes. Man would be without nobility — a brother of the beasts. Envy permeates the struggle for democracy but it does not explain it.

III

The pathetic restlessness with which man tries first one thing and then another in bargaining for the democratic ideal — the sword, the mitre, the ballot, the dollar — is most patent today in America. There are signs that we are losing faith in the ballot and relying more and more on the dollar. Government as an agency for human welfare received a tremendous shock when the governments of the world failed to bring peace out of War. In America for twenty-five years before the War the people had been striving to make government work as a democratic agency. They had faith in the ballot, they believed in political power as an agency for justice, and seemed to feel that if they could put that power, through the ballot, into the hands of the common man, he would use it intelligently, unselfishly, nobly. So in America all kinds of political devices for strengthening the power of the masses: the direct election of United States senators, the primary, the initiative and referendum, the secret ballot, the headless ballot, anti-corruption laws — came into American political life.

Still the millennium receded as we approached it. The

American quest for justice which would bring self-respect to the individual by equalizing the political opportunities of all individuals, proved to be a vain quest. We found some justice, we equalized some opportunities, we checked some iniquities. Probably we have gained a little in our contest with the forces of greed within us which ever seek, and ever have sought since the days of Cain and Abel, to overcome the nobler passions of men in establishment of good will — good will which promotes social peace, which brings justice and self-respect into the hearts of men. The particular form in which the devil in our hearts has become manifest during the last two or three hundred years, the dragon against which the St. George of democracy has been struggling, has been capital. A wiseacre of Broadway declares, "There are many things in this life that are better than money, but it takes money to get them."

In humanity's quest for self-respect man has repeated in his use of capital as a bargaining agent with the gods somewhat the struggle he made with each of the ancient devices by which he has sought to attain his ideal. It is something more than a quest, something less than a bargain, this ceaseless endeavor to find "the pearl of great price." And when man takes up a new device — the sword, the mitre, the ballot, or the dollar — with which to buy his way into Utopia, he always finds that the thing which he believes will save him actually menaces him. The capital of the present age, which has been produced by "many inventions," has, of course, brought the average man far into the realm of social dignity; but as surely as we have advanced far, behind the ægis of capital, so we are now threatened by it, and in America this is particularly true.

America is the paradise of capital. For three hundred years, during the rise of capitalism in the world, America has been the spot to which men from all over the world have been attracted by the love of money. They have called it the love of freedom, but the freedom for the most part has been bought with capital. The continent is rich, the climate salubrious, life abundant. Wealth has piled high and no man or class has been able to hold it all. Somehow, the lavish hand of nature in a virgin continent, rich in alluvial soil and minerals, blessed with a temperate climate, has helped to pile up and yet distribute wealth. Somehow, the very abundance of wealth has made it easy for the average man to acquire a share. So here from all over the earth the poor and oppressed have come and found the self-respect which they have been denied in other places. Government has taken wealth from the few and given its blessings to the many in the form of education, policing, regulatory measures affecting transportation, communication, and human welfare. The government has bought health for the masses out of taxes; the government has engaged in the care of the poor, of the defective, and has organized opportunity in a score of ways undreamed of in other times and places. But with all this public activity, with all the political distribution of wealth, with all our legislation, with all our constitutional prohibition of hereditary caste, vast inequities still remain. Worse than the inequities of life are its ugliness, its disharmonies, and its terrible standardization. Politics, that benevolent goddess who mothers the weak and the oppressed with sheltering institutions, who distributes her largesse in schools, in health, with a certain show of justice in her courts, has another mood and face. She is a corrupt and designing hussy.

American politics are probably no worse than the politics of any other land; but while we are praising what our government has done we should not deny that government also is the shield for special privilege, that government does make it possible for the rich to enjoy privileges in our courts which are denied to the poor, that government does at times act with stupidity, and at times with cupidity. The Declaration of Independence, which is the charter of our liberties, the covenant of our self-respect in America, the source of our idealism, has only been partially realized under our Constitution. Our Constitution, with all its wisdom, still has far to go to institutionalize all the ideals of the Declaration. There remain vast areas untouched in that noble document of 1776; and it is folly to deny that in man's quest for self-respect here in America he is faced continually by the dangers of plutocracy, the dangers of a despotism as cruel and as unjust as any of the despotisms out of which he has struggled in ages past.

But the joyous thing about it is that in America the fight is a fair fight. If we are brave enough and wise enough and honest enough to make the fight for self-respect, even against the centripetal forces of capitalism, we can win out of the very capitalism itself all the liberties which our hearts desire. Granted all that the finical say about and against America. Granted that our politics are corrupt. Granted that much of our standardization is ugly; that in democratizing the arts we have somewhat debased the arts. Granted that in distributing the products of commerce and industry we have quickly elevated millions into living standards which they do not appreciate and cannot evaluate wisely. Granted that democracy is crass, motivated somewhat by envy. Granted all its enemies say of it — still America, more than any other section of the earth, does guarantee to each human being according to his capacity for industry, courage, and intelligence, a right to look squarely into the face of his peers, dream his own dreams, follow his own visions, live his own life, with such abundance, with such beauty, and with such joy as his own heart may contain.

It is that making of potential self-respect which has

drawn the millions to our shores all these three hundred years, the age which has seen the rise of capitalism in the world. Here man may find in his battle against the forces which would crush him into servility a fine field and a fair fight — a fair fight despite all the tremendous prestige and power of aggrandized wealth. For in America aggrandized wealth is not fool proof. It is not established by a legal hereditary caste. Waste may take away from the fool the thing he cherishes and pass his money to the wise. That folly and extravagance cannot do in a legalized aristocracy. The titled fool without his money elsewhere in the world still holds his prestige; the fool without his money in America is just "a fool i' the forest."

IV

That which America has done with humanity is to make the dynamic man — the man eager for change. Throw the whole kit of modern inventions, from steam engine to the radio, into the African jungle or into the midst of Asia, or even into the European peasantry, and these inventions would bring no hope, would change no social or economic status, would bring no relations of man based upon the faith of man in his fellows. Somewhere in a laboratory, working with his tubes and fires, a scientist in an apron is weighing, measuring, trying, changing, poking his fingers into a place along the dead wall that impedes our further progress, and maybe tomorrow, maybe next month, or next year, or the next decade or the next century, he will find the thing that will upset and revolutionize the world. Where will he go with it? It will affect mankind first and in the surest and broadest way in America, because America accepts change. In the golden quest of the ages, the quest for self-respect, we have built actually a new kind of man in America.

There is something in the theory of the Christian theologians that man must be born again. In America he is regenerated. On the North American continent and among the English-speaking colonies, the white man looks at life squarely and without a servile eye. He is no white-winged cherub, no pink angel. By no means has his altruism overcome his eye for the main chance. With all his keen anxiety for change and his profound belief that change is always for the better, with all his institutions taxing the few for the benefit of the many, in education and health, protection and regulation, the American's altruism does not soften him into impotency. He still believes that all things come to him who hustles while he waits, and grabs quickly. But while he grabs he gives. He is a dollar-chaser, certainly; but not for the dollar but for the game rather. He has no sou grip. Pennies and dollars slip through his hands after he has them. He gambles with his gains like a drunken sailor. More than most of his brothers, the American knows that he is his brother's keeper. The thing which has left him in his rebirth is cruelty. He is not callous of suffering and pain; certainly he is not plagued with the sadist's love to hurt. He hits hard, but takes no comfort in revenge. He went into the World War partly in fear, partly prodded by propaganda which worked him into a fine frenzy of altruistic folly. But while he fought like a devil he came out of it with a gay, childish vanity in the fact that he had asked no ransom, that he had exacted no stipend for revenge, or remuneration, and had added nothing to the suffering of mankind. He does not yet realize the implications that follow the collection of what he regards his honest debts; when he does he may make a fine gesture and throw his notes into the sea. And at the end of the episode which began in Serajevo in 1914, the American will be the only man connected with the sad occurrence who has not reaped, consciously and in the sweet solace of revenge, any intentional reward from the

War. This is not because he is better or worse than other men. It is because the American is reborn, regenerated, renewed in self-respect. Another millennium may improve him, may refine him, may quicken his sensibilities and broaden his intellectual and spiritual horizon. Heaven hasten the day. But until that day comes, let us Americans not be fooled and discouraged by those one-eyed critics who see only our faults.

If they say "America has no native art" let them remember that she patronizes the art of the world generously and, upon the whole, intelligently. If her statesmen are cheap, short-sighted, and dull, her inventors are completing the work of civilization where politics has dropped it. If we have produced no musicians except those who jangle jazz, let it not be forgotten that we have orchestras, conducted, if you will, by Europeans, but still patronized by the masses; more good orchestras than any other land. The great composers of other times and other lands find today their largest audiences in America. Our literature may be provincial, but we are cosmopolitan in our taste for literature. Our religion may be dominated to a larger extent than the religions of other lands by a tom-tom evangelism and bull-roaring emotionalism. But where else will the weak find public succor so near him? In what other hundred millions on earth is health being conserved by public institutions; and where else does the cry of distress, from whatever corner of the world it comes, find such quick and wide response? That is the test of our religion, not our yapping, jumping, Hell-spreading evangelists.

It is easy to criticize America, and on the whole it is wise to do so. The gadfly's proboscis injects the serum of progress into our blood with its discontent; but let us also remember, as we listen to our critics, that humanity is wiser than they, and that if America had not some real thing to offer, if America had not "the pearl of great price," America would not be the magnet which is turning to our shores the dreams of the millions from all over the world. Here they come, these eager millions, willing to lay down their lives, their traditions; eager even to give over that dearest of all inheritances — their own nationalities, that they may find joy and salvation in the rebirth which is America. The millions who seek to become Americans are indeed willing to give their lives that they may save them. That great fact is our challenge to the world.

NORMAN THOMAS

After graduation from Princeton in 1905 and the Union Theological Seminary in 1911, Norman Thomas served as pastor in several New York City churches. His liberal sympathies led him gradually into journalism and politics. Long a member of the American Civil Liberties Union, he has fought in many causes for those whom he believed to be oppressed. In 1921–22 he was an associate editor of The Nation; *he is a contributing editor not only to that periodical, but also to* The World Tomorrow, *which he founded, and to* The New Leader. *He has become nationally prominent as Socialist candidate for office: twice for Mayor of New York City (1925, 1929), for Governor of the State of New York, and for President of the United States (1932). Although he has never been elected, he has won the respect of even his political opponents for his characteristic intelligence and courage. Besides his manifold activities as editor and political reformer, he has found time to contribute frequently to magazines and to publish several books, among which may be mentioned* The Conscientious Objector in America *(1923),* The Challenge of War *(1925), and* Socialism of Our Times *(1929).*

The following essay is reprinted from As I See It, *by Norman Thomas, copyright, 1932. By permission of The Macmillan Company, publishers.*

NORMAN THOMAS

THE ESSENTIAL CONDITION OF ECONOMIC PLANNING

A SORELY chastened world is turning to the magic of economic planning as medicine for its wounds. I speak of *magic* advisedly, for in a great deal of what has been said and written there is more of simple faith in a word or a vague idea than of real plan. Nevertheless, the noble army of volunteer planners who do have something more or less specific to offer grows apace. To veterans like Stuart Chase have been added such diverse new recruits as Matthew Woll, acting president of the National Civic Federation and vice-president of the American Federation of Labor, Dean Donham of the Harvard School of Business Administration, President Nicholas Murray Butler, and last and greatest of all, Mr. Gerard Swope of the General Electric. Mr. Donham makes his appeal to business men in whose desire or capacity for planning he has little confidence — less, by his own admission, than in the ability of Russia to produce skilled workers. Mr. Woll generously includes labor (but specifically excludes the government) in his proposal for a conference to set up a plan. Presumably that plan would give respectful attention to Mr. Woll's pet hobbies of even higher tariffs and a world boycott on Russia in which case it should be labelled: "A Plan to Make World War Certain." It must be added that Mr. Woll's inclusion of labor, that is, the A.F. of L., in his proposals for conference, is less significant than it ought to be because of the weakness of the A.F. of L. or any other labor organization in all the key industries except transportation.

So popular is the word "plan" or "planning" that even President Hoover calls his faith that somehow the sturdy economic individualism of America will muddle through to new prosperity, the "American Plan"!

At the opposite pole from such inaccurate looseness in the use of an important word are such detailed plans as Mr. Stuart Chase and Professor Charles A. Beard have placed before us. Mr. Chase draws inspiration from war-time experience and puts much faith in the value of regional boards. Professor Beard has gone even farther into the heart of the problem and proposes (in the July *Forum*) an immediate beginning at setting up syndicates of affiliated corporations in different industries (including agriculture) and their correlation under a National Economic Council, with which a Board of Strategy and Planning will be associated. His plan comes nearer giving us a possible framework for a transitional period of reorganizing a chaotic capitalist system into a virtual socialism than anything proposed by a non-socialist. Under his scheme the private stockholders would be taxed and stripped of power to the point of elimination.

Yet even Mr. Beard does not bring into the forefront of thinking the essential question of purpose. He leans over backward to prove the native, non-Russian origin of planning in general, and the consistency of his own very advanced proposals with American customs and traditions. Most of the other plans avowedly are directed to salvaging capitalism, profits and all. And some of them are not plans at all, but incantations.

The most important of all proposed plans, for the simple reason that it comes from one of our authentic captains of industry, is Mr. Gerard Swope's plan for a kind of capitalist syndicalism, a stabilization of industry by trade associations subject to federal regulation. Elsewhere in this book [1]

[1] See the essay *The Next Decade*, in Mr. Thomas's *As I See It.*

I have suggested that this plan looks to an American Fascism. It cuts the ground from under the older competitive capitalism as completely as socialism. But it is vitally concerned still to preserve private property for power and private profit. It ignores, therefore, all questions of landlordism, market speculation, and the relation of the profit system, no matter how well stabilized, to cyclical depression. It is not an adequate plan, it is not a popular plan even with business, and to the degree that it might work for a time it would give us a certain stability at the price not only of true prosperity and reasonable economic equality but of liberty. It is a sadly belated effort of the new capitalism to save itself.

Nevertheless, this eagerness of a world, that starves because it has produced so much, to find some plan by which to use the machinery it has had the wit to make, is of itself an immensely important sign of the times. It was the essence and the strength of the older economics that it taught faith in automatic processes and laws. Let each man intelligently seek his own good and the ever blessed laws of supply and demand would take care of the rest. Competition assured not only the survival of the strongest but guaranteed that the strongest would be the fittest and the most worthy to survive. Competition — not economic plan — was the guarantor of the general good.

Naturally enough such faith fitted into, and found confirmation from, the prevailing religious beliefs.

Years ago in an old library I came across a little book on theism dating from the early nineteenth century which soberly advanced as one of the soundest arguments for the existence of God the fact that when every man sought his own good the good of all was advanced.

Who but an omnipotent God could arrange matters as nicely as that? Now behold the change. In the very citadels of capitalism, in complete disregard of the assumed efficacy of automatic economic processes, men talk plan.

Nor is it only in the ranks of the capitalists that this great change has occurred. Suppose pre-war anarchists, syndicalists, or even most socialists had been told that by 1931 the great achievement of a communist revolution would have been a five-year plan, not evolved spontaneously by emancipated peasants and workers, but imposed on them from on top by an iron discipline which resorted to the piece-work and speed-up system, made labor unions the creatures of the dictatorship, and reduced nominal workers' control in factories to a shadow — would it not have been a vast and unwelcome surprise to men who had been proclaiming that all that was really necessary was to break the yoke of capitalism and destroy the profit system and set the workers free? Logically in socialism the notion of planning, especially during a transition period, was always implicit. But it certainly assumed no such commanding place in radical thinking as it has assumed today in Russia, and as it must assume if ever power-driven machinery is to be our salvation and not our destruction.

Perhaps the greatest triumph of the Russian dictatorship to date is this: it has taught the lesson that has been implicit in the specialization and interdependence of the machine age — plan or perish. And this lesson has been tragically emphasized for the Western world by a degree of economic insecurity, hunger and actual starvation which we are solemnly told is due to overproduction under our hit-or-miss system.

Now of the necessity of planning no one is more fully persuaded than I. But most talk of planning in our capitalist world leaves me a bit cold and skeptical. Some of this talk of planning is consciously or subconsciously presented as a vague but glorious hope of an earthly heaven to dull the discontent of workers in the present hell of unemployment. It rarely takes account of the immediate emergency.

It almost always ducks the questions: For whom are we planning, investors, speculators, or workers? Are their interests identical, and if so, how far? To men in earnest, the first step in curing our sick society is not plan but purpose. The truly revolutionary decision concerns not the kind of planning commission we shall set up to harness the "billion wild horses" of a machine age, but whether we seriously intend that they shall work for the use of workers rather than the profit of private owners. The Russian Revolution preceded the Five-Year Plan. And while I profoundly hope that we may learn from Russian experience without repeating it in all its details, we cannot possibly beg the question of socialism versus capitalism by appointing a planning commission. That is several degrees worse than the utopian hope of a "scientific" tariff to be devised by a commission irrespective of determining the previous questions, why a tariff, what sort of a tariff, and for whose benefit. A commission on planning may have to compromise on tactics and next steps; it cannot get far and compromise on principles. Principle or philosophy underlies plan.

Stuart Chase, writing on a Ten-Year Plan for America in *Harper's Magazine*, has vividly reminded us of the success with which we went in for planning in war days. He may be right that physically the task of peace planning is easier because it concerns only raising the standard of living, while war planning added to that feeding the maw of the insatiable monster, War itself. But he omits or minimizes two considerations:

1. Economically, war planning did little or nothing to interfere with time-honored methods of financing — liberty loans, etc. — or with profits; witness the 25 per cent average profits of steel companies. These profits did not break down planning while the war was on because War ever cried for more. The crisis inherent in the diver-

sion of profit was postponed to post-war deflations. The economic set-up for successful peace planning must be very different and cannot allow for an orgy of high profits, even with rising wages, if we want to escape recurring crises.

2. Psychologically, the compulsions of war were understood and had traditionally a force that the compulsions of unemployment under a capitalist régime decidedly lack. Even so, notwithstanding the war compulsions and the tradition of discipline for war, the indecent haste with which the planning Mr. Chase praises was scrapped when the Armistice was signed, shows how alien was planning to the spirit of capitalism. It will take a terror not yet inspired by too docile workers to force on capitalism such a degree of planning as will begin to approximate the wartime experiment.

But may not the growing concentration of power to which Mr. Gardner C. Means calls attention alter some of the factors? May we not expect some general planning from "the less than two thousand" directors of the two hundred largest non-financial corporations which in 1927, according to Mr. Means, controlled "over 45 per cent of the assets of all non-financial corporations, received over 40 per cent of corporate income, controlled over 35 per cent of all business wealth, and between 15 and 25 per cent of national wealth"? The *New Republic*, which editorially is somewhat optimistic on this point, is candid enough to admit some of the difficulties. And to its list others can be added. Great as is the control of these corporations, it does not extend to such vital matters as farming, bituminous coal mining, building, and textiles. There is little evidence that these two hundred great corporations have tackled or desire to tackle the general economic problem. Mr. Swope's plan has not met with the universal applause of his fellow industrialists. The most the best of them have done is to make some beginning of stabilization within their own industries. Stabilization of employment has its merits, but the plain truth is that its general adoption at the present level of economic activity and at the present rate of technological advance threatens us with the creation of a standing army of the permanently unemployed. All these great corporations shared in the general speculative debauch; they are dominated by the prevalent acquisitive and competitive temperament. They exist to make profits, and production for profit inevitably means a greater or less degree of both technological and cyclical unemployment. Why, for instance, are new machines installed or new technical processes used save to reduce costs? Which means, almost every time, to cut payrolls by firing workers! Finally, there is no sign at all that the little group in legal control of our two hundred greatest corporations will invite that labor participation in general economic planning which is essential to any reasonable scheme for an economic general staff.

Nevertheless, the persistent discussion of planning, and the fact that big business is strategically and probably psychologically in a better position than a multitude of little businesses to play with this idea, means that we may find ourselves with some sort of planning commission (or commissions) on our hands which may at least spy out the land, make public its findings, and indulge in some useful suggestions. It could conceivably, as Mr. Chase insists, make forecasts that would advise the investor and so guide investment and credits — a guidance without which planning would be nothing but a joke. It might in like fashion aid the correlation of industries. That would be a beginning, and a beginning on which a society resolved to go socialist might well build. It would at least be a denial of the genius of capitalism with its "automatic laws." It is not likely, however, that any scheme of planning under capitalism would make a forthright attack on the heart of our problem which is the redistribution of the national income. Without this the evils of underconsumption will persist.

The basic truth remains: Before society can plan for general use rather than for private profit it must own or at least control the vital economic enterprises for which it plans. All of which is a way of saying that socialism is the essential condition of planning even as planning is the essential tool of successful socialism. There remains the question whether socialism can impose the requisite degree of planning without the power of an iron dictatorship behind it. This in turn divides into two questions, one political or perhaps psychological, and the other economic. The first is: Can planning coexist with political democracy? The second: Can planning on a scale sufficient to banish unemployment and reduce waste permit any effective degree of consumers' choice, or must we all be rationed, fed, clothed, housed, and entertained much as any army is fed, clothed, housed, and entertained, with the inevitable corollary that we shall be assigned jobs much as soldiers are assigned jobs.

Neither question can be answered with absolute certainty. Planning under a democracy will succeed in proportion as the democracy is committed to the philosophy of socialism and to the necessity for intelligence in operating it. If these two ideas become dominant, democracy may provide a more orderly and less dangerous way to determine the human desires and prejudices of which even a dictatorship has to take account. Planning in Russia, notably in agriculture, has traced and retraced its steps as a result of Communist Party conflicts and compromises and Stalin's judgment of the strength of peasant resistance. At no time, not even now, could any economic commission, even with all the power of the dictatorship behind it, move the masses absolutely as they desired. Nevertheless, it will take a democracy capable of understanding and sharing a general interest rather than a democracy immersed in local, sectional and other divisive interests — as our American democracy usually is — to make possible competent and adequate planning. The political democracy that gives sway to log-rolling minorities to make tariff laws and pass pension legislation is not a democracy from which one may hope too much. But then the present democracy is thoroughly capitalist in its philosophy and loyalty.

The other question concerns the possibility of achieving a sufficient degree of economic planning to abolish unemployment without conscripting the workers as producers and rationing them as consumers. I have put this question in an extreme form. Neither the degree of economic planning which served war needs nor the economic planning which serves Russia today has entailed conscription and rationing of workers like soldiers. Indeed, the present tendency in Russia seems to be to increase the inducement of differential rewards of labor as opposed to military conscription and to decrease the amount of rationing of goods that has been necessary. If economic planning means even in a transitional period a degree of bureaucratic control which denies consumers' choice and conscripts workers with the aid of the secret police to the degree now practiced in Russia, it will seem well-nigh intolerable to the average American and it will probably result sooner or later in a dangerous stagnation in the industrial arts. Though I do not think the Russian government gets its astonishing results primarily by terror, I agree, in the main, with Professor Beard's vigorous statement: "One thing, however, is certain: the Russian government rules by tyranny and terror, with secret police, espionage, and arbitrary executions. The system may be adapted to a people

who endured Tsarist despotism for centuries, but to suppose that it could be transported intact to the United
States, even if deemed successful in its own bailiwick, is to
ignore the stubborn facts of American life and experience —
the long practice of self-government in towns, villages, and
states, the traditions of personal liberty, the established
public school system, and a thousand other elements that
stand out like mountains in the American scene."

There is, moreover, a risk that too rigid a degree of
planning will break down of its own weight and paralyze
initiative by red tape. A machine age, already highly col-
lectivized, must increasingly depend upon the initiative of
the engineer rather than of the entrepreneur. But even
the initiative of the engineer can be crushed by routine and
the rigor of a system which tries the vain task of providing
in advance for every conceivable contingency. At present
the Russian dictatorship is bringing vigor and imagination
to planning. It is easier to apply these qualities to catching
up in an industrially backward country than to keeping up.
Rather it is easier in some respects to industrialize a country than to manage the production and distribution of the
things a nation needs after it is industrialized. Moreover,
it is easier for a dictatorship to be vigorous and imaginative
and honest in a revolutionary period than when it has
settled down. These are not arguments against the success
of the Russian experiment; they are reasons why it, and
even more certainly any plan in the United States, must
leave room for meeting emergencies and for developing
initiative. Its very perfection on paper may paralyze it.

The best bureaucracy tends to be static and suspicious
of those new things and new methods which invention
gives us. But I cannot agree with those critics who think
economic planning will either completely paralyze the
consumers' right to turn from, let us say, coal to oil for
domestic heating or will break on a vain attempt at such

control. Logically, planning can reckon with change and leave a margin for experimentation. At any rate, there is more reason to expect this adaptability and to work for it than to endure the wastes of a planless economic order for which technological progress is poor compensation.

The hope of a sufficient economic planning to meet the problems of an interdependent society and still permit a high degree of choice of work and consumers' goods under a political democracy lies in three things: (1) the possibility of learning the average tendency of consumers' choices and even educating it so that a reasonable forecast can be made of the number of factories necessary for shoes, radios, automobiles, etc.; (2) the fact that the productivity of machinery allows for a very considerable amount of waste from an abstract standpoint without breaking down the system; and (3) that, short of conscription, workers can be guided by information and induced by differential rewards to take the necessary jobs. In a country as far advanced industrially as the United States, a country which does not have to pay to industrialize itself out of its food and clothing, a country already disciplined in factory labor, the degree of rationing and conscription practiced in Russia ought not to be necessary. It would at any rate be impossible without a large-scale war.

In short, while production for use rather than profit requires planning and alone makes possible adequate planning for a machine age, such planning will probably be more aided than hurt by keeping money and the mechanism of profit to permit men a very considerable choice both of what goods they will take and at what jobs they will work. That is to say, workers will be paid in money, and goods will be sold, as they are now, by consumers' co-operatives, on a basis of profit, which profit can be refunded either in increased return to the workers, or dividends to purchasers, or reductions of price the next year, or by some combina-

tion of these methods. At the same time, successful planning will enormously enhance the social income of parks,
playgrounds, libraries, museums, and a hundred and one
things that men may enjoy in the increased leisure which
the efficient harnessing of the billion wild horses of machinery will give them. But this will require far more than
trying to plaster planning on our capitalistic chaos. Important, difficult, and deserving of discussion as are questions of the nature of a desirable plan, the way it should
be set up and the manner in which its commissions, regional
and national, should be constituted, the primary questions
for America and the world are not: how shall we plan, but
for whom and for what shall we plan? What sort of society
do we really want?

STUART CHASE

Stuart Chase, born in 1888, *studied for two years at the Massachusetts Institute of Technology, and graduated S.B., cum* laude, *from Harvard in* 1910. *To this training he added practical experience as certified public accountant, as a partner in the firm of Harvey S. Chase Company, from* 1910 *to* 1917. *For five years he was an investigator, for the Federal Trade Commission, of the meat and packing industries; since* 1922 *he has been with the Labor Bureau, Inc. Meanwhile he has become one of our foremost writers on economic and industrial questions, both in books and in current magazines. His prominence in this field is due partly to his thorough knowledge of the problems and partly to his ability to interpret, for the average man, readably and clearly, facts and figures which would with less skillful treatment be of interest only to the specialist. With F. J. Schlink, he helped to expose some of the unfounded claims of advertisers in* Your Money's Worth (1927) *and to found Consumer's Research, Inc., an organization which has had a rapid growth, thanks to its scientific investigation of advertised products. Among Mr. Chase's widely read books are* The Tragedy of Waste (1925), Men and Machines (1929), *and* Mexico (1931).

The following essay is reprinted from The Nemesis of American Business, *by Stuart Chase, copyright,* 1931. *By permission of The Macmillan Company, publishers.*

STUART CHASE

THE NEMESIS OF AMERICAN BUSINESS

I RETURNED from Mexico the first week in April. The taxi from the Pennsylvania Station landed us, about seven o'clock in the morning, in front of an apartment house in the east thirties in New York. We rubbed our eyes. How were we to get into the apartment? For the whole length of the block a solid phalanx of men, six abreast, filled the sidewalk from house wall to gutter. Like a great python, the line curved around the corner of Madison Avenue and, like an act of creation under the microscope of a biologist, cells of humanity from every direction were coagulating into its tail as it twisted and swelled towards Fifth Avenue. A policeman, gently enough, tore a breach through the line and, with suit cases bulging with the serapes of Taxco and the pottery of Puebla, we made our astonished way between the files of stolid, battered men, and up the stairs.

We had come from one of the poorest of lands to the richest under the sun. But among the Aztec villages we found no unemployment and no visible economic suffering, while here on the sidewalk of the Queen City of the Republic, where, it is alleged, thirty mechanical slaves are equipped to serve the needs of every man, woman, and child, were fifteen hundred men without work and without food. For hours they will stand here (one has just swayed and collapsed) until to a thousand of them are given tickets, entitling the holder to tramp some miles to the south, and there hours later receive twenty cents' worth of food.

We have the mechanical slaves truly enough, and this bread line is part of the price that we pay for them. A

bitter paradox. To hold, as some do, that any worthy man
can secure a job if he only applies himself diligently enough
is to be guilty of a total, and almost criminal, misconception of the course of the industrial revolution. Let me
sketch for you if I can a rough parallel.

In the outlying villages of the central plateau of Mexico
I found an almost pure pre-machine culture. Nor was it
by any means a neolithic one. Behind it lay the tradition
of a very great and noble civilization — that of the Aztecs
and the Toltecs who reared their incredible white cities and
stupendous pyramids and temples a thousand years ago.
Much of that culture remains intact in the Indian of today,
bent but not broken by the marchings of Spanish conquerors and of revolutionary armies. A group of these
villages will comprise an almost completely self-sustaining
unit. Houses are built of local materials, clothing is
largely home grown and spun, food comes from the neighboring fields and groves, recreation is a local product in
which all participate, while over the whole economic process
broods a spirit of authentic craftsmanship giving rise to
some of the loveliest pottery, glasswork, masonry, weaving
which the world knows. Nobody has much; a bad harvest
may cause real suffering; you and I would be profoundly
uncomfortable adjusting our bathroom-steam-heat-butter-
plate complexes to actual living in one of these villages;
but there is enough to go around, in the basic biological
sense of the term, leisure to enjoy life, economic independence within the exigencies of climate and food supply,
while unemployment is as rare as a Freudian neurosis.
Indeed, unemployment is a meaningless term in a self-
sustaining pre-machine community. In the fields, in the
forests, about the house there is always work to be done.

Now let us perform a drastic — and mindful of these
kindly Indians — a somewhat ghastly, surgical operation.
Let us graft upon this community the technic which James

Watt set in motion when he solved the problem of the steam engine a century and a half ago. Invested capital comes sweeping into the country and, with it, interest, profits, and wages. Corporations spring like mushrooms. A lumber company takes over the forest and fuel supply. Contractors undertake the building of houses. Mining concerns exploit the silver, copper, and gold of the surrounding mountains. Factories proceed to the manufacture of textiles, agricultural implements, boots and shoes. Serapes and sombreros go into mass production. Banks open their Doric doorways. High-pressure men make the round of the cabins, their portfolios bulging with installment contracts. Radios blare, motor horns grunt, saxophones croon, while down from the mountains two hundred miles away loops the slender wire — which one stroke of a machete might sever — which pumps the life blood of power and light. Self-sufficiency lies in ruins; the region is clamped into world machine economy, drawing its supplies of physical goods from the five continents, and supplies of credit from New York and London.

The Indians will have a higher standard of living: more things — and a perplexing amount of new kinds of trouble. They cease to direct their own economic destinies and go to work for a boss. Money wages supplant their sometime more direct means of subsistence. From diversification they turn to specialization; from cottage craftsmanship to work on the assembly line, or in the machine shop. To eat they must punch a time clock and buy at the Arctic and Antarctic store. Without a job they must fall back upon charity — or indeed upon the grave. And unless the transformation here described is directed by a coordinating intelligence hitherto unknown, morning after bitter morning they will awake to find themselves without a job. And for a great variety of reasons.

A badly managed silver mine fails, disgorging a thousand

workers. Large profits have been made by a concern manufacturing serapes; almost immediately a dozen new mills have invaded the field, competition for weavers has been brisk, wages are good. Then suddenly the serape market is saturated; prices drop, the old mill and half the new ones shut their doors. Another thousand on the street. A panic seizes the stock market in New York, followed by a business depression. American buyers are marking time, imports decline; presently Mexican glass and pottery factories must put their forces on two days a week. The world price of copper takes a slump. Three mines up on the hills give notice to all but the pump men. A new loom room is set up in a cotton factory. Four women can now produce as much as thirty did on the old machines. The twenty-six punch their clocks and march out. Five banks merge, and hundreds of clerks together with a number of high executives find their services no longer needed. An efficiency man is teaching women to fold clothes with ten motions rather than thirty, and the market will not absorb the two hundred per cent increase in output. Half the force is laid off. Meanwhile the systole and diastole of the seasons — the wet and the dry — fill and empty the fields and the canneries which surround them.

Good times come and good times go; men and women are broken in mind and body by the waiting, the uncertainty, the sheer physical deprivation, and join the ranks of the down-and-outers, the unemployables. No longer the rains, the soils, the personal effort on one's environment are the arbiters of the community destiny, but the job. For the reasons spread upon the record — and for a hundred others — the job is untrustworthy and incalculable.

Whether these Aztec Indians would be worse or better off if they submitted to the surgical operation here formulated lies quite outside the discussion. Perhaps they would and perhaps they would not. I should guess the latter, but your guess is as good as mine. The only point I wish to make is that, granting a mechanized environment, normally administered, *they could not escape unemployment.* Where none are unemployed in the pre-machine environment of today, it is safe to assume that after the operation, at least one man out of ten would always be unemployed; and in the troughs of the business cycle the ratio might run as high as two or three out of ten. Under the hit-and-miss methods of free competition and the unlimited pursuit of profit the process implacably takes its toll. Not only does the worker suffer but, by virtue of a ten to thirty per cent decrease in the community's purchasing power, the profit suffers too. Unemployment is the nemesis of modern industry.

II

With the rise of the industrial revolution and the incalculability of the job, at least four kinds of unemployment become chronic phenomena in all nations addicted to the machine:

1. Seasonal unemployment — as experienced by canning factory workers in the winter.

2. Technological unemployment — as experienced by stokers in a liner when one or two white-garbed oil tenders displace them.

3. Cyclical unemployment — as experienced by some two million persons in the United States this winter following the stock market crash. The last great cyclical depression was in 1921.

4. Residual unemployment. The creation through the above misfortunes of a permanent class of unemployables incapable of any disciplined effort.

In recent years, particularly in America, two further

subdivisions of technological unemployment have been in evidence:

5. Stop-watch unemployment — as when, through time-study methods, one bricklayer takes the place of two.

6. Consolidation unemployment — as when, by virtue of a merger, half a dozen vice presidents and a hundred times as many clerks and salesmen find their function as overhead charges irrelevant, incompetent, and immaterial.

The bread line which coiled about my apartment house was an immediate and shattering revelation that these various classes of unemployment were functioning at their best — or worst; that a real business depression had gripped the country; and that the cheerio paragraphs with a Washington date line which I had read in the Mexican papers, were, like the workers caught in a merger, irrelevant, incompetent, and immaterial. It would appear that the administration and the industrial captains had sought by wish fulfillment and holding the right thought to prove the nonexistence of an unpleasant fact. Their efforts were productive of enormous publicity, but something was obviously the matter with the effectiveness of the mental concentration. Here was this bread line. Turning to the back pages of the newspapers, where the optimistic rhetoric gave way to tangible figures, were a number of other unpleasant facts. Let us glance at them.

The United States Department of Labor has for years calculated an index of factory employment, using the year 1926 as 100. What does the index show since the stock market crash?

September	1929	99.3
October	1929	98.3
November	1929	94.8
December	1929	91.9
January	1930	90.2
February	1930	90.3
March	1930	89.8

Down, down, down. For every hundred men working in factories in September only ninety were working in March; ten were on the street. Now compare these figures with some earlier ones. The index figure for March 1929 was 98.6; for March 1923 — also a very busy spring — it was 110.8. The drop between these two prosperous periods of 1923 and 1929 — from 110.8 to 98.6 — illustrates beautifully, and tragically, the inroads of technological unemployment in six years' time. With eleven per cent fewer men, factories were producing more goods in 1929. But the drop from March 1929 to March 1930 was due almost entirely to cyclical unemployment, which in a few months took almost as much toll as six years' growth in technological unemployment. The latter is in the long run the more serious, but the former is the more dramatic. I had read of "corners being turned" week by week in January, in February, in the early spring, but the harsh facts for factory employment showed March the dreariest exhibit of all.

The American Federation of Labor gives us the percentage of unemployment among its membership month by month. This is primarily an accounting for skilled men. The unskilled do not often join trade unions, while experience has repeatedly shown that the unskilled are more subject to unemployment than the skilled. The percentage of unemployed union members runs:

March 1929	14%
September	10
October	11
November	12
December	16
January 1930	20
February	22
March	21

Up, up, up — even as the employment indices went down, down, down. These figures show two appalling things.

First, that even in the best of times one skilled man in ten is without a job. Second, that the number of unemployed more than doubled from September to March.

The back-page reports come soberly in.... Chambers of Commerce in 200 New York State communities in March show ratios of unemployment ranging from 5 to 70 per cent.... The National Urban League reports 330,000 negroes unemployed.... In November 1929 Willys Overland had 4,000 on its payroll as against 28,000 in the peak of 1929.... One-third of the hosiery workers of Philadelphia are out of work.... Fourteen woolen mills shut down in the Albany district, discharging 1,600, and putting 600 on part time.... 150,000 automobile workers jobless in Detroit, the total employed falling from 450,000 to 300,000 with many of the latter on part time.... A special study in Buffalo, based on personal interviews and reported by the *Monthly Labor Review*, shows 11 per cent completely idle, and 18 per cent either idle or on part time.... A 40 per cent reduction in automobile workers is reported by the *Monthy Labor Review* from April to December 1929.... The National Cash Register Company has 6,500 on its payroll on March 7, 1930, as against 8,000 "a few weeks ago.".... Residential construction shows an alarming shrinkage.... The Whitin Machine Works in Massachusetts normally carries a force of 3,500 men; in January 1930 there were 2,000 at work.... And I have hardly made a dent in the clippings and reports before me.

What the grand total of unemployed for the nation was in the early spring of 1930 no man knows. Months from now the computing machines of the Census Bureau may give us a reliable indication. Various estimates have been made, however. Senator Brookhart believes the figure lies between 3,000,000 and 6,000,000. He is probably right. Mr. Darwin J. Meserole of the National Unemployment League hazards 6,600,000 — which is undoubtedly high.

The crash of 1921 probably did not account for more than 5,000,000, and the present slump is, as yet, no worse than 1921; possibly not quite so severe. William Green of the American Federation of Labor estimated 3,700,000 in February. Senator Couzens reports that a high government official told him that within a few weeks after the stock market débâcle unemployment jumped from 700,000 to 3,100,000.... Take your choice. My guess would be at least 4,000,000 in March. The figures cited earlier indicate that unemployment had doubled over its normal rate. If, in the best of times, seven per cent of the 30,000,000 "gainfully employed" are idle — a very conservative figure — this gives us some 2,000,000 in the army of the chronically jobless — the number seeking work in a "good" month like September 1929. Double this, and we reach 4,000,000 for a sinister month like March 1930. This is a reasonably crude guess, but leaning, I think, to the conservative side.

The reasons for the bread line around my house are rapidly coming into focus. In a sense it is a bread line four million strong, that, in single file, three feet apart, would reach from New York to Denver, with 300 miles to spare.

For a bread line there must be bread, and somebody to provide it. Public and private charities say last winter was the worst since 1921, if not since 1914. My particular bread line, organized by The Little Church Around the Corner, had made no such effort since the panic of 1907. It was feeding 1,000 men daily, only 150 of whom were genuine down-and-outers; "the great majority were honest men who would work if they could." Every trade was represented, including musicians and engineers. There were other bread lines in New York, and three in Brooklyn. The 611 rooms of the Salvation Army's flop house on the Bowery were filled every night, with sometimes as many as 400 men sleeping on the floor. "Things are worse than they have been for a good many years. One fact is very noticeable — the majority of homeless and jobless are native-born Americans."

The Russell Sage Foundation, tabulating relief budgets in 77 cities, finds: "Acute demands for outdoor relief, which, beginning in October, have severely taxed the resources of public and private agencies, were unabated in February. During the month $4,676,000 was distributed to 164,000 families." The Charity Organization Society of New York reports more applications for aid from destitute families than at any time since 1921 — 100 per cent greater than in 1929. The Bowery Branch of the Y. M. C. A. distributed as many as 12,000 meal tickets in one day. Five per cent of these applicants held college degrees, and a few were Phi Beta Kappa men. They were largely American born, and their average age was 30. The Welfare Council of New York had to charter an old barge in the East River as an overflow flop house. Twenty-five hundred men were fed daily in Pittsburgh bread lines. The Family Welfare Association of America, tabulating reports from 60 cities, finds a 100 per cent increase in relief administered in January 1930 over January 1929, and a 200 per cent increase in families in distress due to lack of work.

Hospital beds are also an index of unemployment. Bellevue notes an increase of 12 per cent. "Many of these patients are from lodging houses. Out of work and destitute, their resistance has become lowered and has induced an *acute* condition in what are ordinarily chronic complaints that do not require hospitalization."

It has been a bitter winter on the Bowery and a bitter spring. Yet above the flop houses and the bread lines has glared a signboard: "Business is good — Keep it good."

III

As men lose their wages their purchasing power declines. The bulk of purchasing power in the United States con-

sists of wages. This reduces sales in other industries until
they too begin to reduce their working force. The vicious
spiral begins to whirl. The *Annalist's* index of factory
payrolls fell from 109 in September 1929 to 95.6 in January
1930 — the lowest since December 1924. According to the
Annalist, wages have fallen even faster than employment
— indicating a certain lack of sympathy with Mr. Hoover's
recommendation that wage levels be sustained. A further
lack of sympathy is reported from Dayton. Personnel
managers were interviewed in respect to their handling
of lay-offs. Said one, "All they got was ten minutes'
notice. That's not fair, but that's all I got from the New
York office." The tabulations of the Labor Bureau, Inc.,
show a heavy increase in wage cuts in recent months.
Farm wages are the lowest since 1923, with supply far in
excess of demand. Incidentally, demand is considerably
below normal. Mr. William Green, testifying before the
Senate, estimates a loss of purchasing power in the domestic
market of one billion dollars in the first three months of
1930. In the same hearings Senator Wagner introduced
figures to show payroll shrinkages of $200,000,000 a month
in factory employment alone. The repercussion is well
documented by a drop of $86,000,000 in outlays for building
materials in January 1930 as compared with 1929. This
seems to show a certain lack of sympathy with the great
construction program which was to guarantee prosperity.

IV

So much for the tangible evidence as to the economic
state of the nation in the spring of 1930. If you want
more, I am in a position to supply a carload of documents,
more or less. The figures prove that prosperity cannot be
sold like a tooth paste: by making people want it. And
they prove conclusively, I think, that the fifth great era of
American commercial prosperity, which began in 1922,

ran its course in eight short years (rather below the average span) and died on a certain sixteen-million-share day in October, 1929. Many of us at the time saw no logical reason why a stock-market collapse should necessarily undermine business, and indeed there is none; but what most of us did not see was the extent of the black cloud over Detroit which had been gathering all summer. Along about July the nation found itself unable to purchase motor cars as fast as they were being built. Demand began to slacken, and in due time production had to follow suit. The automotive industry was the backbone of the whole prosperity era, and as, faster and faster, it began to slip, it dragged the whole business structure down with it. Thus undoubtedly a depression was in order, though without any stock-market collapse the curve would not have dipped so deep.

It is alleged that factories are now equipped to produce more than 7,000,000 motor cars a year. With safety valves tied down, and selling pressure at the bursting point, not more than 5,000,000 can be absorbed; and in 1930, it is safe to say, sales will be far below that figure. Senator Couzens tells us that radio factories can turn out 15,000,000 units a year, while only 3,000,000 can be marketed. In industry after industry potential output is vastly greater than demand — a condition which grows steadily worse. Sometimes I wonder if the whole mass production, low-unit cost, high-pressure selling formula has not gone almost as far as it can under the present limits of income distribution, and is not destined, if not to collapse, at least to be profoundly modified. The automobile was the keystone of the arch, and the stone has slipped. Nor is there any article on the horizon to take its mighty place. A fool-proof airplane might do it, but where is the fool-proof airplane?

V

Americans want things — lots of them. The raw material is available — as yet — to provide them, together with a willing labor force, a beautiful technic of management, and an abundance of capital. So, whatever happens to the mass-production formula and to the motor car, business will go on. It may stagger for a time, but it is inconceivable that it is permanently crippled. The current depression will pass, and the emergency bread lines fade away. Cyclical unemployment will mark time until the next depression. What threatens to continue unabated, in good times and bad, is technological unemployment with its three faces — the machine, the merger, the stop watch. In four years oil refineries increased output 84 per cent, and laid off 5 per cent of their men while doing it. Tobacco manufacturing output climbed 53 per cent in the same period, with 13 per cent fewer men at the end. This is the trend throughout industry.

It can mean only one thing. An equivalent tonnage of goods can be produced by a declining number of workers, and men must lose their jobs by the thousands — presently by the millions. Heretofore, after a dreary period of searching, they have found other jobs. But how near to saturation are the filling-station industry, bond selling, insurance, hot-dog stands, spear carrying in Hollywood, and the other "blotting paper" trades? How near are we to a genuine attack on the staggering wastes of distribution, with its inevitable result of a reduction in man power? Nobody absolutely knows, but many are guessing — your author included — that the blotting paper is becoming soggy. The automobile industry alone soaked up 4,000,000 new jobs since 1900, but its curve of employment is now definitely downward.

Says the *Iron Age:* "If the productivity of industry through mechanization continues to increase in the next

25 years in the same way and at the same rate as during
the last 25, only 45 men will be needed for the work which
today requires 70, and that formerly required 100.   In
the automobile industry 30 workers were doing in 1925 as
much work as 100 workers in 1914." What are we going
to do with the 25 men out of 70 that are to be displaced
in the next 25 years?   And there may be far more than 25
displaced, as the curve of technology is an accelerating one.
Dr. Wesley C. Mitchell estimates that no less than
650,000 men were added to the ranks of the reserve army
of the unemployed from 1920 to 1927.   We remember too
the drop in the index numbers of employment from March
1923 to March 1929, already quoted.

Here is a new ensilage harvesting machine that cuts
cornstalks in the field and delivers them to the silo without
a human hand touching a single stalk.   Here is a new
tabulating machine capable of doing the work of 100
skilled actuaries.   Here is an automatic mechanism producing 73,000 electric light bulbs every 24 hours, dis-
placing 2,000 hand operators for each machine installed.
Here is Section E of the St. Louis concrete sewer project.
Thirty-three machine operators, aided by 37 laborers, are
doing the work of 7,000 pick and shovel men.   Seventy
men and machines displace 7,000!   The United States
Department of Commerce estimates that combines in the
harvesting of wheat in one area have cut the force of farm
laborers from 50,000 to 20,000.   Here are automatic cigar
makers, dial telephones, the "iron chink" which has re-
volutionized the canning of fish, automatic stokers, mechanical glass blowers, automatic power stations, automatic knitting machines, bookkeeping machines, paint
sprayers, mechanical cotton pickers, the telephonic typewriter, automatic check writers — and a hundred more,
all taking their toll of direct labor.   It must not be forgotten that, in the final balance, the direct labor which is

displaced may find a job in building or servicing the machine — but the margin of jobs permanently lost is reasonably wide, otherwise there would be no point in introducing the mechanism.

Turning to the allies of the iron bouncer, we note a recent statement in *Forbes Magazine:* "Never before were so many salaried men looking for positions. Men formerly receiving $10,000 to $30,000 are now anxious to start at half salary. Thus many bargains in human material are available." Under every merger we shall find a bargain basement.

And here are the indefatigable time-study men. Stop watch in hand, they eliminate enough unnecessary movements in the customary method of dipping chocolate to increase production 88 per cent. Moving on to the next shop, they cut the time of assembling carburetors from 450 minutes to 45. Few markets can absorb such staggering increases in output per man. So the unabsorbed fraction must punch the clock for the last time. In swinging a pick in the coal mines, in sorting potatoes, in picking fruit, in scores of occupations, the time-study brigade is eliminating motions, and with them men. Not only in motions, but in shop arrangement, routing, lighting, ventilating, management generally, is the process rampant. Better conditions — true; fewer men — almost always.

If a machine does not get you, a stop watch will; and if you dodge both there is a merger waiting around the corner — such must be the thought which lies none too lightly in millions of American minds today. If you are alert enough to keep ahead of all three, God knows when you may trip and plunge into the crevasse of a cyclical depression — like that whose somber figures covering the winter of 1930 we have just recorded.

VI

This is no way for a civilized society to behave. Unabated, it will bring most of us to wish that the industrial revolution had never been born. For all our bath tubs, washing machines, and canned asparagus, we may grow more and more envious of the Aztec, who if he has not so many dandy little jiggers, has at least a steady and rewarding job. And quite possibly some of us may start to smash things up. Such a dependable gentleman as Mr. William Green told the Senate that he had no hopes of keeping his hitherto orderly cohorts in line if the conditions which created unemployment were allowed to follow a masterless drift.

If we care enough about it, we can very greatly diminish, if not altogether liquidate unemployment. It will cost something — but consider what it now costs us in charity, in taxes which flow from public charity, in high labor turnover, in broken shop morale, in the quality of work done by men who have no feeling of economic security, in accumulating overhead on closed and partly closed factories and, above all, in reduced markets due to loss of purchasing power. I wonder if the total cost of seizing the situation by the throat would equal the total losses now engendered? I am speaking in strict financial terms for the moment, waiving the whole human cost in suffering, hopelessness, and degradation.

Conceivably, we might start with an intelligent and honest publicity campaign to replace the winter's dishonorable record of prosperity billboards in the Bowery — a campaign which flatly recognizes facts, however harsh, and tries to swing public opinion towards constructive remedies. We have the precedent in the Safety First and the Cancer Control drives. We might even go so far as to hope that some of the advertising fraternity might give a moment or two from their sterner duties and originate some effective slogans:

Six Hours' Work and Work for Everybody.
Give a Job and Get a Customer.
A Steady Job. Ivory Soap Gives It — Why Not Your
Boss?
If Mexicans Can Eat, Why Can't We?
(These are the ravings of a rank amateur. I appeal to
those who know the technic to improve them.)
We need to mobilize public opinion as in the Liberty
Bond drives — with posters, page spreads, four-minute
speakers, radio talks, news reels, editorials, the whole
colorful phenomenon which we Americans do so well, and
which is our equivalent of the poor Mexican's fiesta.

In such an atmosphere concrete measures might have a
chance of success. They may be launched on many fronts.

The logical, sensible, and only final answer to technological unemployment is to shorten working hours. Under
present practice, as the machine advances, fewer men work
equally long (or approximately so). Why not keep the
entire force on the payroll but work them less? Thus the
whole nation would share in technological advances: the
worker in a steady job with fewer hours, the owner in
steadier markets and profits, due to undiminished purchasing power. This is the final goal. I do not deny that
its achievement will take a long time, and more brains and
more co-ordinated planning than have ever as yet blessed
the Republic. It would be something, however, to get it
into the national consciousness.

The regularization of industry lies somewhat short of the
final goal, but concrete beginnings have already been made.
The Procter and Gamble Company, for instance, estimates
its annual production in advance (the variation does not
exceed 3 per cent), divides the total by 48, plans to produce
that much soap in every week of the year, and guarantees
48 weeks' steady employment to every man who has been
in the factory for a term of at least six months. Regulariza-

tion may be approached through four channels: the Business Survey Conference of Mr. Hoover, the trade associations, the industrial manufacturer or contractor, the labor union. For some concerns where seasonal and storage problems have not been solved the program is impossible. For others it may have only partial application. But for thousands it could be put into tangible effect if only their managers could be brought to think about it, and their working force to demand it. Regularization can be only an intermediate goal, because while it provides steady work for those employed, it takes no cognizance of those displaced by machines, time studies, or mergers. It helps the ins enormously, but the outs not at all. What it does in effect is to kill seasonal unemployment and perhaps cripple cyclical; technological it leaves untouched.

Third, there are the long-swing construction programs, optimistically and exhaustively discussed these past few months. In respect to them we need more action and less talk. A construction engineer told me recently that business in his field for the first three months of 1930 had been the worst in his fifteen years' experience. I enquired about the front-page stories, and the figures with the quantities of zeros. "Bosh," he said, "it was stuff they were going to build anyway, except that a lot of it they didn't build!" Carefully prepared, with something of the intelligence with which an army conserves its supplies, construction work both public and private could be nursed in the good years and brought forward when a cyclical depression threatened. It was not so done this winter — but the job was new and the time was short. It could be done, and Senator Wagner has a bill before Congress to expedite it. Beyond the immediate construction programs, consider the vast amount of useful and necessary labor required in a sound national afforestation project, in slum clearance, in regional and beautification work. Some day we must tackle such projects. Why not now?

Fourth, we must have better statistics on unemployment, preferably collected through a nation-wide system of public labor exchanges. No engineer can build a dam until he knows how much dirt he has to move. Meanwhile the exchanges themselves would be enormously valuable in protecting displaced workers from the villainous brigandage of most private exchanges and in informing applicants honorably and specifically of where jobs are to be obtained, if any. This would mitigate the practice of telling a hundred men in Chicago that there is a job in Milwaukee and collecting five dollars from each — with either a single position or a purely fictitious one available when the whole hundred spend their last nickel in reaching Milwaukee.

Fifth, we can raise the age limit at which children are permitted to enter industry, thus salvaging jobs for their elders. If the minimum were placed at sixteen years rather than the prevailing fourteen years (in most states) some hundreds of thousands of jobs would be conserved. The benefit to the children themselves is too obvious to need argument. At the same time studies should be undertaken to find out the type of job that the older worker is especially qualified to fill, and thus halt the vicious and stupid practice of firing , or refusing to hire, men or women because they are thirty-five or forty or forty-five years old. As industry becomes increasingly automatic, the steadiness and dependability of the older worker should be increasingly valuable. Flighty youngsters may have more muscle, but the automatic function needs no muscle; it needs careful inspection, dial watching, checking, and repairing. I am convinced that competent analysis would reveal thousands upon thousands of jobs in the modern world which the older worker is better fitted to perform than the man under forty.

The above programs, if put into energetic effect, will go

far towards liquidating unemployment, but a certain amount of lost time there is bound to be, even under the best of conditions. The industrial machine is not frictionless and never can be. For those who have lost their jobs through no fault of their own, particularly during the transition period, two systems of aid are in order — the dismissal wage and unemployment compensation. The former is a lump sum paid by the company to an employee when forced to give his position to a machine (or for other causes), preferably on a sliding scale based on length of service. The latter is such a system as that set up by the Dennison Manufacturing Company or the Amalgamated Clothing Workers, where reserves are accumulated from profits and payrolls to meet the just debts of industry when the machine or hard times come. State unemployment insurance is another aspect of the same general remedy, and most certainly should be applied if management and labor are themselves unable to provide the necessary funds.

As a certified public accountant, I have been examining corporation balance sheets for many years. Seldom do I find one without a "surplus" account on the credit side, and frequently an appropriated surplus, variously entitled "reserve for dividends," "reserve for depreciation," "reserve for bad debts," "reserve for expansion." But a "reserve for unemployment" I have never seen. The dividends and equities of stockholders have been protected by many ingenious devices. It is time, and more than time, that the flesh and blood which provide them receive at least equal consideration.

Sir *ARTHUR STANLEY EDDINGTON*

Arthur Stanley Eddington was born in 1882, and educated at Owens College, now Manchester University.   Since 1913 he has been Plumian Professor of Astronomy at Cambridge University; since 1914, a Fellow of the Royal Society.   In 1930 he was created knight.   These facts, together with the numerous degrees he has won (including those of M.A., D.Sc., and LL.D.), bear witness to his eminence as a research physicist and astronomer.   He is also eminent, however — and this is important to the general reader — for his interest in the wider significance of modern scientific discoveries. "My principal aim," *he says in the Preface to* The Nature of the Physical World, "has been to show that these scientific developments provide new material for the philosopher."   *That aim was successfully accomplished and the book was widely read because of its author's skill in making lucid what to the lay reader are obscure technicalities in recent physics.   Of this skill, the Introduction, given here, will serve as an example.*   Science and the Unseen World (1929) *and* The Expanding Universe (1933) *also show Sir Arthur Eddington's ability as an expounder of scientific discoveries and their philosophical consequences.*

Sir *ARTHUR STANLEY EDDINGTON*

INTRODUCTION TO *THE NATURE OF THE PHYSICAL WORLD*

I HAVE settled down to the task of writing these lectures and have drawn up my chairs to my two tables. Two tables! Yes; there are duplicates of every object about me — two tables, two chairs, two pens.

This is not a very profound beginning to a course which ought to reach transcendent levels of scientific philosophy. But we cannot touch bedrock immediately; we must scratch a bit at the surface of things first. And whenever I begin to scratch the first thing I strike is — my two tables.

One of them has been familiar to me from earliest years. It is a commonplace object of that environment which I call the world. How shall I describe it? It has extension; it is comparatively permanent; it is coloured; above all it is *substantial*. By substantial I do not merely mean that it does not collapse when I lean upon it; I mean that it is constituted of "substance" and by that word I am trying to convey to you some conception of its intrinsic nature. It is a *thing*; not like space, which is a mere negation; nor like time, which is — Heaven knows what! But that will not help you to my meaning because it is the distinctive characteristic of a "thing" to have this substantiality, and I do not think substantiality can be described better than by saying that it is the kind of nature exemplified by an ordinary table. And so we go round in circles. After all if you are a plain commonsense man, not too much worried with scientific scruples, you will be confident that you understand the nature of an ordinary table. I have even heard of plain men who had the idea that they could better understand the mystery of their own nature if scientists would discover a way of explaining it in terms of the easily comprehensible nature of a table.

Table No. 2 is my scientific table. It is a more recent acquaintance and I do not feel so familiar with it. It does not belong to the world previously mentioned — that world which spontaneously appears around me when I open my eyes, though how much of it is objective and how much subjective I do not here consider. It is part of a world which in more devious ways has forced itself on my attention. My scientific table is mostly emptiness. Sparsely scattered in that emptiness are numerous electric charges rushing about with great speed; but their combined bulk amounts to less than a billionth of the bulk of the table itself. Notwithstanding its strange construction it turns out to be an entirely efficient table. It supports my writing paper as satisfactorily as Table No. 1; for when I lay the paper on it the little electric particles with their headlong speed keep on hitting the underside, so that the paper is maintained in shuttlecock fashion at a nearly steady level. If I lean upon this table I shall not go through; or, to be strictly accurate, the chance of my scientific elbow going through my scientific table is so excessively small that it can be neglected in practical life. Reviewing their properties one by one, there seems to be nothing to choose between the two tables for ordinary purposes; but when abnormal circumstances befall, then my scientific table shows to advantage. If the house catches fire my scientific table will dissolve quite naturally into scientific smoke, whereas my familiar table undergoes a metamorphosis of its substantial nature which I can only regard as miraculous.

There is nothing *substantial* about my second table. It is nearly all empty space — space pervaded, it is true, by fields of force, but these are assigned to the category of "influences," not of "things." Even in the minute part which is not empty we must not transfer the old notion of substance. In dissecting matter into electric charges we have travelled far from that picture of it which first gave rise to the conception of substance, and the meaning of that conception — if it ever had any — has been lost by the way. The whole trend of modern scientific views is to break down the separate categories of "things," "influences," "forms," etc., and to substitute a common background of all experience. Whether we are studying a material object, a magnetic field, a geometrical figure, or a duration of time, our scientific information is summed up in measures; neither the apparatus of measurement nor the mode of using it suggests that there is anything essentially different in these problems. The measures themselves afford no ground for a classification by categories. We feel it necessary to concede some background to the measures — an external world; but the attributes of this world, except in so far as they are reflected in the measures, are outside scientific scrutiny. Science has at last revolted against attaching the exact knowledge contained in these measurements to a traditional picture-gallery of conceptions which convey no authentic information of the background and obtrude irrelevancies into the scheme of knowledge.

I will not here stress further the non-substantiality of electrons, since it is scarcely necessary to the present line of thought. Conceive them as substantially as you will, there is a vast difference between my scientific table with its substance (if any) thinly scattered in specks in a region mostly empty and the table of everyday conception which we regard as the type of solid reality — an incarnate protest against Berkleian subjectivism. It makes all the difference in the world whether the paper before me is poised as it were on a swarm of flies and sustained in shuttle cock fashion by a series of tiny blows from the swarm underneath, or whether it is supported because there is substance below it, it being the intrinsic nature of substance to occupy space to the exclusion of other substance; all the difference in conception at least, but no difference to my practical task of writing on the paper.

I need not tell you that modern physics has by delicate test and remorseless logic assured me that my second scientific table is the only one which is really there — wherever "there" may be. On the other hand I need not tell you that modern physics will never succeed in exorcising that first table — strange compound of external nature, mental imagery and inherited prejudice — which lies visible to my eyes and tangible to my grasp. We must bid good-bye to it for the present for we are about to turn from the familiar world to the scientific world revealed by physics. This is, or is intended to be, a wholly external world.

"You speak paradoxically of two worlds. Are they not really two aspects or two interpretations of one and the same world?"

Yes, no doubt they are ultimately to be identified after some fashion. But the process by which the external world of physics is transformed into a world of familiar acquaintance in human consciousness is outside the scope of physics. And so the world studied according to the methods of physics remains detached from the world familiar to consciousness, until after the physicist has finished his labours upon it. Provisionally, therefore, we regard the table which is the subject of physical research as altogether separate from the familiar table, without prejudging the question of their ultimate identification. It is true that the whole scientific inquiry starts from the familiar world and in the end it must return to the familiar world; but the part of the journey over which the physicist has charge is in foreign territory.

Until recently there was a much closer linkage; the

physicist used to borrow the raw material of his world from the familiar world, but he does so no longer. His raw materials are æther, electrons, quanta, potentials, Hamiltonian functions, etc., and he is nowadays scrupulously careful to guard these from contamination by conceptions borrowed from the other world. There is a familiar table parallel to the scientific table, but there is no familiar electron, quantum or potential parallel to the scientific electron, quantum or potential. We do not even desire to manufacture a familiar counterpart to these things or, as we should commonly say, to "explain" the electron. After the physicist has quite finished his world-building a linkage or identification is allowed; but premature attempts at linkage have been found to be entirely mischievous.

Science aims at constructing a world which shall be symbolic of the world of commonplace experience. It is not at all necessary that every individual symbol that is used should represent something in common experience or even something explicable in terms of common experience. The man in the street is always making this demand for concrete explanation of the things referred to in science; but of necessity he must be disappointed. It is like our experience in learning to read. That which is written in a book is symbolic of a story in real life. The whole intention of the book is that ultimately a reader will identify some symbol, say BREAD, with one of the conceptions of familiar life. But it is mischievous to attempt such identifications prematurely, before the letters are strung into words and the words into sentences. The symbol A is not the counterpart of anything in familiar life. To the child the letter A would seem horribly abstract; so we give him a familiar conception along with it. "A was an Archer who shot at a frog." This tides over his immediate difficulty; but he cannot make serious progress with word-building so long as Archers, Butchers, Captains, dance round the letters. The letters are abstract, and sooner or later he has to realise it. In physics we have outgrown archer and apple-pie definitions of the fundamental symbols. To a request to explain what an electron really is supposed to be we can only answer, "It is part of the A B C of physics."

The external world of physics has thus become a world of shadows. In removing our illusions we have removed the substance, for indeed we have seen that substance is one of the greatest of our illusions. Later perhaps we may inquire whether in our zeal to cut out all that is unreal we may not have used the knife too ruthlessly. Perhaps, indeed, reality is a child which cannot survive without its nurse illusion. But if so, that is of little concern to the scientist, who has good and sufficient reasons for pursuing his investigations in the world of shadows and is content to leave to the philosopher the determination of its exact status in regard to reality. In the world of physics we watch a shadowgraph performance of the drama of familiar life. The shadow of my elbow rests on the shadow table as the shadow ink flows over the shadow paper. It is all symbolic, and as a symbol the physicist leaves it. Then comes the alchemist Mind who transmutes the symbols. The sparsely spread nuclei of electric force become a tangible solid; their restless agitation becomes the warmth of summer; the octave of æthereal vibrations becomes a gorgeous rainbow. Nor does the alchemy stop here. In the transmuted world new significances arise which are scarcely to be traced in the world of symbols; so that it becomes a world of beauty and purpose — and, alas, suffering and evil.

The frank realisation that physical science is concerned with a world of shadows is one of the most significant of recent advances. I do not mean that physicists are to any extent preoccupied with the philosophical implications of this. From their point of view it is not so much a withdrawal of untenable claims as an assertion of freedom for autonomous development. At the moment I am not insisting on the shadowy and symbolic character of the world of physics because of its bearing on philosophy, but because the aloofness from familiar conceptions will be apparent in the scientific theories I have to describe. If you are not prepared for this aloofness you are likely to be out of sympathy with modern scientific theories, and may even think them ridiculous — as, I daresay, many people do.

It is difficult to school ourselves to treat the physical world as purely symbolic. We are always relapsing and mixing with the symbols incongruous conceptions taken from the world of consciousness. Untaught by long experience we stretch a hand to grasp the shadow, instead of accepting its shadowy nature. Indeed, unless we confine ourselves altogether to mathematical symbolism it is hard to avoid dressing our symbols in deceitful clothing. When I think of an electron there rises to my mind a hard, red, tiny ball; the proton similarly is neutral grey. Of course the colour is absurd — perhaps not more absurd than the rest of the conception — but I am incorrigible. I can well understand that the younger minds are finding these pictures too concrete and are striving to construct the world out of Hamiltonian functions and symbols so far removed from human preconception that they do not even obey the laws of orthodox arithmetic. For myself I find some difficulty in rising to that plane of thought; but I am convinced that it has got to come.

In these lectures I propose to discuss some of the results of modern study of the physical world which give most food for philosophic thought. This will include new conceptions in science and also new knowledge. In both respects we are led to think of the material universe in a way very different from that prevailing at the end of the last century. I shall not leave out of sight the ulterior object which must be in the mind of a Gifford Lecturer, the problem of relating these purely physical discoveries to the wider aspects and interests of our human nature. These relations cannot but have undergone change, since our whole conception of the physical world has radically changed. I am convinced that a just appreciation of the physical world as it is understood today carries with it a feeling of open-mindedness towards a wider significance transcending scientific measurement, which might have seemed illogical a generation ago; and in the later lectures I shall try to focus that feeling and make inexpert efforts to find where it leads. But I should be untrue to science if I did not insist that its study is an end in itself. The path of science must be pursued for its own sake, irrespective of the views it may afford of a wider landscape; in this spirit we must follow the path whether it leads to the hill of vision or the tunnel of obscurity. Therefore till the last stage of the course is reached you must be content to follow with me the beaten track of science, nor scold me too severely for loitering among its wayside flowers. That is to be the understanding between us. Shall we set forth?

Sir JAMES HOPWOOD JEANS

James Hopwood Jeans was born in 1877, and studied at Trinity College, Cambridge, where he was Second Wrangler in 1898 and Smith's Prizeman in the following year. Appointed Fellow of Trinity College in 1901, he became University Lecturer in Mathematics three years later. From 1905 to 1909 he was in the United States, as Professor of Applied Mathematics at Princeton University; since that time he has been successively Lecturer in Applied Mathematics in Cambridge University, Secretary of the Royal Society, and Research Associate of the Mount Wilson Observatory. In 1928 he was created knight. Like Sir Arthur Eddington, he holds degrees from universities and memberships in scientific organizations too numerous to mention here; like him, too, he has written much, not only on scientific discoveries but on their wider implications as well. Thus, his bibliography — aside from articles in periodicals — begins with The Dynamical Theory of Gases (1904) *and similar technical discussions, but includes also such general works as* The Universe Around Us (1929), The Mysterious Universe (1930), *and* The Stars in Their Courses (1931).

The following essay is reprinted from The Universe Around Us, *by Sir James Jeans, with the permission of the author and of The Macmillan Company, publishers.*

Sir *JAMES HOPWOOD JEANS*

THE STUDY OF ASTRONOMY

ON THE evening of January 7, 1610, a fateful day for the human race, Galileo Galilei, Professor of Mathematics in the University of Padua, sat in front of a telescope he had made with his own hands.

More than three centuries previously, Roger Bacon, the inventor of spectacles, had explained how a telescope could be constructed so as "to make the stars appear as near as we please." He had shown how a lens could be so shaped that it would collect all the rays of light falling on it from a distant object, bend them until they met in a focus and then pass them on through the pupil of the eye on to the retina. Such an instrument would increase the power of the human eye, just as an ear trumpet increases the power of the human ear by collecting all the waves of sound which fall on a large aperture, bending them, and passing them through the orifice of the ear on to the ear drum.

Yet it was not until 1608 that the first telescope had been constructed by Lippershey, a Flemish spectacle-maker. On hearing of this instrument, Galileo had set to work to discover the principles of its construction and had soon made himself a telescope far better than the original. His instrument had created no small sensation in Italy. Such extraordinary stories had been told of its powers that he had been commanded to take it to Venice and exhibit it to the Doge and Senate. The citizens of Venice had then seen the most aged of their Senators climbing the highest bell-towers to spy through the telescope at ships which were too far out at sea to be seen at all without its help. The telescope admitted about a hundred times as much light as the unaided human eye, and, according to Galileo, it showed an object at fifty miles as clearly as if it were only five miles away.

The absorbing interest of his new instrument had almost driven from Galileo's mind a problem to which he had at one time given much thought. Over two thousand years previously, Pythagoras and Philolaus had taught that the earth is not fixed in space, but rotates on its axis every twenty-four hours, thus causing the alternation of day and night. Aristarchus of Samos, perhaps the greatest of all the Greek mathematicians, had further maintained that the earth not only turned on its axis, but also described a yearly journey around the sun, this being the cause of the cycle of the seasons.

Then these doctrines had fallen into disfavour. Aristotle had pronounced against them, asserting that the earth formed a fixed centre to the universe. Later Ptolemy had explained the tracks of the planets across the sky in terms of a complicated system of cycles and epicycles; the planets moved in circular paths around moving points, which themselves moved in circles around an immoveable earth. The Church had given its sanction and active support to these doctrines. Indeed, it is difficult to see what else it could have done, for it seemed almost impious to suppose that the great drama of man's fall and redemption, in which the Son of God had Himself taken part, could have been enacted on any lesser stage than the very centre of the Universe.

Yet, even in the Church, the doctrine had not gained universal acceptance. Oresme, Bishop of Lisieux, and Cardinal Nicholas of Cusa, had both declared against it, the latter writing in 1440:

> I have long considered that this earth is not fixed, but moves as do the other stars. To my mind the earth turns upon its axis once every day and night.

At a later date those who held these views incurred the active hosti ity of the Church, and in 1600 Giordano Bruno was burned at the stake. He had written:

It has seemed to me unworthy of the divine goodness and power to create a finite world, when able to produce beside it another and others infinite; so that I have declared that there are endless particular worlds similar to this of the earth; with Pythagoras I regard it as a star, and similar to it are the moon, the planets and other stars, which are infinite in number, and all these bodies are worlds.

The most weighty attack on orthodox doctrine had, however, been delivered neither by theologians nor philosophers, but by the Polish astronomer, Nicolaus Copernicus (1473–1543). In his great work *De revolutionibus orbium coelestium* Copernicus had shown that Ptolemy's elaborate structure of cycles and epicycles was unnecessary, because the tracks of the planets across the sky could be explained quite simply by supposing that the earth and the planets all moved round a fixed central sun. The sixty-six years which had elapsed since this book was published had seen these theories hotly debated, but they were still neither proved nor disproved.

Galileo had already found that his new telescope provided a means of testing astronomical theories. As soon as he had turned it on to the Milky Way, a whole crowd of legends and fables as to its nature and structure had vanished into thin air; it proved to be nothing more than a swarm of faint stars scattered like golden dust on the black background of the sky. Another glance through the telescope had disclosed the true nature of the moon. It had on it mountains which cast shadows, and so proved, as Giordano Bruno had maintained, to be a world like our own. What if the telescope should now in some way prove able to decide between the orthodox doctrine that the earth forms the hub of the universe, and the new doctrine that the earth was only one of a number of bodies, all circling round the sun like moths round a candle-flame?

And now Galileo catches Jupiter in the field of his telescope, and sees four small bodies circling round the great mass of the planet — like moths round a candle-flame. What he sees is an exact replica of the solar system as imagined by Copernicus, and it provides direct visual proof that such systems are at least not alien to the architectural plan of the universe. And yet, strangely enough, he hardly sees the full implications of his discovery at once; he merely avers that he has discovered four new planets which chase one another round and round the known planet Jupiter.

Final and complete understanding comes nine months later when he observes the phases of Venus. Venus might have been self-luminous, in which case she would always appear as a full circle of light. If she were not self-luminous, but moved in a Ptolemaic epicycle, then, as Ptolemy had himself pointed out, she could never show more than half her surface illuminated. On the other hand, the Copernican view of the solar system required that both Venus and Mercury should exhibit "phases" like those of the moon, their shining surfaces ranging in appearance from crescent-shape through half moon to full moon, and then back through half moon to crescent-shape. That such phases were not shown by Venus had indeed been urged as an objection to the Copernican theory.

Galileo's telescope now shows that, as Copernicus had foretold, Venus passes through the full cycle of phases, so that, in Galileo's own words, we "are now supplied with a determination most conclusive, and appealing to the evidence of our senses," that "Venus, and Mercury also, revolve around the sun, as do also all the rest of the planets, a truth believed indeed by the Pythagorean school, by Copernicus, and by Kepler, but never proved by the evidence of our senses, as is now proved in the case of Venus and Mercury."

These discoveries of Galileo made it clear that Aristotle, Ptolemy and the majority of those who had thought about these things in the last two thousand years had been utterly and hopelessly wrong. In estimating his position in the universe, man had up to now been guided mainly by his own desires, and his self-esteem; long fed on boundless hopes, he had spurned the simpler fare offered by patient scientific thought. Inexorable facts now dethroned him from his self-arrogated station at the centre of the universe; henceforth he must reconcile himself to the humble position of the inhabitant of a speck of dust, and adjust his views on the meaning of human life accordingly.

The adjustment was not made at once. Human vanity, reinforced by the authority of the Church, contrived to make a rough road for those who dared draw attention to the earth's insignificant position in the universe. Galileo was forced to abjure his beliefs. Well on into the eighteenth century the ancient University of Paris taught that the motion of the earth round the sun was a convenient *but false* hypothesis, while the newer American Universities of Harvard and Yale taught the Ptolemaic and Copernican systems of astronomy side by side as though they were equally tenable. Yet men could not keep their heads buried in the sand for ever, and when at last its full implications were accepted, the revolution of thought initiated by Galileo's observations of January 7, 1610, proved to be the most catastrophic in the history of the race. The cataclysm was not confined to the realms of abstract thought; henceforth human existence itself was to appear in a new light, and human aims and aspirations would be judged from a different standpoint.

This oft-told story has been told once again, in the hope that it may serve to explain some of the interest taken in

astronomy today. The more mundane sciences prove
their worth by adding to the amenities and pleasures of life,
or by alleviating pain or distress, but it may well be asked
what reward astronomy has to offer. Why does the
astronomer devote arduous nights, and still more arduous
days, to studying the structure, motions and changes of
bodies so remote that they can have no conceivable influence on human life?

In part at least the answer would seem to be that many
have begun to suspect that the astronomy of today, like
that of Galileo, may have something to say on the en-
thralling question of the relation of human life to the universe in which it is placed, and on the beginnings, meaning
and destiny of the human race. Bede records how, some
twelve centuries ago, human life was compared in poetic
simile to the flight of a bird through a warm hall in which
men sit feasting, while the winter storms rage without.

> The bird is safe from the tempest for a brief moment, but
> immediately passes from winter to winter again. So man's
> life appears for a little while, but of what is to follow, or of
> what went before, we know nothing. If, therefore, a new doc-
> trine tells us something certain, it seems to deserve to be
> followed.

These words, originally spoken in advocacy of the
Christian religion, describe what is perhaps the main interest in astronomy today. Man,

> only knowing
> Life's little lantern between dark and dark,

wishes to probe further into the past and future than his
brief span of life permits. He wishes to see the universe as
it existed before man was, as it will be after the last man
has passed again into the darkness from which he came.
The wish does not originate solely in mere intellectual
curiosity, in the desire to see over the next range of moun-

tains, the desire to attain a summit commanding a wide view, even if it be only of a promised land which he may never hope himself to enter; it has deeper roots and a more personal interest. Before he can understand himself, man must first understand the universe from which all his sense perceptions are drawn. He wishes to explore the universe, both in space and time, because he himself forms part of it, and it forms part of him.

We may well admit that science cannot at present hope to say anything final on the questions of human existence and human destiny, but this is no justification for not becoming acquainted with the best that it has to offer. It is rare indeed for science to give a final "Yes" or "No" answer to any question propounded to her. When we are able to put a question in such definite form that either of these answers could be given in reply, we are generally already in a position to supply the answer ourselves. Science advances rather by providing a succession of approximations to the truth, each more accurate than the last, but each capable of endless degrees of higher accuracy. To the question, "where does man stand in the universe?" the first attempt at an answer, at any rate in recent times, was provided by the astronomy of Ptolemy: "at the centre." Galileo's telescope provided the next, and incomparably better, approximation: "man's home in space is only one of a number of small bodies revolving round a huge central sun." Nineteenth-century astronomy swung the pendulum still further in the same direction, saying: "there are millions of stars in the sky, each similar to our sun, each doubtless surrounded, like our sun, by a family of planets on which life may be kept in being by the light and heat received from its sun." Twentieth-century astronomy suggests, as we shall see, that the nineteenth century had swung the pendulum too far; life now seems to be more of a rarity than our fathers thought, or would have thought if they had given free play to their intellects.

We are setting out to explain the approximation to the truth provided by twentieth-century astronomy. No doubt it is not the final truth, but it is a step on towards it, and unless we are greatly in error it is very much nearer to the truth than was the teaching of nineteenth-century astronomy. It claims to be nearer the truth, not because the twentieth-century astronomer claims to be better at guessing than his predecessors of the nineteenth century, but because he has incomparably more facts at his disposal. Guessing has gone out of fashion in science; it was at best a poor substitute for knowledge, and modern science, eschewing guessing severely, confines itself, except on very rare occasions, to ascertained facts and the inferences which, so far as can be seen, follow unequivocally from them.

It would of course be futile to pretend that the whole interest of astronomy centres round the questions just mentioned. Astronomy offers at least three other groups of interests which may be described as utilitarian, scientific and æsthetic.

At first astronomy, like other sciences, was studied for mainly utilitarian reasons. It provided measures of time, and enabled mankind to keep a tally on the flight of the seasons; it taught him to find his way across the trackless desert, and later, across the trackless ocean. In the guise of astrology, it held out hopes of telling him his future. There was nothing intrinsically absurd in this, for even today the astronomer is largely occupied with foretelling the future movements of the heavenly bodies, although not of human affairs — a considerable part of the present book will consist of an attempt to foretell the future, and predict the final end, of the material universe. Where the astrologers went wrong was in supposing that terrestrial empires, kings and individuals formed such important items in the scheme of the universe that the motions of the heavenly bodies could be intimately bound up with their fates. As soon as man began to realize, even faintly, his own in-significance in the universe, astrology died a natural and inevitable death.

The utilitarian aspect of astronomy has by now shrunk to very modest proportions. The national observatories still broadcast the time of day, and help to guide ships across the ocean, but the centre of astronomical interest has shifted so completely that the remotest of nebulæ arouse incomparably more enthusiasm than "clock-stars," and the average astronomer totally neglects our nearest neighbours in space, the planets, for stars so distant that their light takes hundreds, thousands, or even millions, of years to reach us.

Recently, astronomy has acquired a new scientific inter-est through establishing its position as an integral part of the general body of science. The various sciences can no longer be treated as distinct; scientific discovery advances along a continuous front which extends unbroken from electrons of a fraction of a millionth of an inch in diameter, to nebulæ whose diameters are measured in hundreds of thousands of millions of millions of miles. A gain of as-tronomical knowledge may add to our knowledge of physics and chemistry, and *vice versa*. The stars have long ago ceased to be treated as mere points of light. Each is now regarded as an experiment on a heroic scale, a high tem-perature crucible in which Nature herself operates with ranges of temperature and pressure far beyond those avail-able in our laboratories, and permits us to watch the results. In so doing, we may happen upon properties of matter which have eluded the terrestrial physicist, owing to the small range of physical conditions at his command. For instance, matter exists in nebulæ with a density at least a million times lower than anything we can approach on earth, and in certain stars at a density nearly a million times

greater. How can we expect to understand the whole nature of matter from laboratory experiments in which we
can command only one part in a million million of the
whole range of density known to nature?

Yet for each one who feels the purely scientific appeal of
astronomy, there are probably a dozen who are attracted
by its æsthetic appeal. Many even of those who seek
after knowledge for its own sake, driven by that intellectual
curiosity which provides the fundamental distinction between themselves and the beasts, find their main interest
in astronomy, as the most poetical and most æsthetically
gratifying of the sciences. They want to exercise their
faculties and imaginations on something remote from
everyday trivialities, to find an occasional respite from "the
long littleness of life," and they satisfy their desires in con-
templating the serene immensities of the outer universe.
To many, astronomy provides something of the vision
without which the people perish.

Before proceeding to describe the results of the modern
astronomers' survey of the sky, let us try to envisage in its
proper perspective the platform from which his observations are made.

Later on, we shall see how the earth was born out of the
sun, something like two thousand millions of years ago.
It was born in a form in which we should find it hard to
recognize the solid earth of today with its seas and rivers,
its rich vegetation and overflowing life. Our home in space
came into being as a globe of intensely hot gas on which
no life of any kind could either gain or retain a foothold.

Gradually this globe of gas cools down, becoming first
liquid, then plastic. Finally its outer crust solidifies, rocks
and mountains forming a permanent record of the irregu-
larities of its earlier plastic form. Vapours condense into
liquids, and rivers and oceans come into being, while the
"permanent" gases form an atmosphere. Gradually the

earth assumes a condition suited to the advent of life, which finally appears, we know not how, whence or why.

It is not easy to estimate the time since life first appeared on earth, but it can hardly have been more than a small fraction of the whole 2000 million years of the earth's existence. Still, there was probably life on earth at least 300 million years ago. The first life appears to have been wholly aquatic, but gradually fishes changed into reptiles, reptiles into mammals, and finally man emerged from mammals. The evidence favours a period of about 300,000 years for this last event. Thus life inhabited the earth for only a fraction of its existence, and man for only a tiny fraction of this fraction. To put it another way, the astronomical time-scale is incomparably longer than the human time-scale — the generations of man, and even the whole of human existence, are only ticks of the astronomer's clock.

Most of the 10,000 or so of generations of men who connect us up with our ape-like ancestry must have lived lives which did not differ greatly from those of their animal predecessors. Hunting, fishing, and warfare filled their lives, leaving but little time or opportunity for intellectual contemplation. Then, at last, man began to wake from his long intellectual slumber, and, as civilization slowly dawned, to feel the need for occupations other than the mere feeding and clothing of his body. He began to discover revelations of infinite beauty in the grace of the human form or the play of light on the myriad-smiling sea, which he tried to perpetuate in carefully chiselled marble or exquisitely chosen words. He began to experiment with metals and herbs, and with the effects of fire and water. He began to notice, and try to understand, the motions of the heavenly bodies, for to those who could read the writing in the sky, the nightly rising and setting of the stars and planets provided evidence that beyond the confines of the earth lay an unknown universe built on a far grander scale.

In this way the arts and sciences came to earth, bringing astronomy with them. We cannot quite say when, but compared even with the age of the human race, they came but yesterday, while in comparison with the whole age of the earth, their age is but a twinkling of the eye.

Scientific astronomy, as distinguished from mere stargazing, can hardly claim an age of more than three thousand years. It is less than this since Pythagoras, Aristarchus, and others explained that the earth moved around a fixed sun. Yet the really significant figure for our present purpose is not so much the time since men began to make conjectures about the structure of the universe, as the time since they began to unravel its true structure by the help of ascertained fact. The important length of time is that which has elapsed since that evening in 1610 when Galileo first turned his telescope on to Jupiter — a mere three centuries or so.

We begin to grasp the true significance of these round-number estimates when we re-write them in tabular form. We have:

Age of earth..................	about 2,000,000,000	years
Age of life on earth............	" 300,000,000	"
Age of man on earth..........	" 300,000	"
Age of astronomical science.....	" 3,000	"
Age of telescopic astronomy....	" 300	"

When the various figures are displayed in this form, we see what a very recent phenomenon astronomy is. Its total age is only a hundredth part of the age of man, only a hundred-thousandth part of the time that life has inhabited the earth. During 99,999 parts out of the 100,000 of its existence, life on earth was hardly concerned about anything beyond the earth. But whereas the task of astronomy is to be measured on the human time-scale, a hundred generations or so of men, there is every reason to expect that its future will be measured on the astronomical time-scale. We shall discuss the probable future stretching before the human race in a later chapter. For the moment it is not unreasonable to suppose that this future will probably be terminated by astronomical causes, so that its length is to be measured on the astronomical time-scale. As the earth has already existed for 2,000 million years, it is *à priori* reasonable to suppose that it will exist for at least something of the order of 2000 million years yet to come, and humanity and astronomy with it. Actually we shall find reasons for expecting it to last far longer than this. But if once it is conceded that its future life is to be estimated on the astronomical time-scale, no matter in what exact way, we see that astronomy is still at the very opening of its existence. This is why its message can claim no finality — we are not describing the mature convictions of a man, so much as the first impressions of a new-born babe which is just opening its eyes. Even so they are better than the idle introspective dreamings in which it indulged before it had learned to look around itself and away from itself.

And so we set out to learn what astronomy has to tell us about the universe in which we live our lives. Our inquiry will not be entirely limited to this one science. We shall call upon other sciences, physics, chemistry and geology, as well as the more closely allied sciences of astrophysics and cosmogony, to give help, when they can, in interpreting the message of observational astronomy. The information we shall obtain will be fragmentary. If it must be compared to anything, let it be to the pieces of a jig-saw puzzle. Could we get hold of all the pieces, they would, we are confident, form a single complete consistent picture, but many of them are still missing. It is too much to hope that the incomplete series of pieces we have already found will disclose the whole picture, but we may at least collect them together, arrange them in some sort of methodical order, fit together pieces which are obviously contiguous, and perhaps hazard a guess as to what the finished picture will prove to be when all its pieces have been found and finally fitted together.

WILLIAM BEEBE

Born in 1877, William Beebe graduated from Columbia University with the degree of B.S., in 1898. In the following year he was appointed Curator of Ornithology for the New York Zoölogical Society, a post which he has held ever since. He also has been Director of that Society's Department of Tropical Research, and a Curator of the American Museum of Natural History. His expeditions in British Guiana, to remote Galápagos, to the Sargasso Sea, and far beneath the surface of the ocean off Bermuda have been extremely valuable for their scientific results alone. Possibly of even greater value for the future of science has been the wide interest of the general public, awakened by Mr. Beebe's essays and books which have told his experiences so vividly as to fascinate his readers. He has an almost unique ability to re-create the scene, to make people who may be quite unscientific themselves see clearly and at least partially comprehend the tropical and marine life of which he writes. Of Mr. Beebe's many books, the following list is perhaps a fair representation: Jungle Peace (1918), Galápagos: Land's End (1924), Jungle Days (1925), The Arcturus Adventure (1926), Beneath Tropic Seas (1928).

The following essay is reprinted from Jungle Days, *by permission of the author and of G. P. Putnam's Sons, publishers.*

WILLIAM BEEBE

A CHAIN OF JUNGLE LIFE

This is the story of Opalina
Who lived in the Tad,
Who became the Frog,
Who was eaten by Fish,
Who nourished the Snake,
Who was caught by the Owl,
But fed the Vulture,
Who was shot by Me,
Who wrote this tale,
Which the Editor took,
And published it here,
To be read by You,
The last in The Chain,
Of Life in the tropical Jungle.

I OFFER a living chain of ten links — the first a tiny delicate being, one hundred to the inch, deep in the jungle, with the strangest home in the world — my last, you the present reader of these lines. Between, there befell certain things, of which I attempt falteringly to write. To know and think them is very worth while, to have discovered them is sheer joy, but to write of them is impertinence, so exciting and unreal are they in reality, and so tame and humdrum are any combinations of our twenty-six letters.

Somewhere today a worm has given up existence, a mouse has been slain, a spider snatched from the web, a jungle bird torn sleeping from its perch; else we should have no song of robin, nor flash of reynard's red, no humming flight of wasp, nor grace of crouching ocelot. In tropical jungles, in Northern home orchards, anywhere you will, unnumbered activities of bird and beast and insect require daily toll of life.

Now and then we actually witness one of these tragedies or successes — whichever point of view we take — appearing to us as an exciting but isolated event. When once we grasp the idea of chains of life, each of these occurrences assumes a new meaning. Like everything else in the world it is not isolated, but closely linked with other similar happenings. I have sometimes traced even closed chains, one of the shortest of which consisted of predacious flycatchers which fed upon young lizards of a species which, when it grew up, climbed trees and devoured the nestling flycatchers!

One of the most wonderful zoölogical "Houses that Jack built" was this of Opalina's, a long, swinging, exciting chain, including in its links a Protozoan, two stages of Amphibians, a Fish, a Reptile, two Birds and (unless some intervening act of legislature bars the fact as immoral and illegal) three Mammals — myself, the Editor, and You.

As I do not want to make it a mere imaginary animal story, however probable, I will begin, like Dickens, in the middle. I can cope, however lamely, with the entrance and participation of the earlier links, but am wholly out of my depth from the time when I mail my tale. The Akawai Indian who took it upon its first lap toward the Editor should by rights have a place in the chain, especially when I think how much better he might tell of the interrelationships of the various links than can I. Still, I know the shape of the owl's wings when it dropped upon the snake, but I do not know why the Editor accepted this; I can imitate the death scream of the frog when the fish seized it, but I have no idea why You purchased this volume nor whether you perceive in my tale the huge bed of ignorance in which I have planted this scanty crop of facts. Nor do I know the future of this book, whether it will go to the garret, to be ferreted out in future years by other links, as I used to do, or whether it will find its way to mid-Asia or the Malay States, or, as I once saw a magazine, half-buried, like the pyramids, in Saharan sands, where it had slipped from the camel load of some unknown traveller.

I left my Kartabo laboratory one morning with my gun, headed for the old Dutch stelling. Happening to glance up I saw a mote, lit with the oblique rays of the morning sun. The mote drifted about in circles, which became spirals; the mote became a dot, then a spot, then an oblong, and down the heavens from unknown heights, with the whole of British Guiana spread out beneath him from which to choose, swept a vulture into my very path. We had a quintet, a small flock of our own vultures who came sifting down the sky, day after day, to the feasts of monkey bodies and wild peccaries which we spread for them. I knew all these by sight, from one peculiarity or another, for I was accustomed to watch them hour after hour, striving to learn something of that wonderful soaring, of which all my many hours of flying had taught me nothing.

This bird was a stranger, perhaps from the coast or the inland savannas, for to these birds great spaces are only matters of brief moments. I wanted a yellow-headed vulture, both for the painting of its marvellous head colors, and for the strange, intensely interesting, one-sided, down-at-the-heel syrinx, which, with the voice, had dissolved long ages ago, leaving only a whistling breath, and an irregular complex of bones straggling over the windpipe. Some day I shall dilate upon vultures as pets — being surpassed in cleanliness, affectionateness and tameness only by baby bears, sloths, and certain monkeys.

But today I wanted the newcomer as a specimen. I was surprised to see that he did not head for the regular vulture table, but slid along the slant of the east wind, banked around its side, spreading and curling upward his wing-finger-tips and finally resting against its front edge. Down this he sank slowly, balancing with the grace of perfect mastery, and again swung round and settled suddenly down shore, beyond a web of mangrove roots. This took me by surprise, and I changed my route and pushed through the undergrowth of young palms. Before I came within sight, the bird heard me, rose with a whipping of great pinions and swept around three-fourths of a circle before I could catch enough of a glimpse to drop him. The impetus carried him on and completed the circle, and when I came out on the Cuyuni shore I saw him spread out on what must have been the exact spot from which he had risen.

I walked along a greenheart log with little crabs scuttling off on each side, and as I looked ahead at the vulture I saw to my great surprise that it had more colors than any yellow-headed vulture should have, and its plumage was somehow very different. This excited me so that I promptly slipped off the log and joined the crabs in the mud. Paying more attention to my steps I did not again look up until I had reached the tuft of low reeds on which the bird lay. Now at last I understood why my bird had metamorphosed in death, and also why it had chosen to descend to this spot. Instead of one bird, there were two, and a reptile. Another tragedy had taken place a few hours earlier, before dawn, a double death, and the sight of these three creatures brought to mind at once the chain for which I am always on the lookout. I picked up my chain by the middle and began searching both ways for the missing links.

The vulture lay with magnificent wings outspread, partly covering a big, spectacled owl, whose plumage was in turn wrapped about by several coils of a moderate-sized anaconda. Here was an excellent beginning for my chain, and at once I visualized myself and the snake, although alternate links, yet coupled in contradistinction to my editor and the vulture, the first two having entered the chain by means of death, whereas the vulture had simply joined in the pacifistic manner of its kind, and as my editor has dealt gently with me heretofore, I allowed myself to believe that his entrance might also be through no more rough handling than a blue slip.

The head of the vulture was already losing some of its brilliant chrome and saffron, so I took it up, noted the conditions of the surrounding sandy mud, and gathered together my spoils. I would have passed within a few feet of the owl and the snake and never discovered them, so close were they in color to the dark reddish beach, yet the vulture with its small eyes and minute nerves had detected this tragedy when still perhaps a mile high in the air, or half a mile up-river. There could have been no odor, nor has this bird any adequate nostrils to detect it, had there been one. It was sheer keenness of vision. I looked at the bird's claws and their weakness showed the necessity of the eternal search for carrion or recently killed creatures. Here in a half minute, it had devoured an eye of the owl and both of those of the serpent. It is a curious thing, this predilection for eyes; give a monkey a fish, and the eyes are the first titbits taken.

Through the vulture I came to the owl link, a splendid bird clad in the colors of its time of hunting; a great, soft, dark, shadow of a bird, with tiny body and long fluffy plumage of twilight buff and ebony night, lit by twin, orange moons of eyes. The name "spectacled owl" is really more applicable to the downy nestling which is like a white powder puff with two dark feathery spectacles around the eyes. Its name is one of those I am fond of repeating rapidly — *Pulsatrix perspicillata perspicillata.* Etymologies do not grow in the jungle and my memory is noted only for its consistent vagueness, but if the owl's title does not mean *The Eye-browed One Who Strikes*, it ought to, especially as the subspecific trinomial grants it two eyebrows.

I would give much to know just what the beginning of the combat was like. The middle I could reconstruct without question, and the end was only too apparent. By a most singular coincidence, a few years before, and less than three miles away, I had found the desiccated remains of another spectacled owl mingled with the bones of a snake, only in that instance, the fangs indicated a small fer-de-lance, the owl having succumbed to its venom. This time the owl had rashly attacked a serpent far too heavy for it to lift, or even, as it turned out, successfully to battle with. The mud had been churned up for a foot in all directions, and the bird's plumage showed that it must have rolled over and over. The anaconda, having just fed, had come out of the water and was probably stretched out on the sand and mud, as I have seen them, both by full sun and in the moonlight. These owls are birds rather of the creeks and river banks than of the deep jungle, and in their food I have found shrimps, crabs, fish, and young birds. Once a few snake vertebrae showed that these reptiles are occasionally killed and devoured.

Whatever possessed the bird to strike its talons deep into the neck and back of this anaconda, none but the owl could say, but from then on the story was written by the combatants and their environment. The snake, like a flash, threw two coils around bird, wings and all, and clamped these tight with a cross-vise of muscle. The tighter the coils compressed the deeper the talons of the bird were driven in, but the damage was done with the first strike, and if the owl and the snake had parted at this moment, neither could have survived. It was a swift, terrible and short fight. The snake could not use its teeth and the bird had no time to bring its beak into play, and there in the night, with the lapping waves of the falling tide only two or three feet away, the two creatures of prey met and fought and died, in darkness and silence, locked fast together.

A few nights before I had heard, on the opposite side of the bungalow, the deep, sonorous cry of the spectacled owl; within a week I had passed the line-and-crescents track of anacondas, one about the size of this snake and another much larger. And now fate had linked their lives, or rather deaths, with my life, using as her divining rod, the focussing of a sky-soaring vulture.

The owl had not fed that evening, although the bird was so well nourished that it could never have been driven to its foolhardy feat by stress of hunger. Hopeful of lengthening the chain, I rejoiced to see a suspicious swelling about the middle of the snake, which dissection resolved into a good-sized fish — itself carnivorous, locally called a basha. This was the first time I had known one of these fish to fall a victim to a land creature, except in the case of a big kingfisher who had caught two small ones. Like the owl and anaconda, bashas are nocturnal in their activities, and, according to their size, feed on small shrimps, big shrimps, and so on up to six or eight inch catfish. They are built on swift, torpedo-like lines, and clad in iridescent silver mail.

From what I have seen of the habits of anacondas, I should say that this one had left its hole high up among the upper beach roots late in the night, and softly wound its way down into the rising tide. Here after drinking, the snake sometimes pursues and catches small fish and frogs, but the usual method is to coil up beside a half-buried stick or log and await the tide and the manna it brings. In the van of the waters comes a host of small fry, followed by their pursuers or by larger vegetable feeders, and the serpent has but to choose. In this mangrove lagoon then,

there must have been a swirl and a splash, a passive holding fast by the snake for a while until the right opportunity
offered, and then a swift throw of coils. There must then
be no mistake as to orientation of the fish. It would be
a fatal error to attempt the tail first, with scales on end
and serried spines to pierce the thickest tissues. It is
beyond my knowledge how one of these fish can be swallowed even head first without serious laceration. But
here was optical proof of its possibility, a newly swallowed
basha, so recently caught that he appeared as in life, with
even the delicate turquoise pigment beneath his scales,
acting on his silvery armor as quicksilver under glass.
The tooth marks of the snake were still clearly visible on
the scales — another link, going steadily down the classes
of vertebrates, mammal, bird, reptile and fish, and still my
magic boxes were unexhausted.

Excitedly I cut open the fish. An organism more unlike
that of the snake would be hard to imagine. There I had
followed an elongated stomach, and had left unexplored
many feet of alimentary canal. Here, the fish had his
heart literally in his mouth, while his liver and lights were
only a short distance behind, followed by a great expanse
of tail to wag him at its will, and drive him through the
water with the speed of twin propellers. His eyes are
wonderful for night hunting, large, wide, and bent in the
middle so he can see both above and on each side. But
all this wide-angled vision availed nothing against the lid-
less, motionless watch of the ambushed anaconda. Searching the crevices of the rocks and logs for timorous small
fry, the basha had sculled too close, and the jaws which
closed upon him were backed by too much muscle, and
too perfect a throttling machine to allow of the least chance
of escape. It was a big basha compared with the moderate-
sized snake but the fierce eyes had judged well, as the
evidence before me proved.

Still my chain held true, and in the stomach of the basha I found what I wanted — another link, and more than I could have hoped for — a representative of the fifth and last class of vertebrate animals living on the earth, an Amphibian, an enormous frog. This too had been a swift-forged link, so recent that digestion had only affected the head of the creature. I drew it out, set it upon its great squat legs, and there was a grandmother frog almost as in life, a Pok-poke as the Indians call it, or, as a herpetologist would prefer, *Leptodactylus caliginosus* — the Smoky Jungle Frog.

She lived in the jungle just behind, where she and a sister of hers had their curious nests of foam, which they guarded from danger, while the tadpoles grew and squirmed within its sudsy mesh as if there were no water in the world. I had watched one of the two, perhaps this one, for hours, and I saw her dart angrily after little fish which came too near. Then, this night, the high full-moon tides had swept over the barrier back of the mangrove roots and set the tadpoles free, and the mother frogs were at liberty to go where they pleased.

From my cot in the bungalow to the south, I had heard in the early part of the night, the death scream of a frog, and it must have been at that moment that somehow the basha had caught the great amphibian. This frog is one of the fiercest of its class, and captures mice, reptiles and small fish without trouble. It is even cannibalistic on very slight provocation, and two of equal size will some-times endeavor to swallow one another in the most appall-ingly matter-of-fact manner.

They represent the opposite extreme in temperament from the pleasantly philosophical giant toads. In out-ward appearance in the dim light of dusk, the two groups are not unlike, but the moment they are taken in the hand all doubt ceases. After one dive for freedom, the toad resigns himself to fate, only venting his spleen in much puffing out of his sides, while the frog either fights until exhausted, or pretends death until opportunity offers for a last mad dash.

In this case the frog must have leaped into the deep water beyond the usual barrier and while swimming been attacked by the equally voracious fish.   In addition to the regular croak of this species, it has a most unexpected and unamphibian yell or scream, given only when it thinks itself at the last extremity.   It is most unnerving when the frog, held firmly by the hind legs, suddenly puts its whole soul into an ear splitting *peent! peent! peent! peent! peent!*

Many a time they are probably saved from death by this cry which startles like a sudden blow, but tonight no utterance in the world could have saved it; its assailant was dumb and all but deaf to aerial sounds.   Its cries were smothered in the water as the fish dived and nuzzled it about the roots, as bashas do with their food — and it became another link in the chain.

Like a miser with one unfilled coffer, or a gambler with an unfilled royal flush, I went eagerly at the frog with forceps and scalpel.   But beyond the meagre residuum of eggs, there was nothing but shrunken organs in its body. The rashness of its venture into river water was perhaps prompted by hunger after its long maternal fast while it watched over its egg-filled nest of foam.

Hopeful to the last, I scrape some mucus from its foodcanal, place it in a drop of water under my microscope, and — discover Opalina, my last link, which in the course of its most astonishing life history gives me still another.

To the naked eye there is nothing visible — the water seems clear, but when I enlarge the diameter of magnification I lift the veil on another world, and there swim into view a dozen minute lives, oval little beings covered with curving lines, giving the appearance of wandering fingerprints. In some lights these are iridescent and they then will deserve the name of Opalina. As for their personality, they are oval and rather flat, it would take one hundred of them to stretch an inch, they have no mouth, and they are covered with a fur of flagella with which they whip themselves through the water. Indeed the whole of their little selves consists of a multitude of nuclei, sometimes as many as two hundred, exactly alike — facial expression, profile, torso, limbs, pose, all are summed up in rounded nuclei, partly obscured by a mist of vibrating flagella.

As for their gait, they move along with colorful waves, steadily and gently, not keeping an absolutely straight course and making rather much leeway, as any rounded, keelless craft, surrounded with its own paddle-wheels, must expect to do.

I have placed Opalina under very strange and unpleasant conditions in thus subjecting it to the inhospitable qualities of a drop of clear water. Even as I watch, it begins to slow down, and the flagella move less rapidly and evenly. It prefers an environment far different, where I discovered it living happily and contentedly in the stomach and intestines of a frog, where its iridescence was lost, or rather, had never existed in the absolute darkness; where its delicate hairs must often be unmercifully crushed and bent in the ever-moving tube, and where air and sky, trees and sun, sound and color were forever unknown; in their place only bits of half-digested ants and beetles, thousand-legs and worms, rolled and tumbled along in the dense gastric stream of acid pepsin; a strange choice of home for one of our fellow living beings on the earth.

After an Opalina has flagellated itself about, and fed for a time in its strange, almost crystalline way on the juices of its host's food, its body begins to contract, and narrow across the center until it looks something like a map of the

New World. Finally its isthmus thread breaks and two Opalinas swim placidly off, both identical, except that they have half the number of nuclei as before. We cannot wonder that there is no backward glance or wave of cilia, or even memory of their body, for they are themselves, or rather it is they, or it is each: our whole vocabulary, our entire stock of pronouns breaks down, our very conception of individuality is shattered by the life of Opalina.

Each daughter cell or self-twin, or whatever we choose to conceive it, divides in turn. Finally there comes a day (or rather some Einstein period of space-time, for there are no days in a frog's stomach!) when Opalina's fraction has reached a stage with only two nuclei. When this has creased and stretched and finally broken like two bits of drawn-out molasses candy, we have the last divisional possibility. The time for the great adventure had arrived, with decks cleared for action, or, as a protozoölogist would put it, with the flagellate's protoplasm uni-nucleate, approximating encystment.

The encysting process is but slightly understood, but the tiny one-two-hundredth-of-its-former-self Opalina curls up, its paddle-wheels run down, it forms a shell, and rolls into the current which it has withstood for a Protozoan's lifetime. Out into the world drifts the minute ball of latent life, a plaything of the cosmos, permitted neither to see, hear, eat, nor to move of its own volition. It hopes (only it cannot even desire) to find itself in water, it must fall or be washed into a pool with tadpoles, one of which must come along at the right moment and swallow it with the débris upon which it rests. The possibility of this elaborate concatenation of events has everything against it, and yet it must occur or death will result. No wonder that the population of Opalinas does not overstock its limited and retired environment!

Supposing that all happens as it should, and that the

only chance in a hundred thousand comes to pass, the encysted being knows or is affected in some mysterious way by entrance into the body of the tadpole. The cyst is dissolved and the infant Opalina begins to feed and to develop new nuclei. Like the queen ant after she has been walled forever into her chamber, the life of the little One-cell would seem to be extremely sedentary and humdrum, in fact, monotonous, until its turn comes to fractionize itself, and again severally to go into the outside world, multiplied and by installments. But as the queen ant had her one superlative day of sunlight, heavenly flight and a mate, so Opalina, while she is still wholly herself, has a little adventure all her own.

Let us strive to visualize her environment as it would appear to her if she could find time and ability, with her single cell, to do more than feed and bisect herself. Once free from her horny cyst, she stretches her drop of a body, sets all her paddle-hairs in motion and swims slowly off. If we suppose that she has been swallowed by a tadpole an inch long, her living quarters are astonishingly spacious or rather elongated. Passing from end to end she would find a living tube two feet in length, a dizzy path to traverse, as it curled in a tight, many-whorled spiral — the stairway, the domicile, the universe at present for Opalina. She is compelled to be a vegetarian, for nothing but masses of decayed leaf tissue and black mud and algae come down the stairway. For many days there is only the sound of water gurgling past the tadpole's gills, or glimpses of sticks and leaves and the occasional flash of a small fish through the thin skin periscope of its body.

Then the tadpole's mumbling even of half-rotted leaves comes to an end, and both it and its guests begin to fast. Down the whorls comes less and less vegetable detritus, and Opalina must feel like the crew of a submarine when the food supply runs short. At the same time something very strange happens, the experience of which eludes our utmost imagination. Poe wrote a memorable tale of a prison cell which day by day grew smaller, and Opalina goes through much the same adventure. If she frequently traverses her tube, she finds it growing shorter and shorter. As it contracts, the spiral untwists and straightens out, while all the time the rations are cut off. A dark curtain of pigment is drawn across the epidermal periscope and as books of dire adventure say, the "horror of darkness is added to the terrible uncertainty." The whole movement of the organism changes; there is no longer the rush and swish of water and the even, undulatory motion alters to a series of spasmodic jerks — quite the opposite of ordinary transition from water to land. Instead of water rushing through the gills of her host, Opalina might now hear strange musical sounds, loud and low, the singing of insects, the soughing of swamp palms.

Opalina, about this time, should be feeling very low in her mind from lack of food, and the uncertainty of explanation of why the larger her host grew, the smaller, more confined became her quarters. The tension is relieved at last by a new influx of provender, but no more inert mold or disintegrated leaves. Down the short, straight tube appears a live millipede, kicking as only a millipede can, with its thousand heels. Deserting for a moment Opalina's point of view, my scientific conscience insists on asserting itself to the effect that no millipede with which I am acquainted has even half a thousand legs. But not to quibble over details, even a few hundred kicking legs must make quite a commotion in Opalina's home, before the pepsin puts a quietus on the unwilling invader.

From now on there is no lack of food, for at each sudden jerk of the whole amphibian there comes down some animal or other. The vegetarian tadpole with its enormously lengthened digestive apparatus, has crawled out on land, fasting while the miracle is being wrought with its plumbing, and when the readjustment is made to more easily assimilated animal food, and it has become a frog, it forgets all about leaves and algae, and leaps after and captures almost any living creature which crosses its path and which is small enough to be engulfed.

With the refurnishing of her apartment and the sudden and complete change of diet, the exigencies of life are past for Opalina. She has now but to move blindly about, bathed in a stream of nutriment, and from time to time, nonchalantly to cut herself in twain. Only one other possibility awaits, that which occurred in the case of our Opalina. There comes a time when the sudden leap is not followed by an inrush of food, but by another leap and still another, and finally a headlong dive, a plash and a rush of water, which, were protozoans given to reincarnated memory, might recall times long past. Suddenly came a violent spasm, then a terrible struggle, ending in a strange quiet, Opalina has become a link.

All motion is at an end, and instead of food comes compression, closer and closer shut the walls and soon they break down and a new fluid pours in. Opalina's cyst had dissolved readily in the tadpole's stomach, but her own body was able to withstand what all the food of tadpole and frog could not. If I had not wanted the painting of a vulture's head, little Opalina, together with the body of her life-long host, would have corroded and melted, and in the dark depths of the tropical waters her multitude of paddle-hairs, her more or fewer nuclei, all would have dissolved and been reabsorbed, to furnish their iota of energy to the swift silvery fish.

This flimsy little, sky scraper castle of Jack's, built of isolated bricks of facts, gives a hint of the wonderland of correlation. Facts are necessary, but even a pack-rat can assemble a gallon of beans in a single night. To link facts together, to see them forming into a concrete whole; to make *A* fit into ARCH and *ARCH* into ARCHITECTURE, that is one great joy of life which, of all the links in my chain, only the Editor, You and I — the Mammals — can know.

ROBERT LOUIS STEVENSON

Born in Edinburgh in 1850, Robert Louis Stevenson died in Samoa, in 1894. From his grandfather and his father, eminent civil engineers, he inherited an interest in science, though ill health kept him from following either their profession or the law, for which he studied. There is no need to tell here of his struggle against consumption, or of the gallant and buoyant spirit, shown in all his books, with which he fought that fight. Still less is it necessary to list his novels and travel sketches, for, as one long-suffering candidate wrote on his examination, "Treasure Island *and* Travels with a Donkey *have not been spoiled even by being taught in school."* *It may be permissible, however, to suggest that those who have known him only as story-teller or poet may find much that is interesting in his essays:* Virginibus Puerisque (1881), Familiar Studies of Men and Books (1882), Memories and Portraits (1887), *and* Across the Plains (1892). *The title of the following essay comes from Horace,* Pulvis et umbra sumus: "*we are dust and shadow."* *The essay itself was first published in* Scribner's Magazine *in* 1888, *and reprinted in* Across the Plains. *Stevenson said of it,* "I might have called it a Darwinian sermon."

ROBERT LOUIS STEVENSON

PULVIS ET UMBRA

WE LOOK for some reward of our endeavors and are disappointed; not success, not happiness, not even peace of conscience, crowns our ineffectual efforts to do well. Our frailties are invincible, our virtues barren; the battle goes sore against us to the going down of the sun. The canting moralist tells us of right and wrong; and we look abroad, even on the face of our small earth, and find them change with every climate, and no country where some action is not honored for a virtue and none where it is not branded for a vice; and we look in our experience, and find no vital congruity in the wisest rules, but at the best a municipal fitness. It is not strange if we are tempted to despair of good. We ask too much. Our religions and moralities have been trimmed to flatter us, till they are all emasculate and sentimentalized, and only please and weaken. Truth is of a rougher strain. In the harsh face of life, faith can read a bracing gospel. The human race is a thing more ancient than the ten commandments; and the bones and revolutions of the Kosmos, in whose joints we are but moss and fungus, more ancient still.

I

Of the Kosmos in the last resort, science reports many doubtful things and all of them appalling. There seems no substance to this solid globe on which we stamp: nothing but symbols and ratios. Symbols and ratios carry us and bring us forth and beat us down; gravity that swings the incommensurable suns and worlds through space, is but a figment varying inversely as the squares of distances; and the suns and worlds themselves, imponderable figures of abstraction, NH_3 and H_2O. Consideration dares not dwell upon this view; that way madness lies; science carries us into zones of speculation, where there is no habitable city for the mind of man.

But take the Kosmos with a grosser faith, as our senses give it us. We behold space sown with rotatory islands, suns and worlds, and the shards and wrecks of systems: some, like the sun, still blazing; some rotting, like the earth; others, like the moon, stable in desolation. All of these we take to be made of something we call matter; a thing which no analysis can help us to conceive; to whose incredible properties no familiarity can reconcile our minds. This stuff, when not purified by the lustration of fire, rots uncleanly into something we call life; seized through all its atoms with a pediculous malady; swelling in tumors that become independent, sometimes even (by an abhorrent prodigy) locomotory; one splitting into millions, millions cohering into one, used as we are to it, yet strikes us with occasional disgust, and the profusion of worms in a piece of ancient turf, or the air of a marsh darkened with insects, will sometimes check our breathing so that we aspire for cleaner places. But none is clean: the moving sand is infected with lice; the pure spring, where it bursts out of the mountain, is a mere issue of worms; even in the hard rock the crystal is forming.

In two main shapes this eruption covers the countenance of the earth: the animal and the vegetable: one in some degree the inversion of the other: the second rooted to the spot; the first coming detached out of its natal mud, and scurrying abroad with the myriad feet of insects or towering into the heavens on the wings of birds: a thing so inconceivable that, if it be well considered, the heart stops. To what passes with the anchored vermin, we have little clue: doubtless they have their joys and sorrows, their delights, and killing agonies: it appears not how. But of the locomotory, to which we ourselves belong, we can tell more. These share with us a thousand miracles, the miracles of sight, of hearing, of the projection of sound, things that bridge space; the miracles of memory and reason, by which the present is conceived, and when it is gone, its image kept living in the brains of man and brute; the miracle of reproduction, with its imperious desires and staggering consequences. And to put the last touch upon this mountain mass of the revolting and the inconceivable, all these prey upon each other, lives tearing other lives in pieces, cramming them inside themselves, and by that summary process, growing fat; the vegetarian, the whale, perhaps the tree, not less than the lion of the desert, for the vegetarian is only the eater of the dumb.

Meanwhile our rotary island loaded with predatory life, and more drenched with blood, both animal and vegetable, than ever mutinied ship, scuds through space with unimaginable speed, and turns alternate cheeks to the reverberation of a blazing world, ninety million miles away.

II

What a monstrous specter is this man, the disease of the agglutinated dust, lifting alternate feet or lying drugged with slumber; killing, feeding, growing, bringing forth small copies of himself; grown upon with hair like grass, fitted with eyes that move and glitter in his face; a thing to set children screaming; — and yet looked at nearlier, known as his fellows know him, how surprising are his attributes! Poor soul, here for so little, cast among so many hardships, filled with desires so incommensurate and so inconsistent, savagely surrounded,

savagely descended, irremediably condemned to prey upon
his fellow lives: who should have blamed him had he been
of a piece with his destiny and a being merely barbarous?   And we look and behold him instead filled with
imperfect virtues: infinitely childish, often admirably
valiant, often touchingly kind, sitting down amidst his
momentary life, to debate of right and wrong and the attributes of the deity; rising up to do battle for an egg or
die for an idea, singling out his friends and his mate with
cordial affection; bringing forth in pain, rearing with long-
suffering solicitude, his young.   To touch the heart of his
mystery, we find in him one thought, strange to the point
of lunacy: the thought of duty; the thought of something
owing to himself, to his neighbor, to his God: an ideal of
deceny, to which he would rise if it were possible; a limit
of shame, below which, if it be possible, he will not stoop.
The design in most men is one of conformity; here and
there, in picked natures, it transcends itself and soars on
the other side, arming martyrs with independence; but
in all, in their degrees, it is a bosom thought: — Not in
man alone, for we trace it in dogs and cats whom we
know fairly well, and doubtless some similar point of
honor sways the elephant, the oyster, and the louse, of
whom we know so little: — But in man, at least, it sways
with so complete an empire that merely selfish things come
second, even with the selfish: that appetites are starved,
fears are conquered, pains supported; that almost the
dullest shrinks from the reproof of a glance, although it
were a child's; and all but the most cowardly stand amid
the risks of war; and the more notable, having strongly
conceived an act as due to their ideal, affront and embrace
death.   Strange enough if, with their singular origin and
perverted practice, they think they are to be rewarded in
some future life: stranger still, if they are persuaded of the
contrary, and think this blow, which they solicit, will strike

them senseless for eternity.   I shall be reminded what a
tragedy of misconception and misconduct man at large
presents: of organized injustice, cowardly violence and
treacherous crime; and of the damning imperfections of the
best.   They cannot be too darkly drawn.   Man is indeed
marked for failure in his efforts to do right.   But where the
best consistently miscarry, how tenfold more remarkable
that all should continue to strive; and surely we should
find it both touching and inspiriting, that in a field from
which success is banished, our race should not cease to
labor.

If the first view of this creature, stalking in his rotatory isle, be a thing to shake the courage of the stoutest,
on this nearer sight he startles us with an admiring wonder.   It matters not where we look, under what climate
we observe him, in what stage of society, in what depth
of ignorance, burthened with what erroneous morality;
by campfires in Assiniboia, the snow powdering his shoulders, the wind plucking his blanket, as he sits, passing the
ceremonial calumet and uttering his grave opinions like a
Roman senator; in ships at sea, a man inured to hardship
and vile pleasures, his brightest hope a fiddle in a tavern
and a bedizened trull who sells herself to rob him, and he
for all that simple, innocent, cheerful, kindly like a child,
constant to toil, brave to drown, for others; in the slums
of cities, moving among indifferent millions to mechanical
employments, without hope of change in the future, with
scarce a pleasure in the present, and yet true to his virtues,
honest up to his lights, kind to his neighbors, tempted
perhaps in vain by the bright gin-palace, perhaps long-
suffering with the drunken wife that ruins him; in India
(a woman this time) kneeling with broken cries and
streaming tears as she drowns her child in the sacred
river; in the brothel, the discard of society, living mainly
on strong drink, fed with affronts, a fool, a thief, the

comrade of thieves, and even here keeping the point of
honor and the touch of pity, often repaying the world's
scorn with service, often standing firm upon a scruple, and
at a certain cost, rejecting riches, everywhere some virtue
cherished or affected, everywhere some decency of thought
and carriage, everywhere the ensign of man's ineffectual
goodness: — ah! if I could show you this! if I could show
you these men and women, all the world over, in every
stage of history, under every abuse of terror, under
every circumstance of failure, without hope, without help,
without thanks, still obscurely fighting the lost fight of
virtue, still clinging, in the brothel or on the scaffold, to
some rag of honor, the poor jewel of their souls! They may
seek to escape, and yet they cannot; it is not alone their
privilege and glory, but their doom; they are condemned
to some nobility; all their lives long, the desire of good is at
their heels, the implacable hunter.

Of all earth's meteors, here at least is the most strange
and consoling: that this ennobled lemur, this hair-crowned
bubble of the dust, this inheritor of a few years and sorrows, should yet deny himself his rare delights, and add
to his frequent pains, and live for an ideal, however misconceived. Nor can we stop with man. A new doctrine,
received with screams a little while ago by canting moralists, and still not properly worked into the body of our
thoughts, lights us a step farther into the heart of this
rough but noble universe. For nowadays the pride of
man denies in vain his kinship with the original dust. He
stands no longer like a thing apart. Close at his heels we
see the dog, prince of another genus: and in him too, we
see dumbly testified the same cultus of an unattainable
ideal, the same constancy in failure. Does it stop with
the dog? We look at our feet where the ground is black-
ened with the swarming ant: a creature so small, so far
from us in the hierarchy of brutes, that we can scarce trace

and scarce comprehend his doings, and here also, in his ordered polities and rigorous justice, we see confessed the law of duty and the fact of individual sin. Does it stop, then, with the ant? Rather this desire of well-doing and this doom of frailty run through all the grades of life: rather is this earth, from the frosty top of Everest to the next margin of the internal fire, one stage of ineffectual virtues and one temple of pious tears and perseverance. The whole creation groaneth and travaileth together. It is the common and the godlike law of life. The browsers, the biters, the barkers, the hairy coats of field and forest, the squirrel in the oak, the thousand-footed creeper in the dust, as they share with us the gift of life, share with us the love of an ideal: strive like us — like us are tempted to grow weary of the struggle — to do well; like us receive at times unmerited refreshment, visitings of support, returns of courage; and are condemned like us to be crucified between that double law of the members and the will. Are they like us, I wonder, in the timid hope of some reward, some sugar with the drug? do they, too, stand aghast at unrewarded virtues, at the sufferings of those whom, in our partiality, we take to be just, and the prosperity of such as in our blindness, we call wicked? It may be, and yet God knows what they should look for. Even while they look, even while they repent, the foot of man treads them by thousands in the dust, the yelping hounds burst upon their trail, the bullet speeds, the knives are heating in the den of the vivisectionist; or the dew falls, and the generation of a day is blotted out. For these are creatures, compared with whom our weakness is strength, our ignorance widsom, our brief span eternity.

And as we dwell, we living things, in our isle of terror and under the imminent hand of death, God forbid it should be man the erected, the reasoner, the wise in his own eyes — God forbid it should be man that wearies in well-doing, that despairs of unrewarded effort, or utters the language of complaint. Let it be enough for faith, that the whole creation groans in mortal frailty, strives with unconquerable constancy: surely not all in vain.

WILL DURANT

Born of French-Canadian parentage, in 1885, *Will Durant was educated in parochial schools, at St. Peter's College, Jersey City, and at Columbia University, from which institution he received the degree of Ph.D. From* 1907 *to* 1911 *he taught Latin and French at Seton Hall College; from* 1914 *to* 1927 *he was a Director of the Labor Temple School. Meanwhile he had spent* 1917 *as instructor in philosophy at Columbia, and was beginning to be well known as lecturer and writer.* The Story of Philosophy (1926) *had an immense popular success, and is today one of the most widely read modern books of non-fiction. Among his later publications have been* Transition (1927), *an autobiography which he calls "a sentimental story of one mind and one era,"* The Mansions of Philosophy (1929), *and* A Program for America (1931).

The following essay is reprinted from The Mansions of Philosophy, *by Will Durant. By permission of Simon and Schuster, Inc., publishers.*

WILL DURANT

IS PROGRESS A DELUSION?

THE Greeks, who seem, in the enchantment of distance, to have progressed more rapidly than any
other people in history, have left us hardly any
discussion of progress in all their varied literature. There
is a fine passage in Æschylus where Prometheus tells how
his discovery of fire brought civilization to mankind, and
where in fifty lines he gives such a summary of the stages
in cultural development as would be considered immorally
modern in Tennessee. And there is a fleeting reference to
progress in a fragment of Euripides (*The Suppliants*).
But there is no mention of the idea in Xenophon's recollec-
tions of Socrates or in Plato; and Aristotle's cold conservatism puts the notion implicitly out of court.

The Greeks conceived history for the most part as a
vicious circle; and the conclusion of Lucretius, that "all
things are always the same" strikes the note of classic
opinion on the subject from Zeno to Aurelius. The Stoics
counselled men to expect nothing of the future. Even the
Epicureans took their pleasures sadly and seem to have
felt, like the late Mr. Bradley, that this is "the best of all
possible worlds, and everything in it is a necessary evil."
Hegesias, the Cyrenaic, pronounced life worthless, and advocated suicide; doubtless he lived as long as Schopenhauer.

Pessimism was to be expected in an Athens that had lost
its freedom; but the same despair sounds in Roman letters
at every stage of Roman history. Horace is a praiser of
times past; Tacitus and Juvenal deplore the degeneracy of
their age; and Virgil turns from his fancies of a new

Saturnian glory to phrase with his melodious felicity the gloomy notion of an Eternal Recurrence, a perpetual cycle and aimless repetition of events: "There will again be a Tiphys and another Argo to carry beloved heroes; there will be also other wars, and great Achilles will again be sent to Troy." The hourglass of æons will turn itself around and pour out the unaltered past into an empty and delusively novel present. There is nothing new under the sun; all is vanity and a chasing after the wind.

What were the causes of the hostility or apathy of the Greeks to the idea of progress? Was it due, as Bury thinks, to the brevity of their historical experience, the very rapidity with which their civilization reached its apex and sank again? Or was it due to their comparative poverty in written records of the past, and a consequent absence of the perspective which might have made them realize the marvel of their own advances? They too had had a Middle Age, and had climbed for a thousand years from barbarism to philosophy; but only towards the end of that ascent had writing graduated from bills of lading to the forms of literature. Parchment was too costly to be wasted on mere history. Or again, was this unconcern with progress due to the arrested development of Greek industry, the failure of the Greeks to move appreciably beyond the technology of Crete, or to produce in quantity those physical comforts which are at the base of the modern belief in progress?

In our own Middle Ages it was a similar dearth of luxuries which kept the notion of progress in abeyance, while the hope of heaven became the center of existence. Belief in another world seems to vary directly with poverty in this one, whether in the individual or in the group. When wealth grows, heaven falls out of focus, and becomes thin and meaningless. But for a thousand years the thought of it dominated the minds of men.

Wealth came to Western Europe with the Renaissance

and the Industrial Revolution; and as it multiplied it displaced the hope of heaven with the lure of progress. That
greatest event in modern history — the Copernican revelation of the astronomic unimportance of the earth —
made many tender souls unhappy; but its reduction of
heaven to mere sky and space compelled the resilient spirit
of man to form for itself a compensatory faith in an earthly
paradise. Campanella, More, and Bacon wrote Utopias,
and announced the coming of universal happiness.
Europe, *nouveau riche*, imported luxuries and exported its
asceticism and its saints. Trade made cities, cities made
universities, universities made science, science made industry, and industry made progress. Gargantua writes to
Pantagruel, "All the world is full of savants, learned
teachers, vast libraries." "In one century" (the fifteenth),
says Pierre de La Ramée, "we have seen a greater progress
in men and works of learning than our ancestors had seen in
the whole course of the previous fourteen centuries." This
has an uncomfortably contemporary sound; what century
has not heard some spacious self-estimate of this kind? But
it was the keynote of the Renaissance; we hear it as an
organ point in every line of Francis Bacon; it strikes the
dominant chord of the modern soul; and the idea of progress is for modern Europe what the hope of heaven was for
medieval Christendom. If man does not really progress,
then the last prop of our faith is fallen, and we stand frus-
trate and ridiculous in the sight of the smiling stars.

This dearest dogma of the modern mind found its most
confident expression in the exuberant optimism of the eighteenth century. Rousseau was out of key, and preferred
America's savages, whom he had not met, to the cruel
Parisians who had rasped his nerves; he thought that thinking was a form of degeneracy, and preached a Golden Age
of the past that was obviously a *Nachschein*, as Teufels-
droeck would say, of the Garden of Eden and the Fall of

Man. But when we come to the irrepressible Voltaire we catch at first breath the exhilarating air of the Enlightenment. This "Grand Seigneur of the mind" had no delusions about the Indians; he knew that man was better off under civilization than under savagery; he was grateful for the slow and imperfect taming of the human brute; and he preferred Paris to the Garden of Eden.

It was his disciples Turgot and Condorcet who made the idea of progress the moving spirit of our day. Condorcet, escaping in 1793 from that consistently savage Rousseauian, Robespierre, wrote, far from his books and his friends, one of the most optimistic books ever penned by man — *Sketch of a Tableau of the Progress of the Human Spirit.* Having finished this magnanimous prophecy of the coming glory of mankind, Condorcet fled from Paris, was captured at a village inn, and confined in the village jail. The next morning he was found dead on the floor of his cell. He had always carried about with him a phial of poison to cheat the guillotine.

To read Condorcet is to realize to what a bitterly disillusioned and skeptical generation we belong. What eloquence he pours forth on the subject of print! — he is sure it will redeem and liberate mankind; he has no premonition of the modern press. "Nature has indissolubly united the advancement of knowledge with the progress of liberty, virtue, and respect for the natural rights of man." Prosperity will "naturally dispose men to humanity, to benevolence, and to justice." And then he formulates one of the most famous and characteristic doctrines of the Enlightenment: "No bounds have been fixed to the improvement of the human faculties; the perfectibility of man is absolutely infinite; the progress of this perfection, henceforth above the control of every power that would impede it, has no other limit than the duration of the globe upon which nature has placed us."

In his final chapter Condorcet draws a tempting picture of the future (by which he means our time). As knowledge spreads, slavery will decrease among classes and among nations; "then will come the moment in which the sun will observe free nations only, acknowledging no other master than their reason; in which tyrants and slaves, priests and their stupid or hypocritical instruments, will no longer exist but in history and upon the stage." Woman will be emancipated from man, the worker from the employer, the subject from the king; perhaps, even, mankind will unlearn war. And Condorcet concludes passionately: "How admirably calculated is this view of the human race to console the philosopher lamenting the errors, the flagrant acts of injustice, the crimes with which the earth is still polluted! It is the contemplation of this prospect that rewards him for all his efforts to assist the progress of reason and the establishment of liberty. He dares to regard these efforts as part of the eternal chain of the destiny of mankind; and in this persuasion he finds the true delight of virtue, the pleasure of having performed a durable service which no vicissitude will ever destroy.... This sentiment is the asylum into which he retires, and to which the memory of his persecutors cannot follow him; he unites himself in imagination with man restored to his rights, delivered from oppression, and proceeding with rapid strides in the path of happiness; he forgets his own misfortunes; ... he lives no longer to adversity, calumny, and malice, but becomes the associate of these wiser and more fortunate beings whose enviable condition he so earnestly contributed to produce." — What courageous optimism! what idealism! what a noble passion for humanity, and for truth! Shall we scorn more the naïve enthusiasm of Condorcet or that intellectual sloth and moral cowardice which have held us back from realizing his prophecies?

Behind these splendid philosophies lay the Commercial

and Industrial Revolutions. Here were machines, new
marvels; they could produce the necessaries, and some of the
luxuries of life at an unprecedented speed, and in un-
dreamed-of quantity; it was only a matter of time when
all vital needs would be met, and poverty would disappear.
Bentham and the elder Mill thought, about 1830, that England could now afford universal education for its people,
and that with universal education all serious social problems
would be solved by the end of the century. Buckle's *History of Civilization* (1857) stimulated the hope that the
spread of knowledge would mitigate human ills. Two
years later Darwin spoke; the secularization of the modern mind was enormously advanced, and the idea of a
coming Utopia replaced not merely the geographical
heaven, but the legendary golden past. Spencer identified progress with evolution, and looked upon it, to a certain point, as an inevitable thing. Meanwhile inventions
poured from a thousand alert minds; riches visibly grew;
nothing seemed hard or impossible to science; the stars
were weighed, and men accepted bravely the age-long
challenge of the bird. What could not man do? What
could we not believe of him, in those happy days before the
War?

II

Of course there had been some philosophic doubts of
progress long before the Great Madness came. Fontenelle,
in his *Dialogues of the Dead* (1683), had pictured Socrates
and Montaigne discussing the question — presumably in
hell, where all philosophers go. Socrates is anxious to hear
of the advances that mankind has made since his fatal cup;
he is astounded to learn that men are still brutes, incapable
of dying without metaphysics. Montaigne assures him
that the world has degenerated; there are no longer such
powerful types as Pericles, Aristides, or Socrates himself.

The old philosopher shrugs his shoulders. "In our days," he says, "we esteemed our ancestors more than they deserved; and now our posterity esteems us more than we deserve. There is really no difference between our ancestors, ourselves, and our posterity. *C'est toujours la même chose.*" And Fontenelle's summary is judicious: "The heart always the same, the intellect perfecting itself; passions, virtues, vices unaltered; knowledge increasing."

"The development of humanity," said Eckermann, "seems to be a matter of thousands of years." "Who knows?" replied Goethe, "perhaps of millions. But let humanity last as long as it will, there will always be hindrances in its way, and all kinds of distress, to make it develop its powers. Men will become cleverer and more intelligent, but not better, nor happier, nor more effective in action, at least except for a limited period. I see the time coming when God will take no pleasure in the race, and must again proceed to a rejuvenated creation." "The motto of history," says Schopenhauer, "should run: *Eadem, sed aliter*" — the same theme, but with variations. Mankind does not progress, said Nietzsche, it does not even exist; or it is a vast physiological laboratory where a ruthless Nature forever makes experiments; where some things in every age succeed, but most things fail. So concludes Romantic Germany.

About 1890 Arthur Balfour suggested, in his genially devastating way, that human behavior and social organization are founded not on thought, which progresses, but on feeling and instinct, which remain almost unchanged; so he explained the apparent failure of our increased knowledge to give us greater happiness or more lasting peace. "He that increaseth knowledge increaseth sorrow." "In all the world," said Anatole France (if we may believe Brousson), "the unhappiest creature is man. It is said, 'Man is the lord of creation.' My friend, man is the lord of suffering."

The socialist critique of modern industry did some damage to our faith in human progress. The endeavor to make people vividly realize the injustices of the present took the form of idealizing the content and peacefulness of the forgotten past. Ruskin, Carlyle, Morris, Kropotkin, and Carpenter painted pictures of the Middle Ages that made one long to be a serf attached to the soil and owing to some lord a share in one's product and one's wife. Meanwhile the liberal critique of modern politics, exposing corruption and incapacity in almost every office, made us doubt the divinity of democracy, which had been for a century our sacred cow. The development of printing and the Hoe press resulted rather in the debasement of the better minds than in the elevation of the worse; mediocrity triumphed in politics, in religion, in literature, even in science (Nordic anthropology, barn-yard eugenics, Viennese psychology, pragmatist philosophy). The "art" of the moving picture replaced the drama; photography drove painting from realism to cubism, futurism, *pointillisme* and other symptoms of cultured neurosis; in Rodin sculpture ceased to carve and tried to paint; in Strauss and Ravel and Scriabine music began to rival the delicate melodies of Chinese pots and pans. And finally came the War.

We discovered then how precariously thin our coat of civilization was, how insecure our security, and how frail our liberties. War had decreased in frequency and had increased in extent. Science, which was to be the midwife of progress, became the angel of death, killing with a precision and a rapidity that reduced the wars of theMiddle Ages to the level of college athletics. Brave aviators dropped bombs upon women and children, and learned chemists described the virtues of poison gas. All the international amity built up by a century of translated literatures, co-operating scientists, educational exchanges, commercial relationships, and financial interdependence melted

away, and Europe fell apart into a hundred hostile nationalities. When it was all over it appeared that the victors
as well as the fallen had lost the things for which they had
fought; that a greedy imperialism had merely passed from
Potsdam to Paris; that violent dictatorships were replacing
orderly and constitutional rule; that democracy was dying,
or dead. Hope faded away; the generation which had lived
through the War could no longer believe in anything; a
wave of apathy and cynicism engulfed all but the youngest
and least experienced souls. The idea of progress seemed
now to be one of the shallowest delusions that had ever
mocked man's misery, or lifted him up to a vain idealism
and a monstrous futility.

III

Perhaps, nevertheless, progress is real?

"If you wish to converse with me," said Voltaire, "define your terms." What shall we mean by "progress"?
Subjective definitions will not do; we must not conceive
progress in terms of the spread of any one religion, or any
one nation, or any one code of morals; an increase of kindness, for example, might scandalize our young Nietzscheans.
Is an objective definition possible — one that would hold
for any individual, any group, even for any species? Let us
provisionally define progress as increasing control of the
environment; and let us mean by environment all the circumstances, external and internal, that condition the
realization of desire. Progress is the domination of matter by form, of chaos by mind and purpose. Spencer was
right and Huxley was wrong; evolution and progress are
one; they are both of them the conquest of the environment by life.

Put in this way, the problem of progress in man is sim-
plified almost to a platitude. By common consent, human
knowledge is increasing; and by common consent knowl-

edge is power; the power of man over his environment grows visibly year by year. What shall we say of this argument?

We must guard against loose thinking. We may not compare the worst (or the best) of our age with the selected best (or worst) of all the past. If we find that our philosophers are slighter than Plato, our sculptors less than Angelo, our painters inferior to Raphael, our poets and composers a little short of Shakespeare and Bach, we need not despair; these stars did not all shine on the same night. Our problem is whether the total and average level of human ability has increased, and is increasing.

That it has increased since the earliest known state of man is hardly to be doubted. Under the complex strains of city life we take imaginative refuge in the quiet simplicity of savage days; but in our sober moments we know that this is a romantic flight-reaction from our actual tasks; like so many of our youthful opinions, this idolatry of barbarism is merely an impatient expression of our adolescent maladaptation. A study of such savage tribes as survive on our sophisticated planet shows their high rate of infantile mortality, their short tenure of life, their inferior speed, their inferior stamina, their inferior will, and their superior plagues. The friendly and flowing savage is like Nature — delightful except for the insects.

But the savage might turn the argument around and inquire how we enjoy our wars and our politics, and whether we think ourselves happier than the tribes whose names resound in the text-books of anthropology. The believer in progress will have to admit that we have made too much progress in the art of war; and that our politicians would have adorned the Roman Forum in the days of Milo and Clodius — though we may consider Mr. Coolidge an appreciable improvement upon Nero. As to happiness, no man can say; it is too elusively subjective to lend itself to measurement. Presumably it depends first upon health and then upon wealth. We are making sufficient progress in wealth. Our thousand fads of diet and drugs predispose us to the belief that we must be ridden with disease as compared with the men of simpler days; but this is an illusion. There is one test of health — and, therefore, in part of happiness — which is objective and reliable; we find it in the mortality statistics of insurance companies, where inaccuracy is ruinous. In some cases these figures extend over three hundred years; in Geneva, for example, they show an average length of life of twenty years in 1600, and of forty years in 1900. In the United States, in 1920, if we may believe Professor Irving Fisher, the tenure of life averaged fifty-three. This is incredible, if true. Taking the figures for granted, we may conclude that if life is a boon at all, we are unquestionably progressing in the quantity of it which we manage to maintain.

Having made these admissions and modifications, let us try to see the matter of progress in that total perspective which is philosophy. When we look at history in the large we see it as a graph of rising and falling culture — nations and civilizations appearing and disappearing as on some gigantic film. But in that irregular movement of countries and that chaos of men certain great moments stand out as the peaks and essence of human history, as the stairway of the progress of mankind. Step by step man has climbed from the savage to the scientist; and these are the stages in his growth.

First, *speech.* Think of it not as a sudden achievement, nor as a gift of the gods, but as the slow development of articulate expression, through centuries of effort, from the mate-calls of animals to the lyric flights of poetry. Without words, generalization would have been stopped in its beginnings, and thought would have stayed where we find it in the brute. The infinite subtlety of the modern mind, as in an Einstein or an Anatole France, was made possible by the development of speech.

Second, *fire*. Fire made man independent of climate, gave him a greater compass on the earth, and offered him as food a thousand things inedible before. But above all it made him master of the night; it shed an animating brilliance over the hours of evening and the dawn. Picture the dark before man conquered it: even now the terrors of that primitive blackness survive in our traditions and perhaps in our blood. Our overspreading of the night with a million man-made stars has brightened the human spirit, and made for a vivacious jollity in modern life. We cannot be too grateful for the light.

Third, *agriculture*. Civilization was impossible in the hunting stage; it needed a permanent habitat, a settled way of life. It came with the home and the school; and these could not be till the products of the field replaced the animals of the forest or the herd as the food of man. The hunter found his quarry with increasing difficulty, while the women whom he left at home tended an ever more fruitful soil. This patient husbandry of the wife threatened to make her independent of the male; and for his own lordship's sake he forced himself at last to bend his back to the prosaic tasks of tillage. So woman domesticated man, as she domesticated the cow and the pig. His domestication, his taming, still goes on, and is far enough from being complete: he is born for hunting rather than for agriculture or industry; hence his cruelty, his orgies of violence, his restlessness, and his occasional relish for war. But woman and civilization are winning; the hunting propensities are weaker; the male is becoming a pacifist and a vegetarian, and discovers the pleasures of the home at the very time when his wife has exhausted them.

Fourth, *the conquest of animals*. Our memories are too

forgetful and our imaginations too unimaginative to let us realize the boon we have in our security from the larger and sub-human beasts of prey. Animals are now our playthings and our helpless food; but there was a time when every step from hut or cave was an adventure, and the mastery of the earth was still undecided between beast and man.

Fifth, *social organization*. Here too is a gift unfelt, because we are born within the charmed circle of its protection, and never understand its value till we wander into the disordered or solitary regions of the earth. God knows that our congresses and parliaments are dubious inventions, the distilled mediocrity of the land; but despite them we manage to enjoy a security of life and property which we shall appreciate more warmly when war or revolution shall have reduced us to primitive "liberty." After all, we must not excite ourselves too much about political corruption or democratic mismanagement; politics is not life, but only a graft upon life; under its vulgar melodrama the traditional order of society gently persists in the family, in the school, in the thousand subtle forces that change our native anarchism into some measure of co-operation and good-will. Without consciousness of it, we partake of a luxurious patrimony of social order built up for us by a hundred generations of trial and error, war and peace, accumulated knowledge and transmitted wealth. What ingrates we mortals are!

Sixth, *morality*. Only a disordered mind can suppose that there is an excess of morality in this world; despite the songs of Zarathustra we see no immediate need of men becoming "more evil." Let us congratulate ourselves on any moral improvement that appears in our race. We are a slightly gentler species than we were; capable of greater kindness, and of generosity even to distant peoples whom we have never seen, or who have been our recent enemies.

We still kill criminals; but we are more uneasy about it, and the number of crimes for which we mete out the ultimate punishment has rapidly decreased.   We still exploit our immigrant labor, but we must soothe our consciences with "welfare work."   Our prevailing mode of marriage, chaotic as it is, represents a pleasant refinement on marriage by capture or purchase, and *le droit de seigneur*.   The emancipation of women, despite the biological problems which it entails, indicates a certain growing gentility in the once-murderous male.   And love, which was unknown to primitive man, or was only a hunger of the flesh, has flowered into a magnificent garden of song and sentiment, in which the passion of a man for a maid, though vigorously rooted in physical need, rises like a fragrance into the realm of living poetry.

Seventh, *tools*.   In the face of the romantics, the machine-wreckers of literature, the pleaders for a return to the primitive soil (dirt, chores, snakes, cobwebs, bugs), we sing the song of the tools, the engines, the machines that are liberating man.   These multiplying inventions are the new organs with which we control our environment; we do not need to grow them on our bodies, as animals must; we make them and use them and lay them aside till we need them again.   We grow gigantic arms that build in a day the pyramids that once enslaved a million men; we make for ourselves great eyes that search out the invisible stars of the sky, and little eyes that peer into the invisible cells of life; we speak, if we wish, with quiet voices that reach across continents and seas; and we move over the land and the air with the freedom of timeless gods.   What more astounding romance could there be than the story of Icarus' dream and Leonardo's patient diagrams, and then that triumphant leap into the air by the modest and un-discourageable Wrights?   Granted that mere speed is worthless: it is as a symbol of persistent human will that the

airplane has its highest meaning for us; long chained, like
Prometheus, to the earth, we have freed ourselves at last,
and now we can look the skylark in the face.... No, these
tools will not conquer us. Our present defeat by the
machinery around us is a transient thing, a plateau in our
progress to a slaveless world. The menial labor that de-
graded both master and man is lifted from human shoulders
and harnessed to the tireless muscles of iron and steel;
power becomes cheaper than brute brawn; soon every
waterfall and every wind will pour their beneficent energy
into factories and homes, and man will be freed for the
tasks of the mind. The slave will be emancipated not by
revolution but by growth. The proletariat will not dictate, it will disappear.

Eighth, *science*. In a large degree Buckle was right: we
progress only in knowledge, and these other gifts are rooted
in the slow enlightenment of the mind. Here in the modest
nobility of research and the silent battles of the laboratory
is a story fit to balance the chicanery of politics and the futile barbarism of war. Here man is at his best, and through
darkness and persecution mounts steadily towards the
light. Behold him standing on a little planet, measuring,
weighing, analyzing invisible constellations; predicting the
vicissitudes of earth and sun and moon and witnessing the
birth and death of worlds. Or here is a seemingly un-
practical mathematician tracking new formulas through
laborious labyrinths, clearing the way for an endless chain
of inventions that will multiply the power of his race.
Here is a bridge: a hundred thousand tons of iron suspended from four ropes of steel flung bravely from shore to
distant shore and bearing the passage of countless men;
here is poetry if your soul is not dead! Or this citylike
building mounting audaciously into the sky, guarded
against every strain by the courage of our calculations, and
shining like diamond-studded granite in the night. Here

shall you find new dimensions, and new elements, and new atoms, and new powers. Here in the rocks is the autobiography of evolving life. Here in the laboratories biology prepares to remake living organisms as physics has remade the face of the earth. Everywhere you come upon them studying, these unpretentious, unrewarded men; you hardly understand where their devotion finds its source and nourishment; they will die before the trees they plant will bear fruit for mankind. But they go on.

Yes, it is true that this victory of man over matter has not been matched with any kindred victory of man over himself. The argument for progress falters here. Psychology has hardly begun to understand, much less control, the desires and actions of men. Today we stand at the cradle of this new and hazardous science; we see it passing through psychoanalysis, behaviorism, glandular mythology, and other diseases of adolescence; and we might well despair of anything so harassed and muddled at its birth. But psychology will survive these storms and ills; it will be matured by the responsibilities which it audaciously undertakes. Three hundred years ago Francis Bacon, standing at the infancy of modern physics, predicted a thousand marvels to be found and formed by physical research. How moderate those predictions seem beside their multiple fulfilment! And what if psychology were entering now upon a like development; what if another Bacon should map its territory, point out the objectives of its attack, and the "fruits and powers" to be won: which of us, knowing the surprises of history and the courage of man, would dare to set a limit to the achievements that will come from our growing knowledge of the mind? Perhaps man, having remade his environment, will turn round at last and begin to remake himself?

Ninth, *education*. More and more completely we pass on to the next generation the gathered wisdom of the past.

It is almost a contemporary innovation, this tremendous expenditure of wealth and labor in the equipment of schools and the provision of instruction for all; perhaps it is the most significant feature of our time. Only a child would complain that the world has not yet been totally remade by our spreading schools, our free colleges, and our teeming universities; in the perspective of history this great experiment but begins. It has not had time to prove itself; it cannot in a generation undo the ignorance and superstition of a thousand years. But already the results appear, like the first green shoots of April's soil. Why is it that, broadly speaking, tolerance and freedom of the mind flourish more easily in the North than in the South, if not because the South has not yet won enough wealth to build enough schools? Who knows how much of our preference for mediocrity in office, and narrowness in leadership, is the result of a generation recruited from impoverished foreign lands, or too occupied with a primitive environment to spare time for the plowing and sowing of the mind? What will the full fruitage be when every one of us knows the happiness of schooldays, and finds an equal access to the intellectual treasures of our race? Consider the instinct of parental love, the profound impulse of every normal parent to raise his children beyond himself; here is the biological leverage of human progress, a force more to be trusted than any legislation, tenoned and mortised in the very nature of man. Adolescence lengthens now with every generation; parental care increases as blind fertility disappears. We began more helplessly, and we grow more completely towards that higher man who struggles to be born out of our imperfect and half-darkened souls. "The young are fortunate; they will see great things."

Tenth, *writing and print*. Again our imagination is too weak-winged to lift us to a full perspective; we cannot vision or recall the long ages of ignorance, impotence, and fear that preceded the coming of letters. Through those numberless generations men could transmit their hard-won lore only by word of mouth from parent to child; if one generation forgot, or misunderstood, the weary ladder of knowledge had to be climbed anew. Writing gave a new permanence to the achievements of the mind; it preserved for thousands of years, and through a millenium of poverty and superstition, the wisdom found by philosophy and the beauty carved out in drama and poetry. It bound the generations together with a common heritage; it created that Country of the Mind in which, because of writing, genius need not die.

And now as writing united the generations, print, despite the thousand prostitutions of it, can bind the civilizations. It is not necessary any more that civilization should disappear. It will change its habitat: doubtless the soil of every nation will refuse at last to yield its fruit to improvident tillage and careless tenancy; inevitably new regions will lure with virgin soil the lustier strains of every race. But a civilization is not a material thing, inseparably bound, like an ancient serf, to a given spot of the earth; it is an accumulation of technical knowledge and cultural creation; if these can be passed on to the new seat of economic power the civilization does not die, it merely makes for itself a new home. Nothing but beauty and wisdom deserve immortality. To a philosopher it is not indispensable that his native city should last forever; he will be content if its achievements shall be passed on, to form part of the permanent possessions of mankind.

Already it is possible to transmit imperfectly a body of culture from one civilization to another, as once it was transmitted from age to age. Australia and New Zealand need not begin at the bottom; they can share in the civilization of the motherland to a degree utterly impossible before the telegraph and the printing press. We are witnessing a new species of parental care exercised by one civilization over another. But it was by parental care that man outgrew the ape; perhaps by a similar solicitude a civilization can enshrine its values in a fresh form and a newer scene before it decays in the place of its birth. Now that dancing wires and leaping waves bind all the world electrically into an intellectual community, it will be a little harder for the accidents of time to destroy the cultural inheritance of the human race.

We need not worry, then, about the future. We are weary with too much war, and in our lassitude of mind we listen readily to a Spengler announcing the downfall of the Western world. But this arrangement of the birth and death of civilizations in cycles of 1800 years is a trifle too exact; we may be sure that the future will play wild pranks with this mathematical despair. There have been wars before, and wars far worse than our Great one. Man and civilization survived them; within fifteen years after Waterloo, defeated France was producing so many geniuses that every attic in Paris was occupied. Never was our heritage of civilization and culture so secure, and never was it half so rich. Let us do our little share to preserve it, augment it, and pass it on, confident that time will wear away chiefly the dross of it, and that what is finally fair and noble in it will escape mortality, to illuminate and gladden many generations.

J. B. S. HALDANE

John Burdon Sanderson Haldane was born in 1892, and educated at Eton and at New College, Oxford.   From beginning to end of the World War he served with the famous Black Watch; he was twice wounded in action, and in 1915 was promoted to a captaincy. Sometime Fellow of New College, he has been since 1922 Sir William Dunn Reader in Biochemistry in the University of Cambridge, since 1927, Fullerian Professor of Physiology in the Royal Institute.   He is also head of the Genetical Department, John Innes Horticultural Institution, Merton.   Besides numerous scientific papers in the field of genetics and human chemistry, Mr. Haldane *has written* Callinicus, *a defense of chemical warfare,* Daedalus, *or* Science and the Future (1924), *and* Science and Ethics (1928).   *Of the essays in* Possible Worlds (1927), *Mr.* Haldane *says: " They have been written in the intervals of research work and teaching, to a large extent in railway trains.   Many scientific workers believe that they should confine their publications to learned journals.   I think, however, that the public has a right to know what is going on inside the laboratories, for some of which it pays.   And it seems to me vitally important that the scientific point of view should be applied, so far as is possible, to politics and religion."*

The following essay is reprinted from Possible Worlds, *by J. B. S. Haldane, with the permission of Harper and Brothers, publishers.*

J. B. S. HALDANE

MAN'S DESTINY

IF, AS I am inclined to suspect, the human will is to some small extent free, there is no such thing as a destiny of the human race. There is a choice of destinies. Even if our actions are irrevocably predetermined we do not know our destiny. In either case, however, we can point to a limited number of probable fates for our species.

First let us consider the stage for our drama. The earth has existed for over a thousand million years. During most of this period its surface temperature has not been very different from that now prevailing. The sun has not cooled down appreciably during that time, and it will probably be only a little cooler a million million years hence, though somewhere about that time it is quite likely that the earth's surface will be destroyed owing to the disruption of the moon by tidal forces. Six hundred million years ago our ancestors were worms, ten thousand years ago they were savages. Both these periods are negligible compared with our possible future. Provided, therefore, that man has a future lasting for more than a few million years we can at once say that our descendants may, for anything we can see to the contrary, excel us a great deal more than we excel worms or jellyfish.

There are, however, several alternatives to this prospect. A catastrophe of an astronomical order, such as a collision with a stray heavenly body, is unlikely. The earth has lasted a long time without any such disasters. The sun may possibly swell up temporarily, as similar stars occasionally do. In this case the human race will be very rapidly roasted. A disease may arise which will wipe out all, or almost all, mankind. But there is nothing in science to make such up-to-date versions of the apocalypse very probable.

Even if man does not perish in this dramatic manner, there is no reason why civilization should not do so. All civilization goes back to a common source less than ten thousand years ago, very probably in Egypt. It is a highly complicated invention which has probably been made only once. If it perished it might never be made again. When in the past its light was extinguished in one area — for example, when the Angles and Saxons wrecked Roman Britain — it could be lit again from elsewhere, as our savage ancestors were civilized from Italy and Ireland. A modern war followed by revolutions might destroy it all over the planet. If weapons are as much improved in the next century as in the last, this will probably happen.

But unless atomic energy can be tapped, which is wildly unlikely, we know that it will never be possible to box up very much more rapidly available energy in a given place, than we can already box up in a high explosive shell, nor has any vapour much more poisonous than "mustard gas" been discovered in the forty-one years that have elapsed since that substance was first produced. I think therefore that the odds are slightly against such a catastrophic end of civilization.

But civilization as we know it is a poor thing. And if it is to be improved there is no hope save in science. A hundred and forty years ago men, women and children were being hanged in England for stealing any property valued at over a shilling, miners were hereditary slaves in Scotland, criminals were publicly and legally tortured to death in France. Europe was definitely rather worse off, whether in health, wealth or morals, than the Roman

Empire under Antoninus Pius in A.D. 150. Since then we have improved very greatly in all these respects. We are far from perfect, but we live about twice as long, and we do not hang starving children for stealing food, raid the coast of Africa for slaves, or imprison debtors for life. These advances are the direct and indirect consequences of science. Physics and chemistry have made us rich, biology healthy, and the application of scientific thought to ethics by such men as Bentham has done more than any dozen saints to make us good. The process can only continue if science continues.

And pure science is a delicate plant. It has never flowered in Spain, and today it is almost dead in Italy. Everywhere there are strong forces working against it. Even where research is rewarded, the usual reward is a professorship with a full-time programme of teaching and administration. The bacteriologist can most easily earn a title and a fortune if he deserts research for medical practice. The potential physicist or chemist can often quadruple his income by taking up engineering or manufacture. In biology and psychology many lines of research are forbidden by law or public opinion. If science is to improve man as it has improved his environment, the experimental method must be applied to him. It is quite likely that the attempt to do so will rouse such fierce opposition that science will again be persecuted as it has been in the past. Such a persecution may quite well be successful, especially if it is supported by religion. A world-wide religious revival, whether Christian or not, would probably succeed in suppressing experimental inquiry into the human mind, which offers the only serious hope of improving it. Again, if scientific psychology and eugenics are used as weapons by one side in a political struggle, their opponents, if successful, will stamp them out. I think that it is quite as likely as not that scientific research may ultimately be strangled in some such way as this before mankind has learnt to control its own evolution.

If so, evolution will take its course. And that course has generally been downwards. The majority of species have degenerated and become extinct, or, what is perhaps worse, gradually lost many of their functions. The ancestors of oysters and barnacles had heads. Snakes have lost their limbs and ostriches and penguins their power of flight. Man may just as easily lose his intelligence.

It is only a very few species that have developed into something higher. It is unlikely that man will do so unless he desires to and is prepared to pay the cost. If, as appears to be the case at present in most parts of Europe and North America, the less intelligent of our species continue to breed more rapidly than the able, we shall probably go the way of the dodo and the kiwi. We do not as yet know enough to avert this fate. If research continues for another two centuries, it is probable that we shall. But if, as is likely enough, the welfare of our descendants in the remote future can only be realized as a very considerable sacrifice of present happiness and liberty, it does not follow that such a sacrifice will be made.

It is quite likely that, after a golden age of happiness and peace, during which all the immediately available benefits of science will be realized, mankind will very gradually deteriorate. Genius will become ever rarer, our bodies a little weaker in each generation; culture will slowly decline, and in a few thousand or a few hundred thousand years — it does not much matter which — mankind will return to barbarism, and finally become extinct. If this happens I venture to hope that we shall not have destroyed the rat, an animal of considerable enterprise which stands as good a chance as any other of evolving towards intelligence.

In the rather improbable event of man taking his own

evolution in hand — in other words, of improving human nature, as opposed to environment — I can see no bounds at all to his progress. Less than a million years hence the average man or woman will realize all the possibilities that human life has so far shown. He or she will never know a minute's illness. He will be able to think like Newton, to write like Racine, to paint like Fra Angelico, to compose like Bach. He will be as incapable of hatred as Saint Francis, and when death comes at the end of a life probably measured in thousands of years he will meet it with as little fear as Captain Oates or Arnold von Winkelried. And every minute of his life will be lived with all the passion of a lover or a discoverer. We can form no idea whatever of the exceptional men of such a future.

Man will certainly attempt to leave the earth. The first voyagers into interstellar space will die, as did Lilienthal and Pilcher, Mallory and Irvine. There is no reason why their successors should not succeed in colonizing some, at least, of the other planets of our system, and ultimately the planets, if such exist, revolving round other stars than our sun. There is no theoretical limit to man's material progress but the subjection to complete conscious control of every atom and every quantum of radiation in the universe. There is, perhaps, no limit at all to his intellectual and spiritual progress.

But, whether any of these possibilities will be realized depends, as far as we can see, very largely on the events of the next few centuries. If scientific research is regarded as a useful adjunct to the army, the factory, or the hospital, and not as the thing of all things most supremely worth doing, both for its own sake and that of its results, it is probable that the decisive steps will never be taken. And unless he can control his own evolution as he is learning to control that of his domestic plants and animals, man and all his works will go down into oblivion and darkness.

SUGGESTIONS FOR READING

Editor's Note. Inasmuch as a selected list of books has been given in each of the preceding introductory notes, the following suggestions do not include works by any of the authors already represented in Group Two. For the sake of convenience, the suggestions have been classified according to ideas, but this classification should not be regarded as rigid, since some overlapping is inevitable. Mr. Lowes Dickinson's *A Modern Symposium*, for instance, might be listed under any of the headings.

The lists are intended to be suggestive, not exhaustive. Magazine articles are identified by the name of the periodical and the date or volume of publication; other titles are those of books.

A. *The Idea of Equality*
    James Bryce: *Equality.* *The Century Magazine*, Vol. XXXIV, p. 459.
    G. Lowes Dickinson: *A Modern Symposium.* See, especially, the first three speeches.
    C. W. Eliot: *The Contemporary American Conception of Equality Among Men.*
    A. T. Hadley: *The Conflict between Liberty and Equality.*
    J. S. Mill: *On Liberty.*
    T. V. Smith: *The American Philosophy of Equality.*
    R. H. Tawney: *Equality.* (The Halley Stewart Lectures.)

B. *Criticisms of Modern America*
    Arnold Bennett: *Your United States.*
    Herbert Croly: *The Promise of American Life.*
    John Dewey: *American Education and Culture.* *The New Republic*, July 1, 1916.
    G. Lowes Dickinson: Ellis's speech in *A Modern Symposium.*
    Katherine Fullerton Gerould: *The Extirpation of Culture.* In *Modes and Morals*, 1920.
    Agnes Repplier: *On a Certain Condescension in Americans.* *The Atlantic Monthly*, May, 1926.
    André Siegfried: *America Comes of Age.*
    T. J. Wertenbaker: *What's Wrong with the United States?* *Scribner's Magazine*, October, 1928.

C. *Man in the Age of Machines*
    Samuel Butler: *Erewhon.* (See, especially, tne three chapters entitled "The Book of the Machines.")

J. M. Clark: *The Empire of Machines.*   *The Yale Review,*
    October, 1922.
R. Flanders: *Pandora's Box.*   *The Forum,* November, 1930.
Julius Klein: *Business.*   (In *Whither Mankind?,* edited by
    C. A. Beard.)
Robert S. and Helen Merrell Lynd: *Middletown.*
W. C. Mitchell: *Economics and Social Engineering.   Mechanical Engineering,* February, 1931.   (A reply to *Pandora's Box.*)
Thorstein Veblen: *The Engineers and the Price System.*
Sidney and Beatrice Webb: *Labor.*   (In *Whither Mankind?,*
    edited by C. A. Beard.)

D. *Science for the Layman*
    E. G. Conklin: *Science and the Faith, of the Modern.   Scribner's Magazine,* November, 1925.
    R. A. Millikan: *Science and Modern Life.   The Atlantic
        Monthly,* April, 1928.
    John Mills: *Within the Atom.*
    E. E. Slosson: *Chats on Science.*
                    Creative Chemistry.
    Sir J. A. Thomson: *The New World of Science.   The Atlantic
                    Monthly,* June, 1930.
                    Modern Science.
                    The Outlines of Science.

E. *The Idea of Progress*
    Duncan Aikman: *Scrapping Perfectibility.   Harper's Magazine,* May, 1927.
    Lincoln Colcord: *Conversation in a Garden.   The Freeman,*
        July 19, 1922.
    H. W. Farnam: *Law, Liberty and Progress.   The Yale Review,*
        April, 1926.
    Archibald Henderson: *Civilization and Progress.   The Virginia Quarterly Review,* April, 1925.
    W. R. Inge: *The Idea of Progress.*   In *Outspoken Essays,
        Second Series.*
    Robert Shafer: *Progress and Science.*
    H. G. Wells: *The Extinction of Man.*   In *Certain Personal
            Matters.*
                    The Next Stage of History.   Final chapter of
                    The Outline of History.

GROUP THREE
FAMILIAR ESSAYS

H. M. TOMLINSON

Henry Major Tomlinson was born in London, in 1873. Early service as office boy and shipping clerk on the London wharves made him familiar with the world of ships, their strange cargoes, and their seamen which he was later to describe with equal accuracy and brilliance in Old Junk *(1919),* London River *(1921), and* Gallion's Reach *(1927). Turning to newspaper work, he joined the staff of* The Morning Leader *in 1904, continuing with* The Daily News *when the two journals merged. In 1914 he was sent as war correspondent to France and Belgium; from 1915 to 1917 he served as Official Correspondent attached to General Headquarters of the British Armies in France. His experiences in this capacity are recorded in* Waiting for Daylight *(1922) and must have furnished some of the chapters in* All Our Yesterdays *(1930), a novel of the War. On his return to England he became, for five years, literary editor of the London* Nation and Athenæum. *As a traveler, Mr. Tomlinson has not only journeyed to remote places, but possesses an unusual skill in conveying to his readers the veritable atmosphere of those places. To read* The Sea and the Jungle *(1912) is perhaps the best possible substitute for an actual voyage up the Amazon; to read* Tide Marks *(1924) is to wander through the Malay Archipelago with an exceedingly observant and penetrating guide.*

The following essay is reprinted from Gifts of Fortune, *by H. M. Tomlinson, with permission of Harper and Brothers, publishers.*

H. M. TOMLINSON

SOME HINTS FOR THOSE ABOUT TO TRAVEL

I

A YEAR or two ago a lively book was published called *The Happy Traveller*. It is not an indispensable work if you have booked your passage, or are on a ship's articles, for only Providence can help you then, yet it is a cheerful guide if you would know what long journeys are like, in parts, without making them. Its author, the Reverend Frank Tatchell, proves he has seen enough of the world to satisfy a crew of able seamen. He has seen it from the byroads, the highroads, the decks of local trading ships, and the windows of third-class railway carriages. He has seen it because, apparently, he wanted to; and he has enjoyed it all, or most of it. He has some heroic advice for those whom he judges may be infected by his own enthusiasm, and indeed his book would induce many young men to pull on their boots forthwith: "Be cheerful and interested in everything," he tells us; and, "Do not bother too much about your inside."

But what I sought in his volume was not the Malay for Thank you — which he gave me — but what set him going. Why did he do it? There is a word, frequently seen in glossy narrative, "Wanderlust." The very lemmings must know it. It excuses almost anything in the way of travel lunacy, even to herding with Russian emigrants for fun. It is used as a flourish by those who hope we will fail to notice that they are uncertain what to do with themselves. Mr. Tatchell, however, does not use it once. Yet you see him hustling through the bazaar at

Bhamo, where you do not meet many tourists; and he discovers that the half-castes of the Society Isles are especially charming, though he does not pretend that it is
worth while voyaging to the South Seas to confirm that;
or he peeps into the Malayan forest long enough to note
"myriads of leeches in all directions humping and hastening towards the traveller." He certainly saw those leeches.
He saw them *hump*. But why did he foregather with
them, and go to smell Bhamo? For out of so varied an
experience he returns but to assure romantic youth sitting
on the bollards of our quays and gazing seaward wistfully, "Elephants dislike having white men approach them
from behind." Or of this: "If you should become in-
fested with fleas, sleep out on a bed of bracken one night,
and in the morning you will be free from the pests."
Such fruits of travel seem hardly enough. Mr. Tatchell
himself was decidedly a happy traveller, and the cause of
happiness in others — his book can be commended in confidence — for he admits that his method of enjoying himself in a strange bed is to sing aloud the aria, "Why do the
Nations?" But he does not tell us what sent him roving,
nor does he produce any collection of treasures, except
oddities such as the warning to white men about approaching the behinds of elephants, and *Vinakka vinakka!*
(Fijian for Bravo.)

Perhaps these little curiosities are enough. We are
pleased to hear of them. What else was there to get? It
would be very hard for most voyagers to explain convinc-
ingly why they became restless, and went to sea. Some
do it to get away from us, some to get away from themselves, and some because they cannot help it. I shall not
forget the silliness which gave me my first sight of Africa.
The office telephone rang. "Oh, is that you? Well, we
want you to go to Algeria at once." I went downstairs
hurriedly to disperse this absurdity. But it was no good.

I had to go. And because I was argumentative about it they added Tripoli and Sicily, which served me right. After all, while in Africa, one is necessarily absent from Fleet Street. I should have remembered that.

Mr. Tatchell tells us that even a poor man, if he does not leave it till he is in bondage to the income-tax or the Poor Law officials, may see all the world. I suppose he may. With sufficient health, enterprise, and impudence, a young fellow could inveigle himself overseas without paying a lot of money to the P. & O. Company; though it wants some doing nowadays, under the present rules of the Mercantile Marine Board and the seafarers' unions. Shipowners do not lightly engage to pay compensation for accidents to inexperienced hands whose sole recommendation is that they want to see the world so wide. As for getting a berth for the voyage cheaply, it would be foolish to suppose that agents for passenger ships are willing to forgive the fact that you are poor, and will shake Cornucopia about freely. Why should they? You have to pay across the counter in exchange for a ticket, and at the post-war rates. If anyone doubts that this is a hard world, let him cut the painter at Port Said, with a shilling in his pocket, and note what will happen. In some difficult regions you must travel on foot with the natives, and live with them; and that costs very little, even in a land otherwise expensive, but those unsophisticated coasts must first be reached. That simple way of a nomad is all very well in the wilderness, but I think any reasonable man, however thirsty he may be for a draught of primitive Life, would hesitate before sequestering himself in native cities like Calcutta and Singapore, counting cannily the lesser coins, and travelling about in third-class carriages. I noticed that even Mr. Tatchell shrank from the prospect of getting from island to island of Indonesia with the deck passengers. I am not surprised. One is easily satisfied with an occasional hour on the lower deck, in converse with a picturesque native elder. But to eat and sleep there for weeks, among the crowing cocks, the banana skins, the babies, the dried fish, and men and women spitting red stuff after chewing betel nut! It has been done, I believe, but the shipping companies and all their officers set their faces against it. They do not encourage Europeans to travel even second class in those seas, though there is hardly any difference between the cabins of the two classes. Of course, if one were anything of an Orientalist, it would be ridiculous to keep to the first saloon with the Europeans when there were Arab and Chinese merchants in an inferior saloon of the ship.

I do not know how one plans a long voyage, and maintains the excellent plan scientifically through all its difficulties. I have never done any planning. A ship seems to have drifted my way at last by chance, and then, if I did not hesitate too long about it, I went in her, though always for a reason very inadequate. One bitter and northerly Easter I read, because gardening was impossible, Bates's *Naturalist on the River Amazons.* The famous illustration of that spectacled entomologist in trousers and a check shirt, standing with an insect net in a tropical forest surrounded by infuriated toucans, fixed me when casually I pulled the volume off a library shelf. The book had not been specially commended to me, but its effect was instant. And the picture that artful naturalist drew of the pleasures of Santa Belem de Para, when contrasted with the sleet of an English spring, made me pensive over a fire. I had never seen the tropics. And what a name it is, the Amazons! And what a delightful book is Bates's!

Yet when I enquired into this enticement, Para might as well have been in another star. One may go cheaply to Canada, and risk it. That trick cannot be played on the

tropics with impunity. I had the propriety to guess that.
Then, one night, a sailor came home from sea, and just before he left he spoke of his next voyage. They were going
to Para, and up the Amazon; and up a tributary of that
river never before navigated by an ocean-going steamer.
"Nonsense," I said, "it cannot be done — not if you
draw, as you say you do, nearly twenty-four feet. And it
means rising about six hundred feet above sea level."

"You can talk," the sailor replied, "but I've seen the
charter. We're going, and I wish we weren't. Sure to be
fevers. Besides, a ship has no right inside a continent."

I began thinking of Bates. My friend turned up the
collar of his coat before going out into the rain. "Look
here," he said, "if you have any doubt about it, you may
take the trip. There's a cabin we don't use."

I never gave that preposterous suggestion a second
thought, but I did write, for a lively morning newspaper,
my sailor's mocking summary of what that strange voyage
might have in store. The editor, a day later, met me on
the office stairs. "That was an amusing lie of yours this
morning," he said. I answered him that it was written
solely in the cause of science and navigation. What was
more, I assured him earnestly, I had been offered a berth
on the ship for the proof of doubters. "Well," said the
editor, "you shall go and prove it." He meant that. I
could see by the challenging look in his eye that nothing
much was left about which to argue. He prided himself
on his swift and unreasonable decisions.

Somehow, as that editor descended the stairs, showing
me the finality of his back, the attractive old naturalist of
the Amazon with his palms at Para, toucans, spectacles,
butterflies, and everlasting afternoon of tranquillity in the
forest of the tropics, was the less alluring. This meant
packing up; and for what? Even the master of the steamer
could not tell me that.

It is better to obey the mysterious index, without any fuss, when it points a new road, however strange that road may be. There is probably as much reason for it, if the truth were known, as for anything else. It would be absurd, in the manner of Browning and Mr. Tatchell, to greet the unseen with a cheer, and thus flatter it, yet when circumstances begin to look as though they intend something different for us, perhaps the proper thing to do is to get into accord with them, to see what will happen.

There was no doubt about that voyage, either. I take this opportunity to thank an autocratic editor for his cruel decision one morning on the office stairs, a trivial episode he has completely forgotten. It is worth the break, and the discomfort of a winter dock, and the drive out in the face of hard westerly weather, to come up a ship's companion one morning, and to see for the first time the glow of sunrise above the palisade of the jungle. You never forget the warm smell of it, and its light; though that simple wonder might not be thought worth a hard fight with gales in the western ocean. Yet later, when by every reasonable estimate of a visitor accustomed to the assumption of man's control of nature the forest should have ended, yet continues as though it were eternal — savage, flamboyant, yet silent and desolate — the voyager begins to feel vaguely uneasy. He cannot meet that lofty and sombre regard with the cheerful curiosity of the early part of the voyage. He feels lost. Saint Paul's Cathedral does not seem so influential as it once did, nor man so important. And perhaps it is not an unhealthful surmise either that man may be only a slightly disturbing episode on earth after all, and had better look out; a hindering and humbling notion of that sort would have done him no harm, if of late years it had given him pause.

Well, something of that sort is about as much as one should expect to get out of the experience, that and the ability to call for a porter in Fijian or Chinese. But is it not sufficient? It is hardly as tangible as hearing earlier than the people at home of the wealth of oil at Balikpapan, or what comes of getting in at the Rand on the ground floor. Even as book material it is not so sparkling as Lady Hester Stanhope, or as exciting as sword-fish angling off the Bermudas. Nor does it provide any inspiration, once you are home again, to get to work to plant the British flag where it will do the lucky ones most good. There seems hardly anything in it, and yet you feel that you could not have done any better, and are not sorry it turned out just so.

Besides, there were the men one met. It would not be easy to analyze the impulse which sent one travelling, an impulse strong enough, if vague, to overcome one's natural desire to be let alone. What did one want, or expect to learn? It would be hard to say. But you are aware, in rare moments, that you have got something almost as good as a word about a new oil-field, through some chance converse with a stranger, about nothing in particular. For it might have been night in the Malacca Strait, with little to give reasonable conviction of the realities except the stars, the tremor of the ship's rail, and the glow of a shipmate's cigar; and the other man might not have said much. You have previously noticed he was not that kind. But his casual relation of an obscure adventure — rather as if the droning of the waters had become a significant utterance — gave an abiding content to the shadows.

II

What right have we to travel, when better men have to stay at home? But it would be unwise to attempt to answer that question, for certainly it would lead, as did the uncorking of the bottle that imprisoned the Genie, to much smoke and confusion. We should not poke about with a naked light amid the props which uphold the august and many-storied edifice of society, even to make sure of our rightful place there. It was a reading of Lord Bryce's *Memories of Travel* that started so odd a doubt in my mind. When I had finished it I did not begin to think of packing a bag. I felt that I had no title to do that. Lord Bryce, that learned man, had been remembering casually Iceland and the tropics, Poland, the Mountains of Moab, and the scenery of North America. But he did not make me feel that those places should be mine. He, that great scholar, made them desirable, yet infinitely remote, and reservations for wiser men, among whom, if I were bold enough to intrude, my inconsequence would be detected instantly. After reading his book of travel I felt that it would be as wrong in me to possess and privily to treasure priceless Oriental manuscripts as to claim the right to see coral atolls in the Pacific or prospects of the Altai.

We may lack the warrant to travel, even if we have the means. Lord Bryce made it coldly clear that few of us are competent to venture abroad. He made me feel that much that would come my way would be wasted on me, for I have little in common with the encyclopædias. The wonders would loom ahead, would draw abeam, would pass astern, and I should not see them; they would not be there. The pleasures of travel, when we are candid about them, are separated by very wide deserts and tedious, where there is nothing but sand and the dreary howling of wild dogs. An Eastern city may grow stale in a night. "'Dear City of Cecrops,' saith the poet; but shall we not say 'Dear City of Zeus'?" There are days when the ocean is a pond. Its relative importance then appears to be that of a newspaper of last week. Sometimes, too, you do not want to hear that there are three miles of water under you; no less. What of it? In nasty weather the end so far below you of the last two miles is of less importance than the beginning of the first.

It may also happen that when at last your ship reaches that far place whose name is as troubling as the name of the star to which you look in solitude, that — what is it you do there? You gaze overside at it from your trite anchorage, unbelievingly. The first mate comes aft, leisurely, rubbing his hands. You do not go ashore. What has become of the magic of a name? You go below with the mate, who has finished his job, for a pipe. Tomorrow will do for Paradise, or the day after. One morning I reached Naples by sea, and I well remember my first sight of it. The stories I had heard of that wonderful bay! The ecstatic letters in my pocket from those who were instructing me how nothing of my luck should be missed! But it was raining. It was cold. I had been travelling for an age. There was hardly any bay, and what I could see of it was as glum as a bad mistake. There was a wet quay, some house fronts that were house fronts, and a few cabs. I took a cab. That was better than walking to the railway station, and quicker. It is quite easy for me to describe my first sight of Naples and its bay.

But Lord Bryce was not an incompetent traveller. He could see through any amount of rain and dirt. He was competent indeed; fully, lightly, and with grace. To other tourists he may have appeared to be one of the crowd, trying hard to get some enjoyment out of a lucky deal in rubber or real estate, and not knowing how to do it. But he was not bored. He was merely quiet because he knew what he was looking at. What to us would have been opaque he could see through; yet I doubt whether he would have said anything about it, unless he had been asked. And why should we ask a fellow-traveller whether he can see through what is opaque? We never do it, because our own intelligence tells us that what is dark cannot be light. What we do not see is not there.

Yet how much we miss, when on a journey, Lord Bryce

reveals. There was not often a language difficulty for him. When he looked at the wilderness of central Iceland he knew the cause of it, and could explain why tuffs and basalts make different landscapes. When he was in Hungary and Poland the problems we should have brushed aside as matters no Englishman ought to be expected to understand, become, in the light of his political and historical lore, simple and relevant. Among the islands of the South Seas, with their unsolved puzzles of an old continental land mass and of race migrations, so learned a traveller was just as much at ease. Once I remarked to an old voyager, who in some ways resembled Lord Bryce, that it was in my dreams to visit Celebes. "But," he remarked coldly, "you are not an ethnologist." No; and I can see now, after these *Memories of Travel,* that I have other defects as a traveller.

Yet I cannot deny that a craving for knowledge, when abroad, may sometimes come over me, with a dim resemblance to a craving for food or sleep. But if I go to my note books in later years and discover that though I had forgotten them I had many interesting facts stored away, nevertheless it is evident the valuable information does very well where it is. It will never be missed. Its importance has faded. There are other things, however, one never entered in a notebook, and never tried to remember, for they were of no seeming importance then or now, things seen for an instant only, or smelt, or heard in the distance, which are never forgotten. They will recur from the past, often irrelevantly, even when memory is not turned that way, as though something in us knew better what to look for in life than our trained eyes.

G. LOWES DICKINSON

Born in London, in 1862, *Goldsworthy Lowes Dickinson was educated at Charterhouse and at King's College, Cambridge. As Fellow of King's College he had ample opportunity to study classical and modern European civilization; in* 1912 *and* 1913 *extensive travel, in China, Japan, and India, gave him a direct observation of the culture of the Orient. Of his unusual advantages in education and native ability he made full use in a long series of books ranging from studies in political history* (From King to King: The Tragedy of the Puritan Revolution, 1891) *to more general criticisms of modern life* (After Two Thousand Years, 1930). *He died on August* 3, 1932.

In an interesting study of the development of Lowes Dickinson's political point of view (Shelburne Essays, Seventh Series), *Paul Elmer More says: "I find in these (writings) a distinction of mere language, a style marked by a rare delicacy of phrase and cadence, even verging at times on a too refined self-consciousness." The reader interested in determining for himself the validity of this criticism should consult, as perhaps the best examples of Dickinson's work,* Letters from a Chinese Official (1901), A Modern Symposium (1908), The Greek View of Life (1896) *and* War: Its Nature, Cause, and Cure (1923).

The following essay comes from Appearances — Notes of Travel, East and West, *by G. Lowes Dickinson, copyright,* 1914, *and reprinted by permission from the publishers, Doubleday, Doran and Company, Inc.*

G. LOWES DICKINSON

A SACRED MOUNTAIN

IT WAS midnight when the train set us down at Tai-an-fu.[1] The moon was full. We passed across fields, through deserted alleys where sleepers lay naked on the ground, under a great gate in a great wall, by halls and pavilions, by shimmering, tree-shadowed spaces, up and down steps, and into a court where cypresses grew. We set up our beds in a veranda, and woke to see leaves against the morning sky. We explored the vast temple and its monuments — iron vessels of the Tang age,[2] a great tablet of the Sungs,[3] trees said to date from before the Christian era, stones inscribed with drawings of these by the Emperor Chien Lung, hall after hall, court after court, ruinous, overgrown, and the great crumbling walls and gates and towers. Then in the afternoon we began the ascent of Tai Shan, the most sacred mountain in China, the most frequented, perhaps, in the world. There, according to tradition, legendary emperors worshiped God. Confucius climbed it six centuries before Christ, and sighed, we are told, to find his native state so small. The great Chin-shih-Huang was there in the third century B.C. Chien Lung in the eighteenth century covered it with inscriptions. And millions of humble pilgrims for thirty centuries at least have toiled up the steep and narrow way. Steep it is, for it makes no detours, but follows straight up

---

[1] Tai-an-fu: a city in the Chinese province of Shantung, near Tai Shan, the sacred mountain.

[2] Tang age: the golden age of Chinese literature, under the rule of the Tang dynasty (A.D. 618–907).

[3] The Sungs: a later dynasty (A.D. 960–1126), noted for its philosophers.

the bed of a stream, and the greater part of the five thousand feet is ascended by stone steps. A great ladder of
eighteen flights climbs the last ravine, and to see it from
below, sinuously mounting the precipitous face to the great
arch that leads on to the summit, is enough to daunt the
most ardent walker. We at least were glad to be chaired
some part of the way. A wonderful way! On the lower
slopes it passes from portal to portal, from temple to
temple. Meadows shaded with aspen and willow border
the stream as it falls from green pool to green pool. Higher
up are scattered pines. Else the rocks are bare — bare, but
very beautiful, with that significance of form which I have
found everywhere in the mountains in China.

To such beauty the Chinese are peculiarly sensitive.
All the way up the rocks are carved with inscriptions
recording the charm and the sanctity of the place. Some
of them were written by emperors; many, especially, by
Chien Lung, the great patron of art in the eighteenth century. They are models, one is told, of caligraphy as well as
of literary composition. Indeed, according to Chinese
standards, they could not be the one without the other.
The very names of favorite spots are poems in themselves.
One is "the pavilion of the phoenixes"; another "the
fountain of the white cranes." A rock is called "the tower
of the quickening spirit"; the gate on the summit is "the
portal of the clouds." More prosaic, but not less charming, is an inscription on a rock in the plain, "the place of the
three smiles," because there some mandarins, meeting
to drink and converse, told three peculiarly funny stories.
Is not that delightful? It seems so to me. And so peculiarly Chinese!

It was dark before we reached the summit. We put up
in the temple that crowns it, dedicated to Yü Huang, the
"Jade Emperor" of the Taoists; [1] and his image and those

---

[1] *Taoists*, one of the chief religious sects of China.

of his attendant deities watched our slumbers. But we
did not sleep till we had seen the moon rise, a great orange
disk, straight from the plain, and swiftly mount till she
made the river, five thousand feet below, a silver streak
in the dim gray levels.

Next morning, at sunrise, we saw that, north and east,
range after range of lower hills stretched to the horizon,
while south lay the plain, with half a hundred streams
gleaming down to the river from the valleys. Full in view
was the hill where, more than a thousand years ago, the
great Tang poet Li-tai-po retired with five companions to
drink and make verses. They are still known to tradition
as the "six idlers of the bamboo grove"; and the morning
sun, I half thought, still shines upon their symposium.
We spent the day on the mountain; and as the hours passed
by, more and more it showed itself to be a sacred place.
Sacred to what god? No question is harder to answer of
any sacred place, for there are as many ideas of the god as
there are worshipers. There are temples here to various
gods: to the mountain himself; to the Lady of the mountain, Pi-hsia-yüen, who is at once the Venus of Lucretius —
"goddess of procreation, gold as the clouds, blue as the
sky," one inscription calls her — and the kindly mother
who gives children to women and heals the little ones of
their ailments; to the Great Bear; to the Green Emperor,
who clothes the trees with leaves; to the Cloud-compeller;
to many others. And in all this, is there no room for God?
It is a poor imagination that would think so. When men
worship the mountain, do they worship a rock, or the
spirit of the place, or the spirit that has no place? It is
the latter, we may be sure, that some men adored, standing
at sunrise on this spot. And the Jade Emperor — is he a
mere idol? In the temple where we slept were three inscriptions set up by the Emperor Chien Lung. They run
as follows:

Without labor, O Lord, Thou bringest forth the greatest things.
Thou leadest Thy company of spirits to guard the whole world.
In the company of Thy spirits Thou art wise as a mighty Lord
   to achieve great works.

These might be sentences from the Psalms; they are as religious as anything Hebraic.   And if it be retorted that the
mass of the worshipers on Tai Shan are superstitious, so
are, and always have been, the mass of worshipers anywhere.   Those who rise to religion in any country are few.
India, I suspect, is the great exception.   But I do not
know that they are fewer in China than elsewhere.   For
that form of religion, indeed, which consists in the worship
of natural beauty and what lies behind it — for the religion
of a Wordsworth — they seem to be preëminently gifted.
The cult of this mountain, and of the many others like it in
China, the choice of sites for temples and monasteries, the
inscriptions, the little pavilions set up where the view is
loveliest — all go to prove this.   In England we have
lovelier hills, perhaps, than any in China.   But where is
our sacred mountain?   Where, in all the country, that
charming mythology which once in Greece and Italy, as
now in China, was the outward expression of the love of
nature?

> Great God, I'd rather be
>   A pagan suckled in a creed outworn;
> So might I, standing on this pleasant lea,
>   Have glimpses that would make me less forlorn.

That passionate cry of a poet born into a naked world would
never have been wrung from him had he been born in
China.

And that leads me to one closing reflection.   When
lovers of China — "pro-Chinese," as they are contemptu-
ously called in the East — assert that China is more
civilized than the modern West, even the candid Westerner,
who is imperfectly acquainted with the facts, is apt to

suspect insincere paradox. Perhaps these few notes on Tai Shan may help to make the matter clearer. A people that can so consecrate a place of natural beauty is a people of fine feeling for the essential values of life. That they should also be dirty, disorganized, corrupt, incompetent, even if it were true — and it is far from being true in any unqualified sense — would be irrelevant to this issue. On a foundation of inadequate material prosperity they reared, centuries ago, the superstructure of a great culture. The West, in rebuilding its foundations, has gone far to destroy the superstructure. Western civilization, wherever it penetrates, brings with it water-taps, sewers, and police; but it brings also an ugliness, an insincerity, a vulgarity never before known to history, unless it be under the Roman Empire. It is terrible to see in China the first wave of this Western flood flinging along the coasts and rivers and railway lines its scrofulous foam of advertisements, of corrugated iron roofs, of vulgar, meaningless architectural forms. In China, as in all old civilizations I have seen, all the building of man harmonizes with and adorns nature. In the West everything now built is a blot. Many men, I know, sincerely think that this destruction of beauty is a small matter, and that only decadent aesthetes would pay any attention to it in a world so much in need of sewers and hospitals. I believe this view to be profoundly mistaken. The ugliness of the West is a symptom of disease of the soul. It implies that the end has been lost sight of in the means. In China the opposite is the case. The end is clear, though the means be inadequate. Consider what the Chinese have done to Tai Shan, and what the West will shortly do, once the stream of Western tourists begins to flow strongly. Where the Chinese have constructed a winding stairway of stone, beautiful from all points of view, Europeans or Americans will run up a funicular railway, a staring scar that will never heal.   Where the Chinese have written poems in exquisite caligraphy, they will cover the rocks with advertisements.   Where the Chinese have built a series of temples, each so designed and placed as to be a new beauty in the landscape, they will run up restaurants and hotels like so many scabs on the face of nature.   I say with confidence that they will, because they have done it wherever there is any chance of a paying investment.   Well, the Chinese need, I agree, our science, our organization, our medicine.   But is it affectation to think they may have to pay too high a price for it, and to suggest that in acquiring our material advantages they may lose what we have gone near to lose, that fine and sensitive culture which is one of the forms of spiritual life?   The West talks of civilizing China.   Would that China could civilize the West!

WILLIAM BOLITHO

William Bolitho (Ryall) was born in 1890 *and died in June,* 1930. *In his thirty-nine years he rose, through varied and exciting experiences, from obscure poverty to a position of distinction in the literary world. Bred in South Africa, he became in turn, a stoker on a liner, a fighter at the front, a patient in a Scottish hospital (he never completely recovered from his injuries during the World War), a critic, a novelist, and a columnist for the* New York World. *In the Preface to* Camera Obscura, *Noel Coward says of Bolitho: "He died young enough to be called 'brilliant,' and not decrepit enough to be called 'great,' which is sad, because he would have enjoyed hugely that particular form of eminence, and I feel that he would have given his wreath of laurels a slightly rakish tilt, however old he was." An editor of* The Nation *(June* 18, 1930) *remarked that "no one could comment upon passing events in a fashion more sprightly than Bolitho's." The zest for living and the scorn of the commonplace which made his comments pungent are shown not only in the following essay but in his other works, among which are* Leviathan (1924), Murder for Profit (1926), *and* Twelve Against the Gods (1929).

The following essay is reprinted from Camera Obscura, *by William Bolitho, with permission of Simon and Schuster, Inc., publishers.*

WILLIAM BOLITHO

BELIEVE IT

HERE is a book,[1] like a boy born with a caul,
doomed to have strange adventures. Long
after it is sold new and net — which is, authors
forget, the least important part of a book's life — it will
drift about the world second-hand, wherever curiosity and
English occur together, turning up in forecastles of ships,
in dentists' waiting rooms, in small town auctions of small
home effects, in barracks and camps, and in temperance
hotels, where traveling salesmen are given special rates.

Wherever it is until the paper crumbles and the strings
wear out, it will automatically make the eye stop and the
hand reach out, and it will never stay in the ten-cent box
outside the used bookstore more than a day. Such books
are rare. They are a sort of currency of reading. A list
of them would be amusing to compile and meditate upon;
I should like to make one myself one day.

The real comparison of Ripley is not at all with Marco
Polo, nor with Sir John Mandeville, which several of his
friends have tried to impose on me. Traveling to him is
an accident, as it was to Herodotus, a mere supplement for
a lack of material, and his real predecessors are the great
bookworms who tunneled the dust of libraries for their
prey. The analogy is the *Anatomy of Melancholy*, Pliny's
Letters, Hone's *Books of Days*, Montaigne, the celebrated Brewer of the *Dictionary of Phrase and Fable*,
the country almanacs of Europe, and many others I could
remember if I had the time, whom, by the way, I recommend to Ripley as mines I suspect he has not yet thoroughly explored.

[1] This essay was a review of Ripley's famous book, *Believe It or Not.*

All these, no doubt, represent the learning of curiosity, and Ripley is not learned. It would be better if he were, as it would often enable him to see the full meaning of a story he has found, or round it out in its full beauty. But I would only wish it, if I were certain it would not blunt the razor edge of his curiosity. That is the main thing and in this, the most important, he is the equal of them all.

He is rightly excited to discover that "manna" is found in the branches of the tamarisk and sold in the Holy Land, where he tasted it. But he is not aware, and it is a pity, that the substance is sold in great quantities in France, where it is — and this is a sufficient reason why his surmise that one day it will be sold in American candy stores is unlikely — the normal, safe aperient for infants and old people.

The book the fantastic Gustave Leblair read daily at the Bibliothèque National in Paris all his lifetime could scarcely have been the life of Saint Apolonius of Tyana, but all the same that is a fascinating book and wonderful, which would delight Ripley's own heart. Also, believe it or not, Gambetta, the great tribune, was even more renowned for his optimistic and enthusiastic stories about himself than for his "ability to repeat all the works of Victor Hugo, word for word," let alone backward.

But I am not making a dash for the honor of the only man successfully to confute one of Ripley's items, but only unconsciously exemplifying the reaction which is one of the most delectable charms of his work on its readers. Which its very title shows that he counts on. He is not merely retailing empty wonders to make yokels gape. His research is for the very highest type of curiosity, the unbelievably true, and when he has found it (as in that sublime "Lindbergh is the 67th") he knows it by the tribute of protests. Be sure he is always waiting with his authority in his hand, like a club, at the top of the stairs.

In this way *Believe It or Not* has a rôle which far exceeds and counteracts that of many a hundred literary upliftings and smartnesses, which I am rebuked for not troubling about. Why should I give a whole column to such a trifle, when I never even acknowledge the receipt of Humbug and Hokum's account of how they think the world ought to be united for dullness? Because this one pricks the sluggish mind and coaxes the doubtful one to a true realization that the world and life are miraculous and interesting.

There never was a time when the illusion of banality was stronger. Literature and religion and even science seem to be united to promote the great illusion of ordinariness and dullness, to put us and keep us in that stupor into which our constitution makes us so liable to fall, in which nothing but the everyday is visible, nothing but the commonplace real. At any rate, in the Middle Ages heaven and hell were near, and that is infinitely more true than that they do not exist. Beginning in a marvel, ending in a marvel, living out a story full of the most outrageous surprises, hazards, shot through and through with the supernatural and the extraordinary, creatures of fire and blood and air every one, we are hypnotized to forget even that we live on a wandering planet whirling through immensity. The very quantity and magic of the instruments which the brains of a small group are shoving into our hands bemuses us, rather than elates us. All, except those who escape by being too low or too high for the gas, are stupefied into boredom. The most malignant heresy, the most idiotic falsehood, that a brick is more existent than an emotional state, than the least overtone of a poem by Shelley, is taught as *a priori*.

Ripley's little book will save you an hour or two at any rate from this life-destroying fiction. The world is ruled by law, certainly; read him and see with what wild eccentricity, what infinite good spirits, what fantastic jokes, it is administered.   Read of fate's jokes in Ripley; they will cure you of ever disbelieving in her again; read of her co-incidences and then laugh for the rest of your life at the naturalist school of fiction which has excluded them from the picture and still claims to be realistic.   This is a pamphlet for truth, for the incontrovertible truth that life is miraculous, breathless, and good to live; that anything but the dull expected is possible, and only the marvelous, predictable and sure, and inexhaustibly enough to go round.

J. B. PRIESTLEY

John Boynton Priestley, born at Bradford, England, in 1894, was educated at Trinity Hall, Cambridge. From 1914 to 1919 he served with the Duke of Wellington's and with the Devon regiment. Since that time he has devoted himself to writing, and has become eminent as essayist, critic, biographer, and novelist. He has published several volumes of essays, including Papers from Lilliput (1922), I for One (1923), *and* The Balconinny (1929). *He has shown himself a judicious and sympathetic critic in* English Comic Characters (1925), *in which he performed the difficult task of commenting wisely and amusingly upon comic characters from Falstaff to the more recent creations. As a biographer he has written studies of his own contemporaries in* Figures in Modern Literature, *and a longer life,* George Meredith, *which he contributed in 1926 to the "English Men of Letters" series. More recently he has turned to the novel, and in 1929 won wide recognition for* The Good Companions.

The following essay is reprinted from The Balconinny, *by J. B. Priestley, with the permission of the author and of Harper and Brothers, publishers.*

J. B. PRIESTLEY

THE DISILLUSIONED

IT WAS our experience at the circus last Tuesday afternoon that compelled me to reflect upon this matter. Even the children were disappointed when we actually visited the circus. For weeks we had been staring at the coloured bills, across which was pasted the startling slip: *For One Day Only*. There was the most artful crescendo of this bill-posting. Every day the children announced that they had seen new pictures of the circus and thereupon reported fresh wonders. Elephants and tigers and ponies and clowns and cowboys, all superb in the three-colour process, claimed more and more space on our hoardings, from which auctioneers and real estate agents and other dull fellows were banished. Nero and Heliogabalus themselves, if they had caught a glimpse of our hoardings, would have decided to stay on in the town.

Now I do not say that it was a bad little travelling circus, but I do say that it was certainly not the circus of the coloured bills. There were no lions and tigers at all. Instead of a whole crazy regiment of clowns, there were only two, and they were rather dingy fellows. The cowboys turned out to be the men who had first shown us our seats, and though their hats and boots undoubtedly came from the Wild West, between these extremities all three of them were too homely for our taste. Where was the long procession of elephants, each of them as big as a house? There were only two elephants and they seemed quite small after those monsters of the hoardings. "I think they must be young elephants," said one of the children. "They're awfully small, aren't they?"

I do not say that our visit was a failure. (The two younger children have been circus ponies ever since and do nothing but trot round in circles.) But I do think it would have been a far greater success if we had never seen all those lying pictures. Our hopes were raised too high, so that disappointment was inevitable. The children naturally assumed they would see in reality all that the poster artists and the printers had contrived for them. They are still puzzled about it. They invent excuses for the proprietor. The other elephants must have gone for a walk or run after the missing lions and tigers. Forty clowns or so — and those that have the nicest costumes too — must not have been feeling very well. It is almost pathetic to hear them thus excusing the cunning old fabulist. These children are growing up in a world of artful advertisement. Only the other day, one of them, who can read quite nicely, chanced to see an advertisement of some domestic commodity and cried: "Mummie, it says it's the *best* in all the world. Why don't you *buy* some?" Here was this precious stuff, the best in the world, to be had for the asking, and we were stupidly doing nothing about it. Soon she will realize that the matter was not quite so urgent as she imagined. Even now she may be thinking in secret that perhaps the man who owned the circus and put out all those false pictures of it had simply taken her in. Disillusion is already dogging her footsteps.

This is, I understand, an age of disillusion. It is also an age in which the business of suggesting that many things are perfect has become a highly organized trade or profession. I suspect that there is some connexion between these two facts. Consider our position. Men have always dreamed of perfection, but in past ages they did not think of perfection as existing at all in the ordinary world. It was always somewhere round the corner. If you could find your way into the Garden of the Hesperides, to the

Isles of the Blest, to that secret Avalon where there is
neither rain nor snow, then there you would come upon
life made perfect. If you were a poet, a dreamer, an
idealist, you found a quiet corner and thought about these
beautiful places. If your wine was sourer than usual and
your new tunic was shredding away, you shrugged your
shoulders, then remembered that in the Hesperides or
Avalon all the wine was unimaginably delicious and
tunics lasted just as long as you wanted them to last. I do
not doubt for a moment that in those days merchants con-
cocted their fables and hucksters cried up their wares most
monstrously. But there was certainly no elaborate machinery for pointing out that all manner of things were
perfect. The whole world was not told to Drink Aristides
Wine and Never Have a Headache, that Trunk Hose From
Richard Whittington's Wear For Ever. There was no
large-scale attempt to introduce the Philosopher's Stone
or the Fountain of Youth into every home. It was not
generally understood that the payment of the first instal-
ment or even the filling in of a coupon would anchor the
Isles of the Blest outside your front door.

Nowadays we do not believe that life that is all goodness,
truth, and beauty is being lived somewhere beyond the
nearest mountains or the western seas. All the en-
chanted islands have vanished. We have stopped singing
about Dixie, which I take to be one — and apparently the
last — of these ideal realms. But have we suddenly forgotten how to dream of perfection? I think not. There
is no perfect life going on round the corner, but now, surely,
it is even nearer than that. In front of me, at this moment, are two magazines, one English and the other
American, the kind with shiny paper and expensive advertisements; and in the pages at the beginning and end of
these magazines I find reports of life that has been made
perfect.

I do not know where to begin.   When I turn over these
pages I am bewildered, mazed with good news.   Reflect on
the irritations, the boredoms, the long grinding tragedies,
of this life of ours.   Be brave for a moment and remember
the dismal antics of our bodies; our fatty tissues and acids
in the stomach, our gout and dyspepsia and startling blood
pressures, our failing sight and thinning hair and rotting
teeth.   Keep steadily in mind the days when you have not
been able to entertain yourself and the nights when you
have not been able even to entertain your friends.   Think
how we suffer from clothes that do not fit, boots that wear
out, raincoats that drink like sponges, tobacco that burns
the tongue, whiskey that is new and raw, cars that will
not take hills in top-gear, mattresses that do nothing but
sag, and trains that are always late.   All these, from the
huge miseries that come crashing into our lives like a
rhinoceros to the little irritations that bite like mosquitoes,
have disappeared.   The people here know nothing about
them.   They are as gods.   Look at the women — seven foot
tall, beautifully slender, exquisitely gowned and hatted,
their hair so cunningly and crisply waved!   Look at the
men — so ruddy of cheek and bright of eye, so broad and
square in the shoulders, so astonishingly tailored and
laundered!   What domestic felicity they enjoy!   "Welcome
home!" they cry, for ever smiling and holding out their
arms.

Examine the children — they are called "Kiddies" here—
and notice their apple-cheeks, their sturdy limbs, their play-
fulness that never, never turns into naughtiness, into
stamping and screaming.   In winter they sit in front of
bright fires (Coal, Gas, Electric) and listen happily to the
World's Masterpieces of Music; they recline in chairs so
marvellously sprung that they would never get up out of
them if they did not know that upstairs were the most
comfortable mattresses ever offered to the public and in-

stant sleep induced by a cup of Whatisit. In summer they sprawl on gamboge sands by the side of a royal blue sea, in perpetual sunshine, and have to hand pipes that will not crack, the aristocrat of cigarettes, bottles of elixir (various brands); and the men look more god-like than ever, partly because their hair has been fixed for the day by a little cream; the women, fully protected against sun-burn, are dazzlingly beautiful and gracious; and the kiddies, well stuffed with a miraculous breakfast food, are growing an inch a day — and all their clothes are growing with them. (Even the suitcases are quietly expanding in the box-room.) And winter or summer, their watches never go wrong and their shoes never pinch; they never worry or mope or quarrel; they never sicken and die. And this, we are told, is not Avalon but our own world.

Alas! we are for ever discovering that it is not our own world, that try as we may — sending off at once, refusing all imitations, filling in coupons, paying first instalments — we cannot reproduce the life of these people in the advertisements. There is always a catch. We are always being taken in. There are only two clowns and two elephants. Thus, living in an age of advertisement, we are perpetually disillusioned. The perfect life is spread before us every day, but it changes and withers at a touch — never a Snark, always a Boojum.

GEORGE MACAULAY TREVELYAN

Born of a distinguished family, in 1876, *George Macaulay Trevelyan received his formal education at Harrow and at Trinity College, Cambridge. Among other duties during the World War he served as Commandant of the First British Ambulance Unit for Italy, and was twice decorated. Returning to civil life, he devoted himself to historical study and teaching, and has been, since* 1927, *Regius Professor of Modern History at Cambridge University. His eminence in his own profession has been won not only by his accurate research, but by his extraordinarily lucid and brilliant style. There is no space here to record the numerous learned societies to which he belongs or the honorary degrees which he holds. His* England Under the Stuarts (1904), British History in the Nineteenth Century (1922), *and* England Under Queen Anne (1930) *are examples of his treatment of special periods; his* History of England (1926) *shows his command of the whole field. According to recent American critics, it combines "scholarship, readability, a unified point of view, and a happy familiarity with the literature." * Garibaldi and the Thousand (1909) *shows that he is equally well versed in modern Italian history. In* Who's Who, *Professor Trevelyan lists, as his recreation, cross country walking. That this is no idle claim will be made evident to every reader.*

The following essay is reprinted from Clio, A Muse, *by G. M. Trevelyan, with permission of Longmans, Green and Company, publishers.*

GEORGE MACAULAY TREVELYAN

WALKING

Wind of the morning, wind of the gloaming, wind of the night,
What is it that you whisper to the moor
All the day long and every day and year,
Resting and whispering, rustling and whispering, hastening and
    whispering
Around, across, beneath
The tufts and hollows of the listening heath?

GEOFFREY YOUNG, Wind and Hills

La chose que je regrette le plus, dans les détails de ma vie
dont j'ai perdu la mémoire, est de n'avoir pas fait des journaux
de mes voyages. Jamais je n'ai tant pensé, tant existé, tant
vécu, tant été moi, si j'ose ainsi dire, que dans ceux que j'ai faits
seul et à pied.[1] ROUSSEAU, *Confessions*, I, IV.

When you have made an early start, followed the coastguard
track on the slopes above the cliffs, struggled through the gold
and purple carpeting of gorse and heather on the moors, dipped
down into quaint little coves with a primitive fishing village,
followed the blinding whiteness of the sands round a lonely bay,
and at last emerged upon a headland where you can settle in
a nook of the rocks, look down upon the glorious blue of the
Atlantic waves breaking into foam on the granite, and see the
distant sea-levels glimmering away until they blend imperceptibly
into cloudland; then you can consume your modest sandwiches,
light your pipe, and feel more virtuous and thoroughly at peace
with the universe than it is easy even to conceive yourself elsewhere. I have fancied myself on such occasions a felicitous blend
of poet and saint — which is an agreeable sensation. What
I wish to point out, however, is that the sensation is confined
to the walker. — LESLIE STEPHEN, *In Praise of Walking.*

---

[1] "What I most regret, in the details of my life which I have forgotten, is that I did not keep a journal of my travels. Never have I thought
so much, existed so much, lived so much, been so much myself, if I may
venture to say so, as on those journeys which I took alone and on foot."

I HAVE two doctors, my left leg and my right. When body and mind are out of gear (and those twin parts of me live at such close quarters that the one always catches melancholy from the other) I know that I have only to call in my doctors and I shall be well again.

Mr Arnold Bennett has written a religious tract called *The Human Machine*. Philosophers and clergymen are always discussing why we should be good — as if anyone doubted that he ought to be. But Mr Bennett has tackled the real problem of ethics and religion — how we can make ourselves be good. We all of us know that we ought to be cheerful to ourselves and kind to others, but cheerfulness is often and kindness sometimes as unattainable as sleep in a white night. That combination of mind and body which I call my soul is often so choked up with bad thoughts or useless worries that

"Books and my food, and summer rain,
    Knock on my sullen heart in vain."

It is then that I call on my two doctors to carry me off for the day.

Mr Bennett's recipe for the blue devils is different. He proposes a course of mental "Swedish exercises" to develop by force of will the habit of "concentrating thought" away from useless angers and obsessions and directing it into clearer channels. This is good, and I hope that everyone will read and practise Mr Bennett's precepts. It is good, but it is not all. For there are times when my thoughts, having been duly concentrated on the right spot, refuse to fire, and will think nothing except general misery; and such times, I suppose, are known to all of us.

On these occasions my recipe is to go for a long walk. My thoughts start out with me like bloodstained mutineers debauching themselves on board a ship they have captured, but I bring them home at nightfall, larking and tumbling over each other like happy little Boy Scouts at play, yet obedient to every order to "concentrate" for any purpose Mr Bennett or I may wish.

"A Sunday well spent
Means a week of content."

That is, of course, a Sunday spent with both legs swinging all day over ground where grass or heather grows. I have often known the righteous forsaken and his seed begging for bread, but I never knew a man go for an honest day's walk, for whatever distance, great or small, his pair of compasses could measure out in the time, and not have his reward in the repossession of his own soul.

In this medicinal use of Walking as the Sabbath-day refection of the tired town worker, companionship is good, and the more friends who join us on the tramp the merrier. For there is not time, as there is on the longer holiday or walking tour, for body and mind to attain that point of training when the higher ecstasies of Walking are felt through the whole being, those joys that crave silence and solitude. And, indeed, on these humbler occasions the first half of the day's walk, before the Human Machine has recovered its tone, may be dreary enough without the laughter of good company, ringing round the interchange of genial and irresponsible verdicts on the topics of the day. For this reason, informal Walking societies should be formed among friends in towns, for week-end or Sabbath walks in the neighboring country. I never get better talk than in these moving Parliaments, and good talk is itself something.

But here I am reminded of a shrewd criticism directed against such talking patrols by a good walker, who has written a book on walking.[1] "In such a case," writes Mr Sidgwick — "in such a case walking goes by the board;

[1] Sidgwick, *Walking Essays*, pp. 10-11. (Author's note.)

the company either loiters and trails in clenched contro-
versy, or, what is worse sacrilege, strides blindly across
country like a herd of animals, recking little of whence
they come or whither they are going, desecrating the face
of nature with sophism and inference and authority, and
regurgitating Blue Book. At the end of such a day, what
have they profited? Their gross and perishable physical
frames may have been refreshed: their less gross but
equally perishable minds may have been exercised: but
what of their immortal being? It has been starved between the blind swing of legs below and the fruitless flickering of the mind above, instead of receiving, through the
agency of quiet mind and a co-ordinated body, the gentle
nutriment which is its due."

Now this passage shows that the author thoroughly
understands the high, ultimate end of Walking, which is
indeed something other than to promote talk. But he
does not make due allowance for times, seasons and circumstances. You cannot do much with your "immortal
soul" in a day's walk in Surrey between one fortnight's
work in London and the next; if "body" can be "refreshed" and "mind exercised," it is as much as can be
hoped for. The perfection of Walking, such as Mr Sidgwick describes in the last sentence quoted, requires longer
time, more perfect training, and, for some of us at least, a
different kind of scenery. Meanwhile let us have good
talk as we tramp the lanes.

Nursery lore tells us that "Charles I. walked and talked:
half-an-hour after his head was cut off." Mr Sidgwick
evidently thinks that it was a case not merely of *post hoc*
but *propter hoc*, an example of summary but just punishment. Yet, if I read Cromwell aright, he no less than his
royal victim would have talked as he walked. And Cromwell reminds me of Carlyle, who carried the art of "walking and talking" to perfection as one of the highest of

human functions. Who does not remember his description of "the sunny summer afternoon" when he and Irving "walked and talked a good sixteen miles"? Those
who have gone walks with Carlyle tell us that then most of
all the fire kindled. And because he talked well when he
walked with others, he felt and thought all the more when
he walked alone, "given up to his bits of reflections in the
silence of the moors and the hills." He was alone when
he walked his fifty-four miles in the day, from Muirkirk
to Dumfries, "the longest walk I ever made," he tells us.
Carlyle is in every sense a patron saint of Walking, and
his vote is emphatically given *not* for the "gospel of
silence"!

Though I demand silent walking less, I desire solitary
walking more than Mr Sidgwick. Silence is not enough; I
must have solitude for the perfect walk, which is very
different from the Sunday tramp. When you are really
walking,[1] the presence of a companion, involving such
irksome considerations as whether the pace suits him,
whether he wishes to go up by the rocks or down by the
burn, still more the haunting fear that he may begin to
talk, disturbs the harmony of body, mind and soul when
they stride along no longer conscious of their separate,
jarring entities, made one together in mystic union with
the earth, with the hills that still beckon, with the sunset
that still shows the tufted moor under foot, with old darkness and its stars that take you to their breast with rapture
when the hard ringing of heels proclaims that you have
struck the final road.

Yet even in such high hours a companion may be good,
if you like him well, if you know that he likes you and the
pace, and that he shares your ecstasy of body and mind.
Even as I write, memories are whispering at my ear how

[1] Is there the same sort of difference between *tramping* and *walking* as
between *paddling* and *rowing*, *scrambling* and *climbing*? (Author's note.)

disloyal I am thus to proclaim only solitary walks as perfect. There comes back to me an evening at the end of a
stubborn day, when, full of miles and wine, we two were
striding towards San Marino over the crest of a high lime-
stone moor — trodden of old by better men in more desperate mood — one of us stripped to the waist, the warm
rain falling on our heads and shoulders, our minds become
mere instruments to register the goodness and harmony of
things, our bodies an animated part of the earth we trod.

And again, from out of the depth of days and nights
gone by and forgotten, I have a vision, not forgettable, of
making the steep ascent to Volterra, for the first time,
under the circling of the stars; the smell of unseen almond
blossom in the air; the lights of Italy far below us; ancient
Tuscany just above us, where we were to sup and sleep,
guarded by the giant walls. Few went to Volterra then;
but years have passed, and now I am glad to think that
many go, *faute de mieux*, in motor-cars; yet so they cannot
hear the silence we heard, or smell the almond blossom we
smelt, or if they did they could not feel them as the walker
can feel. On that night was companionship dear to my
heart, as also on the evening when together we lifted the
view of ancient Trasimene, being full of the wine of Papal
Pienza and striding on to a supper washed down by Monte
Pulciano, itself drawn straight from its native cellars.

Be not shocked, temperate reader! In Italy wine is not
a luxury of doubtful omen, but a necessary part of that
good country's food. And if you have walked twenty-five
miles and are going on again afterwards, you can imbibe
Falstaffian potions and still be as lithe and ready for the
field as Prince Hal at Shrewsbury. Remember also that
in the Latin village tea is in default. And how could you
walk the last ten miles without tea? By a providential
ordering wine in Italy is like tea in England, recuperative
and innocent of later reaction. Then, too, there are wines

in remote Tuscan villages that a cardinal might envy, wines which travel not, but century after century pour forth their nectar for a little clan of peasants, and for any wise English youth who knows that Italy is to be found scarcely in her picture galleries and not at all in her cosmopolite hotels.

Central Italy is a paradise for the walker. I mean the district between Rome and Bologna, Pisa and Ancona, with Perugia for its headquarters, the place where so many of the walking tours of Umbria, Tuscany and the Marches can be ended or begun.[1] The "olive-sandalled Apennine" is a land always of great views, and at frequent intervals of enchanting detail. It is a land of hills and mountains, unenclosed, open in all directions to the wanderer at will, unlike some British mountain game-preserves. And, even in the plains, the peasant, unlike some south-English farmers, never orders you off his ground, not even out of his olive grove or vineyard. Only the vineyards in the suburbs of large towns are concealed, reasonably enough, between high white walls. The peasants are kind and generous to the wayfarer. I walked alone in those parts with great success before I knew more than twenty words of Italian. The pleasure of losing your way on those hills leads to a push over broken ground to a glimmer of light that proves to come from some lonely farmstead, with the family gathered round the burning brands, in honest, cheerful poverty. They will, without bargain or demur, gladly show you the way across the brushwood moor, till the lights of Gubbio are seen beckoning down in the valley beneath. And Italian towns when you enter them, though it be at midnight, are still half

---

[1] The ordnance maps of Italy can be obtained by previous order at London geographers, time allowed, or else bought in Milan or Rome — and sometimes it is possible to get the local ordnance maps in smaller towns. (Author's note.)

awake, and everyone volunteers in the search to find you bed and board.

April and May are the best walking months for Italy. Carry water in a flask, for it is sometimes ten miles from one well to the next that you may chance to find. A siesta in the shade for three or four hours in the midday heat, to the tune of cicada and nightingale, is not the least part of all; and that means early starting and night walking at the end, both very good things. The stars out there rule the sky more than in England, big and lustrous with the honor of having shone upon the ancients and been named by them. On Italian mountain-tops we stand on naked, pagan earth, under the heaven of Lucretius:

"Luna, dies, et nox, et noctis signa severa." [1]

The chorus-ending from Aristophanes' *Frogs*, raised every night from every ditch that drains into the Mediterranean, hoarse and primæval as the raven's croak, is one of the greatest tunes to march by. Or on a night in May one can walk through the too rare Italian forests for an hour on end and never be out of hearing of the nightingale's song.

Once in every man's youth there comes the hour when he must learn, what no one ever yet believed save on the authority of his own experience, that the world was not created to make him happy. In such cases, as in that of Teufelsdröckh, grim Walking's the rule. Every man must once at least in life have the great vision of Earth as Hell. Then, while his soul within him is molten lava that will take some lifelong shape of good or bad when it cools, let him set out and walk, whatever the weather, wherever he is, be it in the depths of London, and let him walk grimly, well if it is by night, to avoid the vulgar sights and

[1] The moon, the day, the night, and the austere symbols of night.

faces of men, appearing to him in his then dæmonic mood, as base beyond all endurance. Let him walk until his flesh curse his spirit for driving it on, and his spirit spend its rage on his flesh in forcing it still pitilessly to sway the legs. Then the fire within him will not turn to soot and choke him, as it chokes those who linger at home with their grief, motionless, between four mean, lifeless walls. The stricken one who has, more wisely, taken to road and field, as he plies his solitary pilgrimage day after day, finds that he has with him a companion with whom he is not ashamed to share his grief, even the Earth he treads, his mother who bore him. At the close of a well-trodden day grief can have strange visions and find mysterious comforts. Hastening at droop of dusk through some remote by-way never to be found again, a man has known a row of ancient trees nodding over a high stone wall above a bank of wet earth, bending down their sighing branches to him as he hastened past for ever, to whisper that the place knew it all centuries ago, and had always been waiting for him to come by, even thus, for one minute in the night.

Be grief or joy the companion, in youth and in middle age, it is only at the end of a long and solitary day's walk that I have had strange, casual moments of mere sight and feeling more vivid and less forgotten than the human events of life, moments like those that Wordsworth has described as his common companions in boyhood, like that night when he was rowing on Esthwaite, and that day when he was nutting in the woods. These come to me only after five-and-twenty miles. To Wordsworth they came more easily, together with the power of expressing them in words! Yet even his vision and power were closely connected with his long daily walks. De Quincey tells us: "I calculate, upon good data, that with these identical legs Wordsworth must have traversed a distance of 175,000 or 180,000 English miles, a mode of exertion which to him stood in the stead of alcohol and all stimulants whatsoever to the animal spirits; to which, indeed, he was indebted for a life of unclouded happiness, and we for much of what is most excellent in his writings."

There are many schools of Walking and none of them orthodox. One school is that of the road-walkers, the Puritans of the religion. A strain of fine ascetic rigor is in these men, yet they number among them at least two poets.[1] Stevenson is *par excellence* their bard:

"Boldly he sings, to the merry tune he marches." It is strange that Edward Bowen, who wrote the Harrow songs, left no walking song, though he himself was the king of the roads. Bowen kept at home what he used to call his "road-map," an index outline of the ordnance survey of our island, ten miles to the inch, on which he marked his walks in red ink. It was the chief pride of his life to cover every part of the map with those red spider-webs. With this end in view he sought new ground every holiday, and walked not merely in chosen hill and coast districts, but over Britain's dullest plains. He generally kept to the roads, partly in order to cover more ground, partly, I

[1] Of the innumerable poets who were walkers we know too little to judge how many of them were *road*-walkers. Shakespeare, one gathers, preferred the foot-path way with stiles to either the highroad or the moor. Wordsworth preferred the lower fell tracks, above the highroads and below the tops of the hills. Shelley we can only conceive of as bursting over or through all obstacles cross-country; we know he used to roam at large over Shotover and in the Pisan forest. Coleridge is known to have walked alone over Scafell, but he also seems to have experienced after his own fashion the sensations of night-walking on roads:

"Like one that on a lonesome road
    Doth walk in fear and dread,
And having once turned round walks on
    And turns no more his head;
Because he knows a frightful fiend
    Doth close behind him tread."

There is a "personal" note in that! Keats, Matthew Arnold and Meredith, there is evidence, were "mixed" walkers — on and off the road. (Author's note.)

suppose, from preference for the free and steady sway of leg over level surface which attracts Stevenson and all devotees of the road. He told me that twenty-five miles was the least possible distance even for a slack day. He was certainly one of the Ironsides.

To my thinking, the road-walkers have grasped one part of the truth. The road is invaluable for pace and swing, and the ideal walk permits or even requires a smooth surface for some considerable portion of the way. On other terms it is hard to cover a respectable distance, and the change of tactile values underfoot is agreeable.

But more than that I will not concede; twenty-five or thirty miles of moor and mountain, of wood and field-path, is better in every way than five-and-thirty, or even forty, hammered out on the road. Early in life, no doubt, a man will test himself at pace Walking, and then of course the road must be kept. Every aspiring Cantab and Oxonian ought to walk to the Marble Arch at a pace that will do credit to the college whence he starts at break of day: [1] the wisdom of our ancestors, surely not by an accident, fixed those two seats of learning each at the same distance from London, and at exactly the right distance for a test walk. And there is a harder test than that: if a man can walk the eighty miles from St Mary Oxon to St Mary Cantab in the twenty-four hours, he wins his place with Bowen and a very few more.

But it is a great mistake to apply the rules of such test Walking on roads to the case of ordinary Walking. The secret beauties of nature are unveiled only to the cross-country walker. Pan could not have appeared to Pheidippides on a road. On the road we never meet the "moving accidents by flood and field": the sudden glory of a woodland glade; the open back-door of the old farmhouse se-

[1] Start at five from Cambridge, and have a second breakfast ordered beforehand at Royston to be ready at eight. (Author's note.)

questered deep in rural solitude; the cow routed up from
meditation behind the stone wall as we scale it suddenly;
the deep, slow, south-country stream that we must jump,
or wander along to find the bridge; the northern torrent of
molten peat-hag that we must ford up to the waist, to
scramble, glowing warm-cold up the farther foxglove bank;
the autumnal dew on the bracken and the blue straight
smoke of the cottage in the still glen at dawn; the rush
down the mountain-side, hair flying, stones and grouse
rising at our feet; and at the bottom the plunge in the pool
below the waterfall, in a place so fair that kings should
come from far to bathe therein — yet is it left, year in
year out, unvisited save by us and "troops of stars."
These, and a thousand other blessed chances of the day,
are the heart of Walking, and these are not of the road.

Yet the hard road plays a part in every good walk, generally at the beginning and at the end.   Nor must we forget the "soft" road, mediating as it were between his hard
artificial brother and wild surrounding nature.   The broad
grass lanes of the low country, relics of mediæval wayfar-
ing; the green, unfenced moorland road; the derelict road
already half gone back to pasture; the common farm track
— these and all their kind are a blessing to the walker, to
be diligently sought out by help of map [1] and used as long
as may be.   For they unite the speed and smooth surface
of the harder road, with much at least of the softness to
the foot, the romance and the beauty of cross-country
routes.

It is well to seek as much variety as is possible in twelve
hours.   Road and track, field and wood, mountain, hill
and plain should follow each other in shifting vision.   The
finest poem on the effects of variation in the day's walk is

---

[1] Compass and colored half-inch Bartholomew is the walker's *vade.
mecum* in the north; the one-inch ordnance is more desirable for the more
enclosed and less hilly south of England.   (Author's note.)

George Meredith's *The Orchard and the Heath.* Some kinds of country are in themselves a combination of different delights, as for example the sub-Lake district, which walkers often see in Pisgah view from Bowfell or the Old Man, but too seldom traverse. It is a land sounding with streams from the higher mountains, itself composed of little hills and tiny plains covered half by hazel woods and heather moors, half by pasture and cornfields; and in the middle of the fields rise lesser islands of rocks and patches of the northern jungle still uncleared. The districts along the foot of mountain ranges are often the most varied in feature, and therefore the best for Walking.

Variety, too, can be obtained by losing the way — a half-conscious process, which in a sense can no more be done of deliberate purpose than falling in love. And yet a man can sometimes very wisely let himself drift, either into love, or into the wrong path out walking. There is a joyous mystery in roaming on, reckless where you are, into what valley, road or farm chance and the hour is guiding you. If the place is lonely and beautiful, and if you have lost all count of it upon the map, it may seem a fairy glen, a lost piece of old England that no surveyor would find though he searched for it a year. I scarcely know whether most to value this quality of aloofness and magic in country I have never seen before, and may never see again, or the familiar joys of Walking grounds where every tree and rock are rooted in the memories that make up my life.

Places where the fairies may still dwell lie for the most part west of Avon. Except the industrial plain of Lancashire, the whole west, from Cornwall to Carlisle, is, when compared to the east of our island, more hilly, more variegated, and more thickly strewn with old houses and scenes, unchanged since Tudor times. The Welsh border, on both sides of it, is good ground. If you would walk away for a while out of modern England, back and away for twice two hundred years, arrange so that a long day's tramp may drop you at nightfall off the Black Mountain on to the inn that nestles in the ruined tower of old Llanthony.   Then go on through

> "Clunton and Clunbury, Clungunford and Clun,
> The quietest places under the sun,"

still sleeping their Saxon sleep with one drowsy eye open for the "wild Welsh" on the "barren mountains" above. Follow more or less the line of Offa's Dyke, which passes, a disregarded bank, through the remotest loveliness of the gorse-covered down and thick, trailing vegetation of the valley bottoms.   Or, if you are more leisurely, stay a week at Wigmore till you know the country round by heart.   You will carry away much, among other things considerable scepticism as to the famous sentence at the beginning of the third chapter of Macaulay's *History*: "Could the England of 1685 be, by some magical process, set before our eyes, we should not know one landscape in a hundred, or one building in ten thousand."   It is doubtful even now, and I suspect that it was a manifest exaggeration when it was written two generations ago.   But Macaulay was not much of a walker across country.[1]

One time with another I have walked twice at least round the coast of Devon and Cornwall, following for the most part the track along the cliff.   The joys of this method of proceeding have been celebrated by Leslie Stephen in the paragraph quoted at the head of this essay. But I note that he used to walk there in the summer, when the heather was "purple."   I prefer Easter for that region, because when spring comes to deliver our island, like the Prince of Orange, he lands first in the south-west. That is when the gorse first smells warm on the cliff-top. Then, too, is the season of daffodils and primroses, which

[1] Like Shelley, he used to *read* as he walked.   I do not think Mr Sidgwick would permit that!   (Author's note.)

are as native to the creeks of Devon and Cornwall as the scalded cream itself. When the heather is "purple" I will look for it elsewhere.

If the walker seeks variety of bodily motion, other than the run down hill, let him scramble. Scrambling is an integral part of Walking, when the high ground is kept all day in a mountain region. To know and love the texture of rocks we should cling to them; and when mountain-ash or holly, or even the gnarled heather root, has helped us at a pinch, we are thenceforth on terms of affection with all their kind. No one knows how sun and water can make a steep bank of moss smell all ambrosia until he has dug foot, fingers and face into it in earnest. And you must learn to haul yourself up a rock before you can visit those fern-clad inmost secret places where the Spirit of the Gully dwells.

It may be argued that scrambling and its elder brother climbing are the essence of Walking made perfect. I am not a climber and cannot judge. But I acknowledge in a climber the one person who, upon the whole, has not good reason to envy the walker. On the other hand, those stalwart Britons who, for their country's good, shut themselves up in one flat field all day and play there, surrounded by ropes and a crowd, may keep themselves well and happy, but they are divorced from nature. Shooting does well when it draws out into the heart of nature those who could not otherwise be induced to go there. But shooters may be asked to remember that the moors give as much health and pleasure to others who do not carry guns. They may, by the effort of a very little imagination, perceive that it is not well to instruct their game-keepers to turn every one off the most beautiful grounds in Britain on those three hundred and fifty days in the year when they themselves are not shooting. Their actual sport should not be disturbed, but there is no sufficient reason for this dog-in-the-manger policy when they are not using the moors. The closing of moors is a bad habit that is spreading in some places though I hope it is disappearing in others. It is extraordinary that a man not otherwise selfish should prohibit the pleasures of those who delight in the moors for their own sakes, on the offchance that he and his guests may kill another stag, or a dozen more grouse in the year. And in most cases an occasional party on the moor makes no difference to the grouse at all. The Highlands have very largely ceased to belong to Britain on account of the deer, and we are in danger of losing the grouse moors as well. If the Alps were British they would long ago have been closed on account of the chamois.

The energetic walker can of course in many cases despise notice-boards and avoid gamekeepers on the moors, but I put in this plea in behalf of the majority of holiday-makers, including women and children. One would have thought that mountains as well as seas were a common pleasure ground. But let us register our thanks to the many who do not close their moors.

And the walker, on his side, has his social duties. He must be careful not to leave gates open, not to break fences, not to walk through hay or crops, and not to be rude to farmers. In the interview always try to turn away wrath, and in most cases you will succeed.

A second duty is to burn or bury the fragments that remain from lunch. To find the neighbourhood of a stream-head, on some well-known walking route like Scafell, littered with soaked paper and the relics of the feast is disgusting to the next party. And this brief act of reverence should never be neglected, even in the most retired nooks of the world. For all nature is sacred, and in England there is none too much of it.

Thirdly, though we should trespass we should trespass only so as to temper law with equity. Private gardens

and the immediate neighbourhood of inhabited houses must
be avoided, or crossed only when there is no fear of being
seen. All rules may be thus summed up: "Give no man,
woman or child reason to complain of your passage."

If I have praised wine in Italy, by how much more shall
I praise tea in England! — the charmed cup that prolongs
the pleasure of the walk and its actual distance by the last,
best spell of miles. Before modern times there was Walking, but not the perfection of Walking, because there was
no tea. They of old time said, "The traveller hasteth
towards evening," but it was then from fear of robbers and
the dark, not from the joy of glad living, as with us who
swing down the darkling road refreshed by tea. When
they reached the forest of Arden, Rosalind's spirits and
Touchstone's legs were weary — but if only Corin could
have produced a pot of tea they would have walked on
singing till they found the Duke at dinner. In that scene
Shakespeare put his unerring finger fine upon the want of
his age — tea for walkers at evening.

Tea is not a native product, but it has become our native drink, procured by our English energy at seafaring
and trading, to cheer us with the sober courage that fits us
best. No, let the swart Italian crush his grape! But
grant to me, ye Muses, for heart's ease, at four o'clock or
five, wasp-waisted with hunger and faint with long four
miles an hour, to enter the open door of a lane-side inn and
ask the jolly hostess if she can give me three boiled eggs
with my tea — and let her answer "yes." Then for an
hour's perfect rest and recovery, while I draw from my
pocket some small, well-thumbed volume, discoloured by
many rains and rivers, so that some familiar, immortal
spirit may sit beside me at the board. There is true luxury of mind and body! Then on again into the night if it
be winter, or into the dusk falling or still but threatened —
joyful, a man remade.

Then is the best yet to come, when the walk is carried on into the night, or into the long, silent, twilight hours which in the northern summer stand in night's place. Whether I am alone or with one fit companion, then most is the quiet soul awake; for then the body, drugged with sheer health, is felt only as a part of the physical nature that surrounds it and to which it is indeed akin; while the mind's sole function is to be conscious of calm delight. Such hours are described in Meredith's *Night Walk*:

> "A pride of legs in motion kept
> Our spirits to the task meanwhile,
> And what was deepest dreaming slept:
> The posts that named the swallowed mile;
> Beside the straight canal the hut
> Abandoned; near the river's source
> Its infant chirp; the shortest cut;
> The roadway missed were our discourse;
> At times dear poets, when some view
> Transcendent or subdued evoked...
> *But most the silences were sweet!*"

Indeed the only reason, other than weakness of the flesh, for not always walking until late at night, is the joy of making a leisurely occupation of the hamlet that chance or whim has selected for the night's rest. There is much merit in the stroll after supper, hanging contemplative at sunset over the little bridge, feeling at one equally with the geese there on the common and with the high gods at rest on Olympus. After a day's walk everything has twice its usual value. Food and drink become subjects for epic celebration, worthy of the treatment Homer gave them. Greed is sanctified by hunger and health. And as with food, so with books. Never start on a walking tour without an author whom you love. It is criminal folly to waste your too rare hours of perfect receptiveness on the magazines you may find cumbering the inn. No one, indeed, wants to read much after a long walk; but for a few

minutes, at supper or after it, you may be in the seventh
heaven with a scene of *Henry IV*, a chapter of Carlyle, a
dozen "Nay, Sirs" of Dr Johnson, or your own chosen
novelist. Their wit and poetry acquire all the richness of
your then condition, and that evening they surpass even
their own gracious selves. Then, putting the volume in
your pocket, go out, and godlike watch the geese.

On the same principle it is good to take a whole day off
in the middle of a walking tour. It is easy to get stale, yet
it is a pity to shorten a good walk for fear of being tired
next day. One day off in a well-chosen hamlet, in the
middle of a week's "hard," is often both necessary to the
pleasure of the next three days, and good in itself in the
same kind of excellence as that of the evening just described. All day long, as we lie *perdu* in wood or field, we
have perfect laziness and perfect health. The body is
asleep like a healthy infant — or, if it must be doing for
one hour of the blessed day, let it scramble a little; while
the powers of mind and soul are at their topmost strength
and yet are not put forth, save intermittently and casually, like a careless giant's hand. Our modern life requires
such days of "anti-worry," and they are only to be obtained in perfection when the body has been walked to a
standstill.

George Meredith once said to me that we should "love
all changes of weather." That is a true word for walkers.
Change in weather should be made as welcome as change in
scenery. "Thrice blessed is our sunshine after rain." I
love the stillness of dawn, and of noon, and of evening, but
I love no less the "winds austere and pure." The fight
against fiercer wind and snowstorm is among the higher
joys of Walking, and produces in shortest time the state
of ecstasy. Meredith himself has described once for all in
The Egoist the delight of Walking soaked through by rain.
Still more, in mist upon the mountains to keep the way,

or to lose and find it, is one of the great primæval games, though now we play it with map and compass. But do not, in mountain mist, "lose the way" on purpose, as I have recommended to vary the monotony of less exciting walks. I once had eight days' walking alone in the Pyrenees, and on only one half-day saw heaven or earth. Yet I enjoyed that week in the mist, for I was kept hard at work finding the unseen way through pine forest and gurgling alp, every bit of instinct and hill knowledge on the stretch. And that one half-day of sunlight, how I treasured it! When we see the mists sweeping up to play with us as we walk mountain crests we should "rejoice," as it was the custom of Cromwell's soldiers to do when they saw the enemy. Listen while you can to the roar of waters from behind the great grey curtain, and look at the torrent at your feet tumbling the rocks down gully and glen, for there will be no such sights and sounds when the mists are withdrawn into their lairs, and the mountain, no longer a giant half seen through clefts of scudding cloud, stands there, from scree-foot to cairn, dwarfed and betrayed by the sun. So let us "love all changes of weather."

I have now set down my own experiences and likings. Let no one be alarmed or angry because his ideas of Walking are different. There is no orthodoxy in Walking. It is a land of many paths and no-paths, where everyone goes his own way and is right.

MAX BEERBOHM

Max Beerbohm was born in London in 1872, and educated at Charterhouse and at Merton College, Oxford. He contributed essays in *"the gay nineties" to* The Yellow Book; *his first volume of essays* (1896) *he entitled* Works of Max Beerbohm *with apparent, but deceptive solemnity.* Hence, *succeeding volumes have been named* More (1899), Yet Again (1909), And Even Now (1920). *In 1898 he accepted the exceedingly difficult task of following George Bernard Shaw as dramatic critic for* The Saturday Review. *The fact that he held the position for twelve years speaks for itself.* In 1911 he *published* Zuleika Dobson; or, An Oxford Love Story. *To describe in a few words this satiric, fantastic, and bewildering novel would be almost beyond the powers of Mr. Beerbohm himself.* His *extraordinary skill as a parodist was shown in* A Christmas Garland (1912). *In several volumes of caricatures he has shown the same exquisite sense of the ridiculous, with the cartoonist's flair for puncturing pomposity wherever shown.* Mr. Osbert Burdett, in The Beardsley Period, *says of Beerbohm's writing: "The style is as fastidious as Whistler's own, and the effects depend more on the manner than the subject."* It is a comment which holds as true for the caricaturist as for the essayist.

The two following essays are taken from And Even Now, *by Max Beerbohm, published by E. P. Dutton and Company, New York., with permission of the publishers.*

MAX BEERBOHM

GOING OUT FOR A WALK

IT IS a fact that not once in all my life have I gone out
for a walk. I have been taken out for walks; but that
is another matter. Even while I trotted prattling by
my nurse's side I regretted the good old days when I had,
and wasn't, a perambulator. When I grew up it seemed
to me that the one advantage of living in London was that
nobody ever wanted me to come out for a walk. London's
very drawbacks — its endless noise and hustle, its smoky
air, the squalor ambushed everywhere in it — assured this
one immunity. Whenever I was with friends in the country, I knew that at any moment, unless rain were actually
falling, some man might suddenly say "Come out for a
walk!" in that sharp imperative tone which he would not
dream of using in any other connexion. People seem to
think there is something inherently noble and virtuous in
the desire to go for a walk. Anyone thus desirous feels
that he has a right to impose his will on whomever he sees
comfortably settled in an armchair, reading. It is easy to
say simply "No" to an old friend. In the case of a mere
acquaintance one wants some excuse. "I wish I could,
but" — nothing ever occurs to me except "I have some
letters to write." This formula is unsatisfactory in three
ways. (1) It isn't believed. (2) It compels you to rise
from your chair, go to the writing-table, and sit improvis-
ing a letter to somebody until the walkmonger (just not
daring to call you liar and hypocrite) shall have lumbered
out of the room. (3) It won't operate on Sunday morn-
ings. "There's no post out till this evening" clinches the
matter; and you may as well go quietly.

Walking for walking's sake may be as highly laudable and exemplary a thing as it is held to be by those who practise it. My objection to it is that it stops the brain. Many a man has professed to me that his brain never works so well as when he is swinging along the high road or over hill and dale. This boast is not confirmed by my memory of anybody who on a Sunday morning has forced me to partake of his adventure. Experience teaches me that whatever a fellow-guest may have of power to instruct or to amuse when he is sitting on a chair, or standing on a hearth-rug, quickly leaves him when he takes one out for a walk. The ideas that came so thick and fast to him in any room, where are they now? where that encyclopædic knowledge which he bore so lightly? where the kindling fancy that played like summer lightning over *any* topic that was started? The man's face that was so mobile is set now; gone is the light from his fine eyes. He says that A. (our host) is a thoroughly good fellow. Fifty yards further on, he adds that A. is one of the best fellows he has ever met. We tramp another furlong or so, and he says that Mrs. A. is a charming woman. Presently he adds that she is one of the most charming women he has ever known. We pass an inn. He reads vapidly aloud to me "The King's Arms. Licensed to sell Ales and Spirits." I foresee that during the rest of the walk he will read aloud any inscription that occurs. We pass a milestone. He points at it with his stick and says "Uxminster. 11 Miles." We turn a sharp corner at the foot of a hill. He points at the wall, and says "Drive slowly." I see far ahead, on the other side of the hedge bordering the high road, a small notice-board. He sees it too. He keeps his eye on it. And in due course "Trespassers," he says, "Will Be Prosecuted." Poor man! — mentally a wreck.

Luncheon at the A.s', however, salves him and floats him in full sail. Behold him once more the life and soul of the party. Surely he will never, after the bitter lesson of this morning, go out for another walk. An hour later, I see him striding forth, with a new companion. I know what he is saying. He is saying that I am rather a dull man to go a walk with. He will presently add that I am one of the dullest men he ever went a walk with. Then he will devote himself to reading out the inscriptions.

How comes it, this immediate deterioration in those who go walking for walking's sake? Just what happens? I take it that not by his reasoning faculties is a man urged to this enterprise. He is urged, evidently, by something in him that transcends reason; by his soul, I presume. Yes, it must be the soul that raps out the "Quick march!" to the body. — "Halt! Stand at ease!" interposes the brain, and "To what destination," it suavely asks the soul, "and on what errand, are you sending the body?" — "On no errand whatsoever," the soul makes answer, "and to no destination at all. It is just like you to be always on the look-out for some subtle ulterior motive. The body is going out because the mere fact of its doing so is a sure indication of nobility, probity, and rugged grandeur of character." — "Very well, Vagula, have your own wayula! But I," says the brain, "flatly refuse to be mixed up in this tomfoolery. I shall go to sleep till it is over." The brain then wraps itself up in its own convolutions, and falls into a dreamless slumber from which nothing can rouse it till the body has been safely deposited indoors again.

Even if you go to some definite place, for some definite purpose, the brain would rather you took a vehicle; but it does not make a point of this; it will serve you well enough unless you are going *for a walk*. It won't, while your legs are vying with each other, do any deep thinking for you, nor even any close thinking; but it will do any number of small odd jobs for you willingly — provided that your legs, also, are making themselves useful, not merely bandying you about to gratify the pride of the soul. Such as it is, this essay was composed in the course of a walk, this morning. I am not one of those extremists who must have a vehicle to every destination. I never go out of my way, as it were, to avoid exercise. I take it as it comes, and take it in good part. That valetudinarians are always chattering about it, and indulging in it to excess, is no reason for despising it. I am inclined to think that in moderation it is rather good for one, physically. But, pending a time when no people wish me to go and see them, and I have no wish to go and see anyone, and there is nothing whatever for me to do off my own premises, I never will go out for a walk.

MAX BEERBOHM

THE GOLDEN DRUGGET

PRIMITIVE and essential things have great power
to touch the heart of the beholder. I mean such
things as a man ploughing a field, or sowing or reaping; a girl filling a pitcher from a spring; a young mother
with her child; a fisherman mending his nets; a light from
a lonely hut on a dark night.

Things such as these are the best themes for poets and
painters, and appeal to aught that there may be of painter
or poet in any one of us. Strictly, they are not so old as
the hills, but they are more significant and eloquent than
hills. Hills will outlast them; but hills glacially surviving
the life of man on this planet are of as little account as hills
tremulous and hot in ages before the life of man had its
beginning. Nature is interesting only because of *us*. And
the best symbols of us are such sights as I have just mentioned — sights unalterable by fashion of time or place,
sights that in all countries always were and never will not
be.

It is true that in many districts nowadays there are
elaborate new kinds of machinery for ploughing the fields
and reaping the corn. In the most progressive districts of
all, I daresay, the very sowing of the grain is done by
means of some engine, with better results than could be
got by hand. For aught I know, there is a patented invention for catching fish by electricity. It is natural that
we should, in some degree, pride ourselves on such triumphs. It is well that we should have poems about them,
and pictures of them. But such poems and pictures cannot touch our hearts very deeply. They cannot stir in us

the sense of our kinship with the whole dim past and the whole dim future. The ancient Egyptians were great at scientific dodges — very great indeed, nearly as great as we, the archæologists tell us. Sand buried the memory of those dodges for a rather long time. How are we to know that the glories of our present civilization will never be lost? The world's coal-mines and oil-fields are exhaustible; and it is not, I am told, by any means certain that scientists will discover any good substitutes for the materials which are necessary to mankind's present pitch of glory. Mankind may, I infer, have to sink back into slow and simple ways, continent be once more separated from continent, nation from nation, village from village. And, even supposing that the present rate of traction and communication and all the rest of it can forever be maintained, is our modern way of life so great a success that mankind will surely never be willing to let it lapse? Doubtless, that present rate can be not only maintained, but also accelerated immensely, in the near future. Will these greater glories be voted, even by the biggest fools, an improvement? We smile already at the people of the early nineteenth century who thought that the vistas opened by applied science were very heavenly. We have travelled far along those vistas. Light is *not* abundant in them, is it? We are proud of having gone such a long way, but... peradventure, those who come after us will turn back, sooner or later, of their own accord. This is a humbling thought. If the wonders of our civilization are doomed, we should prefer them to cease through lack of the minerals and mineral products that keep them going. Possibly they are not doomed at all. But this chance counts for little as against the certainty that, whatever happens, the primitive and essential things will never, anywhere, wholly cease, while mankind lasts. And thus it is that Brown's Ode to the Steam Plough, Jones' Sonnet Sequence on the

Automatic Reaping Machine, and Robinson's Epic of the Piscicidal Dynamo, leave unstirred the deeper depths of emotion in us. The subjects chosen by these three great poets do not much impress us when we regard them *sub specie æternitatis.* Smith has painted nothing more masterly than his picture of a girl turning a hot-water tap. But has he *never* seen a girl fill a pitcher from a spring? Smithers' picture of a young mother seconding a resolution at a meeting of a Board of Guardians is magnificent, as brushwork. But why not have cut out the Board and put in the baby? I yield to no one in admiration of Smithkins' "Façade of the Waldorf Hotel by Night, in Peace Time." But a single light from a lonely hut would have been a finer theme.

I should like to show Smithkins the thing that I call the Golden Drugget. Or rather, as this thing is greatly romantic to me, and that painter is so unfortunate in his surname, I should like Smithkins to find it for himself.

These words are written in war time and in England. There are, I hear, "lighting restrictions" even on the far Riviera di Levante. I take it that the Golden Drugget is not outspread nowanights across the high dark coast-road between Rapallo and Zoagli. But the lonely wayside inn is still there, doubtless; and its narrow door will again stand open, giving out for wayfarers its old span of brightness into darkness, when peace comes.

It is nothing by daylight, that inn. If anything, it is rather an offence. Steep behind it rise mountains that are grey all over with olive trees, and beneath it, on the other side of the road, the cliff falls sheer to the sea. The road is white, the sea and sky are usually of a deep bright blue, there are many single cypresses among the olives. It is a scene of good colour and noble form. It is a gay and a grand scene, in which the inn, though unassuming, is unpleasing, if you pay attention to it. An ugly little box-like inn. A stuffy and uninviting inn. Salt and tobacco, it announces in faint letters above the door, may be bought there. But one would prefer to buy these things elsewhere. There is a bench outside, and a rickety table with a zinc top to it, and sometimes a peasant or two drinking a glass or two of wine. The proprietress is very unkempt. To Don Quixote she would have seemed a princess, and the inn a castle, and the peasants notable magicians. Don Quixote would have paused here and done something. Not so do I.

By daylight, on the way down from my little home to Rapallo, or up from Rapallo home, I am indeed hardly conscious that this inn exists. By moonlight, too, it is negligible. Stars are rather unbecoming to it. But on a thoroughly dark night, when it is manifest as nothing but a strip of yellow light cast across the road from an ever-open door, great always is its magic for me. Is? I mean *was*. But then, I mean also *will be*. And so I cleave to the present tense — the nostalgic present, as grammarians might call it.

Likewise, when I say that thoroughly dark nights are rare here, I mean that they are rare in the Gulf of Genoa. Clouds do not seem to like our landscape. But it has often struck me that Italian nights, whenever clouds *do* congregate, are somehow as much darker than English nights as Italian days are brighter than days in England. They have a heavier and thicker nigritude. They shut things out from you more impenetrably. They enclose you as in a small pavilion of black velvet. This tenement is not very comfortable in a strong gale. It makes you feel rather helpless. And gales can be strong enough, in the late autumn, on the Riviera di Levante.

It is on nights when the wind blows its hardest, but makes no rift anywhere for a star to peep through, that the Golden Drugget, as I approach it, gladdens my heart the most. The distance between Rapallo and my home is rather more than two miles. The road curves and zigzags sharply, for the most part; but at the end of the first mile it runs straight for three or four hundred yards; and, as the inn stands at a point midway on this straight course, the Golden Drugget is visible to me long before I come to it. Even by starlight, it is good to see. How much better, if I happen to be out on a black rough night when nothing is disclosed but this one calm bright thing. Nothing? Well, there has been descriable, all the way, a certain grey glimmer immediately in front of my feet. This, in point of fact, is the road, and by following it carefully I have managed to escape collision with trees, bushes, stone walls. The continuous shrill wailing of trees' branches writhing unseen but near, and the great hoarse roar of the sea against the rocks far down below, are no cheerful accompaniment for the buffeted pilgrim. He feels that he is engaged in single combat with Nature at her unfriendliest. He isn't sure that she hasn't supernatural allies working with her — witches on broomsticks circling closely round him, demons in pursuit of him or waiting to leap out on him. And how about mere robbers and cutthroats? Suppose — but look! that streak, yonder, look! — the Golden Drugget.

There it is, familiar, serene, festal. That the pilgrim knew he would see it in due time does not diminish for him the queer joy of seeing it; nay, this emotion would be far less without that foreknowledge. Some things are best at first sight. Others — and here is one of them — do ever improve by recognition. I remember that when first I beheld this steady strip of light, shed forth over a threshold level with the road, it seemed to me conceivably sinister. It brought Stevenson to my mind: the chink of doubloons and the clash of cutlasses; and I think I quickened pace as I passed it. But now! — now it inspires in me a sense of deep trust and gratitude; and such awe as I have for it is altogether a loving awe, as for holy ground that should be trod lightly. A drugget of crimson cloth across a London pavement is rather resented by the casual passer-by, as saying to him "Step across me, stranger, but not along me, not in!" and for answer he spurns it with his heel. "Stranger, come in!" is the clear message of the Golden Drugget. "This is but a humble and earthly hostel, yet you will find here a radiant company of angels and archangels." And always I cherish the belief that if I obeyed the summons I should receive fulfilment of the promise. Well, the beliefs that one most cherishes one is least willing to test. I do not go in at that open door. But lingering, but reluctant, is my tread as I pass by it; and I pause to bathe in the light that is as the span of our human life, granted between one great darkness and another.

You are

Somebody else

SAMUEL McCHORD CROTHERS

*Samuel McChord Crothers was born in Oswego, Illinois, in 1857.
He received the degree of A.B. from Wittenberg College in 1873, and
from Princeton in 1874.   After three years of study at Union Theological Seminary, he entered the Presbyterian ministry, serving as
pastor of several churches in the West.   In 1881 he came East for
further study at Harvard and entered the Unitarian Church.   From
1894 until his death in 1927 he was pastor of the First Church in
Cambridge, Massachusetts, and was for long time Preacher to Harvard University, in which capacities he was exceedingly successful.
A constant contributor to* The Atlantic Monthly, *he published,
during his lifetime, some eight volumes of collected essays, from* The
Gentle Reader *(1903)* to The Cheerful Giver *(1923).   In* Oliver
Wendell Holmes and His Fellow Boarders *(1909)* and How to
Know Emerson *(1920) are revealed his sympathetic understanding
as critic and interpreter of literature.   His fame, however, rests securely on his familiar essays, which reflect a personality of unusual
charm, grace, and wit.   Among the few readers who did not succumb
to this charm was the late Frank M. Colby: in the third paragraph
of* Our Refinement, *in this volume, will be found an unsympathetic
allusion to the volume of Dr. Crothers' from which the following example has been taken.*

Reprinted from The Dame School of Experience (1919), *by
S. M. Crothers, with permission of Houghton Mifflin Company,
publishers.*

*of us are
end persons made of such
years, That make*

SAMUEL McCHORD CROTHERS

EVERY MAN'S NATURAL DESIRE TO BE SOMEBODY ELSE

SEVERAL years ago a young man came to my study with a manuscript which he wished me to criticize. "It is only a little bit of my work," he said modestly, "and it will not take you long to look it over. In fact it is only the first chapter, in which I explain the Universe."

I suppose that we have all had moments of sudden illumination when it occurred to us that we had explained the Universe, and it was so easy for us that we wondered why we had not done it before. Some thought drifted into our mind and filled us with vague forebodings of omniscience. It was not an ordinary thought, that explained only a fragment of existence. It explained everything. It proved one thing and it proved the opposite just as well. It explained why things are as they are, and if it should turn out that they are not that way at all, it would prove that fact also. In the light of our great thought chaos seemed rational.

Such thoughts usually occur about four o'clock in the morning. Having explained the Universe, we relapse into satisfied slumber. When, a few hours later, we rise, we wonder what the explanation was.

Now and then, however, one of these highly explanatory ideas remains to comfort us in our waking hours. Such a thought is that which I here throw out, and which has doubtless at some early hour occurred to most of my readers. It is that every man has a natural desire to be somebody else.

This does not explain the Universe, but it explains that perplexing part of it which we call Human Nature. It explains why so many intelligent people, who deal skillfully with matters of fact, make such a mess of it when they deal with their fellow creatures. It explains why we get on as well as we do with strangers, and why we do not get on better with our friends. It explains why people are so often offended when we say nice things about them, and why it is that, when we say harsh things about them, they take it as a compliment. It explains why people marry their opposites and why they live happily ever afterwards. It also explains why some people don't. It explains the meaning of tact and its opposite.

The tactless person treats a person according to a scientific method as if he were a thing. Now, in dealing with a thing, you must first find out what it is, and then act accordingly. But with a person, you must first find out what he is and then carefully conceal from him the fact that you have made the discovery. The tactless person can never be made to understand this. He prides himself on taking people as they are without being aware that that is not the way they want to be taken.

He has a keen eye for the obvious, and calls attention to it. Age, sex, color, nationality, previous condition of servitude, and all the facts that are interesting to the census-taker, are apparent to him and are made the basis of his conversation. When he meets one who is older than he, he is conscious of the fact, and emphasizes by every polite attention the disparity in years. He has an idea that at a certain period in life the highest tribute of respect is to be urged to rise out of one chair and take another that is presumably more comfortable. It does not occur to him that there may remain any tastes that are not sedentary. On the other hand, he sees a callow youth and addresses himself to the obvious callowness, and thereby makes himself thoroughly disliked. For, strange to say, the youth prefers to be addressed as a person of precocious maturity.

The literalist, observing that most people talk shop, takes it for granted that they like to talk shop. This is a mistake. They do it because it is the easiest thing to do, but they resent having attention called to their limitations. A man's profession does not necessarily coincide with his natural aptitude or with his predominant desire. When you meet a member of the Supreme Court you may assume that he is gifted with a judicial mind. But it does not follow that that is the only quality of mind he has; nor that when, out of court, he gives you a piece of his mind, it will be a piece of his judicial mind that he gives.

My acquaintance with royalty is limited to photographs of royal groups, which exhibit a high degree of domesticity. It would seem that the business of royalty when pursued as a steady job becomes tiresome, and that when they have their pictures taken they endeavor to look as much like ordinary folks as possible — and they usually succeed.

The member of one profession is always flattered by being taken for a skilled practitioner of another. Try it on your minister. Instead of saying, "That was an excellent sermon of yours this morning," say, "As I listened to your cogent argument, I thought what a successful lawyer you would have made." Then he will say, "I did think of taking to the law."

If you had belonged to the court of Frederick the Great you would have proved a poor courtier indeed if you had praised His Majesty's campaigns. Frederick knew that he was a Prussian general, but he wanted to be a French literary man. If you wished to gain his favor you should have told him that in your opinion he excelled Voltaire.

We do not like to have too much attention drawn to our present circumstances. They may be well enough in their way, but we can think of something which would be more fitting for us. We have either seen better days or we expect them.

Suppose you had visited Napoleon in Elba and had sought to ingratiate yourself with him.

"Sire," you would have said, "this is a beautiful little empire of yours, so snug and cozy and quiet. It is just such a domain as is suited to a man in your condition. The climate is excellent. Everything is peaceful. It must be delightful to rule where everything is arranged for you and the details are taken care of by others. As I came to your dominion I saw a line of British frigates guarding your shores. The evidences of such thoughtfulness are everywhere."

Your praise of his present condition would not have endeared you to Napoleon. You were addressing him as the Emperor of Elba. In his own eyes he was Emperor, though in Elba.

It is such a misapprehension which irritates any mature human being when his environment is taken as the measure of his personality.

The man with a literal mind moves in a perpetual comedy of errors. It is not a question of two Dromios. There are half a dozen Dromios under one hat.

How casually introductions are made, as if it were the easiest thing in the world to make two human beings acquainted! Your friend says, "I want you to know Mr. Stifflekin," and you say that you are happy to know him. But does either of you know the enigma that goes under the name of Stifflekin? You may know what he looks like and where he resides and what he does for a living. But that is all in the present tense. To really know him you must not only know what he is but what he used to be; what he used to think he was; what he used to think he ought to be and might be if he worked hard enough.

You must know what he might have been if certain things had happened otherwise, and you must know what might have happened otherwise if he had been otherwise. All these complexities are a part of his own dim apprehension of himself. They are what make him so much more interesting to himself than he is to anyone else.

It is this consciousness of the inadequacy of our knowledge which makes us so embarrassed when we offer any service to another. Will he take it in the spirit in which it is given?

That was an awkward moment when Stanley, after all his hardships in his search for Dr. Livingstone, at last found the Doctor by a lake in Central Africa. Stanley held out his hand and said stiffly, "Dr. Livingstone, I presume?" Stanley had heroically plunged through the equatorial forests to find Livingstone and to bring him back to civilization. But Livingstone was not particularly anxious to be found, and had a decided objection to being brought back to civilization. What he wanted was a new adventure. Stanley did not find the real Livingstone till he discovered that the old man was as young at heart as himself. The two men became acquainted only when they began to plan a new expedition to find the source of the Nile.

The natural desire of every man to be somebody else explains many of the minor irritations of life. It prevents that perfect organization of society in which everyone should know his place and keep it. The desire to be somebody else leads us to practice on work that does not strictly belong to us. We all have aptitudes and talents that overflow the narrow bounds of our trade or profession. Every man feels that he is bigger than his job, and he is all the time doing what theologians called "works of supererogation."

The serious-minded housemaid is not content to do

what she is told to do.   She has an unexpended balance of
energy.   She wants to be a general household reformer.
So she goes to the desk of the titular master of the house
and gives it a thorough reformation.   She arranges the
papers according to her idea of neatness.   When the poor
gentleman returns and finds his familiar chaos transformed
into a hateful order, he becomes a reactionary.

The serious manager of a street railway company is not
content with the simple duty of transporting passengers
cheaply and comfortably.   He wants to exercise the functions of a lecturer in an ethical culture society.   While the
transported victim is swaying precariously from the end
of a strap he reads a notice urging him to practice Christian courtesy and not to push.   While the poor wretch
pores over this counsel of perfection, he feels like answer-
ing as did Junius to the Duke of Grafton, "My Lord, injuries may be atoned for and forgiven, but insults admit
of no compensation."

A man enters a barber shop with the simple desire of
being shaved.   But he meets with the more ambitious
desires of the barber.   The serious barber is not content
with any slight contribution to human welfare.   He insists that his client shall be shampooed, manicured, mas-
saged, steamed beneath boiling towels, cooled off by electric fans, and, while all this is going on, that he shall have
his boots blacked.

Have you never marveled at the patience of people in
having so many things done to them that they don't want,
just to avoid hurting the feelings of professional people
who want to do more than is expected of them?   You
watch the stoical countenance of the passenger in a Pull-
man car as he stands up to be brushed.   The chances are
that he doesn't want to be brushed.   He would prefer to
leave the dust on his coat rather than to be compelled to
swallow it.   But he knows what is expected of him.   It is

a part of the solemn ritual of traveling.   It precedes the
offering.

The fact that every man desires to be somebody else
explains many of the aberrations of artists and literary
men.   The painters, dramatists, musicians, poets, and
novelists are just as human as housemaids and railway
managers and porters.   They want to do "all the good
they can to all the people they can in all the ways they
can."   They get tired of the ways they are used to and like
to try new combinations.   So they are continually mixing
things.   The practitioner of one art tries to produce effects
that are proper to another art.

A musician wants to be a painter and use his violin as
if it were a brush.   He would have us see the sunset glories
that he is painting for us.   A painter wants to be a musician and paint symphonies, and he is grieved because the
uninstructed cannot hear his pictures, although the colors
do swear at each other.   Another painter wants to be an
architect and build up his picture as if it were made of
cubes of brick.   It looks like brick-work, but to the natural
eye it doesn't look like a picture.   A prose-writer gets
tired of writing prose, and wants to be a poet.   So he begins every line with a capital letter, and keeps on writing
prose.

You go to the theater with the simple-minded Shakespearean idea that the play's the thing.   But the playwright wants to be a pathologist.   So you discover that
you have dropped into a gruesome clinic.   You sought
innocent relaxation, but you are one of the non-elect and
have gone to the place prepared for you.   You must see
the thing through.   The fact that you have troubles of
your own is not a sufficient claim for exemption.

Or you take up a novel expecting it to be a work of
fiction.   But the novelist has other views.   He wants to
be your spiritual adviser.   He must do something to your

mind, he must rearrange your fundamental ideas, he must
massage your soul, and generally brush you off.   All this
in spite of the fact that you don't want to be brushed off
and set to rights.   You don't want him to do anything to
your mind.   It's the only mind you have and you need it
in your own business.

But if the desire of every man to be somebody else ac-
counts for many whimsicalities of human conduct and for
many aberrations in the arts, it cannot be lightly dismissed
as belonging only to the realm of comedy.   It has its
origin in the nature of things.   The reason why every man
wants to be somebody else is that he can remember the
time when he was somebody else.   What we call personal
identity is a very changeable thing, as all of us realize when
we look over old photographs and read old letters.

The oldest man now living is but a few years removed
from the undifferentiated germ-plasm, which might have
developed into almost anything.   In the beginning he was
a bundle of possibilities.   Every actuality that is developed
means a decrease in the rich variety of possibilities.   In
becoming one thing it becomes impossible to be something
else.

The delight in being a boy lies in the fact that the possibilities are still manifold.   The boy feels that he can be
anything that he desires.   He is conscious that he has
capacities that would make him a successful banker.   On
the other hand, there are attractions in a life of adventure
in the South Seas.   It would be pleasant to lie under a
bread-fruit tree and let the fruit drop into his mouth, to
the admiration of the gentle savages who would gather
about him.   Or he might be a saint — not a commonplace
modern saint who does chores and attends tiresome committee meetings, but a saint such as one reads about, who
gives away his rich robes and his purse of gold to the first
beggar he meets, and then goes on his carefree way through

the forest to convert interesting robbers. He feels that he might practice that kind of unscientific charity, if his father would furnish him with the money to give away.

But by and by he learns that making a success in the banking business is not consistent with excursions to the South Seas or with the more picturesque and unusual forms of saintliness. If he is to be in a bank he must do as the bankers do.

Parents and teachers conspire together to make a man of him, which means making a particular kind of man of him. All mental processes which are not useful must be suppressed. The sum of their admonitions is that he must pay attention. That is precisely what he is doing. He is paying attention to a variety of things that escape the adult mind. As he wriggles on the bench in the school-room, he pays attention to all that is going on. He attends to what is going on out-of-doors; he sees the weak points of his fellow pupils, against whom he is planning punitive expeditions; and he is delightfully conscious of the idiosyncrasies of the teacher. Moreover, he is a youthful artist and his sketches from life give acute joy to his contemporaries when they are furtively passed around.

But the schoolmaster says sternly, "My boy, you must learn to pay attention; that is to say, you must not pay attention to so many things, but you must pay attention to one thing, namely the second declension."

Now the second declension is the least interesting thing in the room, but unless he confines his attention to it he will never learn it. Education demands narrowing of attention in the interest of efficiency.

A man may, by dint of application to a particular subject, become a successful merchant or real-estate man or chemist or overseer of the poor. But he cannot be all these things at the same time. He must make his choice. Having in the presence of witnesses taken himself for bet-

ter for worse, he must, forsaking all others, cleave to that
alone.   The consequence is that, by the time he is forty,
he has become one kind of a man, and is able to do one
kind of work.   He has acquired a stock of ideas true
enough for his purposes, but not so transcendentally true
as to interfere with his business.   His neighbors know
where to find him, and they do not need to take a spiritual
elevator.   He does business on the ground floor.   He has
gained in practicality, but has lost in the quality of inter-
estingness.

The old prophet declared that the young men dream
dreams and the old men see visions, but he did not say
anything about the middle-aged men. *They* have to look
after the business end.

But has the man whose working hours are so full of responsibilities changed so much as he seems to have done?
When he is talking shop is he "all there"?   I think not.
There are elusive personalities that are in hiding.   As the
rambling mansions of the old Catholic families had secret
panels opening into the "priest's hole," to which the family resorted for spiritual comfort, so in the mind of the
most successful man there are secret chambers where are
hidden his unsuccessful ventures, his romantic ambitions,
his unfulfilled promises.   All that he dreamed of as possible
is somewhere concealed in the man's heart.   He would not
for the world have the public know how much he cares for
the selves that have not had a fair chance to come into the
light of day.   You do not know a man until you know his
lost Atlantis, and his Utopia for which he still hopes to set
sail.

When Dogberry asserted that he was "as pretty a piece
of flesh as any is in Messina" and "one that hath two
gowns and everything handsome about him," he was pointing out what he deemed to be quite obvious.   It was in a
more intimate tone that he boasted, "and a fellow that
hath had losses."

When Julius Cæsar rode through the streets of Rome in his chariot, his laurel crown seemed to the populace a symbol of his present greatness. But gossip has it that Cæsar at that time desired to be younger than he was, and that before appearing in public he carefully arranged his laurel wreath so as to conceal the fact that he had had losses.

Much that passes for pride in the behavior of the great comes from the fear of the betrayal of emotions that belong to a simpler manner of life. When the sons of Jacob saw the great Egyptian officer to whom they appealed turn away from them, they little knew what was going on. "And Joseph made haste, for his bowels did yearn upon his brother: and he sought where to weep; and he entered into his chamber, and wept there. And he washed his face, and went out, and refrained himself." Joseph didn't want to be a great man. He wanted to be human. It was hard to refrain himself.

What of the lost arts of childhood, the lost audacities and ambitions and romantic admirations of adolescence? What becomes of the sympathies which make us feel our kinship to all sorts of people? What becomes of the early curiosity in regard to things which were none of our business? We ask as Saint Paul asked of the Galatians, "Ye began well; who did hinder you?"

The answer is not wholly to our discredit. We do not develop all parts of our nature because we are not allowed to do so. Walt Whitman might exult over the Spontaneous Me. But nobody is paid for being spontaneous. A spontaneous switchman on the railway would be a menace to the traveling public. We prefer some one less temperamental.

As civilization advances and work becomes more specialized, it becomes impossible for any one to find free and full development for all his natural powers in any recognized occupation. What then becomes of the other selves? The answer must be that playgrounds must be provided for them outside the confines of daily business. As work becomes more engrossing and narrowing the need is more urgent for recognized and carefully guarded periods of leisure.

The old Hebrew sage declared, "Wisdom cometh from the opportunity of leisure." It does not mean that a wise man must belong to what we call the leisure classes. It means that if one has only a little free time at his disposal, he must use that time for the refreshment of his hidden selves. If he cannot have a sabbath rest of twenty-four hours, he must learn to sanctify little sabbaths, it may be of ten minutes' length. In them he shall do no manner of work. It is not enough that the self that works and receives wages shall be recognized and protected; the world must be made safe for our other selves. Does not the Declaration of Independence say that every man has an inalienable right to the pursuit of happiness?

To realize that men are not satisfied with themselves requires imagination, and we have had a terrible example of what misfortunes come from the lack of imagination. The Prussian militarists had a painstaking knowledge of facts, but they had a contempt for human nature. Their tactlessness was almost beyond belief. They treated persons as if they were things. They treated facts with deadly seriousness, but had no regard for feelings. They had spies all over the world to report all that could be seen, but they took no account of what could not be seen. So, while they were dealing scientifically with the obvious facts and forces, all the hidden powers of the human soul were being turned against them. Prussianism insisted on highly specialized men who have no sympathies to interfere with their efficiency. Having adopted a standard, all variation must be suppressed. It was against this effort to suppress the human variations that the world fought. We did not want all men to be reduced to one pattern. And against the effort to produce a monotonous uniformity we must keep on fighting. It was of little use to dethrone the Kaiser if we submit to other tyrants of our own making.

C. E. MONTAGUE

Born at Ealing, Middlesex, England, in 1867, Charles Edward Montague received a careful education at home, at the City of London School, and at Balliol College, Oxford, where he was not only a classical exhibitioner, but an oarsman and rugby player. Joining the staff of The Manchester Guardian *soon after leaving the university, he continued with that great Liberal journal, as reporter, dramatic critic, and editorial writer, until the outbreak of the World War. In 1914 Montague was forty-seven, married, and the devoted father of seven children. Refusing to consider exemption, he managed to enlist as a private in the Royal Fusiliers, and served throughout the War, emerging as Captain and Assistant Press Officer engaged in censorship. He had thus exceptional opportunities, not only to partake of active service in the trenches, but also to learn the point of view of the staff, and of the distinguished visitors to the Front, to entertain whom was at one time his duty. His ability to stand the strain of service was due partly to his love of outdoor sports; he was an enthusiastic mountain climber, a member of the Alpine Club from 1901 on. After the War, he returned to* The Guardian *for six years more, retiring in 1925 to devote himself to writing. He died in 1928. Of his books,* Rough Justice (1926), *a novel of the War,* Dramatic Values (1911), *a collection of his criticisms, and* Disenchantment (1922), *a remarkable series of essays and sketches revealing the disillusionment of those who fought to end war, are perhaps the best known, although it is not easy to select from the works of a man who invariably wrote with insight and distinction.*

The following essay is reprinted from Disenchantment, *by C. E. Montague, published by Chatto and Windus, London, with permission of the Montague Estate.*

o

C. E. MONTAGUE

AUTUMN TINTS IN CHIVALRY

I

IN EITHER of two opposite tempers you may carry on war. In one of the two you will want to rate your enemy, all round, as high as you can. You may pursue him down a trench, or he you; but in neither case do you care to have him described by somebody far, far away as a fat little short-sighted scrub. Better let him pass for a paladin. This may at bottom be vanity, sentimentality, all sort of contemptible things. Let him who knows the heart of man be dogmatic about it. Anyhow, this temper comes, as they would say in Ireland, of decent people. It spoke in Porsena of Clusium's whimsical prayer that Horatius might swim the Tiber safely; it animates Velasquez' knightly *Surrender of Breda;* it prompted Lord Roberts' first words to Cronje when Paardeberg fell — "Sir, you have made a very gallant defense"; it is avowed in a popular descant of Newbolt's —

> To honor, while you strike him down,
> The foe who comes with eager eyes.

The other temper has its niche in letters, too. There was the man that "wore his dagger in his mouth." And there was Little Flanigan, the bailiff's man in Goldsmith's play. During one of our old wars with France he was always "damning the French, the parle-vous, and all that belonged to them." "What," he would ask the company, "makes the bread rising? The parle-vous that devour us. What makes the mutton fivepence a pound? The parle-vous that eat it up. What makes the beer threepence-halfpenny a pot?"

Well, your first aim in war is to hit your enemy hard, and the question may well be quite open — in which of these tempers can he be hit hardest? If, as we hear, a man's strength be "as the strength of ten because his heart is pure," possibly it may add a few foot-pounds to his momentum in an attack if he has kept a clean tongue in his head. And yet the production of heavy woolens in the West Riding, for War Office use, may, for all that we know, have been accelerated by yarns about crucified Canadians and naked bodies of women found in German trenches. There is always so much, so bewilderingly much, to be said on both sides. All I can tell is that during the war the Newbolt spirit seemed, on the whole, to have its chief seat in and near our front line, and thence to die down westward all the way to London. There Little Flanigan was enthroned, and, like Montrose, would bear no rival near his throne, so that a man on leave from our trench system stood in some danger of being regarded as little better than one of the wicked. Anyhow, he was a kind of provincial. Not his will, but that of Flanigan, had to be done. For Flanigan was the center of things; he had leisure, or else volubility was his trade; and he had got hold of the megaphones.

II

In the first months of the war there was any amount of good sportsmanship going; most, of course, among men who had seen already the whites of enemy eyes. I remember the potent emetic effect of Flaniganism upon a little blond Regular subaltern maimed at the first battles of Ypres. "Pretty measly sample of the sin against the Holy Ghost!" the one-legged child grunted savagely, showing a London paper's comic sketch of a corpulent German running away. The first words I ever heard uttered in palliation of German misdoings in Belgium came

from a Regular N.C.O., a Dragoon Guards sergeant, holding forth to a sergeants' mess behind our line. "We'd
have done every damn thing they did," he averred, "if it
had been we." I thought him rather extravagant, then.
Later on, when the long row of hut hospitals, jammed between the Calais-Paris Railway at Etaples and the great
reinforcement camp on the sandhills above it, was badly
bombed from the air, even the wrath of the R.A.M.C.
against those who had wedged in its wounded and nurses
between two staple targets scarcely exceeded that of our
Royal Air Force against war correspondents who said the
enemy must have done it on purpose.

Airmen, no doubt, or some of them, went to much
greater lengths in the chivalrous line than the rest of us.
Many things helped them to do it. Combatant flying was
still new enough to be almost wholly an officer's job; the
knight took the knocks, and the squire stayed behind and
looked after his gear. Air-fighting came to be pretty well
the old duel, or else the medieval mêlée between little
picked teams. The clean element, too, may have counted
— it always looked a clean job from below, where your
airy notions got mixed with trench mud, while the airman
seemed like Sylvia in the song, who so excelled "each
mortal thing upon the dull earth dwelling." Whatever
the cause, he excelled in his bearing towards enemies, dead
or alive. The funeral that he gave to Richthofen in
France was one of the few handsome gestures exchanged
in the war. And whenever Little Flanigan at home began
squealing aloud that we ought to take some of our airmen
off fighting and make them bomb German women and
children instead, our airmen's scorn for these ethics of the
dirt helped to keep up the flickering hope that the post-
war world might not be ignoble.

Even on the dull earth it takes time and pains to get a
cleanrun boy or young man into a mean frame of mind.

A fine N.C.O. of the Grenadier Guards was killed near
Laventie — no one knows how — while going over to
shake hands with the Germans on Christmas morning.
"What! not shake on Christmas Day?"   He would have
thought it poor, sulky fighting.   Near Armentières at the
Christmas of 1914 an incident happened which seemed
quite the natural thing to most soldiers then.   On Christmas Eve the Germans lit up their front line with Chinese
lanterns.   Two British officers thereupon walked some
way across No Man's Land, hailed the enemy's sentries,
and asked for an officer.   The German sentries said, "Go
back, or we shall have to shoot."   The Englishmen said
"Not likely!" advanced to the German wire, and asked
again for an officer.   The sentries held their fire and sent
for an officer.   With him the Englishmen made a one-day
truce, and on Christmas Day the two sides exchanged
cigarettes and played football together.   The English intended the truce to end with the day, as agreed, but decided not to shoot next day till the enemy did.   Next
morning the Germans were still to be seen washing and
breakfasting outside their wire; so our men, too, got out
of the trench and sat about in the open.   One of them,
cleaning his rifle, loosed a shot by accident, and an English
subaltern went to tell the Germans it had not been fired
to kill.   The ones he spoke to understood, but as he was
walking back a German somewhere wide on a flank fired
and hit him in the knee, and he has walked lame ever since.
Our men took it that some German sentry had misunderstood our fluke shot.   They did not impute dishonor.
The air in such places was strangely clean in those distant
days.   During one of the very few months of open warfare
a cavalry private of ours brought in a captive, a gorgeous
specimen of the terrific Prussian Uhlan of tradition.   "But
why didn't you put your sword through him?" an officer
asked, who belonged to the school of Froissart less obvi-

ously than the private. "Well, sir," the captor replied, "the gentleman wasn't looking."

III

At no seat of war will you find it quite easy to live up to Flanigan's standards of hatred towards an enemy. Reaching a front, you find that all you want is just to win the war. Soon you are so taken up with the pursuit of this aim that you are always forgetting to burn with the gemlike flame of pure fury that fires the lion-hearted publicist at home.

A soldier might have had the Athanasian ecstasy all right till he reached the firing line. Every individual German had sunk the *Lusitania;* there was none righteous, none. And yet at a front the holy passion began to ooze out at the ends of his fingers. The bottom trouble is that you cannot fight a man in the physical way without somehow touching him. The relation of actual combatants is a personal one — no doubt, a rude, primitive one, but still quite advanced as compared with that between a learned man at Berlin who keeps on saying *Delenda est Britannia!* at the top of his voice and a learned man in London who keeps on saying that every German must have a black heart because Cæsar did not conquer Germany as he did Gaul and Britain. Just let the round head of a German appear for a passing second, at long intervals, above a hummock of clay in the middle distance. Before you had made half a dozen sincere efforts to shoot him the fatal germ of human relationship had begun to find a nidus again: he had acquired in your mind the rudiments of a personal individuality. You would go on trying to shoot him with zest — indeed, with a diminished likelihood of missing, for mere hatred is a flustering emotion. And yet the hatred business had started crumbling. There had begun the insidious change that was to send you home, on your first leave, talking unguardedly of "old Fritz" or of "the good old Boche" to the pain of your friends, as if he were a stout dog fox or a real stag or a hare.

The deadliest solvent of your exalted hatreds is laughter. And you can never wholly suppress laughter between two crowds of millions of men standing within earshot of each other along a line of hundreds of miles. There was, in the Loos salient in 1916, a German who, after his meals, would halloo across to an English unit taunts about certain accidents of its birth. None of his British hearers could help laughing at his mistakes, his knowledge, and his English. Nor could the least humorous priest of ill-will have kept his countenance at a relief when the enemy shouted: "We know you are relieving," "No good hiding it," "Good-by, Ox and Bucks," "Who's coming in?" and some hurried humorist in the obscure English battalion relieving shouted back, with a terrific assumption of accent, "Furrst Black Watch!" or "Th' Oirish Gyards!" and a hush fell at the sound of these great names. Comedy, expelled with a fork by the dignified figure of Quenchless Hate, had begun to steal back of herself.

At home that tragedy queen might do very well; she did not have these tenpenny nails scattered about on her road to puncture the nobly inflated tires of her chariot. The heroes who spoke up for shooing all the old German governesses into the barbed wire compounds were not exposed to the moral danger of actually hustling, *propria persona*, these formidable ancients. But while Hamilcar at home was swearing Hannibal and all the other little Hamilcars to undying hatred of the foe, an enemy dog might be trotting across to the British front line to sample its rats, and its owner be losing in some British company's eyes his proper quality as an incarnation of all the Satanism of Potsdam and becoming simply "him that lost the dog."

If you took his trench it might be no better; perhaps In-

carnate Evil had left its bit of food half-cooked, and the
muddy straw, where it lay last, was pressed into a hollow
by Incarnate Evil's back as by a cat's.   Incarnate Evil
should not do these things that other people in trenches do.
It ought to be more strange and beastly and keep on making
beaux gestes with its talons and tail, like the proper dragon
slain by Saint George.   Perhaps Incarnate Evil was extinct and you went over its pockets.   They never contained
the right things — no poison to put in our wells, no practical
hints for crucifying Canadians; only the usual stuffing of
all soldiers' pockets — photographs and tobacco and bits
of string and the wife's letters, all about how tramps were
always stealing potatoes out of the garden, and how the
baby was worse, and was his leave never coming?   No
good to look at such things.

IV

With this guilty weakness gaining upon them our
troops drove the Germans from Albert to Mons.   There
were scandalous scenes on the way.   Imagine two hundred German prisoners grinning inside a wire cage while a
little Cockney corporal chaffs them in half the dialects of
Germany!   His father, he says, was a slop tailor in White-
chapel; most of his journeymen came from somewhere or
other in Germany — "Ah! and my dad sweated 'em
proper," he says proudly; so the boy learnt all their kinds
of talk.   He convulses Bavarians now with his flow of
Silesian.   He fraternizes grossly and jubilantly.   Other
British soldiers laugh when one of the Germans sings, in
return for favors received, the British ballad "Knocked
'em in the Ol' Kent Road."   By the time our men had
marched to the Rhine there was little hatred left in them.
How can you hate the small boy who stands at the farm
door visibly torn between dread of the invader and deep delight in all soldiers, as soldiers?   How shall a man not offer

a drink to the first disbanded German soldier who sits next
to him in a public house at Cologne, and try to find out if
he was ever in the line at the Brickstacks or near the Big
Crater? Why, that might have been his dog!

The billeted soldier's immemorial claim on "a place by
the fire" carried on the fell work. It is hopelessly bad for
your grand Byronic hates if you sit through whole winter
evenings in the abhorred foe's kitchen and the abhorred foe
grants you the uncovenanted mercy of hot coffee and discusses without rancor the relative daily yields of the British
and the German milch cow. And then comes into play the
British soldier's incorrigible propensity, wherever he be, to
form virtuous attachments. "Love, unfoiled in the war,"
as Sophocles says. The broad road has a terribly easy
gradient. When all the great and wise at Paris were making
peace, as somebody said, with a vengeance, our command on
the Rhine had to send a wire to say that unless something
was done to feed the Germans starving in the slums it could
not answer for discipline in its army; the men were giving
their rations away, and no orders would stop them. Rank
"Pro-Germanism," you see — the heresy of Edith Cavell;
"Patriotism is not enough; I must have no hatred or bitterness in my heart." While these men fought on, year after
year, they had mostly been growing more void of mere
spite all the time, feeling always more and more sure that
the average German was just a decent poor devil like everyone else. One trembles to think what the really first-class
haters at home would have said of our army if they had
known at the time.

V

Even at places less distant than home the survival of old
English standards of fighting had given some scandal. In
that autumn of the war when our generalship seemed to
have explored all its own talents and found only the means

to stage in an orderly way the greatest possible number of
combats of pure attrition, the crying up of unknightliness
became a kind of fashion among a good many Staff Officers
of the higher grades. "I fancy our fellows were not taking
many prisoners this morning," a Corps Commander would
say with a complacent grin, on the evening after a battle.
Jocose stories of comic things said by privates when getting rid of undesired captives became current in messes far
in the rear. The other day I saw in a history of one of the
most gallant of all British divisions an illustration given
by the officer who wrote it of what he believed to be the
true martial spirit. It was the case of a wounded High-
lander who had received with a bomb a German Red Cross
orderly who was coming to help him. A General of some
consequence during part of the war gave a lecture, towards
its end, to a body of officers and others on what he called
"the fighting spirit." He told with enthusiasm an anecdote of a captured trench in which some of our men had
been killing off German appellants for quarter. Another
German appearing and putting his hands up, one of our
men — so the story went — called out, "'Ere! Where's
'Arry? 'E ain't 'ad one yet." Probably someone had
pulled the good general's leg, and the thing never happened. But he believed it, and deeply approved the
"blooding" of 'Arry. That, he explained, was the "fighting spirit." Men more versed than he in the actual hand-
to-hand business of fighting this war knew that he was mistaken, and that the spirit of trial by combat and that of
pork-butchery are distinct. But that is of course. The
notable thing was that such things should be said by anyone wearing our uniform. Twenty years before, if it had
been rumored, you would, without waiting, have called the
rumor a lie invented by some detractor of England or of
her army. Now it passed quite unhissed. It was the
latter-day wisdom. Scrofulous minds at home had long

been itching, publicly and in print, to bomb German women and children from aeroplanes, and to "take it out of"
German prisoners of war. Now the disease had even
affected some parts of the non-combatant Staff of our
army.

VI

You know the most often quoted of all passages of
Burke. Indeed, it is only through quotations of it that
most of us know Burke at all —

> But the age of chivalry is gone... the unbought grace of
> life, the cheap defense of nations, the nurse of manly sentiment
> and heroic enterprise is gone! It is gone, that sensibility of
> principle, that chastity of honor, which felt a stain like a wound,
> which inspired courage whilst it mitigated ferocity, which en-
> nobled whatever it touched, and under which vice itself lost
> half its evil by losing all its grossness.

Burke would never say a thing by halves. And as
truth goes by halves, and declines to be sweeping like
rhetoric, Burke made sure of being wrong to the tune of
some fifty per cent. The French Revolution did not, as
his beautiful language implies, confine mankind for the
rest of its days to the procreation of curs. And yet his
words do give you, in their own lush, Corinthian way, a
notion of something that probably did happen, a certain
limited shifting of the center of gravity of West European
morals or manners.

One would be talking like Burke — talking, perhaps you
might say, through Burke's hat — if one were to say that
the war found chivalry alive and left it dead. Chivalry is
about as likely to perish as brown eyes or the moon. Yet
something did happen, during the war, to which these wild
words would have some sort of relation. We were not all
Bayards in 1914; even then a great part of our Press could
not tell indignation from spite, nor uphold the best cause

in the world without turpitude.   Nor were we all, after
the Armistice, rods of the houses of Thersites and Cleon;
Haig was still alive, and so were Gough and Hamilton and
thousands of Arthurian subalterns and privates and of
like-minded civilians, though it is harder for a civilian not
to lose generosity during a war.   But something had happened; the chivalrous temper had had a set-back; it was no
longer the mode; the latest wear was a fine robust shabbi-
ness.   All through the war there had been a bear movement in Newbolts and Burkes, and, corresponding to this,
a bull movement in stocks of the Little Flanigan group.

ROBERT BENCHLEY

Robert Benchley was born in 1889 *and graduated from Harvard in* 1912. *It will be no surprise to his readers to learn that he was editor of* The Harvard Lampoon. *After some years in advertising and industrial personnel work, he became an associate editor of the Sunday Magazine of the* New York Tribune (1916). *Since that time he has been Managing Editor of* Vanity Fair, *columnist for* The New York World, *and an editor of* Life (*from* 1920 *to* 1929); *he is now on the staff of* The New Yorker. *No mention of Mr. Benchley's humorous activities would be complete without reference to his performances in the* Music Box Revue *during the season of* 1923–24, *or his appearances in movietone "shorts" for the Fox Film Company. From time to time he has published collections of his essays:* Of All Things (1921), Love Conquers All (1922), Pluck and Luck (1925), *and* The Treasurer's Report (1930). *Of their popularity and of the eagerness with which his weekly articles in* The New Yorker *are awaited, it is hardly necessary to speak.*

The following essay is reprinted from The Treasurer's Report, *and Other Aspects of Community Singing, by Robert Benchley, with permission of Harper and Brothers, publishers.*

ROBERT BENCHLEY

CLEANING OUT THE DESK

THE first thing I have got to do in my campaign to make this bright new year a better one for all of us is to clean out my desk. I started on this a little over a week ago, but, so far, I have got only to the second drawer on the left hand side. I think that people must have been sneaking up during the last three or four years and putting things in my desk drawers while I have been asleep (they couldn't have done it while I was awake, for I have been working here every minute and would most certainly have noticed them at it, that is, unless they were dressed like gnomes. I never pay any attention to gnomes fussing around my desk when I am working. In fact, I rather like it). But somebody has been at work, and hard at work, putting little objects and bits of paper in my desk drawers since the last time I went through them. And I don't know whether to throw them away or not.

For instance, what would I ever have wanted with an old mitten that I should have tucked it 'way back in that upper left hand drawer? It was right up against the back partition of the drawer, under a program of the six-day bicycle race of February, 1923, and clinging to it, almost a part of it, was half a life-saver (clove flavor). Now, I never wear mittens, and even if I did it certainly wouldn't be a mitten like this. Furthermore, it has no mate. I haven't tried it on, for I would rather not have much to do with it in its present state, but I think it is for the right hand only. As I lift it gingerly out of the drawer (I was at first afraid it was a small beaver) it seems to have some lumpy object tucked away up in the very tip, but I am not going in to find out what it is. I may have a man come up with a ferret and get the whole thing settled once and for all, but for the present both the mitten and the piece of life-saver are over in the corner of the room where I tossed them. I almost wish that they were back in the drawer again.

Just in front of the mitten, and a little to the left, I came upon a pile of old check book stubs (1926–'28 inclusive, with February, April, July and August of 1926, and September to December of 1927 missing). On thumbing these over I was fascinated to see how many checks I had made out to "cash" and for what generous amounts. I must have been a pretty prodigal boy in those days. Dear me, dear me! Here is one made out to the Alsatian Novelty Company for $11.50 on October 5, 1926. What traffic was I having with the Alsatian Novelty Company, do you suppose? Whatever it was, it wasn't enough of a novelty to make an impression on me — or on anyone else, I guess. Maybe it was that rubber girdle that I sent for when I first began to notice that I was putting on weight. Whatever became of that, I wonder? I know what became of the weight, because it is right there where it was, but the girdle never did much but make me look bulky. Maybe the girdle is in the bottom drawer which I haven't come to yet.

Now about those old check stubs. I suppose that they might as well be thrown away, but then supposing the Alsatian Novelty Company should come around and say that I never paid the $11.50! I would be in a pretty pickle, wouldn't I? Of course, no jury would acquit me merely on the evidence of a check stub, but I don't know where the cancelled checks are and this would at least show that I was systematic about the thing. Then, too, the income tax people never get around to complaining about your payments until three or four years after they are made, and it might come in handy to be able to write to them and say: "On March 15, 1928, according to my records, sent you a

check for $45.60. It is up to you to find it." It might
frighten them a little, anyway. So I guess the best thing
to do is to put the stubs right back in the drawer and sit
tight. All I hope is that no trouble arises over the checks
drawn during those months which are lost. I wouldn't
have a leg to stand on in that case.

In with the pile of check stubs I found a pamphlet entitled, "The Control of the Root Knot," issued by the U.S.
Department of Agriculture in 1923. Now "root knot" is
something that I never have had much trouble with (knock
wood) and why I should have been saving a pamphlet on
its control for seven years is something that not only mysti-
fies, but irritates me a little. I read some of it and even
then I didn't see why.

However, in 1923 I evidently thought that it might come
in handy some day, and if I throw it away now it would be
just my luck to come down with root knot next week and
need it very badly. It is possible, of course, that I never
had any hand in sending for the pamphlet at all and that
it has been put in my desk by those mysterious agencies
which I suspected at first (gnomes, or people representing
themselves to be gnomes), in which case I am just making
a fool of myself by hoarding it for another seven years. I
guess that I will put it aside and read it thoroughly some
day before throwing it away. Maybe my name is mentioned in it somewhere.

One article, however, which I recognized almost immediately is an old German pipe, one of those with a long
crooked stem and a bowl covered with straw. I think that
I bought that myself; at any rate I remember trying to
smoke it once or twice. But as soon as I got the tobacco
into it and the fire started so that it would draw, it went out.
This, I figured, was owing to my shutting the lid down over
the bowl. The lid was evidently meant to be shut down, as
there was a hinge on it (now fortunately broken so that it

hangs loosely to one side), but I guess that I didn't quite have the knack of the thing. I remember thinking that sometimes I might want to dress up in German costume for a lark or something, and then if I saved the pipe all I would have to get would be the German costume. So I saved it, and, as luck would have it, have never been called upon to dress up. There is still some of the original to- bacco in it — some is in it and some is in the drawer — and I got a little sentimental over the memories of the old days in Munich where I bought it. (I was in Munich for three hours, between trains.) I even tried to smoke a little of it without clamping down the lid, but either the tobacco wasn't very good or my stomach isn't what it used to be, for I didn't go through with the scheme. "Wer nicht die Sehnsucht kennt —" and whatever the rest of the quota- tion is.

All of this, you will see, took up quite a lot of time. It is necessary that I get the desk cleaned out if I am ever going to start fresh now, but, with the first two drawers giving up such a wealth of sentimental memorabilia, I must evi- dently give over several days to it. There is, for instance, the letter from my insurance company, dated June 15, 1928, saying that as I have allowed policy No. 4756340 to lapse it will be necessary for me to take another physical examination before I can be reinstated. Now the question arises: Did I ever take the examination, and am I rein- stated? I remember taking an examination, but I think it was for the war. I certainly don't think that I have had my shirt off before a doctor since 1928 and I am afraid that if I call them up about it to find out they will make me do it right away, and that would be too bad because I wouldn't get anywhere near such a good mark now as I would when the policy first lapsed. I might even have to do a lot of homework in order to catch up with my class. I think what I will do is set about right now getting into condition again and then call them up.   I don't see how that letter ever got so far back in the drawer.

There is one thing, however, that I shall never be short of again, and that is matches, I have never seen so many matches in one place as there were in my desk drawer. Here I have sat day after day, unable to work because I was out of matches with which to light my pipe, and all the time there were enough matches right under my nose (if I had put my nose in the upper left hand drawer) to do parlor tricks with for 10 years.   They are all in those little paper covers, some containing five matches, some none, but, added together, a magnificent hoard.   I don't right now see the advantage of saving empty match covers, but I suppose I had some good reason at the time.   Perhaps I liked the pictures on them.   There are some with pictures of hotels on them which I never visited in my life (Atlantic City has a marvellous representation) and I am afraid that I would have a difficult time denying that I had ever been to the Five Devils Inn in Tia Juana with such damning evidence as two match covers bearing its advertisement staring the examiners in the face.   But honestly, I haven't. However, there are seven matches left in one and one match in the other; so I am going to save them anyway.   And what a lot of fun I am going to have with my new found treasures!   It might even be the means of my becoming a pyromaniac.

But there!   I mustn't think of such things now.   All I have to do is to get those other four drawers cleaned out and the papers which are on the back of my desk sorted out (I am a little nervous about tackling those papers, as I have heard a strange rustling in there lately and there might be field mice) and I shall be all spick and span and ready for the new year.   All I hope is that the other drawers don't take as long as the first two have, or it will be 1931, and then I would have to wait until 1940 for another good, even year to start fresh.

STEPHEN BUTLER LEACOCK

Although Stephen Leacock was born in England, in 1869, *his family brought him to Canada when he was only seven years old, and as he has since made his home on this side of the Atlantic, he is able to understand, with equal clarity and humor, the point of view of the American or Canadian tourist in England and that of the English visitor to America. He received the B.A. degree from the University of Toronto in* 1891, *taught for eight years at his old school, Upper Canada College, studied for three years more at the University of Chicago, where he took his Ph.D. degree in* 1903, *and has been since that time at McGill University, as Lecturer in Political Science and as Head of the Department of Economics and Political Science. He is distinguished, professionally, both as teacher and as author of several books, from* Elements of Political Science (1906) *to* Economic Prosperity in the British Empire (1930). *To the general reading public, however, he is known as a delightfully humorous essayist. The discerning have found that there is a method in even his most apparent madness. He has satirized modern authors and fiction in such parodies as* Literary Lapses (1910), Nonsense Novels (1911) *and* Frenzied Fiction (1917). *He has ridiculed other foibles of contemporary life and thought in* Behind the Beyond (1913) *and* Moonbeams from the Larger Lunacy (1915). *Beneath the fun of* My Discovery of England (1922) *is a series of shrewd and penetrating criticisms, not only of the natives, but of the complacent travelers as well.*

STEPHEN BUTLER LEACOCK

OXFORD AS I SEE IT

M Y PRIVATE station being that of a university professor, I was naturally deeply interested in the system of education in England. I was therefore led to make a special visit to Oxford and to submit the place to a searching scrutiny. Arriving one afternoon at four o'clock, I stayed at the Mitre Hotel and did not leave until eleven o'clock next morning. The whole of this time, except for one hour spent in addressing the undergraduates, was devoted to a close and eager study of the great university. When I add to this that I had already visited Oxford in 1907 and spent a Sunday at All Souls with Colonel L. S. Amery, it will be seen at once that my views on Oxford are based upon observations extending over fourteen years.

At any rate I can at least claim that my acquaintance with the British university is just as good a basis for reflection and judgment as that of the numerous English critics who come to our side of the water. I have known a famous English author to arrive at Harvard University in the morning, have lunch with President Lowell, and then write a whole chapter on the Excellence of Higher Education in America. I have known another one to come to Harvard, have lunch with President Lowell, and do an entire book on the Decline of Serious Study in America. Or take the case of my own university. I remember Mr. Rudyard Kipling coming to McGill and saying in his address to the undergraduates at 2.30 P.M., "You have here a great institution." But how could he have gathered this information? As far as I know he spent the entire morning with Sir Andrew Macphail in his house beside the campus, smoking cigarettes.   When I add that he distinctly refused to visit the Palæontologic Museum, that he saw nothing of our new hydraulic apparatus, or of our classes in Domestic Science, his judgment that we had here a great institution seems a little bit superficial.   I can only put beside it, to redeem it in some measure, the hasty and ill-formed judgment expressed by Lord Milner, "McGill is a noble university": and the rash and indiscreet expression of the Prince of Wales, when we gave him an LL.D. degree, "McGill has a glorious future."

To my mind these unthinking judgments about our great college do harm, and I determined, therefore, that anything that I said about Oxford should be the result of the actual observation and real study based upon a bona fide residence in the Mitre Hotel.

On the strength of this basis of experience I am prepared to make the following positive and emphatic statements. Oxford is a noble university.   It has a great past.   It is at present the greatest university in the world: and it is quite possible that it has a great future.   Oxford trains scholars of the real type better than any other place in the world. Its methods are antiquated.   It despises science.   Its lectures are rotten.   It has professors who never teach and students who never learn.   It has no order, no arrangement, no system.   Its curriculum is unintelligible.   It has no president.   It has no state legislature to tell it how to teach, and yet — it gets there.   Whether we like it or not, Oxford gives something to its students, a life and a mode of thought, which in America as yet we can emulate but not equal.

If anybody doubts this let him go and take a room at the Mitre Hotel (ten and six for a wainscoted bedroom, period of Charles I) and study the place for himself.

These singular results achieved at Oxford are all the

more surprising when one considers the distressing conditions under which the students work. The lack of an adequate building fund compels them to go on working in the same old buildings which they have had for centuries. The buildings at Brasenose College have not been renewed since the year 1525. In New College and Magdalen the students are still housed in the old buildings erected in the sixteenth century. At Christ Church I was shown a kitchen which had been built at the expense of Cardinal Wolsey in 1527. Incredible though it may seem, they have no other place to cook in than this and are compelled to use it today. On the day when I saw this kitchen, four cooks were busy roasting an ox whole for the students' lunch: this at least is what I presumed they were doing from the size of the fire-place used, but it may not have been an ox; perhaps it was a cow. On a huge table, twelve feet by six and made of slabs of wood five inches thick, two other cooks were rolling out a game pie. I estimated it as measuring three feet across. In this rude way, unchanged since the time of Henry VIII, the unhappy Oxford students are fed. I could not help contrasting it with the cosy little boarding houses on Cottage Grove Avenue where I used to eat when I was a student at Chicago, or the charming little basement dining-rooms of the students' boarding houses in Toronto. But then, of course, Henry VIII never lived in Toronto.

The same lack of a building-fund necessitates the Oxford students' living in the identical old boarding houses they had in the sixteenth and seventeenth centuries. Technically they are called "quadrangles," "closes" and "rooms"; but I am so broken in to the usage of my student days that I can't help calling them boarding houses. In many of these the old stairway has been worn down by the feet of ten generations of students: the windows have little latticed panes: there are old names carved here and there upon the stone, and a thick growth of ivy covers the walls. The boarding house at St. John's College dates from 1509, the one at Christ Church from the same period. A few hundred thousand pounds would suffice to replace these old buildings with neat steel and brick structures like the normal school at Schenectady, N.Y., or the Peel Street High School at Montreal. But nothing is done. A movement was indeed attempted last autumn towards removing the ivy from the walls, but the result was unsatisfactory and they are putting it back. Anyone could have told them beforehand that the mere removal of the ivy would not brighten Oxford up, unless at the same time one cleared the stones of the old inscriptions, put in steel fire-escapes, and in fact brought the boarding houses up to date.

But Henry VIII being dead, nothing was done. Yet in spite of its dilapidated buildings and its lack of fire-escapes, ventilation, sanitation, and up-to-date kitchen facilities, I persist in my assertion that I believe that Oxford, in its way, is the greatest university in the world. I am aware that this is an extreme statement and needs explanation. Oxford is much smaller in numbers, for example, than the State University of Minnesota, and is much poorer. It has, or had till yesterday, fewer students than the University of Toronto. To mention Oxford beside the 26,000 students of Columbia University sounds ridiculous. In point of money, the $39,000,000 endowment of the University of Chicago, and the $35,000,000 one of Columbia, and the $43,000,000 of Harvard seem to leave Oxford nowhere. Yet the peculiar thing is that it is not nowhere. By some queer process of its own it seems to get there every time. It was therefore of the very greatest interest to me, as a profound scholar, to try to investigate just how this peculiar excellence of Oxford arises.

It can hardly be due to anything in the curriculum or

program of studies. Indeed, to anyone accustomed to the best models of a university curriculum as it flourishes in the United States and Canada, the program of studies is frankly quite laughable. There is less Applied Science in the place than would be found with us in a theological college. Hardly a single professor at Oxford would recognize a dynamo if he met it in broad daylight. The Oxford student learns nothing of chemistry, physics, heat, plumbing, electric wiring, gas-fitting or the use of a blow-torch. Any American college student can run a motor-car, take a gasoline engine to pieces, fix a washer on a kitchen tap, mend a broken electric bell, and give an expert opinion on what has gone wrong with the furnace. It is these things indeed which stamp him as a college man, and occasion a very pardonable pride in the minds of his parents. But in all these things the Oxford student is the merest amateur.

This is bad enough. But after all one might say this is only the mechanical side of education. True: but one searches in vain in the Oxford curriculum for any adequate recognition of the higher and more cultured studies. Strange though it seems to us on this side of the Atlantic, there are no courses at Oxford in Housekeeping, or in Salesmanship, or in Advertising, or on Comparative Religion, or on the influence of the Press. There are no lectures whatever on Human Behaviour, on Altruism, on Egotism, or on the Play of Wild Animals. Apparently, the Oxford student does not learn these things. This cuts him off from a great deal of the larger culture of our side of the Atlantic. "What are you studying this year?" I once asked a fourth year student at one of our great colleges. "I am electing Salesmanship and Religion," he answered. Here was a young man whose training was destined inevitably to turn him into a moral business man: either that or nothing. At Oxford Salesmanship is not taught and Religion takes the feeble form of the New Testament.   The more one looks at these things the more amazing it becomes that Oxford can produce any results at all.

The effect of the comparison is heightened by the peculiar position occupied at Oxford by the professors' lectures.   In the colleges of Canada and the United States the lectures are supposed to be a really necessary and useful part of the student's training.   Again and again I have heard the graduates of my own college assert that they had got as much, or nearly as much, out of the lectures at college as out of athletics or the Greek letter society or the Banjo and Mandolin Club.   In short, with us the lectures form a real part of the college life.   At Oxford it is not so. The lectures, I understand, are given and may even be taken.   But they are quite worthless and are not supposed to have anything much to do with the development of the student's mind.   "The lectures here," said a Canadian student to me, "are punk."   I appealed to another student to know if this was so.   "I don't know whether I'd call them exactly punk," he answered, "but they're certainly rotten."   Other judgments were that the lectures were of no importance: that nobody took them: that they don't matter: that you can take them if you like: that they do you no harm.

It appears further that the professors themselves are not keen on their lectures.   If the lectures are called for they give them; if not, the professor's feelings are not hurt.   He merely waits and rests his brain until in some later year the students call for his lectures.   There are men at Oxford who have rested their brains this way for over thirty years: the accumulated brain power thus dammed up is said to be colossal.

I understand that the key to this mystery is found in the operations of the person called the tutor.   It is from him, or rather with him, that the students learn all that they know: one and all are agreed on that. Yet it is a little odd to know just how he does it. "We go over to his rooms," said one student, "and he just lights a pipe and talks to us." "We sit round with him," said another, "and he simply smokes and goes over our exercises with us." From this and other evidence I gather that what an Oxford tutor does is to get a little group of students together and smoke at them. Men who have been systematically smoked at for four years turn into ripe scholars. If anybody doubts this, let him go to Oxford and he can see the thing actually in operation. A well-smoked man speaks and writes English with a grace that can be acquired in no other way.

In what was said above, I seem to have been directing criticism against the Oxford professors as such: but I have no intention of doing so. For the Oxford professor and his whole manner of being I have nothing but a profound respect. There is indeed the greatest difference between the modern up-to-date American idea of a professor and the English type. But even with us in older days, in the bygone time when such people as Henry Wadsworth Longfellow were professors, one found the English idea; a professor was supposed to be a venerable kind of person, with snow-white whiskers reaching to his stomach. He was expected to moon around the campus oblivious of the world around him. If you nodded to him he failed to see you. Of money he knew nothing; of business, far less. He was, as his trustees were proud to say of him, "a child."

On the other hand he contained within him a reservoir of learning of such depth as to be practically bottomless. None of this learning was supposed to be of any material or commercial benefit to anybody. Its use was in saving the soul and enlarging the mind.

At the head of such a group of professors was one whose

beard was even whiter and longer, whose absence of mind was even still greater, and whose knowledge of money, business, and practical affairs was below zero. Him they made the president.

All this is changed in America. A university professor is now a busy, hustling person, approximating as closely to a business man as he can do it. It is on the business man that he models himself. He has a little place that he calls his "office," with a typewriter machine and a stenographer. Here he sits and dictates letters, beginning after the best business models, "in re yours of the eighth ult. would say, etc., etc." He writes these letters to students, to his fellow professors, to the president, indeed to any people who will let him write to them. The number of letters that he writes each month is duly counted and set to his credit. If he writes enough he will get a reputation as an "executive," and big things may happen to him. He may even be asked to step out of the college and take a post as an "executive" in a soap company or an advertising firm. The man, in short, is a "hustler," an "advertiser" whose highest aim is to be a "live-wire." If he is not, he will presently be dismissed, or, to use the business term, be "let go," by a board of trustees who are themselves hustlers and live-wires. As to the professor's soul, he no longer needs to think of it as being handed over along with all the others to a Board of Censors.

The American professor deals with his students according to his lights. It is his business to chase them along over a prescribed ground at a prescribed pace like a flock of sheep. They all go humping together over the hurdles with the professor chasing them with a set of "tests" and "recitations," "marks" and "attendances," the whole apparatus obviously copied from the time-clock of the business man's factory. This process is what is called "showing results." The pace set is necessarily that of the slow-est, and thus results in what I have heard Mr. Edward Beatty describe as the "convoy system of education."

In my own opinion, reached after fifty-two years of profound reflection, this system contains in itself the seeds of destruction. It puts a premium on dulness and a penalty on genius. It circumscribes that latitude of mind which is the real spirit of learning. If we persist in it we shall presently find that true learning will fly away from our universities and will take rest wherever some individual and enquiring mind can mark out its path for itself.

Now the principal reason why I am led to admire Oxford is that the place is little touched as yet by the measuring of "results," and by this passion for visible and provable "efficiency." The whole system at Oxford is such as to put a premium on genius and to let mediocrity and dulness go their way. On the dull student Oxford, after a proper lapse of time, confers a degree which means nothing more than that he lived and breathed at Oxford and kept out of jail. This for many students is as much as society can expect. But for the gifted students Oxford offers great opportunities. There is no question of his hanging back till the last sheep has jumped over the fence. He need wait for no one. He may move forward as fast as he likes, following the bent of his genius. If he has in him any ability beyond that of the common herd, his tutor, interested in his studies, will smoke at him until he kindles him into a flame. For the tutor's soul is not harassed by herding dull students, with dismissal hanging by a thread over his head in the class room. The American professor has no time to be interested in a clever student. He has time to be interested in his "department," his letter-writing, his executive work, and his organizing ability and his hope of promotion to a soap factory. But with that his mind is exhausted. The student of genius merely means to him a student who gives no trouble, who passes all his "tests," and is present at all his "recitations." Such a student also, if he can be trained to be a hustler and an advertiser, will undoubtedly "make good." But beyond that the professor does not think of him. The everlasting principle of equality has inserted itself in a place where it has no right to be, and where inequality is the breath of life.

American or Canadian college trustees would be horrified at the notion of professors who apparently do no work, give few or no lectures and draw their pay merely for existing. Yet these are really the only kind of professors worth having — I mean, men who can be trusted with a vague general mission in life, with a salary guaranteed at least till their death, and a sphere of duties entrusted solely to their own consciences and the promptings of their own desires. Such men are rare, but a single one of them, when found, is worth ten "executives" and a dozen "organizers."

The excellence of Oxford, then, as I see it, lies in the peculiar vagueness of the organization of its work. It starts from the assumption that the professor is a really learned man whose sole interest lies in his own sphere: and that a student, or at least the only student with whom the university cares to reckon seriously, is a young man who desires to know. This is an ancient mediæval attitude long since buried in more up-to-date places under successive strata of compulsory education, state teaching, the democratization of knowledge and the substitution of the shadow for the substance, and the casket for the gem. No doubt, in newer places the thing has got to be so. Higher education in America flourishes chiefly as a qualification for entrance into a money-making profession, and not as a thing in itself. But in Oxford one can still see the surviving outline of a nobler type of structure and a higher inspiration.

I do not mean to say, however, that my judgment of

Oxford is one undiluted stream of praise. In one respect at least I think that Oxford has fallen away from the high ideals of the Middle Ages. I refer to the fact that it admits women students to its studies. In the Middle Ages women were regarded with a peculiar chivalry long since lost. It was taken for granted that their brains were too delicately poised to allow them to learn anything. It was presumed that their minds were so exquisitely hung that intellectual effort might disturb them. The present age has gone to the other extreme: and this is seen nowhere more than in the crowding of women into colleges originally designed for men. Oxford, I regret to find, has not stood out against this change.

To a profound scholar like myself, the presence of these young women, many of them most attractive, flittering up and down the streets of Oxford in their caps and gowns, is very distressing.

Who is to blame for this and how they first got in I do not know. But I understand that they first of all built a private college of their own close to Oxford, and then edged themselves in foot by foot. If this is so they only followed up the precedent of the recognized method in use in America. When an American college is established, the women go and build a college of their own overlooking the grounds. Then they put on becoming caps and gowns and stand and look over the fence at the college athletics. The male undergraduates, who were originally and by nature a hardy lot, were not easily disturbed. But inevitably some of the senior trustees fell in love with the first year girls and became convinced that coeducation was a noble cause. American statistics show that between 1880 and 1900 the number of trustees and senior professors who married girl undergraduates or who wanted to do so reached a percentage of — I forget the exact percentage; it was either a hundred or a little over.

I don't know just what happened at Oxford but presumably something of the sort took place. In any case the women are now all over the place. They attend the college lectures, they row in a boat, and they perambulate the High Street. They are even offering a serious competition against the men. Last year they carried off the ping-pong championship and took the chancellor's prize for needlework, while in music, cooking, and millinery the men are said to be nowhere.

There is no doubt that unless Oxford puts the women out while there is yet time, they will overrun the whole university. What this means to the progress of learning few can tell and those who know are afraid to say.

Cambridge University, I am glad to see, still sets its face sternly against this innovation. I am reluctant to count any superiority in the University of Cambridge. Having twice visited Oxford, having made the place a subject of profound study for many hours at a time, having twice addressed its undergraduates, and having stayed at the Mitre Hotel, I consider myself an Oxford man. But I must admit that Cambridge has chosen the wiser part.

Last autumn, while I was in London on my voyage of discovery, a vote was taken at Cambridge to see if the women who have already a private college nearby, should be admitted to the university. They were triumphantly shut out; and as a fit and proper sign of enthusiasm the undergraduates went over in a body and knocked down the gates of the women's college. I know that it is a terrible thing to say that any one approved of this. All the London papers came out with headings that read — ARE OUR UNDERGRADUATES TURNING INTO BABOONS? and so on. The *Manchester Guardian* draped its pages in black and even the London *Morning Post* was afraid to take bold ground in the matter. But I do know also that there was a great deal of secret chuckling and jubilation in the London clubs. Nothing was expressed openly. The men of England have been too terrorized by the women for that. But in safe corners of the club, out of earshot of the waiters and away from casual strangers, little groups of elderly men chuckled quietly together. "Knocked down their gates, eh?" said the wicked old men to one another, and then whispered guiltily behind an uplifted hand, "Serve 'em right." Nobody dared to say anything outside. If they had some one would have got up and asked a question in the House of Commons. When this is done all England falls flat upon its face.

But for my part when I heard of the Cambridge vote, I felt as Lord Chatham did when he said in parliament, "Sir, I rejoice that America has resisted." For I have long harbored views of my own upon the higher education of women. In these days, however, it requires no little hardihood to utter a single word of criticism against it. It is like throwing half a brick through the glass roof of a conservatory. It is bound to make trouble. Let me hasten, therefore, to say that I believe most heartily in the higher education of women; in fact, the higher the better. The only question to my mind is: What is "higher education" and how do you get it? With which goes the secondary enquiry, What is a woman and is she just the same as a man? I know that it sounds a terrible thing to say in these days, but I don't believe she is.

Let me say also that when I speak of coeducation I speak of what I know. I was coeducated myself some thirty-five years ago, at the very beginning of the thing. I learned my Greek alongside of a bevy of beauty on the opposite benches that mashed up the irregular verbs for us very badly. Incidentally, those girls are all married long since, and all the Greek they know now you could put under a thimble. But of that presently.

I have had further experience as well. I spent three

years in the graduate school of Chicago, where coeducational girls were as thick as autumn leaves — and some thicker. And as a college professor at McGill University in Montreal, I have taught mingled classes of men and women for twenty years.

On the basis of which experience I say with assurance that the thing is a mistake and has nothing to recommend it but its relative cheapness. Let me emphasize this last point and have done with it. Coeducation is of course a great economy. To teach ten men and ten women in a single class of twenty costs only half as much as to teach two classes. Where economy must rule, then, the thing has got to be. But where the discussion turns not on what is cheapest, but on what is best, then the case is entirely different.

The fundamental trouble is that men and women are different creatures, with different minds and different aptitudes and different paths in life. There is no need to raise here the question of which is superior and which is inferior (though I think, the Lord help me, I know the answer to that too). The point lies in the fact that they are different.

But the mad passion for equality has masked this obvious fact. When women began to demand, quite rightly, a share in higher education, they took for granted that they wanted the same curriculum as the men. They never stopped to ask whether their aptitudes were not in various directions higher and better than those of the men, and whether it might not be better for their sex to cultivate the things which were best suited to their minds. Let me be more explicit. In all that goes with physical and mathematical science, women, on the average, are far below the standard of men. There are, of course, exceptions. But they prove nothing. It is no use to quote to me the case of some brilliant girl who stood first in physics at Cornell. That's nothing. There is an elephant in the zoo that can count up to ten, yet I refuse to reckon myself his inferior.

Tabulated results spread over years, and the actual experience of those who teach show that in the whole domain of mathematics and physics women are outclassed. At McGill the girls of our first year have wept over their failures in elementary physics these twenty-five years. It is time that some one dried their tears and took away the subject.

But, in any case, examination tests are never the whole story. To those who know, a written examination is far from being a true criterion of capacity. It demands too much of mere memory, imitativeness, and the insidious willingness to absorb other people's ideas. Parrots and crows would do admirably in examinations. Indeed, the colleges are full of them.

But take, on the other hand, all that goes with the æsthetic side of education, with imaginative literature and the cult of beauty. Here women are, or at least ought to be, the superiors of men. Women were in primitive times the first story-tellers. They are still so at the cradle side. The original college woman was the witch, with her incantations and her prophecies and the glow of her bright imagination, and if brutal men of duller brains had not burned it out of her, she would be incanting still. To my thinking, we need more witches in the colleges and less physics.

I have seen such young witches myself — if I may keep the word: I like it — in colleges such as Wellesley in Massachusetts and Bryn Mawr in Pennsylvania, where there isn't a man allowed within the three mile limit. To my mind, they do infinitely better thus by themselves. They are freer, less restrained. They discuss things openly in their classes; they lift up their voices, and they speak, whereas a girl in such a place as McGill, with men all about her, sits for four years as silent as a frog full of shot.

But there is a deeper trouble still. The careers of the men and women who go to college together are necessarily different, and the preparation is all aimed at the man's career. The men are going to be lawyers, doctors, engineers, business men, and politicians. And the women are not.

There is no use pretending about it. It may sound an awful thing to say, but the women are going to be married. That is, and always has been, their career; and, what is more, they know it; and even at college, while they are studying algebra and political economy, they have their eye on it sideways all the time. The plain fact is that, after a girl has spent four years of her time and a great deal of her parents' money in equipping herself for a career that she is never going to have, the wretched creature goes and gets married, and in a few years she has forgotten which is the hypotenuse of a right-angled triangle, and she doesn't care. She has much better things to think of.

At this point someone will shriek: "But surely, even for marriage, isn't it right that a girl should have a college education?" To which I hasten to answer: most assuredly. I freely admit that a girl who knows algebra, or once knew it, is a far more charming companion and a nobler wife and mother than a girl who doesn't know x from y. But the point is this: Does the higher education that fits a man to be a lawyer also fit a person to be a wife and mother? Or, in other words, is a lawyer a wife and mother? I say he is not. Granted that a girl is to spend four years in time and four thousand dollars in money in going to college, why train her for a career that she is never going to adopt? Why not give her an education that will have a meaning and a harmony with the real life that she is to follow?

For example, suppose that during her four years every girl lucky enough to get a higher education spent at least six months of it in the training and discipline of a hospital as a nurse. There is more education and character making in that than in a whole bucketful of algebra.

But no, the woman insists on snatching her share of an education designed by Erasmus or William of Wykeham or William of Occam for the creation of scholars and lawyers; and when later on in her home there is a sudden sickness or accident, and the life or death of those nearest to her hangs upon skill and knowledge and a trained fortitude in emergency, she must needs send in all haste for a hired woman to fill the place that she herself has never learned to occupy.

But I am not here trying to elaborate a whole curriculum. I am only trying to indicate that higher education for the man is one thing, for the woman another. Nor do I deny the fact that women have got to earn their living. Their higher education must enable them to do that. They cannot all marry on their graduation day. But that is no great matter. No scheme of education that anyone is likely to devise will fail in this respect.

The positions that they hold as teachers or civil servants they would fill all the better if their education were fitted to their wants.

Some few, a small minority, really and truly "have a career" — husbandless and childless — in which the sacrifice is great and the honor to them, perhaps, all the higher. And others no doubt dream of a career in which a husband and a group of blossoming children are carried as an appendage to a busy life at the bar or on the platform. But all such are the mere minority, so small as to make no difference to the general argument.

But there — I have written quite enough to make plenty of trouble except perhaps at Cambridge University.

So I return with relief to my general study of Oxford. Viewing the situation as a whole, I am led then to the conclusion that there must be something in the life of Oxford itself that makes for higher learning. Smoked at by his tutor, fed in Henry VIII's kitchen, and sleeping in a tangle of ivy, the student evidently gets something not easily obtained in America. And the more I reflect on the matter the more I am convinced that it is the sleeping in the ivy that does it. How different it is from student life as I remember it!

When I was a student at the University of Toronto thirty years ago, I lived — from start to finish — in seventeen different boarding houses. As far as I am aware these houses have not, or not yet, been marked with tablets. But they are still to be found in the vicinity of McCaul and Darcy, and St. Patrick Streets. Anyone who doubts the truth of what I have to say may go and look at them.

I was not alone in the nomadic life that I led. There were hundreds of us drifting about in this fashion from one melancholy habitation to another. We lived as a rule two or three in a house, sometimes alone. We dined in the basement. We always had beef, done up in some way after it was dead, and there were always soda biscuits on the table. They used to have a brand of soda biscuits in those days in the Toronto boarding houses that I have not seen since. They were better than dog biscuits but with not so much snap. My contemporaries will all remember them. A great many of the leading barristers and professional men of Toronto were fed on them.

In the life we led we had practically no opportunities for association on a large scale, no common rooms, no reading rooms, nothing. We never saw the magazines — personally I didn't even know the names of them. The only interchange of ideas we ever got was by going over

to the Cær Howell Hotel on University Avenue and inter-
changing them there.

I mention these melancholy details not for their own
sake but merely to emphasize the point that when I speak
of students' dormitories, and the larger life which they
offer, I speak of what I know.

If we had had at Toronto, when I was a student, the
kind of dormitories and dormitory life that they have at
Oxford, I don't think I would ever have graduated. I'd
have been there still. The trouble is that the universities
on our Continent are only just waking up to the idea of
what a university should mean. They were, very largely,
instituted and organized with the idea that a university
was a place where young men were sent to absorb the contents of books and to listen to lectures in the class rooms.
The student was pictured as a pallid creature, burning
what was called the "midnight oil," his wan face bent over
his desk. If you wanted to do something for him you gave
him a book: if you wanted to do something really large on
his behalf you gave him a whole basketful of them. If
you wanted to go still further and be a benefactor to the
college at large, you endowed a competitive scholarship
and set two or more pallid students working themselves
to death to get it.

The real thing for the student is the life and environment that surrounds him. All that he really learns he
learns, in a sense, by the active operation of his own intellect and not as the passive recipient of lectures. And
for this active operation what he really needs most is the
continued and intimate contact with his fellows. Students
must live together and eat together, talk and smoke together. Experience shows that that is how their minds
really grow. And they must live together in a rational
and comfortable way. They must eat in a big dining room
or hall, with oak beams across the ceiling, and the stained

glass in the windows, and with a shield or tablet here or there upon the wall, to remind them between times of the men who went before them and left a name worthy of the memory of the college. If a student is to get from his college what it ought to give him, a college dormitory, with the life in common that it brings, is his absolute right. A university that fails to give it to him is cheating him.

If I were founding a university — and I say it with all the seriousness of which I am capable — I would found first a smoking room; then when I had a little more money in hand I would found a dormitory; then after that, or more probably with it, a decent reading room and a library. After that, if I still had money over that I couldn't use, I would hire a professor and get some text books.

This chapter has sounded in the most part like a continuous eulogy of Oxford with but little in favor of our American colleges. I turn therefore with pleasure to the more congenial task of showing what is wrong with Oxford and with the English university system generally, and the aspect in which our American universities far excel the British.

The point is that Henry VIII is dead. The English are so proud of what Henry VIII and the benefactors of earlier centuries did for the universities that they forget the present. There is little or nothing in England to compare with the magnificent generosity of individuals, provinces and states, which is building up the colleges of the United States and Canada. There used to be. But by some strange confusion of thought the English people admire the noble gifts of Cardinal Wolsey and Henry VIII and Queen Margaret, and do not realize that the Carnegies and Rockefellers and the William Macdonalds are the Cardinal Wolseys of today. The University of Chicago was founded upon oil. McGill University rests largely on a basis of tobacco. In America the world of commerce and business levies on itself a noble tribute in favor of the higher learning. In England, with a few conspicuous exceptions, such as that at Bristol, there is little of the sort. The feudal families are content with what their remote ancestors have done: they do not try to emulate it in any great degree.

In the long run this must count. Of all the various reforms that are talked of at Oxford, and of all the imitations of American methods that are suggested, the only one worth while, to my thinking, is to capture a few millionaires, give them honorary degrees at a million pounds sterling apiece, and tell them to imagine that they are Henry the Eighth. I give Oxford warning that if this is not done the place will not last another two centuries.

SUGGESTIONS FOR READING

Editor's Note.   Books by authors already represented in Group Three have in general been omitted from these suggestions, since the separate introductory notices contain hints for further reading in the works of these authors.   To attempt any elaborate classification, in a field so wide and so vaguely defined as that of the personal essay, would be pedantic.   Readers familiar with the field will doubtless perceive many omissions, some due to ignorance on the part of the editor, and some, to his effort to suggest chiefly books which undergraduates have found enjoyable and profitable reading.

A. *Essays of Places and of Travel*
   Havelock Ellis: *The Soul of Spain.*
   R. B. Cunninghame Graham: *The Ipané.*
   Mogreb-el-Achsa.
   Philip Guedalla: *Argentine Tango.*
   J. Norman Hall: *On the Stream of Travel.*
   W. H. Hudson: *Idle Days in Patagonia.*
   A Traveller in Little Things.
   E. V. Lucas: *Traveller's Luck.*
   A Wanderer in Holland.
   William McFee: *Swallowing the Anchor.*
   C. E. Montague: *The Right Place.*
   Osbert Sitwell: *Discursions on Travel, Art, and Life.*

B. *Personal Essays*
   A. C. Benson: *From a College Window.*
   Augustine Birrell: *Obiter Dicta.*
   Thomas Burke: *East of Mansion House.*
   H. S. Canby: *Definitions.*
   G. K. Chesterton: *Generally Speaking; Tremendous Trifles.*
   Katherine Fullerton Gerould: *Modes and Morals.*
   Kenneth Grahame: *Pagan Papers; The Golden Age.*
   E. V. Lucas: *Lemon Verbena.*
   Robert Lynd: *It's a Fine World.*
   Rose Macaulay: *A Casual Commentary.*
   Arthur Machen: *Dreads and Drolls.*
   Don Marquis: *The Almost Perfect State.*
   A. A. Milne: *By Way of Introduction.*

Christopher Morley: *Mince Pie.*
H. W. Nevinson: *Essays in Freedom and Rebellion.*
Meredith Nicholson: *The Man in the Street.*
Agnes Repplier: *Compromises; Points of Friction.*
Logan Pearsall Smith: *Trivia.*
Simeon Strunsky: *The Rediscovery of Jones; Belshazzar Court.*
H. G. Wells: *An Englishman Looks at the World.*

GROUP FOUR
ON LITERARY TYPES

CARL VAN DOREN

Carl Van Doren, born in 1885, *graduated from the University of Illinois in* 1907, *and received the degree of Ph.D. from Columbia University in* 1911. He taught English for a time at Illinois, but has been since 1916 Associate in English at Columbia. *Meanwhile he has been Headmaster of the Brearley School* (1916–1919), Literary Editor of The Nation (1919–1922), *of* The Century Magazine (1922–1925), *and on the board of* The Literary Guild *since* 1926, *as well as managing editor of* The Cambridge History of American Literature (1917–1921). *In spite of these editorial and administrative duties he has found time to contribute frequently to periodicals and to write many books. A novelist himself* (The Ninth Wave, 1926), *he can criticize as well as create.* The American Novel (1921) *remains the most comprehensive study in its field; it has been followed by* Contemporary American Novelists (1922), *and by* American and British Literature Since 1890 (1925), *written in collaboration with his brother Mark.* The Life of Thomas Love Peacock (1911), James Branch Cabell (1925), *and* Lucifer from Nantucket (1926), *an analysis of Melville's* Moby Dick *which appeared in W. A. Drake's* American Criticism, *may be mentioned among his criticisms of individual writers and books, while* Many Minds (1924) *is a collection of critical essays.*

The following essay appeared in The New Pearson's; *it is reprinted by permission of the author, Carl Van Doren.*

CARL VAN DOREN

A NOTE ON THE ESSAY

THE sonnet has a standard form very much as a man has. Leave off the sestet of your sonnet and you do about what a god does when he leaves the legs off a man. The drama has a standard form very much as a rendezvous has. Write a drama in which no spark is exchanged between the audience and the action, and you have done what fate does when it keeps lovers from their meeting. The novel has a standard form very much as a road has. You may set out anywhere you like and go wherever you please, at any gait, but you must go somewhere, or you have made what is no more a novel than some engineer's road would be a road if it had neither beginning, end, nor direction. But the essay! It may be of any length, breadth, depth, weight, density, color, savor, odor, appearance, importance, value, or uselessness which you can or will give it. The epigram bounds it on one side and the treatise on the other, but it has in its time encroached upon the territory of both of them, and it doubtless will do so again. Or, to look at the essay from another angle, it is bounded on one side by the hell-fire sermon and on the other by the geometrical demonstration; and yet it ranges easily between these extremes of heat and cold and occasionally steals from both of them. It differs from a letter by being written to more — happily a great many more — than one person. It differs from talk chiefly by being written at all.

Having to obey no regulations as to form, the essay is very free to choose its matter. The sonnet, by reason of its form, tends to deal with solemn and not with gay themes. The drama, for the same reason, tends to look for intense and not for casual incidents. The novel tends to feel that it must carry a considerable amount of human life on its back. The essay may be as fastidious as a collector of carved emeralds or as open-minded as a garbage-gatherer. Nothing human, as the platitude says, is alien to it. The essay, however, goes beyond the platitude and dares to choose matter from numerous non-human sources. Think of the naturalists and their essays. Think, further, of the range of topics for essayists at large. Theodore Roosevelt in an essay urges the strenuous life; Max Beerbohm in an essay defends cosmetics. De Quincey expounds the fine art of murder, Thoreau the pleasures of economy, William Law the blisses of prayer, Hudson the sense of smell in men and in animals, Schopenhauer the ugliness of women, Bacon the advantages of a garden, Plutarch the traits of curiosity, and A. C. Benson the felicity of having nothing much in the mind. All, in fact, an essayist needs to start with is something, anything, to say. He gets up each morning and finds the world spread out before him, as the world was spread out before Adam and Eve the day they left paradise. With the cosmos, past, present, and future, to pick from, the essayist goes to work. If he finds a topic good enough he may write a good essay, no matter how he writes it.

He may. There is still, however, the question of his manner. Thousands of dull men have written millions of true things which no one but their proof-readers, wives, or pupils ever read. If each essayist could take out a patent on each subject into which he dips his pen, and could prevent any other pen from ever dipping into it after him, he might have better luck. But there are no monopolists in this department. Would research find in all the hoards of books or all the morgues of manuscripts a single observation which has never been made twice? Competition in such affairs is free and endless. The only law which gives an essayist a right to his material is the law which rules that the best man wins. The law does not say in what fashion he must be best. Any fashion will do. Let him be more sententious, like Bacon; or more harmonious, like Sir Thomas Browne; or more elegant, like Addison; or more direct, like Swift; or more hearty, like Fielding; or more whimsical, like Lamb; or more impassioned, like Hazlitt; or more encouraging, like Emerson; or more Olympian, like Arnold; or more funny, like Mark Twain; or more musical, like Pater; or more impish, like Max Beerbohm; or more devastating, like Mencken. Let the essayist be any of these things and he may have a copyright till someone takes it away from him. What matters is the manner. If he has good matter, he *may* write a good essay; if he has a good manner he probably *will* write a good essay.

An essay is a communication. If the subject of the discourse were the whole affair, it would be enough for the essayist to be an adequate conduit. If the manner were the whole affair, any versatile fellow might try all the manners and have a universal triumph. But back of matter and manner both lies the item which is really significant. The person who communicates anything in any way must be a person. His truth must have a tone, his speech must have a rhythm which are his and solely his. His knowledge or opinions must have lain long enough inside him to have taken root there; and when they come away they must bring some of the soil clinging to them. They must, too, have been shaped by that soil — as plants are which grow in cellars, on housetops, on hillsides, in the wide fields, under shade in forests. Many kinds of men, many kinds of essays! Important essays come from important men.

ELIZABETH A. DREW

Miss Drew studied at Lady Margaret Hall, Oxford. From 1919 to 1921 she served as Head of the Women's Staff, Department of Education, for the British Army of the Rhine. She has lectured frequently, both in the United States and in England, and is now Lecturer in English at the University of Cambridge. A most amusing account of some of her experiences on a lecture tour in this country appeared in The Outlook *for October 19, 1927. Besides contributions to other magazines, notably* The Atlantic Monthly, *Miss Drew has written* Jane Welsh and Jane Carlyle (1928), *a penetrating study of the character of Mrs. Carlyle, and* The Modern Novel (1926). *The Conclusion to this latter volume consists of the following quotation from Boswell's* Life of Johnson, *which suggests at once her critical frankness and her modesty:*

"A lady once asked him how he came to define Pastern *the knee of a horse: instead of making an elaborate defence, as she expected, he at once answered, 'Ignorance, Madam, pure ignorance.'"*

As this collection goes to press, comes the announcement of Miss Drew's most recent book, Discovering Poetry (1933).

The following essay is a chapter from The Modern Novel, *by Elizabeth A. Drew. Copyright, 1926, by Harcourt, Brace and Company, Inc.*

ELIZABETH A. DREW

THE PLAIN READER

If all the good people were clever
And all the clever people were good,
The world would be better than ever
We thought that it possibly could;

But somehow 'tis seldom or never
The two hit it off as they should,
The good are so harsh to the clever
The clever so rude to the good.

ELIZABETH WORDSWORTH

AND the rudeness of the clever to the good is expressed nowhere more caustically than when the æsthetes address the general public on the subject of literary appreciation. "Anyone who has anything to say cannot fail to be misunderstood," says Mr. Cardan in *Those Barren Leaves*. "The public only understands the things with which it is perfectly familiar. Something new makes it lose its orientation." Or we can hear Mr. Mencken cackling triumphantly as he scores hit upon palpable hit on the subject of the Nordic incapacity to comprehend art and the artist. It is all quite true. The vast majority of the public are in the position of Florence in *The Constant Nymph* as she argues with her artist husband.

"You put the wrong things first. Music, all art — What is it for? What is its justification? After all..."

"It's not for anything. It has no justification."

"It's only part of the supreme art, the business of living beautifully. You can't put it on a pedestal above decency and humanity and civilization."

"I know. You want to use it like electric light... I've
seen it; my father's cultured ——"

"That is a much abused word, but it means an important thing which we can't do without."

"Can't we? I can! By God, I can!"

The pure artist claims, as Lewis Dodd claims here, to be
creator and nothing else, and demands to be judged as
such. Literature, however, with the possible exception of
what Mr. George Moore calls pure poetry, differs from the
other major arts by its far closer approach to the terms of
actual life. In a sense this makes it easier for the general
public to appreciate, but in another sense it complicates
the outlook. It has led to the unending strife among the
critics as to the plane on which the enjoyment of literature
should function, and the poor reading public, sincerely
anxious to know what books to read, and what to look for
in the books it reads, finds itself confused and fuddled by
the contradictory advices of the experts. It knows, from
the rude things which the superior intellectuals say about
it, that its natural instinct to regard literary values exactly as if they were moral values, and to judge books as
it would judge human conduct, is inadequate and mislead-
ing; but how is it to choose an alternative? It reads books
in a straightforward way, and wants to criticize them in a
straightforward way, but there are the Art for Art's sakers
who demand a purely æsthetic standard, making of literature, as of the fine arts, an exclusive cult for exclusive people. The intellectual theorists are not very much more
helpful, even though Matthew Arnold and Pater, the literary philosophers, with their somewhat vague talk of ab-
stractions like Beauty and Good and Sweetness and Light
and hard gemlike flames of the mind, have been followed
by the newer race of literary psychologists; then there are
the social historians like Taine, generalizing all individual-

ity into a national and social significance, with the anatomists to whom technique means everything, and finally the mere gossips who deal in nothing but the froth of personalities.

It is no wonder if the patient dies while all these doctors disagree, yet the holding of some standard of appreciation is essential to the intelligent enjoyment of reading, even of novel reading. The novel may be an amusement for an idle hour, but it may equally be, as Jane Austen claims for it, "a work in which the greatest powers of the mind are displayed: in which the most thorough knowledge of human nature, the happiest delineations of its varieties, the liveliest effusions of wit and humour, are conveyed to the world in the best chosen language." It is worth considering, therefore, how a novel which is a serious work of literature should be approached, for it is an inquiry which is of importance to all readers and to all writers of novels, that is, to a majority of the inhabitants of the English-speaking world.

It may, I think, be of some help if, before arguing further about literary appreciation, we go back another step, to the root of the matter, and ask the basic question what literature *is*. Sir Arthur Quiller-Couch has defined it, "what sundry men and women have said memorably concerning life," which is, perhaps, as good a working definition as it is possible to find. As modern scholarship enables us to see further and further into past civilizations and "the dark backward and abyss of time," the more apparent does it become that human nature remains essentially unchanged. Egyptian, Greek, Chinese, Hindu, medieval, Renaissance or modern European thinkers and creators, tell the same stories, and distil the same comments from them as to the nature of life and of mankind. Men and women all down the ages have faced the same eternal human problems and have asked the same eternal human questions as they found themselves confronted by the same harsh interplay of human venture and event, the same clash of opposites which forever thwart and jar each other in human existence: aspiration and achievement, physical and spiritual, actual and ideal, good and evil, life and death. Meanwhile, all those who have had what we vaguely call the gift of expression, have always striven to describe in words something of what they have seen, something of what they have heard, something of what they have thought, something of what they have felt, in this eternal and unchanging drama, the author of the Book of Job crying with the same voice as Oedipus or Milton's Samson, "God of our Fathers, what is Man?" No writer can ever solve the riddle: the characters he creates are but comments suggested by his own mind, the stories he tells are but illustrations evolved by his own mind, and these comments and illustrations vary with every age and nationality and individual. But the aim of each in turn is always and eternally the same: to give some created vision of what life is, it may be to fall into the baffling fascination of attempting to explain its why; and the unfading interest for the reader is to compare epochs and peoples and personalities as they practise this single aim: to watch each one, from Confucius to Conrad, from Sophocles to Shaw, as he illustrates and interprets human existence in the terms of his own times and his own temperament. We are all, as Galsworthy says, little bits of continuity, and "the still sad music of humanity" remains the same melody, whether we listen to it as the Song of Solomon or in the latest jazz tempo, interpreted through shawm or lyre, spinet or saxophone.

All art, since it cannot use as its material anything but what already exists in the universe, must in some degree be a comment and interpretation of that universe, but literature has a relationship to life far more close than that of any of the other arts, since it uses the same medium by whose help we carry on our human intercourse, the medium of language. The media of colour, sound, mass or line are not used as natural bases for human communication except in the world of cinema, where the art of miming and making faces must perforce replace human speech. Average human beings live their lives with the help of words, conveying their experiences, expressing their thoughts, and interpreting their emotions through them. The literary artist uses exactly the same material, hence the impossibility of detaching the experiences of literature entirely from those of actual living. Oscar Wilde declares that, to the elect, beautiful things mean only Beauty, but I think we can safely say that there is no human being to whom *Hamlet* or the *Odyssey* means only Beauty. The artistic emotion the most cultivated and sensitive mind experiences on reading them is complicated by direct emotional, intellectual, and moral impressions which it inevitably receives at the same time.

More than ever is this so with the novel, since the novel is almost entirely concerned with problems and situations common to all men, so that it is more than ever inevitable that questions of content alone should intrude in our judgment of it, as well as the æsthetic questions of the fusion of subject matter and form. The novel, dealing as it does with the actions and passions of human beings whom we think of in the terms of fellow living creatures, and telling of crisis, incident, character and circumstance within the observation of us all, is bound to express certain of the moral values men live by, and by implication, if not directly, the attitude of the author towards those values, so that it is almost as difficult to divorce a discussion of the novel from questions of conduct as for a blind man with one arm to get out of a bunker with a toothpick — as Mr. P. G. Wodehouse would say!

But this brings us at once to the central difficulty of intelligent appreciation of the modern English and American novel, and the ground of attack by the intellectuals and the æsthetes.   Human life, as all experiencers of it are agreed, is a sorry scheme.   We are all comrades in distress and dissatisfaction, united in a tragic community of longing to lighten "the weary weight of all this unintelligible world."   Hence, since the novel portrays so many of the riddles of life as we meet them in life itself, great numbers of readers go to the novel in much the same spirit in which they would go to a fortune teller.   They do not really want to be told the truth about life, or to listen to speculation about life, they want to be reassured about it: to get some comforting "message."   There is a certain American magazine which sends out slips for its contributors' guidance, stating: "Humour, tragedy and pathos are acceptable, but not stories that are morbid or that leave the reader uncomfortable."   The editor of this magazine reads the average reader aright.   Hence the inanities of the ordinary magazine story and the glut of popular love romances, where, in place of the pessimism "more black than ash buds in the front of March" (which is so popular among the intellectuals, but which leaves the average reader uncomfortable), we find a sincere sentimentalism more sticky than chestnut buds in the front of April, which apparently somehow convinces him, and still more, her, that she herself some day will be clothed with the heavens and crowned with the stars.

This craving for a certain emotional effect in fiction goes deeper than the demand for sentimental romance, and involves the whole matter of "uplift."   There is, says Mr. Edwin Muir, one great orthodox heresy about the universe which makes it such a dull place to live in, and that is the dogma that if a thing is not useful it cannot be important. It is a heresy imbedded with peculiar tenacity in the Anglo-

Saxon mind, which makes it demand perpetually that the meaning of life and the message of art shall lie in its own especial code of conduct, and which makes it distrust any manifestation of human energy unless a definite lesson can be drawn from it. Readers who hold this heresy seem to regard literature as the Polonius of life, a sort of mine of useful and helpful and improving maxims and truisms, whose sole purpose is to be the mouthpiece of established order and the bourgeois virtues: the missing link between God and suburbia. It arises from a failure to distinguish between literary and moral values, between conduct in life and the representation of conduct in writing. Now this *is* difficult for the general reader, because as I have already said it is not possible entirely to divorce literature from moral questions. There is, of course, always the extreme logical position of Plato, the first Puritan, who argued that since art is imitation, and of bad no less than good, therefore there must be evil in it: that the same person cannot at the same time devote himself to the development of pure good and be creating characters of evil. Hence his ideal republic must banish entirely all art and all artists. But if we accept the Aristotelian view that the universe is rationally organized, and that the existence of art in it as one of the natural functions of human nature proves that it has a proper place in life and a part in the ultimate perfection of life, we must decide what that place is. "You confuse two things," says Tchekov, "solving a problem, and stating it correctly. It is only the second that is obligatory for the artist." This is the whole kernel of the matter. When the artist is creating he no more thinks of the purely moral qualities of his creation than passionate lovers think of the moral qualities of the child that may spring from their ecstatic union. Creation is creation, not something else. The artist takes as much pains and is as much absorbed in his creation of evil as of

good, of ugliness as of beauty. He lavishes as much work
and care, and exactly the same *sort* of work and care, on
Iago as on Othello, on Medea as on Alkestis, on a gargoyle
as on the Venus of Milo. He looks on experience as an
end in itself, while the moralist regards it as a symptom
which must be treated in relation to some general manifestation of truth, and requires that a book shall conform to
some special ethical formula. We might illustrate the
point from that very brilliant recent novel, from which I
have already quoted, *The Constant Nymph.* The implacable reporter of human experience who is the creator
of that book chooses a group of human beings to play her
story, notes the inevitable outcome of the clashes of character and circumstance she has planned, and is concerned
only to present that interplay of character and circumstance with all the intensity of realization, clarity of outline and economy of language of which she is capable.
She has no other aim. Were she a sentimentalist we should
be presented with an Ethel M. Dell or a Maud Diver
solution and Florence would have a convenient railway
accident so that Teresa could marry Lewis Dodd and live
happily ever afterwards. Sentimental readers, no doubt,
wished this had happened. Or again, if she were a social
moralist, like the late Mrs. Humphry Ward, Lewis would
conform his music to the immediate claims of his environment, and we should have an end typifying Art rendering
Service to Humanity through the Sacrifice of Selfish Aims.
And social moralists, no doubt, wish *that* had happened.
But as it is the book stands as a piece of literature and must
be discussed as such. It is neither a dream nor a tract.

   To say that a serious novel must be discussed as a
piece of creative art and not as a piece of life is to contra-
dict what we have already said as to the impossibility
of divorcing the discussion of literature from questions of
conduct. The novel is concerned with the statement of

human truths and problems and cannot get away from them, but the point always to be remembered is that the author is concerned with the *creation* of those truths and problems and not primarily with any *comment* on them. The illustrations of conduct which he creates concern us (in our character as critics of literature) only in so far as they involve a criticism of the *literary* treatment of such conduct, and an understanding of the author's mind. It is just as much a sin against *literature* to read a book for nothing but a useful moral lesson, as to read it for nothing but a sensual thrill, and to judge a work to be defective *as literature* because it leaves no helpful message and encouragement for living, is as stupid as to judge a chrysanthemum to be defective because it does not eat as well as a cauliflower.

Perhaps the point will be clearer if we again look for a moment at the past and consider some accepted masterpieces and our attitude to them. We shall then be aware at once that our enjoyment of them depends not at all on our agreement or disagreement with their ethical standards. Since public opinion is now agreed about the artistic value of these works, we instinctively leave any personal view of their morality out of account in reading them and concentrate our attention on feeling their literary qualities. For example, suppose we found this paragraph in the police news of a daily paper:

MIXED MARRIAGE
MURDER AND SUICIDE
Finds Truth Too Late, Says Colored Husband

An inquest was held on Wednesday last to investigate the circumstances attending the deaths of a Moor and his wife (a white woman) which took place Monday night last under tragic circumstances. It appeared from the evidence of the deceased man's secretary, Michael Cassio, that the couple, who had only recently been married, had lived together very happily, until his employer had come under the influence of his manager, a man of the name of Iago. This man, who was now in hospital as a result of wounds received on the night of the murder, had convinced his employer of his wife's improper intimacy with himself (the witness). Inflamed by jealousy, and without waiting to carefully investigate the charge, the Moor had suffocated his wife in bed, and on discovering from her maid that his suspicions had been groundless, had stabbed himself to death in the presence of the police who were about to take him into custody.

On reading this sordid tale of lust and jealousy we should probably comment on the problems of marriages of mixed races, and the baseness of human instincts, and so on: if it appeared as a modern novel, the American Society for the Suppression of Vice would certainly try to get it suppressed, and a great number of readers would say that they didn't want to hear about that sort of people and that life was unpleasant enough without meeting that sort of thing in fiction. But when we read the play of *Othello* we are not concerned to discuss the facts of the plot as such, because we allow ourselves to be concerned with the validity of Shakespeare's imagination in dealing with them: the literary and not the moral question. Or again, the fact that there are very few people nowadays who would agree with Milton's theology or believe literally the story of *Paradise Lost* does not impair our literary enjoyment of the epic. In the same way Shelley's *Prometheus Unbound* can be fully appreciated by someone who is neither a Socialist or a pantheist: Burns's *Jolly Beggars* can be read with pleasure by a member of the Charity Organization Society, and Cowley's delightful lines on drinking not only by any citizen of the United States in general, but I believe by even the strictest inhabitant of Kansas! It will be found, indeed, that none of us demands standards of use from accepted works of art: we do not ask the cubic con-

tents of Keats's Grecian Urn, or require that Shelley's
West Wind shall grind corn.

It is time, though, to leave the negative discussion of
what intelligent criticism is not, and to attempt to form
some standard of what it is: to try to answer that continually recurring and teasing question of what to look for in
a book, and how the average man and woman can get all
that can be got out of his or her general reading.

Appreciation depends on partnership, on the establishment of understanding between writer and reader. "What
is a book?" says Anatole France. "A series of little
printed signs, essentially only that. It is for the reader
himself to supply the forms and colors and sentiments to
which these signs correspond. It will depend on him
whether the book be dull or brilliant, hot with passion or
cold as ice." It is true that the reader gets what he de-
serves out of a book. As we have seen, the writer of a novel
is trying to interpret something of human existence as it
appears to his temperament, to give some created vision
of what life seems to him to be. At the same time the
reader unconsciously contributes his own view and his
own personality, and the result of the fusion is criticism.
And there are always two main positions from which
criticism springs. On the one hand the reader's view of
his partnership with the writer may be that it should
merely supply a duplication of his own ideas. He may
desire, not a stimulus to further thought, but certainty,
and assurance about his own pre-established codes of
decision, which shall make any further search for reality
unnecessary to him. Or, on the other hand, he may possess the experiencing faculty, the love of mental and emotional adventure for its own sake, the knowledge that
there is always something to be discovered about the
world we live in, that it must necessarily be larger than any
one view of it, and that to have an ardor for such discovery

is to make life full of an inexhaustible interest.   Such a reader will not be concerned only with the sort of people and the sort of conventions and codes to which he is accustomed and of which he approves.   He is not a Puritan but he loves *The Pilgrim's Progress*; not a sentimentalist, but he delights in the analysis of *Clarissa*; not a libertine, but a happy reader of Byron; not a Catholic, but enraptured by *The Hound of Heaven*; not a Jew, but profoundly stirred by the drama of Job and Jehovah.   And although he has likes and dislikes, he makes them give an account of themselves; using his intellectual faculties to make his criticism self-conscious, aware of itself, and of the reason for its pleasures and rebellions.   "A good hater" if need be, but not a mere helpless victim of prejudice.

From this latter position springs Taste.   In other words, to have a gusto for life is its essential root.   To be able, with Fielding, to address humanity as "thou jolly substance."   Art is communication of experience; the novel is direct communication of human experience, and the fascination of its study lies first of all in an unquenchable and detached curiosity to meet and appraise as many as possible of the multitudinous existing varieties of character, situation, action and opinion.   It follows, then, that from the emotional and intellectual point of view, the matter of supreme importance in criticizing a novel is the answer to the question: from what kind of mind does this writing come?   Out of how deep and wide an experience was it born?   This, and not the mere question of the subject matter, is the all-important starting point for discussion. Here again, perhaps, illustrations are best first from literary classics.   Let us take Shakespeare's tragedies. Judged merely as a picture of human existence, nothing could be more ghastly than the spectacle of the cosmos they present.   We see innocence murdered and trust betrayed, cruelty torturing old age and treachery triumphing over honesty. Nobility, courage, generosity, truth, are dashed to pieces under the wheels of Fate. Man, struggling in the grip of circumstance and character, is beaten in that struggle every time. Evil always triumphs over good: Iago is proved stronger than Othello and Desdemona, Goneril and Regan vanquish Lear, Hamlet is overthrown, so is Brutus, so is Antony, so is poor young Romeo. Yet the flavor of life which is left on the mental palate after reading Shakespeare is not that of the despair which a play like Galsworthy's *Justice*, for instance, leaves, but something much nearer exaltation — a very strange effect to be produced by the spectacle of the world's illusion! Shakespeare's mind being rich, sure, intense, powerful and comprehensive, it is the impress of the qualities of richness, sureness, intensity, power and understanding which is left upon the mind of the reader. The same magic is achieved by Hardy, whose mind is such that his treatment of the mockery of life and the ignoble bludgeonings of Fate, his picture of this "show God ought surely to shut up soon," becomes a thing of grandeur, its pettiness transmuted into dignity, its baseness ennobled. If again, we look at the world with the eyes and mind of George Moore, we see it as a place for little more than varied opportunities for various kinds of sensation; if we look at it with Shaw, we see it from the point of view of inspired common sense; if we look at it with Dickens, from that of inspired common sensibility. Coming to the modern novel, we can illustrate the same truth by seeing the various ways in which one theme can be treated by different personalities. Let us take that ever-popular situation in fiction, the theme of illicit love. The moralist will simply disapprove of any novel dealing with an "unpleasant theme," and dismiss it at that. The possessor of taste, very well aware that it is a part of life and cannot be ignored so easily, is interested to mark all the tones and degrees of its representation in the terms of various mentalities. He can see it handled by a detached artistic mind like Arnold Bennett or Rose Macaulay or Willa Cather; or by a pictorial mind like Hergesheimer; or by a scientific, analytic mind like Shaw or Wells; or a pitiful, gentle mind, like Galsworthy; or a sincerely sentimental mind, like A. S. M. Hutchinson, or a cynically sentimental mind like Michael Arlen; or a commonplace and rather base mind, as is usual in any of the Legs and Lingerie School; or perhaps one might say, by a vacuum in place of a mind, as is usual in any of the writers of sentimental romances.

Individual preferences must always exist, in literature as in life, and they have to be accepted in the same spirit. Just as sometimes we simply cannot understand how our friends choose their mates as they do, so, maybe, we cannot understand what they see in, say Miss Dorothy Richardson. It does not really help matters, however, to echo Dr. Johnson as he discussed a book with Boswell, and to bellow as if it were a convincing argument, "You, Sir, may think it excellent, but that it does not make it so." Tastes differ, and if you are all for steak and onions, caviar and peaches is unsatisfying. Beyond opinion about the merits of individual writers, there are always the two great types of mind which we label Romantic and Realistic. When all the recent criticism which argues against the academic exactitude of the labels has been accepted, there still remain two types of mind, and most readers have a bias towards one or the other. Some naturally prefer looking through magic casements opening on the foam of perilous seas in faëry lands forlorn: their Pegasus is like that of Edward Lear's old Person of Bazing,

> Whose presence of mind was amazing,
> He purchased a steed,
> Which he rode at full speed
> And escaped from the people of Bazing.

(A poem which might stand as a symbolist rendering of that literature of escape the psychologists tell us so much about.) This class of readers generally regards the novels of Jane Austen or of Ethel Sidgwick or of Trollope or of Arnold Bennett, much as du Maurier's Frenchman regarded the fox-hunt, "no promenade, no band of music, nossing," while to those who enjoy that kind of thing the commonplace brings its own excitement and thrill, and a book like Walter de la Mare's *Memoirs of a Midget*, or Cabell's tales of romance, and stories in general of "elves, fairies and such like mummery," as Fielding would say, are about as comforting as a cold crumpet. It is useless to argue about it, because the extremists on either side cannot understand each other, just as the mystic cannot understand the cynic's profound indifference to inner realities, and the intellectual ironist cannot understand anyone really bothering much about the soul. The critic can only follow that excellent advice, "Do not call the tortoise unworthy, because she is not something else," and recognize the fact, true again in literature as in life, that it is quite possible to have a detached admiration without affection and complete sympathy.

So much for the human appeal of the novel and its capacity to satisfy the human curiosity of its readers. That curiosity is the essential basis of all enjoyment of fiction, but it is not possible fully to appreciate it without a further quality — the sense of craftsmanship and style. The difference between art and life is one of Form. Every day of our existence we meet, and realize quite well that we meet, both in our own lives and in those of others, the materials for drama or fiction. But the experiences of living are blurred and confused by a mass of superfluous detail and dialogue, by a bewildering medley of extraneous character and action, which interfere constantly with the development and statement of any single situation. To try to report the thoughts, speech, and activities of one single day in a man's life has spread over nearly a thousand pages of print in *Ulysses*. The function of art is to select, clarify and isolate the experiences of life within a certain form. "Life is like a blind and limitless expanse of sky, forever dividing into tiny drops of circumstance that rain down, thick and fast, a ceaseless, meaningless drip. Art is like the dauntless plastic force that builds up stubborn, amorphous substance, cell by cell, into the frail geometry of a cell." This subject will be treated at greater length in a later chapter, and now it is enough to say that in the novel this means bringing character, situation, point of view, setting and background under the discipline of outline, enclosing both the raw material and the creative vision of the artist towards his material in a certain structure of expression. Critics of the novel in textbooks which profess to teach novel-writing in twelve lessons (or words to that effect), often speak as if there were a right or a wrong form for the novel. This cannot be. The purpose of the serious novel (I mean a novel which is a serious piece of literary work, though it may be a pure comedy) is to give interest and enjoyment to the reader — not the merely superficial enjoyment and interest of something which amuses him when he is tired, but the true enjoyment of having his faculties energized and vitalized by being called into play in a comparison of the experience of another mind with that of his own. That novel is a good novel which succeeds in communicating vividly the writer's experience, and there can be no rules for what form succeeds in doing that — except the rule of success! We might quote Mr. Kipling on tribal lays, and apply the same remark to the novel.

> There are nine and sixty ways of constructing tribal lays.
> And every single one of them is right.

The novelist may convey his effects by the rambling, enormously patient reporting of James Joyce in *Ulysses*, or by the rigid selection of Willa Cather in *A Lost Lady*, by the architectural massiveness of Arnold Bennett's *The Old Wives' Tale* or by the brilliant impressionism of Aldous Huxley's *Antic Hay*. He may be as direct as Wells or as elusive as Virginia Woolf: he may set chronology at defiance, as in *Lord Jim*, or he may make the lives of a group of characters centre in one night as in *Nocturne*: he may make his action live at four removes from the teller of the tale, as when, in *Chance*, we listen to what Marlow said that Mrs. Fyne said that Flora said the governess said, or he may be as frankly autobiographical as Samuel Butler in *The Way of All Flesh*. Provided that the reader feels that he simply must finish the book, the novelist has succeeded in his aim and his form has justified itself.

G. K. CHESTERTON

Gilbert Keith Chesterton was born in 1874 *and educated at St. Paul's School, England.* For a time he worked as an office clerk and attended the Slade School of Art, but he soon began to contribute literary criticism to The Bookman *and launched out on the sea of journalism.* He has become one of the most prolific as well as most popular writers of today, with a list of productions in fiction, biography, poetry, and the essay far too long to reproduce here. *Among his books may be mentioned his critical studies of Dickens* (1906) *and Browning (in the "English Men of Letters" series);* The Victorian Age in Literature (1913) *is a stimulating and witty review of that period.* The creator of one of the most original detectives, *Father Brown (*The Innocence of Father Brown *appeared in* 1911 *and there have been several later collections), Mr. Chesterton is well qualified to write upon detective novels.* Curiously, however, the book discussing the mechanics of the detective story, the lack of which he complains of in the essay, had already been written, and by the very lady he praised *(*The Technique of the Mystery Story, *by Carolyn Wells, was published in* 1913). *Collections of his shorter essays began with* Heretics (1905) *and have continued to appear almost annually ever since, reprinted from the various periodicals including his own weekly, to which he is a contributor.* Tremendous Trifles (1909), Generally Speaking (1928), *and* Come to Think of It (1930) *are characteristic examples.*

The following essay is reprinted from Generally Speaking, *by G. K. Chesterton. Copyright,* 1929, *by Dodd, Mead and Company, Inc. By permission of the author and Dodd, Mead and Company, Inc., publishers.*

G. K. CHESTERTON

ON DETECTIVE NOVELS

IT IS now some years since Mrs. Carolyn Wells, the American lady who has produced some of our most charming stories of murder and mystification, wrote to a magazine to complain of the unsatisfactory sort of review accorded to that sort of book; but not yet has the abuse been corrected. She said it is only too obvious that the task of reviewing detective stories is given to people who do not like detective stories. She says, and I think not unreasonably, that this is very unreasonable: a book of poems is not sent to a man who hates poetry; an ordinary novel is not reviewed by a rigid moralist who regards all novels as immoral. If mystery stories have any right to be reviewed at all, they have a right to be reviewed by the sort of person who understands why they were written. And the lady proceeds to say that, by this neglect, the nature of the technique really required in such a tale is never adequately discussed. I, for one, agree with her that it is a matter well worthy of discussion. There is no better reading, and in the true sense no more serious reading, than the few critical passages which great critics have devoted to this literary question; such as Edgar Allan Poe's disquisition on analysis at the beginning of the beautiful idyll about the murderous ape; or the studies of Andrew Lang on the problem of Edwin Drood; or the remarks of Stevenson on the police novel at the end of *The Wrecker*. Any such discussion, clearly conducted, will soon show that the rules of art are as much involved in this artistic form as in any other; and it is not any objection to such a form that people can enjoy it who cannot criticize it. The same is true of any good song or any sound romance. By a curious confusion, many modern critics have passed from the proposition that a masterpiece may be unpopular to the other proposition that unless it is unpopular it cannot be a masterpiece. It is as if one were to say that because a clever man may have an impediment in his speech, therefore a man cannot be clever unless he stammers. For all unpopularity is a sort of obscurity; and all obscurity is a defect of expression like a stammer. Anyhow, I am in this matter on the popular side; I am interested in all sorts of sensational fiction, good, bad and indifferent, and would willingly discuss it with a much less capable exponent of it than the author of *Vicky Van*. And if anyone likes to say that my tastes are vulgar and inartistic and illiterate, I can only say I am quite content to be as vulgar as Poe and as inartistic as Stevenson and as illiterate as Andrew Lang.

Now, it is all the more curious that the technique of such tales is not discussed, because they are exactly the sort in which technique is nearly the whole of the trick. It is all the more odd that such writers have no critical guidance, because it is one of the few forms of art in which they could to some extent be guided. And it is all the more strange that nobody discusses the rules, because it is one of the few cases in which some rules could be laid down. The very fact that the work is not of the highest order of creation makes it possible to treat it as a question of construction. But while people are willing to teach poets imagination, they seem to think it hopeless to help plotters in a matter of mere ingenuity. There are textbooks instructing people in the manufacture of sonnets, as if the visions of bare ruined quires where late sweet birds sang, or of the ground-whirl of the perished leaves of hope, the wind of death's imperishable wing, were things to be explained like a conjuring trick. We have monographs expounding the art of the Short Story, as if the dripping horror of the *House of Usher* or the sunny irony of the *Treasure of Franchard* were recipes out of a cookery book. But in the case of the only kind of story to which the strict laws of logic are in some sense applicable, nobody seems to bother to apply them, or even to ask whether in this or that case they are applied. Nobody writes the simple book which I expect every day to see on the bookstalls, called *How to Write a Detective Story*.

I myself have got no farther than discovering how not to write one. But even from my own failures I have gained stray glimpses of what such a scheme of warnings might be. Of one preliminary principle I am pretty certain. The whole point of a sensational story is that the secret should be simple. The whole story exists for the moment of surprise; and it should be a moment. It should not be something that it takes twenty minutes to explain, and twenty-four hours to learn by heart, for fear of forgetting it. The best way of testing it is to make an imaginative picture in the mind of some such dramatic moment. Imagine a dark garden at twilight, and a terrible voice crying out in the distance, and coming nearer and nearer along the serpentine garden paths until the words become dreadfully distinct; a cry coming from some sinister yet familiar figure in the story, a stranger or a servant from whom we subconsciously expect some such rending revelation. Now, it is clear that the cry which breaks from him must be something short and simple in itself, as, "The butler is his father," or "The Archdeacon is Bloody Bill," or "The Emperor has cut his throat," or what not. But too many otherwise ingenious romancers seem to think it their duty to discover what is the most complicated and improbable series of events that could be combined to produce a certain result. The result may be logical, but it is not sensational. The servant cannot rend

the silence of the twilight garden by shrieking aloud:
"The throat of the Emperor was cut under the following
circumstances: his Imperial Majesty was attempting to
shave himself and went to sleep in the middle of it, fa-
tigued with the cares of state; the Archdeacon was attempting at first in a Christian spirit to complete the shaving
operation on the sleeping monarch when he was suddenly
tempted to a murderous act by the memory of the Dis-
establishment Bill, but repented after making a mere
scratch and flung the razor on the floor; the faithful butler,
hearing the commotion, rushed in and snatched up the
weapon, but in the confusion of the moment cut the Emperor's throat instead of the Archdeacon's; so everything
is satisfactory, and the young man and the girl can leave
off suspecting each other of assassination and get married."
Now, this explanation, however reasonable and complete,
is not one that can be conveniently uttered as an exclama-
tion or can sound suddenly in the twilight garden like the
trump of doom. Anyone who will try the experiment of
crying aloud the above paragraph in his own twilight
garden will realize the difficulty here referred to. It is
exactly one of those little technical experiments, illustrated
with diagrams, with which our little text-book would
abound.

Another truth to which our little text-book would at
least tentatively incline is that the *roman policier* should
be on the model of the short story rather than the novel.
There are splendid exceptions: *The Moonstone* and one
or two Gaboriaus are great works in this style; as are, in
our own time, Mr. Bentley's *Trent's Last Case*, and
Mr. Milne's *Red House Mystery*. But I think that the
difficulties of a long detective novel are real difficulties,
though very clever men can by various expedients get
over them. The chief difficulty is that the detective story
is, after all, a drama of masks and not of faces. It de-

pends on men's false characters rather than their real characters. The author cannot tell us until the last chapter any of the most interesting things about the most interesting people. It is a masquerade ball where everybody is disguised as somebody else, and there is no true personal interest until the clock strikes twelve. That is, as I have said, we cannot really get at the psychology and philosophy, the morals and religion, of the thing until we have read the last chapter. Therefore, I think it is best of all when the first chapter is also the last chapter. The length of the short story is about the legitimate length for this particular drama of the mere misunderstanding of fact. When all is said and done, there have never been better detective stories than the old series of Sherlock Holmes; and though the name of that magnificent magician has spread over the whole world, and is perhaps the one great popular legend made in the modern world, I do not think that Sir Arthur Conan Doyle has ever been thanked enough for them. As one of many millions, I offer my own mite of homage.

LUDWIG LEWISOHN

Born in Berlin, Germany, in 1882, *Ludwig Lewisohn came with his family to the United States eight years later. After graduating from the College of Charleston (South Carolina) in* 1901, *Mr. Lewisohn came to Columbia University for further study, receiving the degree of M.A. in* 1903. *He was on the editorial staff of Doubleday, Page and Company for two years, and after further experience as a free-lance magazine writer, became Assistant Professor of German Language and Literature at Ohio State University. In* 1919 *he returned to New York, to serve first as dramatic editor and later as associate editor and contributor to* The Nation. *He has since traveled widely, residing for some years in Paris. In the list of his published books are some twenty-five items, including translations from Continental literature, poetry, criticism, fiction, and autobiography. In* Upstream *and* Mid-Channel (1922, 1929) *he has told the story of his own life, often with beauty if not always without bitterness. In* The Spirit of Modern German Literature (1916) *and in* Poets of Modern France (1918) *he has shown critical acumen and wide reading.* Expression in America (1932) *is an exceedingly stimulating study of the whole field of American literature.*

The following selections are reprinted from The Drama and the Stage, *by Ludwig Lewisohn. Copyright,* 1922, *by Harcourt, Brace and Company, Inc.*

LUDWIG LEWISOHN

A NOTE ON TRAGEDY

IT HAS been said many times, and always with an air
of authority, that there is no tragedy in the modern
drama. And since tragedy, in the minds of most
educated people, is hazily but quite firmly connected with
the mishaps of noble and mythical personages, the statement has been widely accepted as true. Thus very tawdry
Shakespearean revivals are received with a traditional
reverence for the sternest and noblest of all the art-forms
that is consciously withheld from *Ghosts* or *Justice* or *The
Weavers*. Placid people in college towns consider these
plays painful. They hasten to pay their respects to awkward chantings of Gilbert Murray's Swinburnian verse
and approve the pleasant mildness of the pity and terror
native to the Attic stage. The very innocuousness of
these entertainments as well as the pain that Ibsen and
Hauptmann inflict should give them pause. Pity and
terror are strong words and stand for strong things. But
our public replies in the comfortable words of its most
respectable critics that tragedy has ceased to be written.

These critics reveal a noteworthy state of mind. They
are aware that tragedy cuts to the quick of life and springs
from the innermost depth of human thinking because it
must always seek to deal in some intelligible way with the
problem of evil. But since it is most comfortable to
believe that problem to have been solved, they avert their
faces from a reopening of the eternal question and declare
that the answer of the Greeks and the Elizabethans is
final. They are also aware, though more dimly, that all
tragedy involves moral judgments. And since they are

unaccustomed to make such judgments, except by the light of standards quite rigid and quite antecedent to experience, they are bewildered by a type of tragic drama that transfers its crises from the deeds of men to the very criteria of moral judgment, from guilt under a law to the arraignment of the law itself.

Macbeth represents in art and life their favorite tragic situation. They can understand a gross and open crime meeting a violent punishment. When, as in *King Lear*, the case is not so plain, they dwell long and emphatically on the old man's weaknesses in order to find satisfaction in his doom. In the presence of every tragic protagonist of the modern drama they are tempted to play the part of Job's comforters. They are eager to impute to him an absoluteness of guilt which shall, by implication, justify their own moral world and the doctrine of moral violence by which they live. The identical instinct which in war causes men to blacken the enemy's character in order to justify their tribal rage and hate, persuades the conventional critic to deny the character of tragedy to every action in which disaster does not follow upon crime. Yet, rightly looked upon, man in every tragic situation is a Job, incapable and unconscious of any degree of voluntary guilt that can justify a suffering as sharp and constant as his own.

Thus modern tragedy does not deal with wrong and just vengeance, which are both, if conceived absolutely, pure fictions of our deep-rooted desire for superiority and violence. It is inspired by compassion. But compassion without complacency is still, alas, a very rare emotion. And it seeks to derive the tragic element in human life from the mistakes and self-imposed compulsions, not from the sins, of men. The central idea of *Ghosts*, for instance, is not concerned with the sin of the father that is visited upon the son. It is concerned, as Ibsen sought to make abundantly clear, with Mrs. Alving's fatal conformity to a social tradition that did not represent the pureness of her will. Her tragic mistake arises from her failure to break the law. The ultimate and absolute guilt is in the blind, collective lust of mankind for the formulation and indiscriminate enforcement of external laws.

To such a conception of the moral world, tragedy has but recently attained. That both the critical and the public intelligence should lag far behind is inevitable. Every morning's paper proclaims a world whose moral pattern is formed of terrible blacks and glaring whites. How should people gladly endure the endless and pain-touched gray of modern tragedy? They understand the Greek conception of men who violated the inscrutable will of gods; they understand the renaissance conception that a breach of the universal law sanctioned and set forth by God, needed to be punished. They can even endure such situations as that of Claudio and Isabella in the terrible third act of *Measure for Measure*. For that unhappy brother and sister never question the right of the arbitrary power that caused so cruel a dilemma, nor doubt the absolute validity of the virtue that is named. These two strike at each other's hearts and never at the bars of the monstrous cage that holds them prisoner. Do they not, therefore, rise almost to the dignity of symbols of that moral world in which the majority of men still live?

But it is precisely with the bars of the cage that modern tragedy is so largely and so necessarily concerned. It cannot deal with guilt in the older sense. For guilt involves an absolute moral judgment. That, in its turn, involves an absolute standard. And a literally absolute standard is unthinkable without a super-human sanction. Even such a sanction, however, would leave the flexible and enlightened spirit in the lurch. For if it were not constantly self-interpretative by some method of progressive and objectively embodied revelation, its interpretation would again become a mere matter of human opinion, and the absoluteness of moral guilt would again be gravely jeopardized. Not only must God have spoken; He would need to speak anew each day. The war has overwhelmingly illustrated how infinitely alien such obvious reflections still are to the temper of humanity. We must have guilt. Else how, without utter shame, could we endure punitive prisons and gibbets and battles? Is it suprising that audiences are cold to Ibsen and Hauptmann and Galsworthy, and that good critics who are also righteous and angry men deny their plays the character of tragedy?

But the bars of the absolutist cage are not so bright and firm as they were once. The conception of unrelieved guilt and overwhelming vengeance has just played on the stage of history a part so monstrous that its very name will ring to future ages with immitigable contrition and grief. And thus in the serener realm of art the modern idea of tragedy is very sure to make its gradual appeal to the hearts of men. Guilt and punishment will be definitely banished to melodrama, where they belong. Tragedy will seek increasingly to understand our failures and our sorrows. It will excite pity for our common fate; the terror it inspires will be a terror lest we wrong our brother or violate his will, not lest we share his guilt and incur his punishment. It will seek its final note of reconciliation not by delivering another victim to an outraged God or an angry tribe, but through a profound sense of that community of human suffering which all force deepens and all freedom assuages.

LUDWIG LEWISOHN

A NOTE ON COMEDY

THE pleasure that men take in comedy arises from their feeling of superiority to the persons involved in the comic action. The Athenian who laughed with Aristophanes over the predicament of the hungry gods, the contemporary New Yorker who laughs over a comedian blundering into the wrong bedroom, are stirred by an identical emotion. The difference in the intellectual character of the two inheres in the nature of the stimulus by which the emotion is in each case aroused. In the former the pleasure was conditioned in a high and arduous activity of mind; in the latter it arises from a momentary and accidental superiority of situation. High and low comedy are dependent in all ages upon the temper of the auditor whose pleasurable emotions of superiority must be awakened. He who has brought a critical attitude of mind to bear upon the institutions and the ways of men will coöperate with the creative activity of a faculty which he himself possesses and has exercised; he to whom all criticism is alien can evidently find no causes for superiority within himself and must be flattered by the sight of physical mishaps and confusions which, for the moment, are not his own. Pure comedy, in brief, and that comedy of physical intrigue which is commonly called farce, cannot from the nature of things differ in the effect they strive to produce. But they must adapt their methods of attaining this common end to the character of the spectator whose emotions they desire to touch.

It follows that pure comedy is rare. Historically we find it flourishing in small, compact, and like-minded groups: the free citizens of Athens, the fashionables of Paris and London who applauded Molière and Congreve. But in all three instances the reign of pure comedy was brief, and in the latter two precarious and artificial at best. With the loss of Athenian freedom, intrigue took the place of social and moral criticism; no later poet dared, as Aristophanes had done in *The Acharnians*, to deride warlikeness in the midst of war. In the New Comedy public affairs and moral criticism disappeared from the Attic stage. In Rome there was no audience for pure comedy. Its function was exercised by the satirists alone, precisely as a larger and nobler comic force lives in the satires of Dryden than in the plays of Congreve. Nor should it be forgotten that Molière himself derives from a tradition of farce which reaches, through its Italian origin, to Latin comedy and the New Comedy of Greece, and that the greater number of his own pieces depends for effectiveness on the accidents and complications of intrigue. When he rose above this subject matter and sought the true sources of comic power and appeal in *L'École des Femmes* and *Tartuffe*, he aroused among the uncritical a hatred which pursued him beyond the grave.

The modern theatre, which must address itself primarily to that bulwark of things as they are, the contented middle classes, is, necessarily, a bleak enough place for the spirit of comedy. These audiences will scarcely experience a pleasurable feeling of superiority at the comic exposure of their favorite delusions. Hence Shaw is not popular on the stage; a strong comic talent, like Henri Lavedan's, begins by directing its arrows at those grosser vices which its audience also abhors and then sinks into melodrama; isolated exceptions, such as the success of Hauptmann's massive satire of bureaucratic tyranny in *The Beaver Coat*, scarcely mitigate the loneliness of comedy on the stage of our time. The comic spirit which once sought refuge in satire now seeks it in the novel — that great, inclusive form of art which can always find the single mind to which its speech is articulate.

But since men still desire to laugh in the theatre, there has arisen out of a long and complicated tradition the sentimental comedy. Here the basic action is pseudo-realistic and emotional. Into it are brought, however, odd and absurd characters whose function is the same as that of Shakespeare's Fools in tragedy. They break the tension and release the pleasurable feeling of superiority. More often, however, they encroach largely on the sentimental action, and then we have the most popular form of theatrical entertainment among us — a reckless mixture of melodrama and farce. And this form caters, beyond all others, to its huge audience's will to superiority. Men and women laugh at the fools whom they despise, at the villains whose discomfiture vindicates their peculiar sense of social and moral values; they laugh with the heroes in whom those values are embodied and unfailingly triumphant.

From such facile methods pure comedy averts its face. It, too, arouses laughter; it, too, releases the pleasurable emotion of superiority. But it demands a superiority that is hard won and possessed by few. It is profoundly concerned with the intellect that has in very truth risen above the common follies and group delusions of mankind; it seeks its fellowship among those who share its perceptions or are prepared to share them. It demands not only moral and intellectual freedom in its audience; it demands a society in which that freedom can be exercised. It cannot flourish, as the central example of Attic comedy illustrates, except in a polity where art and speech are free. And anyone who reflects on the shifting panorama of political institutions will realize at once how few have been the times and places in history in which, even given a critically minded audience, the comic dramatist could have spoken to that audience in a public playhouse.

The immediate example in our own period is that of Bernard Shaw. Whatever the ultimate value of his plays may be, he is to us the truest representation of the comic spirit. Some of his plays have, on occasion, quite frankly been removed from the stage by the police power; none are truly popular except in the study. The bourgeois audiences who at times witness their performance have set up between themselves and Shaw the protective fiction that he is a high-class clown. Since they cannot, in self-defense, laugh with him, they attempt to laugh at him, and thus save their pleasure and their reputation for cleverness at once. True comedy, in a word, is a test both of the inner freedom of the mind and of the outer freedom of the society in which men live. Its life has always been brief and hazardous. Nor is it likely to flourish unless the liberties of mankind are achieved in a new measure and with a new intensity. For the great comic dramatist, if he would gain the most modest success, must gather in a single theatre as many free minds in a free state as Lucian or Swift or Heine seek out and make their own in a whole generation.

JOHN GALSWORTHY

*Born at Coombe, Surrey, in 1867, John Galsworthy was educated
at Harrow and at New College, Oxford, where he took an honor degree
in law, and where he later served as Honorary Fellow.   Although
admitted to the bar in 1890, he gave up his practice for the sake of
travel and of writing.   On a voyage between Australia and South
Africa he met a seaman named Joseph Conrad, not yet famous, and
the friendship which resulted proved to be lasting.   Before his death,
in February, 1933,* Mr. *Galsworthy had published some twenty
novels, at least an equal number of plays, and several collections of
essays and short stories, through which he had become one of the best
known and most loved authors of his day.   Of his novels, including*
The Forsyte Saga *(1922), there is no room to speak here.   In them,
as in his plays, he showed himself warmly in sympathy with the
victims of social injustice, but his understanding of human nature
was such as to prevent him from undue bitterness, and his irony was
always tempered by restraint.   Among his collected essays are*
A Commentary (1908), A Motley (1910), The Inn of Tranquillity (1912), *and* A Sheaf (*Volume I,* 1916, *Volume II,* 1919).
*The title of his essay on drama is characteristically modest, although
it comes from one who was a prolific and successful dramatist.*

The following essay is reprinted from The Inn of Tranquillity, *by
John Galsworthy.   Copyright, 1912, by Charles Scribner's Sons.
By permission of the publishers.*

JOHN GALSWORTHY

SOME PLATITUDES CONCERNING DRAMA

A DRAMA must be shaped so as to have a spire of meaning. Every grouping of life and character has its inherent moral; and the business of the dramatist is so to pose the group as to bring that moral poignantly to the light of day. Such is the moral that exhales from plays like *Lear*, *Hamlet*, and *Macbeth*. But such is not the moral to be found in the great bulk of contemporary Drama. The moral of the average play is now, and probably has always been, the triumph at all costs of a supposed immediate ethical good over a supposed immediate ethical evil.

The vice of drawing these distorted morals has permeated the Drama to its spine; discoloured its art, humanity, and significance; infected its creators, actors, audience, critics; too often turned it from a picture into a caricature. A Drama which lives under the shadow of the distorted moral forgets how to be free, fair, and fine — forgets so completely that it often prides itself on having forgotten.

Now, in writing plays, there are, in this matter of the moral, three courses open to the serious dramatist. The first is: To definitely set before the public that which it wishes to have set before it, the views and codes of life by which the public lives and in which it believes. This way is the most common, successful, and popular. It makes the dramatist's position sure, and not too obviously authoritative.

The second course is: To definitely set before the public those views and codes of life by which the dramatist him-

self lives, those theories in which he himself believes, the
more effectively if they are the opposite of what the public
wishes to have placed before it, presenting them so that
the audience may swallow them like powder in a spoonful
of jam.

There is a third course: To set before the public no cut-
and-dried codes, but the phenomena of life, selected and
combined, *but not distorted*, by the dramatist's outlook,
set down without fear, favour, or prejudice, leaving the
public to draw such poor moral as nature may afford.
This third method requires a certain detachment; it requires a sympathy with, a love of, and a curiosity as to,
things for their own sake; it requires a far view, together
with patient industry, for no immediately practical result.

It was once said of Shakespeare that he had never done
any good to anyone, and never would. This, unfortunately, could not, in the sense in which the word "good"
was then meant, be said of most modern dramatists. In
truth, the good that Shakespeare did to humanity was of
a remote, and, shall we say, eternal nature; something of
the good that men get from having the sky and the sea to
look at. And this partly because he was, in his greater
plays at all events, free from the habit of drawing a distorted moral. Now, the playwright who supplies to the
public the facts of life distorted by the moral which it
expects, does so that he may do the public what he considers an immediate good, by fortifying its prejudices;
and the dramatist who supplies to the public facts distorted by his own advanced morality, does so because he
considers that he will at once benefit the public by sub-
stituting for its worn-out ethics, his own. In both cases
the advantage the dramatist hopes to confer on the public
is immediate and practical.

But matters change, and morals change; men remain —
and to set men, and the facts about them, down faithfully,

so that they may draw for us the moral of their natural actions, may also possibly be of benefit to the community. It is, at all events, harder than to set men and facts down, as they ought, or ought not to be. This, however, is not to say that a dramatist should, or indeed can, keep himself and his temperamental philosophy out of his work. As a man lives and thinks, so will he write. But it is certain, that to the making of good drama, as to the practice of every other art, there must be brought an almost passionate love of discipline, a white-heat of self-respect, a desire to make the truest, fairest, best thing in one's power; and that to these must be added an eye that does not flinch. Such qualities alone will bring to drama the selfless character which soaks it with inevitability.

The word "pessimist" is frequently applied to the few dramatists who have been content to work in this way. It has been applied, among others, to Euripides, to Shakespeare, to Ibsen; it will be applied to many in the future. Nothing, however, is more dubious than the way in which these two words "pessimist" and "optimist" are used; for the optimist appears to be he who cannot bear the world as it is, and is forced by his nature to picture it as it ought to be, and the pessimist one who cannot only bear the world as it is, but loves it well enough to draw it faithfully. The true lover of the human race is surely he who can put up with it in all its forms, in vice as well as in virtue, in defeat no less than in victory; the true seer he who sees not only joy but sorrow, the true painter of human life one who blinks nothing. It may be that he is, also, its true benefactor.

In the whole range of the social fabric there are only two impartial persons, the scientist and the artist, and under the latter heading such dramatists as desire to write not only for today, but for tomorrow, must strive to come.

But dramatists being as they are made — past remedy

— it is perhaps more profitable to examine the various points at which their qualities and defects are shown.

The plot! A good plot is that sure edifice which slowly rises out of the interplay of circumstance on temperament, and temperament on circumstance, within the enclosing atmosphere of an idea. A human being is the best plot there is; it may be impossible to see why he is a good plot, because the idea within which he was brought forth cannot be fully grasped; but it is plain that *he is a good plot.* He is organic. And so it must be with a good play. Reason alone produces no good plots; they come by original sin, sure conception, and instinctive after-power of selecting what benefits the germ. A bad plot, on the other hand, is simply a row of stakes, with a character impaled on each — characters who would have liked to live, but came to untimely grief; who started bravely, but fell on these stakes, placed beforehand in a row, and were transfixed one by one, while their ghosts stride on, squeaking and gibbering, through the play. Whether these stakes are made of facts or of ideas, according to the nature of the dramatist who planted them, their effect on the unfortunate characters is the same; the creatures were begotten to be staked, and staked they are! The demand for a good plot, not unfrequently heard, commonly signifies: "Tickle my sensations by stuffing the play with arbitrary adventures, so that I need not be troubled to take the characters seriously. Set the persons of the play to action, regardless of time, sequence, atmosphere, and probability!"

Now, true dramatic action is what characters do, at once contrary, as it were, to expectation, and yet because they have already done other things. No dramatist should let his audience know what is coming; but neither should he suffer his characters to act without making his audience feel that those actions are in harmony with temperament, and arise from previous known actions, together with the temperaments and previous known actions of the other characters in the play. The dramatist who hangs his characters to his plot, instead of hanging his plot to his characters, is guilty of cardinal sin.

The dialogue! Good dialogue again is character, marshalled so as continually to stimulate interest or excitement. The reason good dialogue is seldom found in plays is merely that it is hard to write, for it requires not only a knowledge of what interests or excites, but such a feeling for character as brings misery to the dramatist's heart when his creations speak as they should not speak — ashes to his mouth when they say things for the sake of saying them — disgust when they are "smart."

The art of writing true dramatic dialogue is an austere art, denying itself all license, grudging every sentence devoted to the mere machinery of the play, suppressing all jokes and epigrams severed from character, relying for fun and pathos on the fun and tears of life. From start to finish good dialogue is hand-made, like good lace; clear, of fine texture, furthering with each thread the harmony and strength of a design to which all must be subordinated.

But good dialogue is also spiritual action. In so far as the dramatist divorces his dialogue from spiritual action — that is to say, from progress of events or towards events which are significant of character — he is stultifying τὸ δρᾶμα the thing done; he may make pleasing disquisitions, he is not making drama. And in so far as he twists character to suit his moral or his plot, he is neglecting a first principle, that truth to Nature which alone invests Art with hand-made quality.

The dramatist's license, in fact, ends with his design. In conception alone he is free. He may take what character or group of characters he chooses, see them with what eyes, knit them with what idea, within the limits of his temperament; but once taken, seen, and knitted, he is bound to treat them like a gentleman, with the tenderest consideration of their mainsprings. Take care of character; action and dialogue will take care of themselves! The true dramatist gives full rein to his temperament in the scope and nature of his subject; having once selected subject and characters, he is just, gentle, restrained, neither gratifying his lust for praise at the expense of his offspring, not using them as puppets to flout his audience. Being himself the nature that brought them forth, he guides them in the course predestined at their conception. So only have they a chance of defying Time, which is always lying in wait to destroy the false, topical, or fashionable — all in a word — that is not based on the permanent elements of human nature. The perfect dramatist rounds up his characters and facts within the ring-fence of a dominant idea which fulfils the craving of his spirit; having got them there, he suffers them to live their own lives.

Plot, action, character, dialogue! But there is yet another subject for a platitude. Flavour! An impalpable quality, less easily captured than the scent of a flower, the peculiar and most essential attribute of any work of art! It is the thin, poignant spirit which hovers up out of a play, and is as much its differentiating essence as is caffeine of coffee. Flavour, in fine, is the spirit of the dramatist projected into his work in a state of volatility, so that no one can exactly lay hands on it, here, there, or anywhere. This distinctive essence of a play, marking its brand, is the one thing at which the dramatist cannot work, for it is outside his consciousness. A man may have many moods, he has but one spirit; and this spirit he communicates in some subtle, unconscious way to all his work. It waxes and wanes with the currents of his vitality, but no more alters than a chestnut changes into an oak.

For, in truth, dramas are very like unto trees, springing

from seedlings, shaping themselves inevitably in accordance with the laws fast hidden within themselves, drinking sustenance from the earth and air, and in conflict with the natural forces round them. So they slowly come to full growth, until, warped, stunted, or risen to fair and gracious height, they stand open to all the winds. And the trees that spring from each dramatist are of different race; he is the spirit of his own sacred grove, into which no stray tree can by any chance enter.

One more platitude. It is not unfashionable to pit one form of drama against another — holding up the naturalistic to the disadvantage of the epic; the epic to the belittlement of the fantastic; the fantastic to the detriment of the naturalistic. Little purpose is thus served. The essential truth, beauty, and irony of things may be revealed under all these forms. Vision over life and human nature can be as keen and just, the revelation as true, inspiring, delight-giving, and thought-provoking, whatever fashion be employed — it is simply a question of doing it well enough to uncover the kernel of the nut. Whether the violet come from Russia, from Parma, or from England matters little. Close by the Greek temples at Paestum there are violets that seem redder, and sweeter, than any ever seen — as though they have sprung up out of the footprints of some old pagan goddess; but under the April sun, in a Devonshire lane, the little blue scentless violets capture every bit as much of the spring. And so it is with drama — no matter what its form — it need only be the "real thing," need only have caught some of the precious fluids, revelation, or delight, and imprisoned them within a chalice to which we may put our lips and continually drink.

And yet, starting from this last platitude, one may perhaps be suffered to speculate as to the particular forms that our renascent drama is likely to assume. For our drama is renascent, and nothing will stop its growth. It is not renascent because this or that man is writing, but because of a new spirit. A spirit that is no doubt in part the gradual outcome of the impact on our home-grown art, of Russian, French, and Scandinavian influences, but which in the main rises from an awakened humanity in the conscience of our time.

What, then, are to be the main channels down which the renascent English drama will float in the coming years? It is more than possible that these main channels will come to be two in number and situate far apart.

The one will be the broad and clear-cut channel of naturalism, down which will course a drama poignantly shaped, and inspired with high intention, but faithful to the seething and multiple life around us, drama such as some are inclined to term photographic, deceived by a seeming simplicity into forgetfulness of the old proverb, "Ars est celare artem," and oblivious of the fact that, to be vital, to grip, such drama is in every respect as dependent on imagination, construction, selection, and elimination — the main laws of artistry — as ever was the romantic or rhapsodic play. The question of naturalistic technique will bear, indeed, much more study than has yet been given to it. The aim of the dramatist employing it is obviously to create such an illusion of actual life passing on the stage as to compel the spectator to pass through an experience of his own, to think, and talk, and move with the people he sees thinking, talking, and moving in front of him. A false phrase, a single word out of tune or time, will destroy that illusion and spoil the surface as surely as a stone heaved into a still pool shatters the image seen there. But this is only the beginning of the reason why the naturalistic is the most exacting and difficult of all techniques. It is easy enough to *reproduce* the exact conversation and movements of persons in a room; it is desperately hard to *produce* the perfectly natural conversations and movements of those persons, when each natural phrase spoken and each natural movement made has not only to contribute toward the growth and perfection of a drama's soul, but also to be a revelation, phrase by phrase, movement by movement, of essential traits of character. To put it another way, naturalistic art, when alive, indeed to be alive at all, is simply the art of manipulating a procession of most delicate symbols. Its service is the swaying and focussing of men's feelings and thoughts in the various departments of human life. It will be like a steady lamp, held up from time to time, in whose light things will be seen for a space clearly and in due proportion, freed from the mists of prejudice and partisanship.

And the other of these two main channels will, I think, be a twisting and delicious stream, which will bear on its breast new barques of poetry, shaped, it may be, like prose, but a prose incarnating through its fantasy and symbolism all the deeper aspirations, yearning, doubts, and mysterious stirrings of the human spirit; a poetic prose-drama, emotionalising us by its diversity and purity of form and invention, and whose province will be to disclose the elemental soul of man and the forces of Nature, not perhaps as the old tragedies disclosed them, not necessarily in the epic mood, but always with beauty and in the spirit of discovery.

Such will, I think, be the two vital forms of our drama in the coming generation. And between these two forms there must be no crude unions; they are too far apart, the cross is too violent. For, where there is a seeming blend of lyricism and naturalism, it will on examination be found, I think, to exist only in plays whose subjects or settings — as in Synge's *Playboy of the Western World*, or in Mr. Masefield's *Nan* — are so removed from our ken that we cannot really tell, and therefore do not care, whether an absolute illusion is maintained. The poetry

which may and should exist in naturalistic drama, can
only be that of perfect rightness of proportion, rhythm,
shape — the poetry, in fact, that lies in all vital things.
It is the ill-mating of forms that has killed a thousand
plays.   We want no more bastard drama; no more attempts to dress out the simple dignity of everyday life in
the peacock's feathers of false lyricism; no more straw-
stuffed heroes or heroines; no more rabbits and goldfish
from the conjurer's pockets, nor any limelight.   Let us
have starlight, moonlight, sunlight, and the light of our
own self-respects.

ANDRÉ MAUROIS

André Maurois (Emile Herzog) was born in Elbeuf, France, in 1885. After his education at the Lycée in Elbeuf, the Lycée Corneille at Rouen — where he won prizes in Latin, Greek, and Philosophy — and at the university of Caen, he fulfilled his term of military service, and then entered the cloth factory of Fraenkel et Herzog, which had been built up by several generations of his family. Already he had begun to write, as an avocation, and increased by travel his knowledge of England and the English. When the War broke out he was detailed as liaison officer with the Ninth Scottish Division. The acute and kindly discrimination with which he watched his allies is apparent in Les Discours du Colonel Bramble, *which appeared in* 1918. *Ostensibly a narrative, made up chiefly of the conversations of British, Scottish, and Irish officers in a regiment on active service, it is actually a witty and penetrating study of varieties in the insular temperament. The pseudonym of André Maurois was adopted to avoid the difficulties which would have been inevitable had he published under his own name while still an officer in the French Army; the success of the book, which was extraordinary, made it wise to retain the pseudonym for his later work.* Les Discours du Dr. O'Grady (1922), *a sequel in which several characters reappear, has met with even higher praise. In America, however, M. Maurois is best known through his biographies:* Ariel, or the Life of Shelley (1923), Disraeli (1927), *and* Byron (1930). *Since* 1926 *he has retired from business to devote himself to writing. His bibliography, too long to give here, includes fiction, essays, and criticism, besides the works noted; he has lectured in this country and in England with great success.*

In his note granting permission to reprint the accompanying essay, M. Maurois requested that there should be some indication that the English was that of a Frenchman, and asked for the indulgence of the reader. In recording this fact, the editor fulfills his promise; he feels certain, however, that no indulgence on the part of the reader will be found necessary.

The following essay is reprinted from the January, 1928, Yale Review, *copyright* Yale University Press, *by permission of the editors, and of M. Maurois.*

ANDRÉ MAUROIS

THE MODERN BIOGRAPHER

IS THERE such a thing as modern biography? Can one name a year in which suddenly the old biography ceased to exist and modern biography came into being? And if so, what is the difference between old and modern biography?

The first question, Is there such a thing as modern biography? can be answered in the affirmative. Read a page of Plutarch or Izaak Walton, of Dr. Johnson, or of a Victorian biographer like Trevelyan or Froude, and read after this a page of Strachey. You will see at once that you have before you two different types of book. You will find the same difference if you read biographers of other countries. Compare, in America, the traditional life of George Washington, of Abraham Lincoln, with the latest lives written. Compare, in Germany, the biographies of the beginning of the nineteenth century with Ludwig's *Kaiser Wilhelm* or with his *Goethe*. As regards France, the comparison is difficult, because biography with us is a new art, but we seem to be making up for lost opportunities by a period of mass production, and biographies built after the Stracheyan pattern have been turned out by the dozen in the last three or four years.

If now we come to the second question, Can one name a year in which suddenly the old biography ceased to exist and modern biography came into being? we shall perhaps find an answer in a quotation from the great English novelist, Virginia Woolf. She hazards an assertion that "on or about December, 1910, human character changed." "I am not saying," she writes, "that one went out, as one might into a garden, and there saw that a rose had flowered, or that a hen had laid an egg. The change was not sudden and definite like that. But a change there was, never-theless;... let us date it about the year 1910. The first signs of it are recorded in the books of Samuel Butler, in *The Way of All Flesh* in particular; the plays of Bernard Shaw continue to record it. In life one can see the change, if I may use a homely illustration, in the character of one's cook. The Victorian cook lived like a leviathan in the lower depths, formidable, silent, obscure, inscrutable; the Georgian cook is a creature of sunshine and fresh air; in and out of the drawing-room, now to borrow the *Daily Herald*, now to ask advice about a hat. Do you ask for more solemn instances of the power of the human race to change?... All human relations have shifted — those between masters and servants, husbands and wives, parents and children. And when human relations change there is at the same time a change in religion, conduct, politics, and literature. Let us agree to place one of these changes about the year 1910."

Making allowance for the conscious exaggerations of a delightful writer, there is a great deal of truth in this paradox. In other countries, the great change took place later, in 1918; but it is, I think, indisputable that the outlook on life of the cultured part of humanity, whether in Europe or in America, has undergone deep transformations in the course of the last decade. Has this change been for better or for worse? This remains to be seen, but the fact cannot be denied by an impartial observer that biography, like the novel — like all forms of literature — has been affected by these changes.

As to the third question, What is the difference between old and modern biography? the differences are of two kinds — difference in motive and difference in method. Let us begin with the motive. Why did the biographers of the old days write? We find an answer in one of them: "Biography sets before us the lives of eminent men that we may imitate their virtues and avoid their vices." The object of Plutarch is to teach morality. The object of Walton is a twofold one — "an honor due to the virtuous dead and the lesson in magnanimity to those who shall succeed them." Walton writes about his friends a few years after their deaths, and his charming lives are nothing but monuments to the memories of those friends.

Sir Sidney Lee, in his *Principles of Biography*, tells us with unconscious humor that biography exists to satisfy a natural instinct in man, the commemorative instinct. This reminds one of the theory of the Doctor in Molière's *Malade Imaginaire*: "Opium facit dormire quia est in eo virtus dormitiva." The creation of instincts makes psychology an easy science. Nevertheless, it is true that most of the old writers of biographies worked, as Sir Sidney says, to keep alive the memories of those who by character and deeds have distinguished themselves from the mass of humanity.

It must not be forgotten that the old biographer had sometimes another motive, which was simply that such lives had been ordered from him by a publisher. Dr. Johnson, for instance, never considered it as a duty towards humanity to write the lives of the British poets. He was asked to do so, and he did so extremely well, because his was a splendid mind, and he could not help giving life and color to everything he wrote.

In the Victorian era, after the death of any great Englishman, his family and his friends chose with care a writer who, they thought, would give suitable praise to the deceased hero. The process was the same in America. "When any distinguished citizen, lawyer or judge, merchant or writer, died," wrote William Roscoe Thayer, "it was taken for granted that his clergyman, if he had one, would write his life, unless his wife, sister, or cousin were preferred." Prudent men, before their death, appointed a biographer just as they appointed an executor of their will. Such choices were sometimes unfortunate. Thus Carlyle found Froude an intimate and dangerous enemy. Byron was hopelessly misunderstood by Moore. The Prince Consort and Cardinal Manning were made ridiculous by two well-meaning biographers. Other choices were happy; for example, the appointment of Monypenny by the trustees of Lord Beaconsfield; or the appointment of Charles Whibley by the family of Lord John Manners. But in the old Victorian biographies the quality most appreciated by the families of the heroes was respect of the proprieties. The intimate life of a man, his everyday doings, his weaknesses and follies and mistakes, were not to be mentioned. Even if his life had been notoriously scandalous, this should only be vaguely alluded to. "What business," says Tennyson, "has the public to know about Byron's wildnesses? He has given them fine work, and they ought to be satisfied." The author was given all the information available; letters, even private diaries, were generously put at his disposal; but such generosity forced upon him a loyalty which compelled him to be secretive and laudatory. If there was a widow, she kept a careful eye both on the portrait of her deceased husband and on the figure she herself cut in the book before posterity. The results are too well known — "Books so stuffed with virtue," one writer says of them, "that I began to doubt the existence of any virtue."

Of course, such a hard judgment is unfair to the good books of that period. A great deal could be said in favor of the old type of life and letters in three volumes, with notes and appendix. It was an invaluable mass of material, where the modern biographer is very glad to go and dig for precious metal. It was even sometimes fine work of real literary value. Macaulay's life, by Trevelyan, is a very readable book. The custom is to praise Lockhart's life of Scott and Forster's life of Dickens; these are useful books, full of interesting documents; but shall I confess that I do not admire them unreservedly? They are long and badly constructed. On the other hand, Dowden's life of Shelley seems to me perfect.

Even when the Victorian biographer is a good historian and a good writer, we have a grievance against him, which is his attitude of hero-worship. A public man, whether he is an artist or a statesman, always wears a mask. We find in him two characters; one is the man known to the public, or at least the man he would like the public to believe in; the other is the man as he is known to his friends or to himself, if he is sincere. The Victorian biographer always describes a mask, and refuses to look behind it. Read Moore's life of Byron. It is only a mask of Byron. Nobody has ever dared to write about the real Dickens or the real Thackeray. Who has described the real Herbert Spencer, human, rather comical, as we find him in the unconsciously delightful little book, *Home Life with Herbert Spencer*? The tradition was to glide over the real facts if they spoiled the rigid perfection of the mask. Victorian biographers were sculptors of commemorative monuments. Few of them were good sculptors.

We now come to Strachey, who is, I think, by common agreement to be considered as the father and master of modern biography. At once we perceive a difference. Strachey is no hero-worshipper. On the contrary, he is a hero-wrecker, an idol-breaker. Before him the great Victorians were sacred to an English gentleman of letters. General Gordon, great puritan and great soldier, was treated as a sort of national saint. Queen Victoria had Gordon's Bible placed in one of the corridors at Windsor, enclosed in a crystal case. As to the Queen herself, people knew there might be some faint essence of the comic about her, but they preferred not to think about it, and especially not to talk about it.

Then Strachey wrote *Eminent Victorians*. Nobody could complain about the title of the book. The men and women he spoke about were eminent, and they were Victorians. But as soon as one began to read, one perceived that the title was ironic. With great skill, Strachey described these Victorian giants, Cardinal Manning, Thomas Arnold, General Gordon. He did not say a word against them; he never judged; he remained objective; but he portrayed the men as they had been, without hiding anything. He gave us extracts from their letters, from their diaries, and he grouped such extracts in such a cunning way that the intimate life of his unfortunate models was revealed. For instance, he tells us that Cardinal Manning in his diary notes that, having decided to mortify himself, he determined during Lent "to use no pleasant bread except on Sundays and feasts, such as cake and sweetmeat." "But," says Strachey, "a few days later the Cardinal added in the margin 'I do not include plain biscuits.'" No comments from Strachey, but the shaft has gone home.

In Strachey's *Queen Victoria*, you cannot find a single sentence against the Queen, but the quotations and facts collected evoke the image of a fat and resolute little woman, full of pride, accessible to flattery, at the same time touching and ridiculous. The literary method of Strachey is the method of the great humorists. He does not appear himself in his book; he does not judge his model; he walks behind her, imitates her gestures, remains serious, and obtains by such tricks excellent effects of comedy. The fact that he imitates the habits of the queen, that he underlines like herself all the words of a sentence, that he writes, like her, "Lord M." instead of Lord Melbourne,

"Dear Albert" instead of Prince Albert, all these little details create a very natural and very human image. Even the exact quotation of an official document produces an effect of cruel humor. For instance, when he comes to the construction of the Albert Memorial, the ugliest monument in England, Strachey does not say that it is ugly; he simply describes the thing as it is, and gives us the very words of the sculptor: "I have chosen the sitting posture as best conveying the idea of dignity befitting the royal personage.... The aim has been, with the individuality of portraiture, to embody rank, character, and enlightenment, and to convey a sense of that responsive intelligence indicating an active, rather than a passive, interest in those pursuits of civilisation illustrated in the surrounding figures, groups, and relieves.... To identify the figure with one of the most memorable undertakings of the public life of the Prince — the International Exhibition of 1851 — a catalogue of the works collected in that first gathering of the industry of all nations, is placed in the right hand." "The statue was of bronze gilt," Strachey continues, "and weighed nearly ten tons. It was rightly supposed that the simple word 'Albert,' cast on the base, would be a sufficient means of identification."

But it would be unfair to see nothing in Strachey but an idol-breaker. He is also a very deep psychologist. As a painter, he has a curious method. He begins by designing a rather crude portrait; then he corrects a line, then another, and he keeps on making it more involved, more confused, but at the same time nearer to life. He often uses expressions like "and yet, and yet," or "There was something — what was it?" — which give the reader the impression that he pursues an indefinable character just as he would do in real life.

Remember the wonderful portrait of the Prince Consort:

Albert, certainly, seemed to be everything that Stockmar could have wished — virtuous, industrious, persevering, intelligent. And yet — why was it? — all was not well with him. He was sick at heart.

For in spite of everything he had never reached to happiness. His work, for which at last he came to crave with an almost morbid appetite, was a solace and not a cure.... The causes of his melancholy were hidden, mysterious, unanalysable perhaps — too deeply rooted in the innermost recesses of his temperament for the eye of reason to apprehend. There were contradictions in his nature, which, to some of those who knew him best, made him seem an inexplicable enigma: he was severe and gentle; he was modest and scornful; he longed for affection and he was cold. He was lonely, not merely with the loneliness of exile but with the loneliness of conscious and unrecognised superiority. He had the pride, at once resigned and over-weening, of a doctrinaire. And yet to say that he was simply a doctrinaire would be a false description; for the pure doctrinaire rejoices always in an internal contentment, and Albert was very far from doing that. There was something that he wanted and that he could never get. What was it? Some absolute, some ineffable sympathy? Some extraordinary, some sublime success? Possibly, it was a mixture of both. To dominate and to be understood! To conquer, by the same triumphant influence, the submission and the appreciation of men — that would be worth while indeed! But, to such imaginations, he saw too clearly how faint were the responses of his actual environment. Who was there who appreciated him, really and truly? Who *could* appreciate him in England? And, if the gentle virtue of an inward excellence availed so little, could he expect more from the hard ways of skill and force? The terrible land of his exile loomed before him a frigid, an impregnable mass.... He believed that he was a failure and he began to despair.

One cannot admire too much the skill of the artist and the way in which the description of a mind slowly becomes a monologue of the mind itself. The stream of consciousness, so often alluded to by the modern novelist, is described in the work of Strachey and also in the work of his followers. Nobody, perhaps, has done it better than Harold

Nicolson in his *Byron*.   Here we follow the moods of the
man, just as we would in one of James Joyce's novels —
and at the same time every thought attributed to Byron is
a thought that Byron really had.   Take, for instance, the
impressions of Byron when the family of Leigh Hunt
invades his house.

> Leigh Hunt was Shelley's fault entirely: Shelley was like
> that, he let one in for things.   One would just mention an
> idea, and expand it a little, and before one knew what had
> happened Shelley had shrilled off into another of his enthusi-
> asms.   That was the worst of Shelley: he could never see the
> difference between an idea and a proposal; obviously there
> was a very great difference.   Byron, that hot night at Ravenna
> when they had sat up together drinking gin and water, had
> merely suggested that, in certain circumstances, it would be
> great fun if he and Shelley and Leigh Hunt were all to edit
> a radical newspaper together from Italy, which could be
> published by John Hunt in London.   Shelley had called it
> a "generous proposal": it *wasn't* a proposal, it was only an
> idea; on second thoughts it was a devilish bad idea.   And
> there was Shelley writing to him from Pisa saying "Poor
> Hunt is delighted by your *noble* offer."   Had Byron ever
> made an offer?   He certainly had never intended to: at least
> not exactly an offer, only an idea.   And then, before he could
> explain it all away, there was the Hunt family already em-
> barked and well on their way to Italy.

Or, better still, perhaps, take the impressions of Byron
at a time when he starts on his Greek adventure.

> It would be idle to pretend that Byron set out upon this his
> last journey with any very spirited enthusiasm.... For when
> it had come to packing up, and destroying old letters, and
> explaining to Barry what was to be done with the books, and
> toting up the accounts, and sending the horses down to the
> harbour, and finding everything at the Casa Saluzzo hourly
> more disintegrated and uncomfortable, he began, definitely
> and indignantly, to curse the whole undertaking.   It was
> always like that: people never left one alone; there he was,
> good-natured and kindly, and they came along and took
> advantage of him, and extracted promises, and imposed upon

him generally. Once again he had been caught in a chain of circumstances: there had been his first visit to Greece, and *Childe Harold*, and *The Corsair*, and that silly passage about the "hereditary bondsmen"; and there had been Hobhouse (damn Hobhouse!), and that egregious ass Trelawny. And as a result here was he, who had never done any harm to anyone, sitting alone in the Casa Saluzzo, with his household gods once again dismantled around him, and his bulldog growling now and then at the distant voice of Trelawny thundering orders to the servants.

Of all forms of cant, this cant of romanticism was the most insufferable. There was Trelawny, for instance, trying to look like Lara, with his sham eagle eyes, his sham disordered hair, his sham abrupt manners. Why couldn't Trelawny behave quietly and like a man of decent breeding? Surely, if they were committed to this Greek scrape it would be better to take the thing soberly and calmly, instead of all this dust and bustle, of all this cant about Causes, and Liberty, and Adventure. How he *loathed* adventures! At the mere word he ground his teeth in fury.

In the case of Nicolson, just as in the case of Strachey, there is a curious mixture of irony and tenderness; but such tenderness is rather grim. Even when Strachey pats his heroes on the back, you feel that he is ready to scratch them. To treat a great man as a human being, even if this human being is a lovable one, is to make the great man smaller. The statue is brought down from its pedestal. Yes, it cannot be denied, Strachey and his pupils are idol-breakers.

It seems natural that such a school of biographers should be born in England, because a reaction against the excess of propriety of the Victorians was inevitable. After too much hero-worship, the reaction was even necessary. Strachey, Nicolson, Guedalla, have done in biography what Huxley, Forster, Virginia Woolf, have done in the novel. But though the school was born in England, it was imitated in other countries. In the United States, biographers are now rewriting the lives of most of the illustrious statesmen, and the new lives are more frank, more outspoken, than the old ones. We discover a new Franklin, a new Washington; and as to the men who lend themselves to comic treatment, they are treated without mercy by the new generation. As a good example I may mention the very remarkable life of Brigham Young by Werner.

Is this new type of biography written for the pleasure of destroying heroes? If it were so, it would be a rather despicable art. Humanity has always found a source of consolation in the lives of its great men, and one ought to consider very seriously before one destroys a perhaps useful illusion. It cannot be denied that in some instances the new biographer has overdone it. Strachey himself must be admitted in some instances to be a shade nastier than is really fair. His Disraeli is a courtier without scruples, who dominates through flattery a rather unintelligent old woman. Indeed, Disraeli was apt to pay the Queen hyperbolical compliments; but he also knew how to resist her. On the other hand, the letters of the Queen are not only made of the sentences — of the very amusing sentences — so admirably chosen by Strachey, but also of very wise comments on the political situation and a sort of middle-class wisdom that was not without useful effect upon the fate of the British Empire.

Strachey is so good a psychologist that truth in his hands is never in real danger; but some of his disciples, without imitating his deep insight, have only got hold of his familiar tricks. Instead of choosing, as heroes for biographies, "eminent men, so that we may imitate their virtues," they restrict themselves to individualities which are susceptible of treatment in their favorite mode of irony. The writer treats his hero with an unheard-of familiarity. There is a biography of Longfellow in which the biographer persists in calling the poet Henry. We have regretted in France during the last years the publication of several books where great writers are treated by much lesser writers as rather contemptible schoolmates. They even take the liberty of inventing conversations between well-known men and of putting in their mouths sentences they never pronounced. Some of these books would make us regret the three-volume life and letters which, after all, was an historical and a scholarly work. We sometimes get tired of "the plucking of dead lions by the beard."

But when we judge the modern biographer, we must consider that he represents a reaction, and that a reaction always goes too far. It was necessary to remind the last of the Victorians that a mask is not a man; it is now necessary to remind our contemporaries that a man is never entirely ridiculous, and that his life is very serious for himself.

If some of the writers of the present day have adopted the habit of choosing a hero because they do not quite like him, others, on the contrary, choose him because they are attracted to him and because they think and feel that by writing the lives of great men they may, to a certain extent, express sentiments that they have felt themselves. We all know that art is for the artist an outlet and a mode of self-expression. It is particularly true of the novelist. The novelist, through his hero, gets rid of emotions which, if they could not find such an outlet, would torment him. Samuel Butler when he writes *The Way of All Flesh* builds a hero who is an image of himself. Flaubert, when he was asked who Madame Bovary was, answered, "Madame Bovary, c'est moi."

It may happen that you find in the life of another real man certain similarities of character and idea to your own, which make you think that by writing his life you might explain to yourself some of the difficulties that you have met with. I have — to take an example from my own work — written a life of Shelley. It would, of course, be absurd to say that I find any resemblance between Shelley's life and my own. Shelley was a great poet and I am not; Shelley was the son of an English baronet at the beginning of the nineteenth century, and I am a French commoner of the twentieth. Nevertheless, Shelley was a romantic who, having begun life with certain ideals, attempted to live up to them and found himself confronted by a hard and hostile world. This in a much smaller way had happened to me. I had left school with an idealistic outlook, when I found myself in a practical world of business, where the theories of my adolescence refused to work. It was a very painful experience, so that when I first read a life of Shelley, I felt a sympathy with him, a great desire to know him better, and to understand better what had happened. Going into details, I saw that Shelley was much more human than the beautiful and ineffectual angel depicted by Matthew Arnold. It gave me pleasure to find him human. The superman is not a companion; he is too different from us; we cannot understand him. Happily, he does not exist. Shelley was a great man, but he was not a superman. I did my best to describe him exactly as I had seen him. I did not want to make fun of him. I like and admire him too much for that; but I did not want to conceal any of his weaknesses and errors, because I felt that what made him lovable was that very mixture of greatness and humanity.

In the case of Disraeli, the inducement was the same. Disraeli is again the romantic who attempts to transform ideals into reality. But Shelley died very young and had no time to succeed, whereas Disraeli managed to combine the romantic and the man of action, and died an unrepenting and partly successful romantic. Considered from that point of view, biography becomes an art similar to the art of the novel — not in its treatment but with regard to the spirit in which the work is approached.

Whether they work from the motives of Strachey (reaction) or from the motives that have just been analyzed (self-expression), modern biographers have one thing in common; that is their refusal to paint masks, their desire to get to the real man. Is this a good or a bad thing? Some critics say, Why do away with hero-worship? It is quite true, perhaps, that a hero is at the same time a man, but why say so? Is it not healthier for humanity to keep in view an image of the better type of man, an image which will help us to climb on our own shoulders? Do you not fear that the spectacle of the weaknesses of great men will lead minor men to be easily satisfied with their own conduct? Plutarch was not, perhaps, quite true to life, but he produced Montaigne, and Napoleon.

Yes; but the danger of the old type of biography is that nobody believes in it. We all know that Gladstone was not exactly the man painted by Morley. Would it not be more inspiring to meet real human beings and to treat them as such? This man Byron was not the man Moore makes him out to be; he was full of pride; he was hard on women; he was a strange mixture of his own *Manfred* and a typical English gentleman; but he was a very lovable character just the same. I wonder if make-believe is ever a good policy, and if there is any real greatness outside of perfect truth. In spite of his somewhat brutal sincerity, we must give credit to the modern biographer for his genuine respect of truth.

We shall now try to find out what are the methods of the new biographer. The essential point about him is that his aim is to build a work of art. When historians accumulated masses of documents without choice or discrimination, the result might be an interesting book, but the works produced were of considerable length, unreadable for the average man, and certainly they were not works of art. The question will be raised, Should a biography be a work of art?

"Art is essentially," Bacon said, "man added to Nature"; that is, facts ordered by a human mind. The novel is constructed; the idea of symmetry, of rhythm, plays an important part in the building of any good novel. But how can symmetry and form be achieved when the author deals with real life? Real life is what it is. We cannot alter it. How shall we give shape to this monster? The author finds himself confronted with long periods in the life of his hero when nothing happens, and then suddenly in the space of a few months events crowd in. Also it may happen that the real life ends where the story begins. Once, in London, an old bookseller said to me, "Well, sir, your life of Shelley — it isn't such a bad book; but I'll give you some advice. Next time, don't make your hero die so young. The public doesn't like it." The sentence sounds absurd, but there is something in it. The real subject of any novel is conflict between man and the universe — what Goethe called the Years of Learning; but the real conclusion of the Years of Learning is reached only in the maturity of man. For Shelley, one does not know what the conclusion might have been had he lived through this maturity.

However, consider the portrait-painter. He also has to deal with a given reality and to build a harmony of colors and lines with this given material. How does he do it? He selects; he leaves out a great many things; he does not add to the face of his model lines that are not there, but he builds by suppression, by concentrating the interest of the onlooker on the important features of the face. This is exactly what the biographer should do. He must not invent anything, but his art is to forget. If he has at his disposal two hundred letters and a long diary, he must

know how to extract the few sentences that will convey a
general impression.

In any life, there is always a well-hidden harmony; the
historian has to discover the mysterious rhythm in that
existence. He can give an impression of unity by repeating certain themes, as Wagner does in music. In the
biography of Shelley, for instance, there must be a theme
of water; water plays a great part in Shelley's life. As a
boy he is attracted by it; as a man he spends his life in
fragile boats. From the beginning, you feel that he will
die by drowning. The writer should give this impression
of impending fate. In the life of Disraeli, rain is a poetical
element. Implacable, steady rain is a symbol of the
universe fighting the romantic. Peacocks also play a
curious part in this life. By a careful handling of such
themes, the biographer can hope to achieve some sort of
musical construction.

Such construction must, of course, coincide with a respect for facts. A strict adherence to historical truth is
necessary to the biographer, but after he has collected his
facts, he has a right to eliminate some of them.

Now, there are certain rules which practice has proved
useful. The first is that one should follow a chronological
order. Ancient biographers like Plutarch had no idea of
chronology. They started with a recital of facts, and,
after they had told us about the death of their hero, they
began again with anecdotes and analysis of character.
Then came an ethical judgment. This method gave a
painful impression of repetition. It was copied from
Plutarch by Walton and also by Johnson; they all tell you
from the first that their hero was a great man. The Victorian biographer writes "This great poet was born in
1788." This, I think, is wrong. A man is not born a
great poet, and he will not interest us if he is shown as a
great man from his babyhood. What is interesting is to

see the child Byron, the young man at Harrow, at Cambridge, and to discover slowly how he became *Manfred* and *Don Juan*.

Of course, this idea of chronological development is new. It comes from the fact that we now believe in the evolution of an individual mind as well as of a race. A biographer like Walton did not feel the need of chronology because he did not believe that a man's nature could change very much. All arts react one upon another. In the last twenty years, Marcel Proust has taught us how to avoid drawing static characters. Some of his heroes are unpleasant at the beginning of the novel and delightful at the end. In the case of other characters, the process is reversed. We want the biographer to be as true to life as the novelist. "My object," says Miss Lowell, "has been to make the reader feel as though he were living with Keats, subject to the same influences that surrounded him, moving in his circle, watching the advent of poems as from day to day they sprang into being." In biography, as in the novel, it is important that the minor characters should be seen from the point of view of the central figure. They should not even be allowed to appear until the very moment when the hero discovers them.

The second rule is to avoid pronouncing moral judgments. The essential difference between art and action is that art builds a world where no real events occur, and where, therefore, man feels that he has no moral decision to make. The characters in *Hamlet* would be painful to meet in real life, because something would have to be done about them, but we accept them on the stage because no moral problem arises for us. If an artist gives the impression that the world he describes is a world where we must act and decide, he may be a great moralist, but he is no more a great artist. A biographer must tell his story in objective and impartial style.

The third rule is to read every word that has ever been written on the subject and to collect all available testimony.   What the modern historian wants to describe is not the statue but the man.   In official documents, very often he finds nothing but the statue.   It may be in the letters or the journal of an unknown woman that he will come across the anecdote that will suddenly reveal a character.   He must hunt for details if he wants truth. Of course, the question arises, What is truth?   Is there indeed a truth about character?   You remember Walt Whitman's —

When I read the book, biography famous,
And is this, then (said I), what the author calls a man's life?
And so will some one, when I am dead and gone, write my life?
As if any man really knew aught of my life;
Why, even I myself, I often think, know little or nothing of my
   real life.

Whitman is partly right.   If we think of our own lives, we realize that some of our most important acts have been accomplished by us without any real motivation.   Perhaps we have said words which meant more than we thought; and a few months later we found ourselves involved in actions which did not coincide with our real wishes.   This is true of Byron.   Byron never meant to die in Greece, or even to go to Greece.   He had played with the idea because he was bored, because he thought it would relieve him of the tedium of his Italian life.   Then the moment came when words were turned into acts and Byron lived up to them.

The writer should be careful not to make the life of his hero appear too well constructed.   A human life is very rarely the conscious accomplishment of the will.   It is that partly, but you must always leave a certain margin for the action of circumstance.   A "tale told by an idiot," says Shakespeare.   There is always something of that

madness in the lives of great men of action. If you leave
out the strange atmosphere of fate, you miss all the real
poetry of human life.

Of course, one of the best technical rules to follow in
order to avoid showing the life of the hero as too squarely
built is to allow the reader to see him through the eyes of
friends and enemies who judge him differently. There the
biographer can learn much from the modern novelist.
Read a novel like Forster's *Passage to India*; there you see
the English as they appear to a Hindu, the Hindu as
seen by the English, and the Hindu as seen by himself.
In the same way, I have attempted as well as I could to
show Disraeli as seen by Gladstone, and Gladstone as seen
by Disraeli. You cannot say that there was one Gladstone; there were as many Gladstones as there were people
who knew him, and it is the sum of these portraits which
enables the reader to form an idea of the average Gladstone.

There is one more question to deal with, How is one to
select the subject of a biography? Sir Sidney Lee says
that the theme should be of a certain magnitude. This
has been contradicted. Many writers contend that if you
could know every thought that crosses the mind of a beggar, you could write a better book than any life of Caesar.
Perhaps; but a great life makes better food for a human
soul. Moreover, the life of the beggar leaves very few
traces. It may be written by the novelist, not by the
biographer, who needs documents, letters, diaries. The
man who leaves behind him an historical record is either
the great man of thought or the great man of action. In
some cases, the theme may be of sufficient magnitude
though the man himself is not a great man. This happens
when the chosen hero has been the centre of important
events. A good example is Mr. Shane Leslie's *George the
Fourth*. In such cases, the poetical element might be

found in the contrast between the magnitude of the tragedy and the misery of the tragedians.

At the end of his biography of his wife, Alice Freeman
Palmer, Mr. Palmer says: "If my portrait of her is correct,
invigoration will go forth from it and disheartened souls
be cheered." This should apply to any biography worth
writing. Such books should help us to bear the difficulties
of life. They should help us to understand them. Carlyle said that "a well-written life is almost as rare as a well-
spent one." This is true, but "great men, taken up in
any way, are profitable company."

IOLO A. WILLIAMS

Born in Middlesborough, England, in 1890, *Iolo Aneurin Williams was educated at Rugby and at King's College, Cambridge. He entered the army at the outbreak of the War, and served until* 1920, *retiring as captain. Two collections of his verse had already appeared:* Poems (1915), *and* New Poems (1919). *Since* 1920 *he has been bibliographical correspondent of* The London Mercury, *and has contributed frequently to such magazines as* The Observer, The Listener, *and* The Library. *His interest in bibliography is further indicated by his publication of* Seven Eighteenth Century Bibliographies (1924) *and* Elements of Book Collecting (1927). *He has edited two unique anthologies:* Shorter Poems of the Eighteenth Century (1923) *and* Byways Round Helicon (1922), *an exceedingly interesting collection of good work by minor poets, chiefly of the eighteenth century. He has thus shown himself a discriminating student and critic, as well as practitioner, of the art of poetry.*

The following selection is reprinted from Poetry Today *by I. A. Williams, by permission of the publishers, Herbert Jenkins, Ltd. The final paragraph of the original essay, which serves chiefly to introduce the subsequent chapter, has been omitted.*

IOLO A. WILLIAMS

POETRY TODAY

IT IS usually wise, when writing upon a subject, to begin by defining it, as exactly as possible, so that the
reader may be made to understand what it is that the
author is proposing to discuss. *Poetry Today*, which is
to be the subject of this brochure, presents, however, to
the unhappy writer who endeavours to follow such a pro-
cedure, this difficulty — that while it is quite possible to
define the word "Today," it is not necessary, and that, on
the other hand, it is most desirable to define "Poetry,"
but unfortunately impossible. Many persons have tried
to say what poetry is. Wordsworth (I think) approached
pretty near to one aspect of the truth when he said that
poetry was emotion recollected in tranquillity, a remark
which at least contains a realisation of the fact that poetry
is not a thing created hastily, thoughtlessly almost, by a
mind violently agitated by some strong emotion. The
public loves to believe, and has been encouraged to do so
by some poets, that a poem is the instantaneous outcome
of inspiration, that the poet has but to have his soul
stirred by some sight, to strike his breast with one hand, to
throw the other before him into the air, and — heigh pres-
to! — the poem is ready to be written out and sent to the
printer. Wordsworth knew better than that. He knew
that an art needs more from its practitioner than inspiration, it needs labour and thought. The emotion which is
the seed of the poem must lie in the poet's mind for some
time before it germinates, and as it grows it must be
tended and trimmed so that the grown plant may be as
shapely and perfect as possible.

It is perhaps for this reason that so many of the best
poems are melancholy, for melancholy is not an emotion
roused, like anger, or indignation, or laughter, upon the
immediate contemplation of a particular event, but a
quality of thought and feeling that (for some reason which
we need not consider here) more or less constantly per-
vades the minds of a large number of the most sensitive
and intelligent people. The scene, which arouses the
poet's original emotion, may be gay and lively enough;
but he does not immediately convert his emotion into a
poem; he lets it lie in his mind for perhaps years, and when
the poem finally emerges, it may show that the writer's
melancholy has permeated the whole thing, and converted
some brilliantly shining and happy vision into a reflection,
perhaps even more exquisitely beautiful, but sad and sub-
dued — transposed, as it were, into a minor key. Thus
"emotion recollected in tranquillity" tends usually to
change its character in the process, and very often, from
the nature of the human mind, the change is from gay to
grave, from joy to wistfulness. How pervasive is melancholy in English poetry may be shown by the instance of
Mr. Belloc, who is usually reckoned a cheerful writer, but
yet cannot avoid converting to sadness such a scene as that
of a girl dancing in a Spanish inn:

> Glancing,
> Dancing,
> Backing and advancing,
> Snapping of the clapper to the spin
> Out and in —
> And the Ting, Tong, Tang of the guitar!
> Do you remember an Inn,
> Miranda?
> Do you remember an Inn?

It is safe to surmise that, when Mr. Belloc witnessed
that dance, he did not weep, rather, I should guess, he
rejoiced; but in converting its recollection into a poem he

achieves a slow, sad music that wrings the very heart of the reader. The emotion is, in essence, that which is always aroused by man's yearning to give one more day of life to things desirable but — of their nature — transient and fugitive. It is perhaps the most generally pervading of all human feelings, save that of love; it is the "Eheu fugaces" of Horace, and — equally — the instinct that leads us to recall, almost with tears, the comic songs of years gone by and to think wistfully of "At Trinity Church I met my doom" and "Her golden hair was hanging down her back." It is an emotion that rouses us, when we meet it, even, in the foolish, as Shakespeare very well knew:

> Jesu! Jesu! dead! a' drew a good bow; and dead! a' shot a fine shoot; John a Gaunt loved him well, and betted much money on his head. Dead!

Shallow was a fool, but, nevertheless, he makes us share his feeling.

We have reason to suppose, then, that when emotion is recollected in tranquillity it is also very frequently transmuted by the temperament and prevailing cast of mind of the poet. Even so, however, there is more than this necessary for the making of a poem, for it is clear that recollected emotion could quite as well be expressed in prose as in poetry. Prose, indeed, may have a poetical quality, but it cannot be poetry, for there is, as a perfectly sound instinct tells us, somewhere a dividing line between the two, though we do not know its exact position. In trying to clarify our ideas as to the nature of prose and poetry, we are like the scientist who believes that such a thing as a species exists, but cannot define it. Yet we are, I think, in a position to say not only that there is an essential distinction between the two forms of writing, but also that this lies in the element of repetition which is present in all poetry. Sometimes the repetition is of sounds, as in rhymed or alliterative verse, sometimes of rhythms, as in blank and other unrhymed verses; usually there is a combination of both kinds of repetition. But the repetition must be there for a piece of writing to be poetry. There must be an arrangement of the words so planned as to bring about, at more or less regular intervals, the re-iteration of certain recognisable units, whether those units be combinations of the sounds of vowels and consonants, or of stressed and unstressed syllables. Whatever the nature of the unit of repetition, it must be there, and must contribute to the impression created by — in other words to the *sense* of — the composition as a whole. In prose the actual arrangement of words is planned merely, as it were, to liberate most easily the meaning of the writer. In poetry, on the other hand, the words are so arranged as to produce by their very arrangement, as opposed to their dictionary definitions, a particular impression on the reader's mind.

It is difficult to see how this can be done except by the use of repetition, and certainly that has, in the past, always been the method adopted by poets. To write prose that is not like other prose is a thing that is not difficult of achievement, and I am inclined to wonder whether certain modern writers, in their attempts to evolve a new kind of poetry, are not merely writing an odd kind of prose. Perhaps it is that my mind is not sufficiently alert to grasp the unit of repetition (which I suggest must be present in all poetry) in the work of such writers as Mr. Carl Sandburg. Mr. Sandburg, who has a considerable reputation in America, is a writer of much vigour, with a keen eye for those details in a scene which are essential to its presentation in words, and a quick mind. My only fear is that he has never given that mind to the consideration of the essentials of poetry and prose, and that, in his eagerness to write an original kind of poetry, he is writing something which has none of the essentials of

poetry and few of the merits of prose. Here are a few
lines, from one of Mr. Sandburg's pieces:

> There is something terrible
> about a hurdy-gurdy,
> a gipsy man and woman,
> and a monkey in red flannel
> all stopping in front of a big house
> with a sign "For Rent" on the door
> and the blinds hanging loose
> and nobody home.
> I never saw this.
> I hope to God I never will.

That passage avoids many of the worst faults of bad
poetry; it is not obscure, for instance; it contains an amusing thought, and it is not false in sentiment. Yet I find
difficulty in resisting the belief that Mr. Sandburg is bark-
ing up the wrong tree, or rather, perhaps, that he is bark-
ing up a very small shrub in the mistaken belief that it is
a tree. Such lines as those I have just quoted seem rather
to be notes for a piece of prose than part of a poem; and,
indeed, Mr. Sandburg, and writers of his school, by omit-
ting from their work that which is an essential thing in
poetry, give us nothing to show that they are poets at all.
It is as if a man were to build a pig-stye and then invite
us to admire his skill in domestic architecture. Yet perhaps the saddest thing about much so-called "free-verse"
is that it does not even substitute good prose for poetry,
but a sort of hybrid which seems, like most hybrids, to be
born sterile.

It is easy to deride the poetical form of any particular
literary period, and it is a healthy thing that poets should
constantly be seeking new forms; for since form is not
merely a mould in which a poem is cast, but something
which becomes a part of its content, since form is not an
external thing to a poem, but something internal, it is
clear that no poet can be writing truly original verse who

is not in some degree an innovator in form. The difference is not always one that can be measured, or set down in feet, or displayed in a scheme of rhymes — A B B A, or what not — but certainly every poet, to give his work value, must contrive to give a shape of his own to those subtle but recognisable internal rhythms which are part of the life and being of a poem. In other words he must, as the journalists say, "Strike a note of his own."

This brings me, naturally enough I trust, to a point which can be studied in the light of another favourite definition of poetry. Prose, we are sometimes told, is the right words in the right order, but poetry is "the best words in the best order." The antithesis has, I must admit, always struck me as foolish. What, I pray, is the difference between "the right words" and "the best words"? But in any case, the answer to that question does not much matter, for words (like most other things) are not absolutely, and without qualification, best or worst. They are only best for a particular purpose, and, before we can make any such antithesis as that which I have quoted, we must consider whether the purposes of poetry and of prose are the same. It does not, I think, take very long for us to decide that they are by no means the same. The primary object of written prose is, I take it, to put the reader in possession of certain facts; the best prose is that which uses words with the greatest individual precision and collective lucidity. It would almost be fair to say that the more one notices the style of a prose-writer, the worse it is. With poetry, however, the chief aim is not mere information. It is true that before the invention of printing much purely informative literature was written in verse. Treatises on husbandry, for example, were written by poets, and epics and ballads were versified history. But the reason for this was not that poetry was better suited than prose to the exposition of these subjects, but that, once written, it was more easily remembered. Today, however, the printing press has made it unnecessary for us to carry all our knowledge in our heads, and poetry is no longer used as a mnemonic — except for such things as the gender rhymes which all small boys learn at school. Of these, however, I will take leave to omit consideration. Broadly speaking, poetry today is not intended to be informative, and those forms of it which originally won their position because verse was easier to remember than prose — the epic, the ballad, and the didactic poem — have, each of them, fallen upon comparatively evil days.

Those kinds of poetry which, at the present time, have the greatest attraction for us, and are most successfully practised, are those which aim, not so much at telling us something, but at arousing in us some emotion — pity, or anger, or laughter, or scorn, or exultation; and poetry does this not only by the words it uses, but by the way it uses them, and by the tune it makes with them as it arranges them. It is hard to resist using a musical metaphor, for, indeed, in some ways poetry is essentially more nearly allied to music than to written prose, and, as music does, approaches the brain by way of the sense of hearing. Poetry has in its appeal a physical quality which is none the less potent because we find difficulty in saying of the emotion which a beautiful poem excites in us, how much is caused by the mere sound of the words, and how much by the sense which our brain attaches to them. The two appeals are, however, certainly there, and the perfection of a poem depends upon the blending and interadjustment of the one and the other. It is this mutual relation of sound to meaning that makes any comparison of what is the best word for poetry with what is the right word for prose meaningless, for the words are wanted for different purposes.

It is impossible to create anything which is a blend of two different things, and still to keep each of those things at its highest individual perfection and purity. To do so would be to produce a mixture, in which the elements jostled one another crude and unaltered, rather than a compound. Therefore in poetry words are used neither at their highest precision of meaning and arrangement, nor at their greatest value as mere sounds. There must be compromise between the two elements, for the poet has to remember that he is relying for his effect upon their combined action upon the reader. The result is that in no poem, however great, can the choice and order of words be exactly that of prose; yet the poet must remember that the words which he is using, are things which have well known and accepted meanings in everyday prose, and he must not select, for their mere sound, words which have meanings that make them, in that place, either ludicrous or colourless. Similarly, he must reject words which, though admirable in sense, by their sound break his rhythm or otherwise jar with the musical effect at which he is aiming. There has been much misunderstanding and loose thinking on this subject, and one is constantly seeing poets struggling as hard as they can to over-emphasise one or the other of the two elements. Swinburne, for instance, was liable to be carried away by the sound of his words and to write verses that, often enough, made very little sense. Some of his disciples have succeeded in making no sense at all; and it is an interesting thing to note, incidentally, that Swinburne has had less influence on the technique of others than any poet of equal eminence, and that when his influence is apparent the result is usually deplorable. On the other hand, by neglecting the sound of their verses, many poets have failed as badly. I quoted, a page or two back, a few lines by Mr. Carl Sandburg, in which I felt this writer had made the mistake of deliberately neglecting the appeal of sound by excluding that repetitive element which I believe to be essential to the form of poetry. Others have, indeed, retained the form of the thing, but have forced their meaning too roughly into the mould. Even so great a man as Browning did this at times, so that, for the moment at least, he versified clumsily, instead of writing poetry:

> No harm! It was not my fault
> If you never turned your eye's tail up
> As I shook upon E *in alt*,
> Or ran the chromatic scale up.

Perhaps in these particular lines the effect was deliberate on Browning's part; but, deliberate or not, they furnish an admirable example of what I mean.

Now, by way of contrast, let me quote a stanza from one of the loveliest of all modern poems, Mr. Walter de la Mare's *All That's Past*, a piece the very thought of which never fails to recall the thrill it gave me when first I read it, about the year 1910 I suppose, in a short-lived magazine called (somewhat unhappily) *The Thrush*. This poem, to my mind, is a perfect example of the blending of the elements which are necessary in poetry. It consists of three stanzas, of which the last runs thus:

> Very old are we men;
> Our dreams are tales
> Told in dim Eden
> By Eve's nightingales;
> We wake and whisper awhile,
> But, the day gone by,
> Silence and sleep like fields
> Of amaranth lie.

If ever there was a stanza which was calculated to destroy the notion that poetry is only another kind of prose, or that it aims at the same object as prose, it is this one. Try, for a moment, to shut your ears to the poetry of the thing, and force yourself to read the words as prose, taking account only of their prose meanings; you will find that, not only is the prose not the best prose, but it is pretty well meaningless.   One could recast in prose a part of the meaning of the stanza, by talking of complexes, subconscious egos, and inherited characteristics; but a greater part would escape us.   In truth, the force of the whole is a thing compounded of the meanings of the words used, and of the rhythms and sounds which they form.   Only by the arrangement of these particular words in this particular poetic form can the whole of the poet's intention be made clear; and there is no way of paraphrasing what his verse says.   Yet no violence is done either to the prose sense, or to the prose order, of the words; so that the reader's mind is not distressed (or entertained) by any such incongruities as inept versifiers are forever producing in their verses. The poet here has kept a perfect balance between the two media — words as sound, and words as vehicles of definite ideas — in which he is, when he is writing a poem, simultaneously working.

I wonder if we are now any nearer — not, indeed, to defining poetry, for that I believe to be impossible — but to understanding it and some of its essentials.   I trust so; but, however that may be, the subject cannot be pursued here at much further length, for this booklet is not, primarily, an essay on the nature of poetry, but a discussion of the present state of the art.   Yet one thing more must be said, before we pass on to our main task, and that is that poetry can be written on any subject which is susceptible to emotional treatment — which means, in practice, almost any subject in the world.   Too often attempts have been made to limit the subject matter of poetry.   All such attempts are fundamentally unsound, for anything which is capable of being presented in some other way than as a bald statement of fact, is capable of being the subject

of a poem. The eighteenth century realised this, but —
taken as a whole — the nineteenth century did not, and
was inclined to limit poetry to an admiring contemplation
of the soul soaring, and to a discreet lament over the dis-
solution of the body. These things are, of course, perfectly proper subjects for poetry, but they are by no means
the only ones.

Happily, modern poets are beginning to realise that
exaltation and melancholy, though they may be the commonest, are not the only states of mind suited to poetical
expression. A poem may just as well be funny as sad,
and is not then necessarily to be classed, somewhat con-
temptuously, as mere verse. Poetry, as I have tried to
show, is a method of expression in which the sense of the
words, and their rhythms and sounds, work together to
produce an effect on the reader's mind. So long as there
is true harmony between the two elements, the result is a
poem, whatever the emotion governing them both may be.
It is only when the comic effect is produced by a deliberate
incongruity between rhythm and sense, when the result
is in fact a parody, that we are justified in classing it as
verse, a thing produced by mere cleverness and without
depth of feeling — though not necessarily without inspiration (whatever that may be) — for when a writer
feels deeply it is, I conceive, impossible for him to play
with his emotion and, as it were, make fun of it, or, if it is
possible, and he does it, he is deliberately refraining from
writing poetry. It is within our daily experience that the
emotions of laughter, or of disgust, to mention only two,
can affect us just as strongly as sorrow or joy; and they
not only can be, but are, made into poetry. It would not
be difficult to choose from modern poetry a series of quotations which would show the emotions which, generally
speaking, the nineteenth century held to be unpoetical,
made into poems. Let me quote, not a long series, but

just two or three. As I write this essay there arrives on
my desk a slender book, *The Dispassionate Pilgrim*, by
a poet of whom I have never previously heard, and of
whom I now know nothing, except that he shows considerable skill in writing just the kind of lightly witty
poetry with which it suits me to illustrate my present
point.

This poet's name is Mr. Colin D. B. Ellis, and this is how
he begins one of his poems:

> Though my heart is bound to Chloris
> (Chloe, Amaryllis, Doris),
> Though I stoutly should condemn
> All inconstancy to — them,
> Though my love will never falter
> And my heart will never alter
> Till — I do not like to vow;
> Not, at any rate, just now —
> Yet I see no valid reason
> Why I should account it treason
> If at times, and by the way,
> I should let my glances stray
> And appreciate the graces
> Shown in unfamiliar faces.

Light enough, in all conscience; but it expresses a genuine
feeling, and expresses it through the technique of poetry
with an effect which could not otherwise be achieved.
Therefore, I believe these lines to be poetry.   Perhaps my
reader may object that there is nothing very new in this
kind of poetry, that it is a legitimate line of descent from
Prior and Praed and Austin Dobson.   That is true, but the
thing to be considered is this — how much was Prior read
thirty years since, and has there not too often been a
tendency to consider him, and Praed, and Dobson, and a
dozen other poets who wrote lightly and wittily, as different *in kind* from their more solemn brothers?   It is the
general realisation that poetry can express a multitude of

emotions that is a new thing today, or, rather, the revival
of an old thing; it is not, except in a lesser degree, the existence of humorous poetry.

Now let us turn to another kind of poem, the political
satire, which has often been looked down upon as a sort of
poor relation of the better class of poem, though none has
ever been able to deny altogether its kinship to poetry.
Through the nineteenth century political satire was
hardly written, if at all; but now one could put together
quite a large body of verse of this kind, which would have
great and obvious merits as poetry. There would be
things by Mr. Belloc. There would be others by Mr.
Chesterton, among them that masterful piece of political
disgust, to which he was moved by the then Mr. F. E.
Smith's extravagant remark that the Welsh Disestablish-
ment Bill had "shocked the conscience of every Christian
community in Europe." This is the last stanza of it:

> It would greatly, I must own,
> Soothe me, Smith,
> If you left this theme alone,
> Holy Smith!
> For your legal cause or civil
> You fight well and get your fee;
> For your God or dream or devil
> You will answer, not to me.
> Talk about the pews and steeples
> And the Cash that goes therewith!
> But the souls of Christian peoples...
> — Chuck it, Smith!

There would, I think, also be this war-time epigram by Mr.
J. C. Squire:

> Customs die hard in this our native land;
> And still in Northern France, I understand,
> Our gallant boys, as through the fray they forge,
> Cry "God for Harmsworth! England and Lloyd George!"

And there would be other such things, which are poetry

because their verse form is an essential part of the expression of some violent emotion of indignation, or disgust, aroused by the contemplation of current politics.

Our living poets are also realising that poetry is a language that includes even the broadly comic — as it did to some extent in the seventeenth and eighteenth centuries. Here it is more difficult to select an example, for there is also such a thing as humorous verse, which is not what I am speaking about. Mr. Chesterton, however, will once more give me exactly what I want:

Old Noah he had an ostrich farm and fowls on the largest scale,
He ate his egg with a ladle in an egg-cup big as a pail,
And the soup he took was Elephant Soup and the fish he took
    was Whale,
But they all were small to the cellar he took when he set out to
    sail,
And Noah he often said to his wife when he sat down to dine,
"I don't care where the water goes if it doesn't get into the wine."

Perhaps because, as a teetotaller, I do not share Mr. Chesterton's, and Noah's, enthusiasm for wine, I feel that I am all the more likely to be giving a true and unbiassed opinion when I say that nothing on earth will persuade me that that exuberant and uproarious stanza is not poetry. Mr. Squire has put it — and quite rightly — in an anthology of modern poetry, side by side with the loveliest things of Mr. de la Mare, Rupert Brooke, James Elroy Flecker, Mr. Ralph Hodgson, and a dozen others. Would any anthologist of the nineteenth century have done that? And, if not, may we not congratulate ourselves that our appreciation of poetry is becoming more catholic, better able to recognise perfection in whatever form we find it? It is a strange thing, this attempt which the nineteenth century made to limit the sphere of poetry, for there was no similar attempt to limit that of prose. A man might "dare to write as funny as" he could, and yet have no cause to fear for his reputation as a great prose-writer; in fact, the readers of prose rather liked it, and encouraged him to do it again; but let him dare to be funny, even rather funny, in a poem, and he was regarded as a trifler — a verdict which only such occasional robust and careless spirits as R. H. Barham dared to brave. In a sense, I suppose, this was intended as a compliment to poetry, which was held to be the nobler of the two arts, and therefore to be applied to the expression only of lofty thoughts. But if poetry is nobler than prose, is it not a good thing that we should laugh in poetry, and the more nobly the better?

CHAUNCEY BREWSTER TINKER

Born at Auburn, Maine, in 1876, Chauncey Brewster Tinker received the degree of B.A. in 1899, and that of Ph.D. in 1902, from Yale University. He began his career as teacher of English at Bryn Mawr College; since 1903 he has continued it at Yale, where, in 1924, he was appointed Sterling Professor of English. *During the War he served as captain in the Military Intelligence Division, attached to the General Staff, U.S.A.* In 1930 he was Lecturer on Fine Arts at Harvard. *Through his courses at Yale and through a series of publications ranging from* Dr. Johnson and Fanny Burney (1911) *to an edition of the* Letters of James Boswell (1924), *he is perhaps best known as an interpreter of the life and literature of the eighteenth century.* That in 1902 he published a notable translation *of* Beowulf *and that in 1929 he published* The Good Estate of Poetry — *essays on modern literature* — *are facts which indicate significantly the unusual range of his knowledge.* In the Preface *to this latter volume, from which the accompanying selection has been taken, Professor Tinker has stated his plan (page vii):* "to examine certain tendencies in poetry and criticism against the background of what may be termed the tradition of English literature." *For such an examination it would be difficult to suggest anyone better qualified.*

The following essay is reprinted from The Good Estate of Poetry, *by Chauncey Brewster Tinker.* An Atlantic Monthly Press Publication. *Reprinted by permission of Little, Brown and Company, and by the courtesy of the author.*

CHAUNCEY BREWSTER TINKER

FIGURES IN A DREAM

POETRY AND THE FASHIONS

How doth the city sit solitary, that was full of people! how
is she become as a widow! she that was great among the nations,
and princess among the provinces, how is she become tributary!
— LAMENTATIONS OF JEREMIAH

WHEN, towards the end of May, 1770, *The
Deserted Village* issued from the press, its author was, with but a single exception, the best
known of living English poets. Thomas Gray, indeed,
was still alive, but no longer productive, and was, moreover, at the threshold of the last year of his life. Gray
read the poem and praised its author — Gray was chary
of praise — and may well have detected in it that rare
union of high literary distinction and wide popular appeal
that marked his own *Elegy*. The *Elegy* had appeared
twenty years before, and had been at once received into
the hearts of men. *The Deserted Village*, like its great
predecessor, has kept its place in the esteem of critics and
in the affection of readers in a way that may properly
challenge the attention of all persons who are seriously
concerned for the welfare of poetry.

Evidences of its popularity and influence appeared at
once. So many editions of it were issued that they have
constituted ever since a bibliographical problem. It
begot, soon after its appearance, an imitation by one
"A.K." of the Middle Temple, who inscribed his verses
"with much respect" to "Dr. Oliver Goldsmith (in whose
acquaintance he [the author] is personally honored)," and
entitled them, rather presumptuously, *The Frequented*

Village. This of course is a mere literary curiosity; but the influence of Goldsmith's poem is writ large elsewhere. It exerted an influence truly creative on the Romantic Movement, not only in England but on the Continent. This is not the place to dwell on the indebtedness of German literature to Oliver Goldsmith; but we may mention two interesting events which occurred within two years of the publication of the poem in England. In the first place, in 1771 the youthful Goethe translated the poem into German — a work which has unfortunately disappeared. Secondly, in the next year, probably in the month of May, he had the original English text published at Darmstadt, "printed for a friend of the Vicar." In the same year there appeared a French imitation of the poem at Brussels, entitled, *Le Retour du Philosophe, ou le Village abandonné.* A long line of translations and imitations followed this.

Among the careful students of the poem was Robert Burns, whose *Cotter's Saturday Night* and a dozen other poems exist to show that the "pastoral simplicity" of rural life, though it may have departed from England, is still to be found in Scotland. When George Crabbe, in revolt from the warm pastoral romanticism of his time, attacked the idealization of rural life, he called his bitter *exposé The Village,* in obvious reminiscence of Goldsmith's poem, and summed up his views in the line —

Auburn and Eden can be found no more.

But the poet would certainly not have been content with a merely literary influence. He aspired to draw effective attention to an alarming evidence of national decay. He was disturbed, and he might well be disturbed, by the condition of the English countryside. As a result of the vast accumulation of wealth, he saw an increasing number of great estates with large tracts "improved" by the new art of landscape gardening, and exhibiting long, picturesque prospects, which were often enriched with a glimpse of a Gothic ruin, sometimes genuine, sometimes an imitation of the antique in lath and plaster. It was all got up to look very fine; but cottages formerly occupied by peasants and busy tillers of the soil had at times to be swept away wholesale in order to open out the fine views.[1] Still other tracts of land had to be "preserved" for game.

> Yet count our gains. This wealth is but a name
> That leaves our useful products still the same.
> Not so the loss. The man of wealth and pride,
> Takes up a space that many poor supplied;
> Space for his lake, his park's extended bounds,
> Space for his horses, equipage, and hounds.

This criticism of the rapidly developing luxury of the middle classes was not new in the poet's work. He had written essays on the menace of luxury. He had even deplored the decay of villages in verse before:

> Have we not seen, at pleasure's lordly call,
> The smiling long-frequented village fall;
> Beheld the duteous son, the sire decay'd,
> The modest matron, and the blushing maid,
> Forc'd from their homes, a melancholy train,
> To traverse climes beyond the western main;
> Where wild Oswego spreads her swamps around,
> And Niagara stuns with thund'ring sound?

The Deserted Village, therefore, had made its first appearance in verse near the end of *The Traveller*, and had been developing ever since in the mind of the poet. It is the result of long meditation on the change in British life which we have since learned to call the beginning of the Industrial Era, with its coal and machinery and factory hands.

How odd to find a poem germinating from such medita-

---

[1] "It is too much the interest of a parish, both landlords and tenants, to decrease the cottages in it — and, above all, to prevent their increase, that, in a process of time, habitations are extremely difficult to be procured." A. Young, *Farmer's Letters* (1767), p. 173. (Author's note.)

tion as that! What has poetry, we instinctively inquire today, to do with local, economic conditions such as these? We feel an irrepressible tendency to apologize for Goldsmith's sentimentality and ignorance of economic law — *The Deserted Village* antedates Smith's *Wealth of Nations* by six years — and defend the poem as a cento of beautiful descriptions such as those of the parson, the schoolmaster, the village inn, the broken soldier, the peasants at play. I must confess that I myself long regarded the poem as saved by the excellence of such details; but of late I have come to feel the inadequacy of such a view. It concedes too much. A poem which has exhibited such vitality must be sound at the core. There must be something universal in the central theme to explain the enduring appeal of the poem. And such a universality of theme may, I believe, be found. What we love in the poem is not merely the beauty of the lines about the parson, passing rich with forty pounds a year, who allured to brighter worlds and led the way; not the schoolmaster, though he is as true to type as one of Chaucer's pilgrims — whose pupils laughed "with counterfeited glee at all his jokes, for many a joke had he." These and the rest we hold in memory with that peculiar warmth of affection which Goldsmith always elicits; but the touching beauty of these and the other descriptions is derived from the central theme, out of which the poem rose. These persons and all the dear simplicity of their lives are no more. The beauty of the deserted village is that pensive grace which clings in memory to blessings lost long since. There is a sadness inseparable from the changes, inevitable though they be, which are wrought by Time; and in particular is such regret stimulated by the recollection of the house which we loved at another period of life. Who that has spark of affection for the home of his boyhood can conquer a bitter dismay at its alterations? Such change seems always the work of vandals. And now if our emotions can be kindled by so simple a thing as the recollection of our old home, why should not profounder depths of being stir into life as we meditate with the poet upon the sad beauty of a whole village in decay, fallen into ruin under the triumphant wheels of Luxury and Progress?

It is not essential to think ourselves back into the eighteenth century in order to appreciate all this. The conditions lie about us still. If we could produce a Goldsmith in Connecticut, he would find material ready to his hand in the abandoned farms. Do you fancy that Auburn was more beautiful — or more deserted — than Old Lyme or Hadley, Massachusetts? One given over to artists, the other abandoned to the Poles. It may well be irrational to bewail such changes; but Goldsmith was irrational. Poets often are. Poetry is seldom the handmaid of rationalism. In the pleasant valleys of Connecticut, abandoned by our grandfathers only to be rediscovered by Italian market gardeners and millionaires, who would fain retire from the ugliness which their factories have created — in such phenomena, no doubt, there is much to inspire confidence in the future of such a nation as ours; but they do not still the longings of the New England heart for the tender grace of a day that is dead. Do you recall that day? The day of the village before it was quite deserted? The simple white dwelling with green shutters and syringa bushes on either side of the plain front porch — a house wholly unaware that it was in any way picturesque or worthy of being painted by Mr. Childe Hassam. "The decent church that topped the neighbouring hill," where simple folk prayed to a God who seemed to be very near them. The fields beyond, with straggling stone walls over which a boy could scramble to pick raspberries, or even escape for a run in the patch of woods beyond. Do you recall the half-patriarchal life that centred in the vil-

lage? The aristocracy of the minister, the easy association, acquaintance with almost everybody in the place.
Quaint figures like Miss Fanny who lived down by the
river and was "Aunt Fanny" to every boy in town. The
village idiot and the philosophic tramp and the wise old
shoemaker; the myths and the feuds and the haunted
house! And above all, the faith in New England, her poets
and her railroads and her destiny in this new world of ours.
Do you, I ask, remember it? If you accuse me of idealizing, I shall reply that I have done so deliberately, for I am
speaking of poetry, and what is poetry without it? I am
confident that I have not heightened and colored the picture more than did Goldsmith when he drew his Auburn,
"loveliest village of the plain, where health and plenty
cheered the labouring swain."

As long as there are poets, they will lament the passing
of earth's loveliness, inevitable though that passing may
be. But there is, in the poem, evidence of something else
that has disappeared, the departure of which it is not
fashionable to deplore. The subject of Goldsmith's poem
is, I have tried to show, deathless, but not so the form in
which he embodied it. *The Deserted Village* is a kind of
essay, or discussion in verse, sometimes placid, sometimes
passionate, but never heedless of the main theme; never
disdaining argument, and never forgetful of the necessity
of an orderly progression to a conclusion; always mindful
of the reader, and eagerly concerned to persuade him,
point by point. The essayist aspires to clarity and order,
and has nothing occult or queer in his verses. If he found
a trace of such mannerism, he would be concerned to erase
it, for he has no wish to tease the reader's emotions or
bewilder his mind. As a matter of fact, Goldsmith disliked the new "romantic" poetry of his day, and described
it thus:

A parcel of gaudy images pass on before his [the reader's]

imagination like the figures in a dream; but curiosity, induction, reason, and the whole train of affections, are fast asleep.

Strange words these would seem to Mr. De la Mare or Mr.
Edwin Arlington Robinson, if ever their eye fell upon them.
Poetry, you see, eschewing vagueness and the evanescent
phantasma of dreams, should stimulate the reader's curiosity and proceed inductively to a conclusion, awakening
meanwhile all the "affections" of the human heart.
Hence the poet, far from "striking the poem out" in an
ecstasy, labored over it tirelessly and doggedly. He
sketched his ideas in prose, versified them, polished and
repolished the lines, and then submitted them to friends
for criticism. He aspired to make the verses live in our
memory as happy summaries of the truth, *multum in
parvo*, "what oft was thought, but ne'er so well expressed";
and knew that, if he was successful in a high degree, his
work would at moments have the ring of a proverb, and
would enter into the living speech of men.

Now this was a type of poetry that had summoned
forth the best efforts of poets since the days of Dryden, or,
may we not say, of Horace. Pope's *Essay on Man*,
Johnson's *Vanity of Human Wishes*, and Goldsmith's
Traveller, to mention only three, were all of this species.
Each poem had a thesis to propound, to illustrate, to
prove, and to recommend. Lesser poets, as though to
show to what strange use the type might be put, wrote on
all subjects from "The Art of Preserving the Health" to
the "Philosophy of Melancholy." Time has buried
thousands and thousands of them, but the best remain, as
the best of any type will always do. By the nineteenth
century the style had begun to fail. No supreme examples of it were produced unless we reckon in Wordsworth's *Prelude, or Growth of the Poet's Mind*, which, as a
spiritual autobiography in verse, would, I imagine, display
nothing which, to an eighteenth-century mind, would seem

inappropriate to that species of poem.   It was, however, in
New England that it was to make its last appearance and
bid adieu — perhaps only a temporary farewell — to the
literary stage.   I refer to Dr. Holmes's poems, *Urania:
a Rhymed Lesson* (1846) and *Astræa, or the Balance of Illusions* (1850), the latter a typically eighteenth-century
theme.   It was written for the Phi Beta Kappa Society of
Yale College, and remains a readable poem today, though
Dr. Holmes, for some reason which he never seems to have
divulged, did not care to include it in his collected works,
but broke it up into a number of fragmentary poems, with
no obvious connections.   His act is symbolic of the passing
of the species.

Now, however ardent we may be in our loyalty to modern
poets, we cannot witness the disappearance of a great
type of poetry without regret.   No such type, which has
had a noble history and summoned forth the full power of
great poets, can disappear from literature without grave
misfortune to us.   In the disuse of this polished clarity,
this discussion, now urbane, now passionate, of matters
that concern all mankind, we are all the poorer.   The poets,
however much they may congratulate themselves upon
their superior subtleties and the finer discernment of
modern readers, are, in particular, the losers, for their
readers are few and ever fewer.   A whole class of men who
once read verse, using their minds as they read and finding
themselves presently stirred to unsuspected depths of
emotion, now read verse no longer.   Occasionally they
may be caught unaware, as by the *Spoon River Anthology;*
but they find themselves uneasy in reading poetry which,
for aught that they can see, is addressed to connoisseurs,
intended exclusively for the initiate.   Such men are not
to be thought of as turning from poetry in contempt, for
they are generally willing enough to concede that poetry is
very fine, only "beyond them."   They fancy that they

have no power of assimilating such ethereal food. And so they keep away from the poet, and the work that he might have wrought upon their spirit is not even begun. Goldsmith would have won them all.

More serious still is the loss to the reading world of any literary type in which a poet may pass from grave meditation to passionate argument and glowing dream. Even the prose essay, in which exposition may mingle with "appreciation" of a highly individual sort, is no proper medium for the intenser moments of personal expression. Yet all these moods and many more find a natural channel of expression in the kind of verse here discussed. In *The Deserted Village*, for instance, a poem which begins as a description of "Sweet Auburn" develops into a dissertation on the evils of luxury, touches on the problem of emigration, laments the depopulation of villages, and ends with the author's impassioned farewell to Poetry, which is conceived of as departing with the peasants to America. This touching and eloquent adieu to the Muse, like the less successful appeal to the throne in *The Traveller*, could hardly have been introduced into a prose essay, of however intimate a character:

> And thou, sweet Poetry, thou loveliest maid,
> Still first to fly where sensual joys invade;
> Unfit in these degenerate times of shame,
> To catch the heart, or strike for honest fame;
> Dear charming nymph, neglected and decried,
> My shame in crowds, my solitary pride,
> Thou source of all my bliss and all my woe,
> That found'st me poor at first, and keep'st me so;
> Thou guide by which the nobler arts excel,
> Thou nurse of every virtue, fare thee well.

There are subjects, no longer considered "poetical," but which may one day reclaim their right to the poet's attention, which require for their adequate treatment just such a medium as *The Deserted Village*. At the present stage

of our poetical development they go unhonored and un-
sung. Out of a thousand that might be specified, I select
one, Democracy. Here is a theme of universal interest and
appeal. For the past twelve or fifteen years we have been
asking ourselves if the ideal of our forefathers has been
tried and found wanting, whether government of the people, by the people, and for the people is destined to perish.
No newspaper has failed to discuss the question — however inconclusively. Cartoons have been suggested by the
query, Has civilization gone wrong? And we have asked
ourselves so often whether democracy is safe for the world
or the world safe for democracy that the question has become a byword and a jest.

In the eighteenth century the theme would have been
seized upon by a poet as a noble subject worthy of that
exalted treatment which is possible in poetry alone. He
would have sketched in rapid outline the history of democracy, its career in Greece and Rome, in the Italian cities
of the Middle Ages, and in the mountains of Switzerland.
He would have described its dark hours during the French
Revolution, and would have hailed the young republic of
the New World. Such a poet, had he known the history
of the past fifteen years, would have blazed into what the
eighteenth century called "generous indignation" at the
mention of Russia, where a new tyranny has again arrayed
class against class, lifted the standard of hatred, ignorance,
and atheism, and promised to return civilization to the
chaos out of which it rose. He would have ended all with
a passionate appeal to the hearts of his countrymen with
such fervor as Lowell breathed into his fine stanzas beginning —

Oh beautiful, my country!

We do not encourage ourselves to be emotional about
such matters nowadays, and unexpressed emotion tends
to disappear altogether, or finds an outlet in channels per-

verse and strange. A degree of poetic eloquence, addressed to the hearts of men, was once permitted to oratory, but oratory, as conceived by Burke and by Webster, has disappeared along with the kind of verse here considered. Under the influence of the scientific specialist and the deterministic philosopher, we have opened a rift between our reason and our other faculties, as though it were possible to discharge all the functions of living with our minds alone, to the exclusion of such emotion as brings the glow of pride to the cheek and the tear of sensibility to the eye. Such stimulus has been at best confined to our hours of relaxation and amusement. Poetry has been increasingly confined to our bosoms and excluded from our business.

As an example of the increasing involution of romantic poetry and the increasing subtlety demanded of the reader, it will be sufficient to cite examples of the modern treatment of the theme of ruin or desolation which may fairly be contrasted with Goldsmith's. It is not necessary to dwell on the popularity of this *motif* among the poets of the Romantic School. What poem of Shelley's is more popular than *Ozymandias*?

> Nothing beside remains. Round the decay
> Of that colossal wreck, boundless and bare
> The lone and level sands stretch far away!

What stanza in the *Rubáiyát* lovelier than this?

> They say the Lion and the Lizard keep
> The Courts where Jamshyd gloried and drank deep,
> And Bahrám, that great Hunter, the Wild Ass
> Stamps o'er his Head, but cannot break his Sleep.

None of the poets is more insistent (for obvious reasons) upon the theme of desolation than is Byron. The fourth canto of *Childe Harold* is a very epic of ruin. Rome herself is, in one aspect, a Titanic image of the desolation of the poet's soul.

Oh Rome! my country! city of the soul!
The orphans of the heart must turn to thee,
Lone mother of dead empires! and control
In their shut breasts their petty misery.
What are our woes and sufferance?   Come and see
The cypress, hear the owl, and plod your way
O'er steps of broken thrones and temples, Ye!
Whose agonies are evils of a day —
A world is at our feet as fragile as our clay.

Here is a typically romantic exaltation of the "sufferance" of a great capital as compared with the petty misery
of a mere man, whose years are brief.   The woes of Rome
are eternal, like her years.   Despite what may be deemed
a somewhat exaggerated emotionalism, the stanza is yet
perfectly intelligible.   The ordinary reader may not care
to indulge so intense an emotion for the majestic past, but
there is nothing to elude his understanding or even to make
him feel that the poet is "beyond him."   He may reject
the stanza and the canto of which it is a part as deficient
in thought, but he will never contend that it is unintelligible.

When we pass on to Browning's "Love among the
Ruins," which was the introductory poem in *Men and Women* (1855), we encounter a poem so sublimated that the
reader's problem is now to bring his emotion to a state
where he may be worthy of communion with the poet.
If he attempt to use his reason, he will discover that he is
confronted with an asseveration which may very likely
require a shift in all the standards which he has hitherto
instinctively accepted.   Browning, having selected the
familiar scene of peasant lovers amidst the ruins of ancient
grandeur, proceeds to the interesting conclusion that the
love of the two is somehow the answer to "whole centuries
of folly, noise and sin."   So eloquently does he set the
shepherd boy's passion before us that the sympathetic
reader experiences a temporary "suspension of disbelief"